DC/YOUNG ANIMAL:
MILK WARS

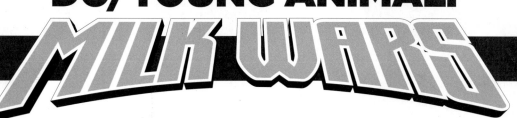

DC/YOUNG ANIMAL:
MILK WARS

Written by

STEVE ORLANDO
GERARD WAY
JODY HOUSER
CECIL CASTELLUCCI
JON RIVERA
MAGDALENE VISAGGIO

Art by

ACO
TY TEMPLETON
MIRKA ANDOLFO
LANGDON FOSS
DALE EAGLESHAM
NICK DERINGTON
SONNY LIEW

Coloring by

TAMRA BONVILLAIN
MARISSA LOUISE
KEIREN SMITH
NICK FILARDI

Lettering by

CLEM ROBINS
JOHN WORKMAN
SAIDA TEMOFONTE
TODD KLEIN

Cover art by

FRANK QUITELY

Original series covers by

FRANK QUITELY
RIAN HUGHES
CLAY MANN and MARISSA LOUISE

DOOM PATROL created by **ARNOLD DRAKE**
SUPERMAN created by **JERRY SIEGEL** and **JOE SHUSTER**
By special arrangement with the Jerry Siegel family
BATMAN created by **BOB KANE** with **BILL FINGER**
MOTHER PANIC created by **GERARD WAY,**
JODY HOUSER and **TOMMY LEE EDWARDS**
WONDER WOMAN created by
WILLIAM MOULTON MARSTON
SHADE THE CHANGING MAN created by **STEVE DITKO**
SWAMP THING created by **LEN WEIN**
and **BERNIE WRIGHTSON**

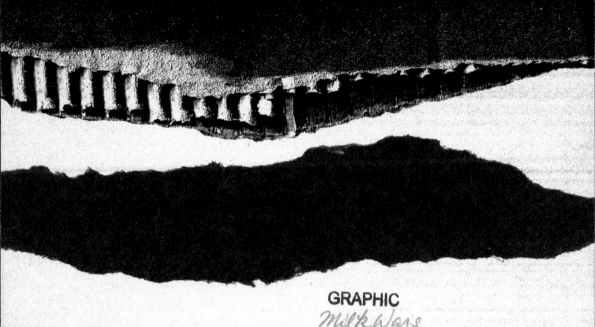

GRAPHIC

Milk Wars

Jamie S. Rich Group Editor – Vertigo Comics and Editor – Original Series
Molly Mahan Editor – Original Series
Jeb Woodard Group Editor – Collected Editions
Scott Nybakken Editor – Collected Edition
Steve Cook Design Director – Books
Megen Bellersen Publication Design

Bob Harras Senior VP – Editor-in-Chief, DC Comics
Mark Doyle Executive Editor, Vertigo

Diane Nelson President
Dan DiDio Publisher
Jim Lee Publisher
Geoff Johns President & Chief Creative Officer
Amit Desai Executive VP – Business & Marketing Strategy, Direct to Consumer
& Global Franchise Management
Sam Ades Senior VP & General Manager, Digital Services
Bobbie Chase VP & Executive Editor, Young Reader & Talent Development
Mark Chiarello Senior VP – Art, Design & Collected Editions
John Cunningham Senior VP – Sales & Trade Marketing
Anne DePies Senior VP – Business Strategy, Finance & Administration
Don Falletti VP – Manufacturing Operations
Lawrence Ganem VP – Editorial Administration & Talent Relations
Alison Gill Senior VP – Manufacturing & Operations
Hank Kanalz Senior VP – Editorial Strategy & Administration
Jay Kogan VP – Legal Affairs
Jack Mahan VP – Business Affairs
Nick J. Napolitano VP – Manufacturing Administration
Eddie Scannell VP – Consumer Marketing
Courtney Simmons Senior VP – Publicity & Communications
Jim (Ski) Sokolowski VP – Comic Book Specialty Sales & Trade Marketing
Nancy Spears VP – Mass, Book, Digital Sales & Trade Marketing
Michele R. Wells VP – Content Strategy

DC/YOUNG ANIMAL: MILK WARS

Published by DC Comics. Compilation and all new material Copyright
© 2018 DC Comics. All Rights Reserved.

Originally published in single magazine form in JLA/DOOM PATROL
SPECIAL 1, MOTHER PANIC/BATMAN SPECIAL 1, SHADE, THE CHANGING
GIRL/WONDER WOMAN SPECIAL 1, CAVE CARSON HAS A CYBERNETIC
EYE/SWAMP THING SPECIAL 1 and DOOM PATROL/JLA SPECIAL 1.
Copyright © 2018 DC Comics. All Rights Reserved. All characters,
their distinctive likenesses and related elements featured in this
publication are trademarks of DC Comics. The stories, characters and
incidents featured in this publication are entirely fictional. DC Comics
does not read or accept unsolicited submissions of ideas, stories or
artwork.

DC Comics
2900 West Alameda Avenue
Burbank, CA 91505
Printed by LSC Communications, Owensville, MO, USA. 5/11/18.
First Printing.
ISBN: 978-1-4012-7733-8

Library of Congress Cataloging-in-Publication Data is available.

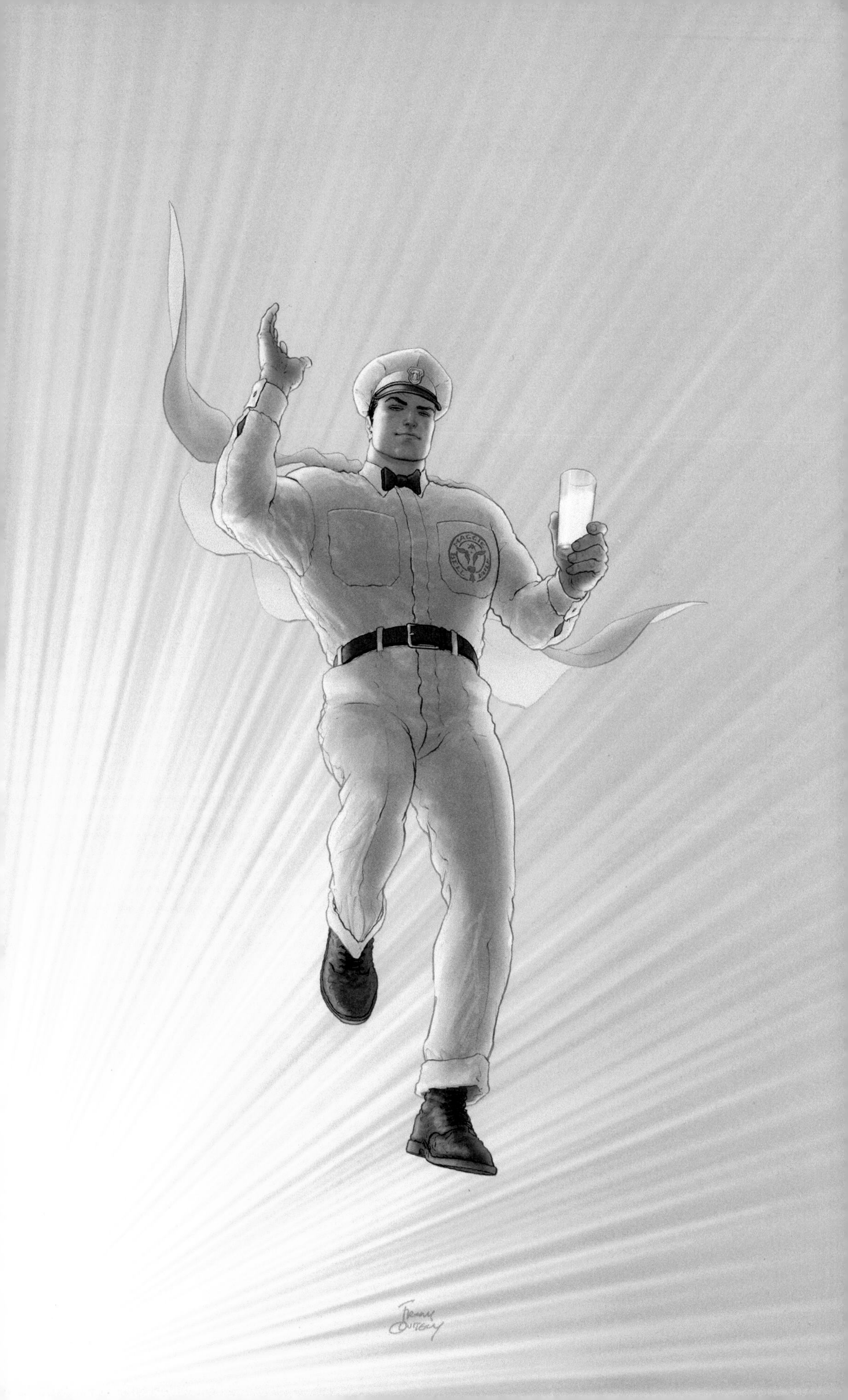
MAGGIE
BELL
FRANK QUITELY

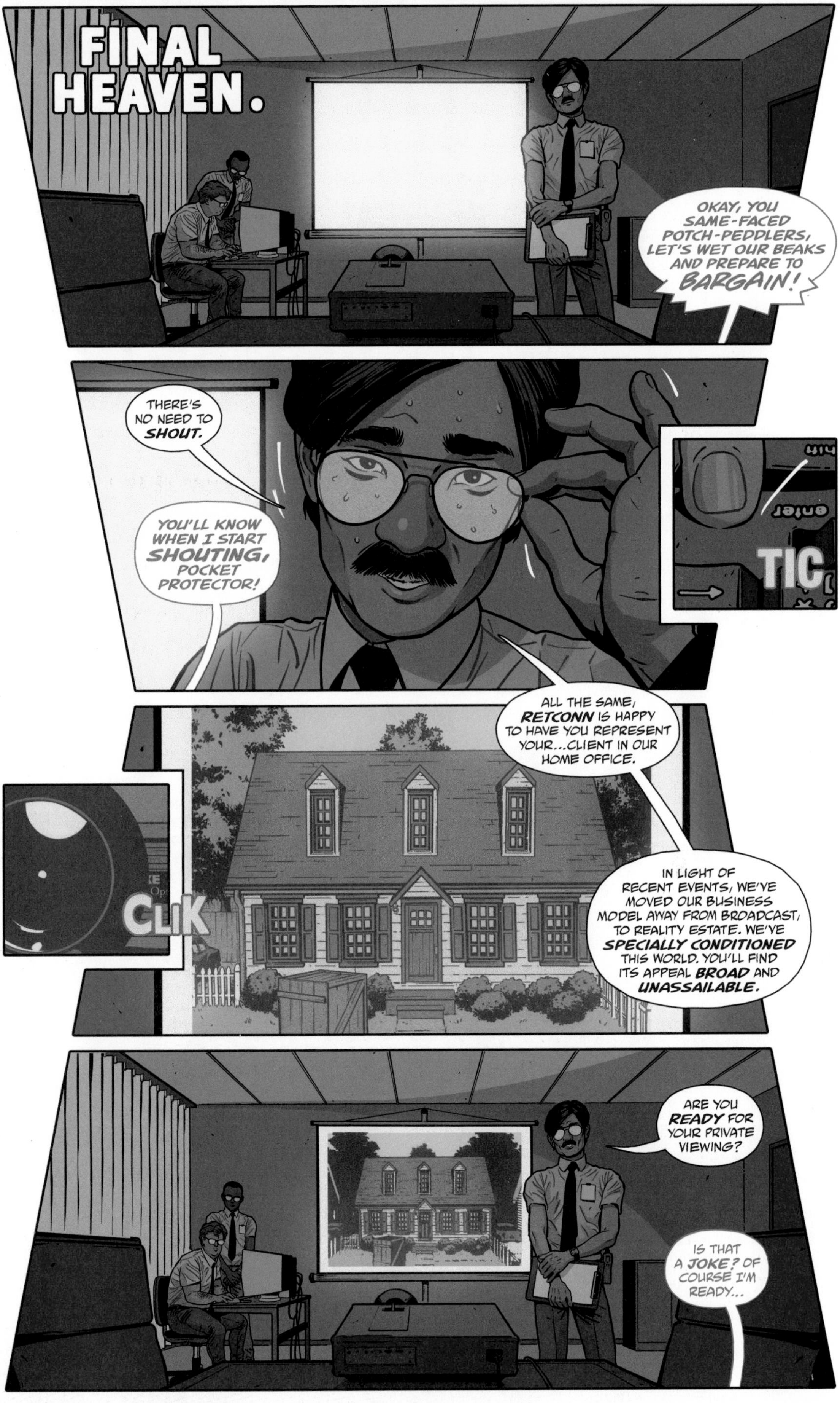
FINAL HEAVEN.
OKAY, YOU SAME-FACED POTCH-PEDDLERS, LET'S WET OUR BEAKS AND PREPARE TO BARGAIN!
THERE'S NO NEED TO SHOUT.
YOU'LL KNOW WHEN I START SHOUTING, POCKET PROTECTOR!
TIC
ALL THE SAME, RETCONN IS HAPPY TO HAVE YOU REPRESENT YOUR...CLIENT IN OUR HOME OFFICE.
CLIK
IN LIGHT OF RECENT EVENTS, WE'VE MOVED OUR BUSINESS MODEL AWAY FROM BROADCAST, TO REALITY ESTATE. WE'VE SPECIALLY CONDITIONED THIS WORLD. YOU'LL FIND ITS APPEAL BROAD AND UNASSAILABLE.
ARE YOU READY FOR YOUR PRIVATE VIEWING?
IS THAT A JOKE? OF COURSE I'M READY...

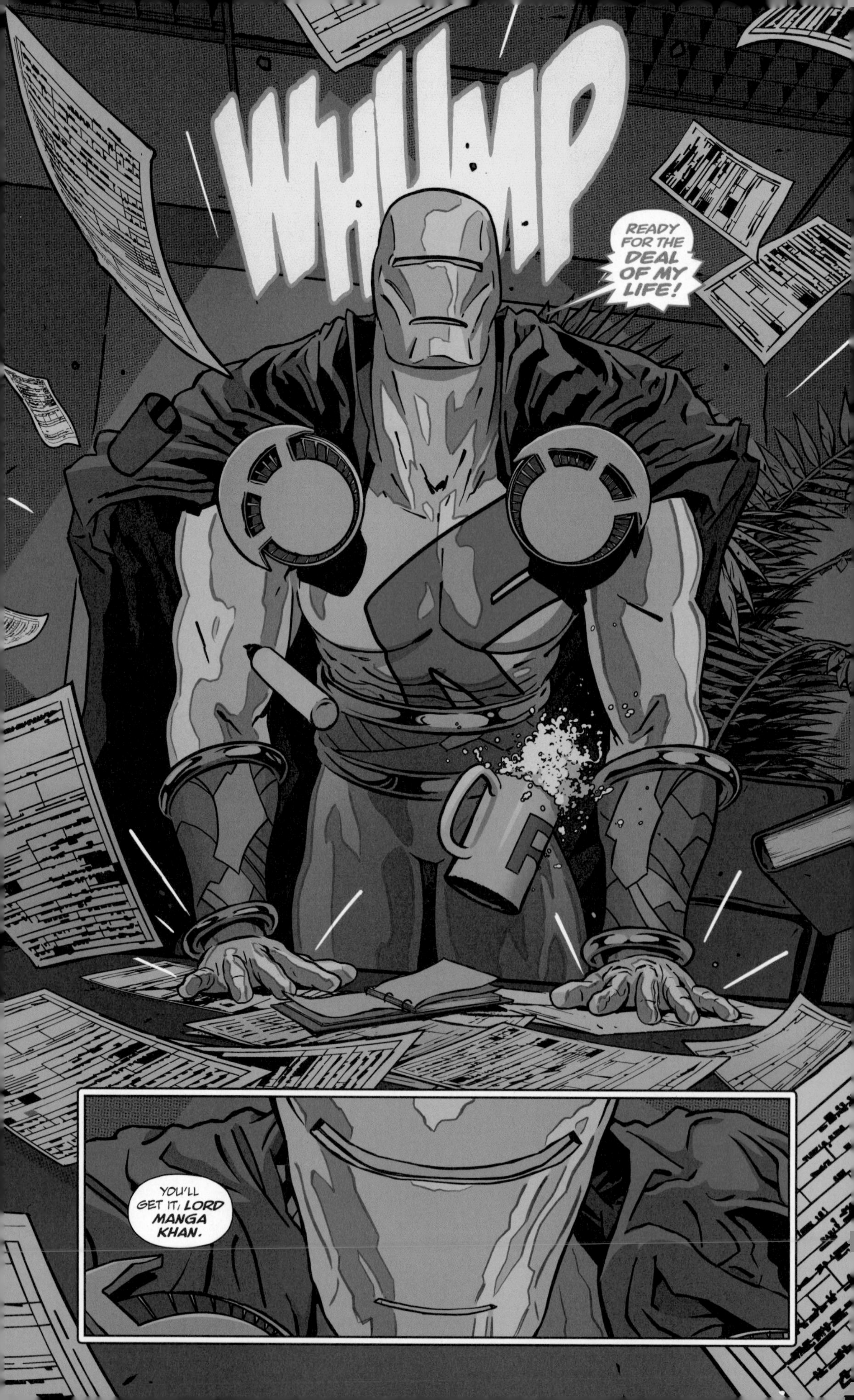
WHUMP
READY FOR THE DEAL OF MY LIFE!
YOU'LL GET IT, LORD MANGA KHAN.

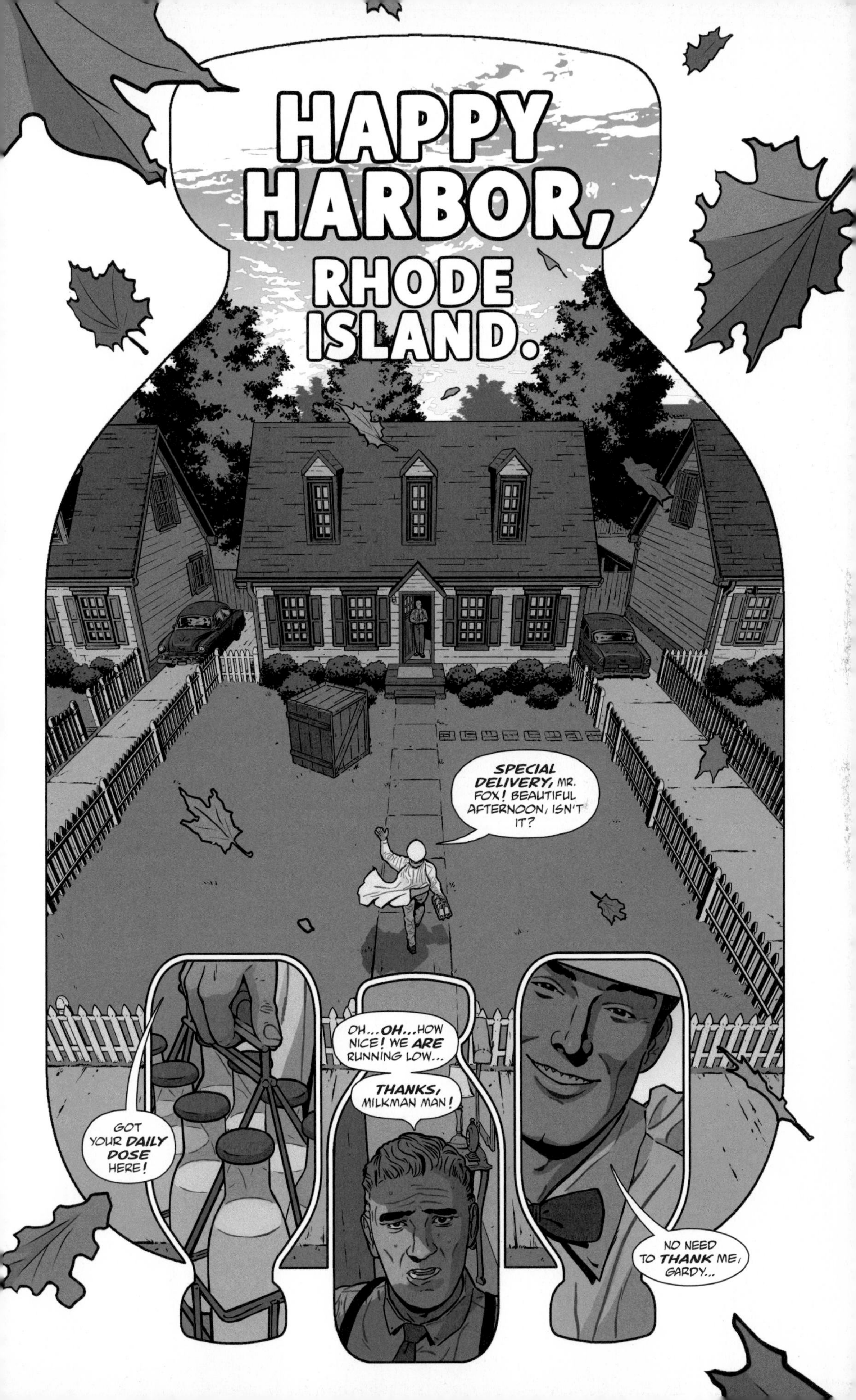
HAPPY HARBOR, RHODE ISLAND.
SPECIAL DELIVERY, MR. FOX! BEAUTIFUL AFTERNOON, ISN'T IT?
GOT YOUR DAILY DOSE HERE!
OH... OH... HOW NICE! WE ARE RUNNING LOW...
THANKS, MILKMAN MAN!
NO NEED TO THANK ME, GARDY...

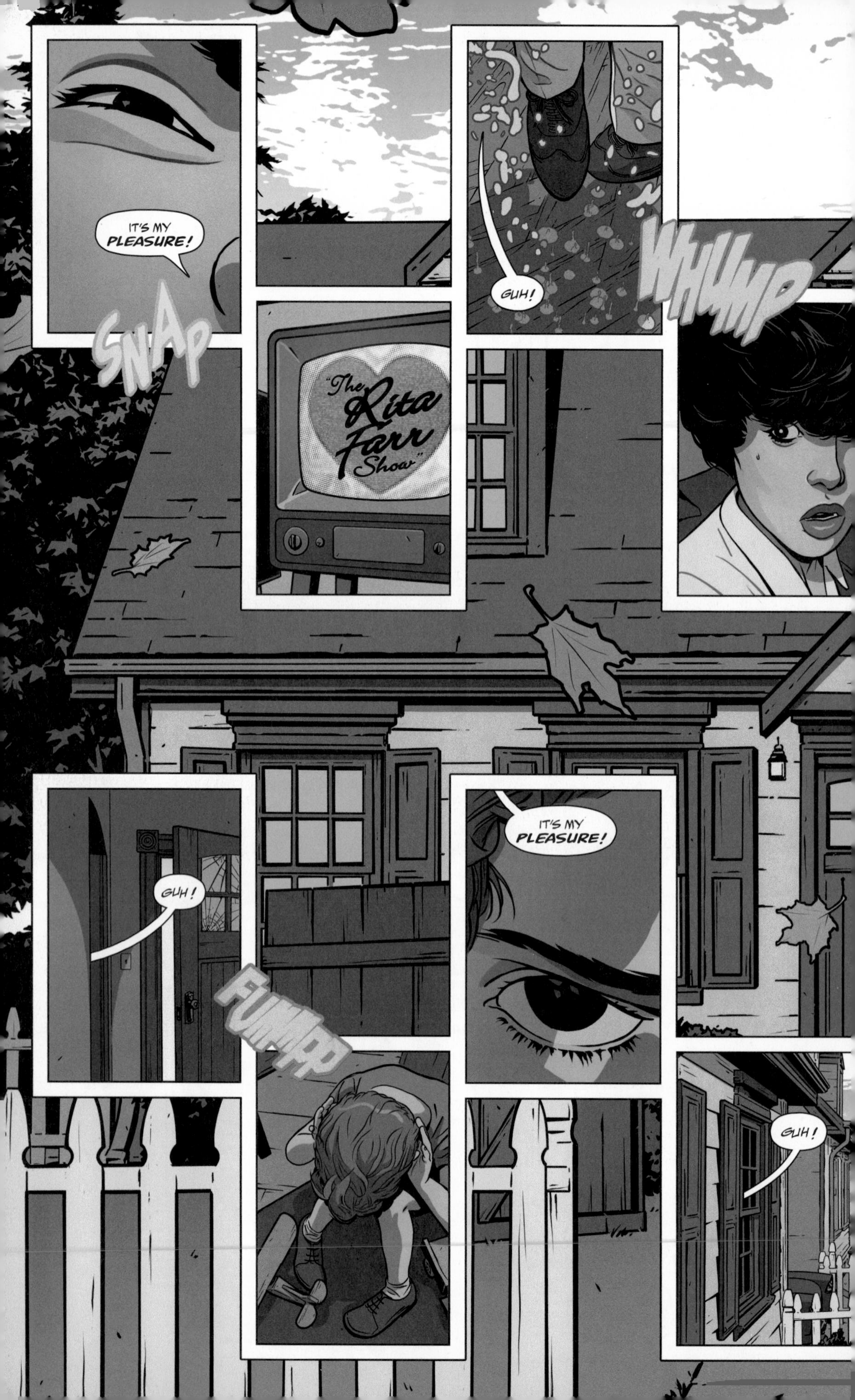
IT'S MY PLEASURE!
SNAP
GUH!
WHUMP
"The Rita Farr Show"
GUH!
FUMPP
IT'S MY PLEASURE!
GUH!

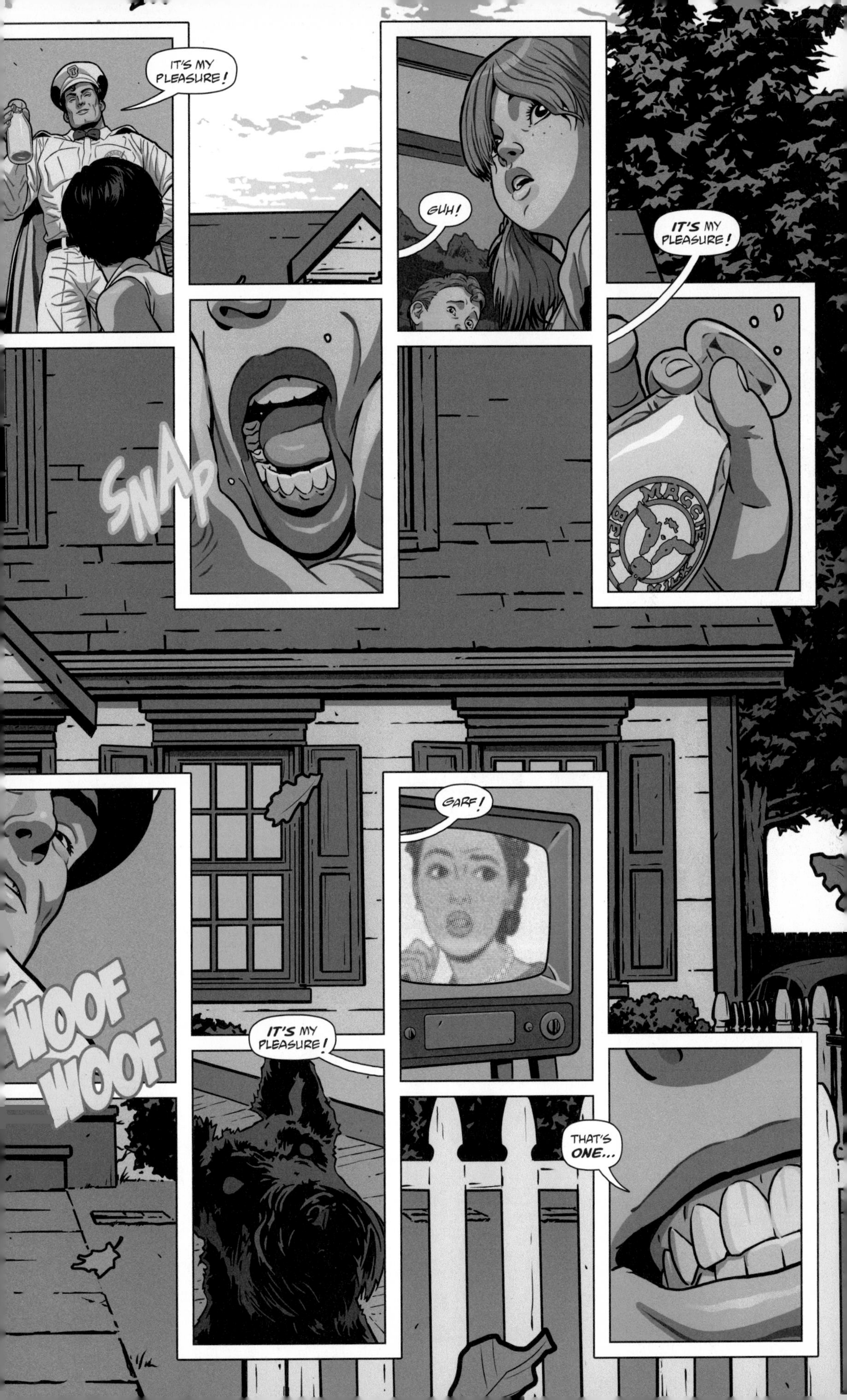

IT'S MY PLEASURE!
GUH!
SNAP
IT'S MY PLEASURE!
MAGGIE
GARF!
WOOF WOOF
IT'S MY PLEASURE!
THAT'S ONE...

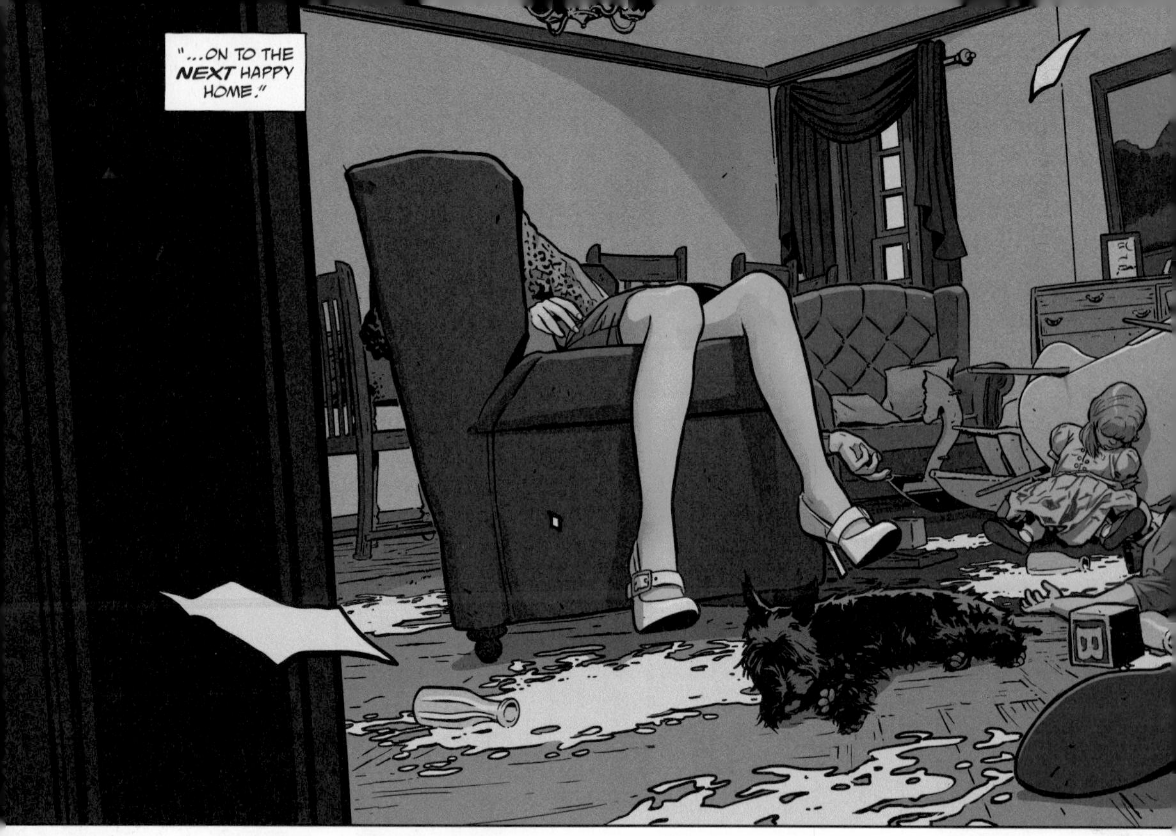
"...ON TO THE NEXT HAPPY HOME."

MILK W

STEVE ORLANDO & GERARD WAY
WRITERS

ACO
ILLUSTRATOR

PG 12 BY
HUGO PETRUS

TAMRA BONVILLAIN & MARISSA LOUISE
COLORISTS

CLEM ROBINS
LETTERER

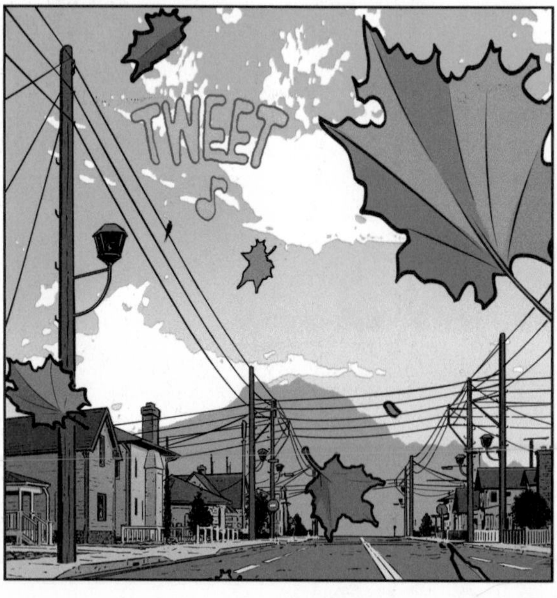
TWEET

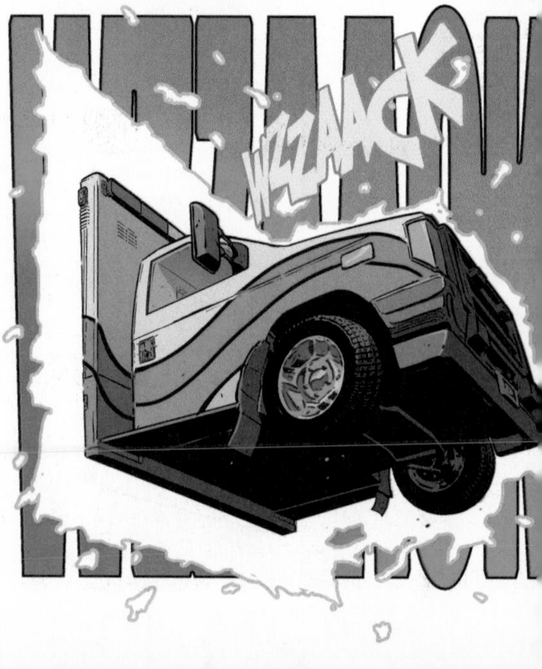
WZZAACK

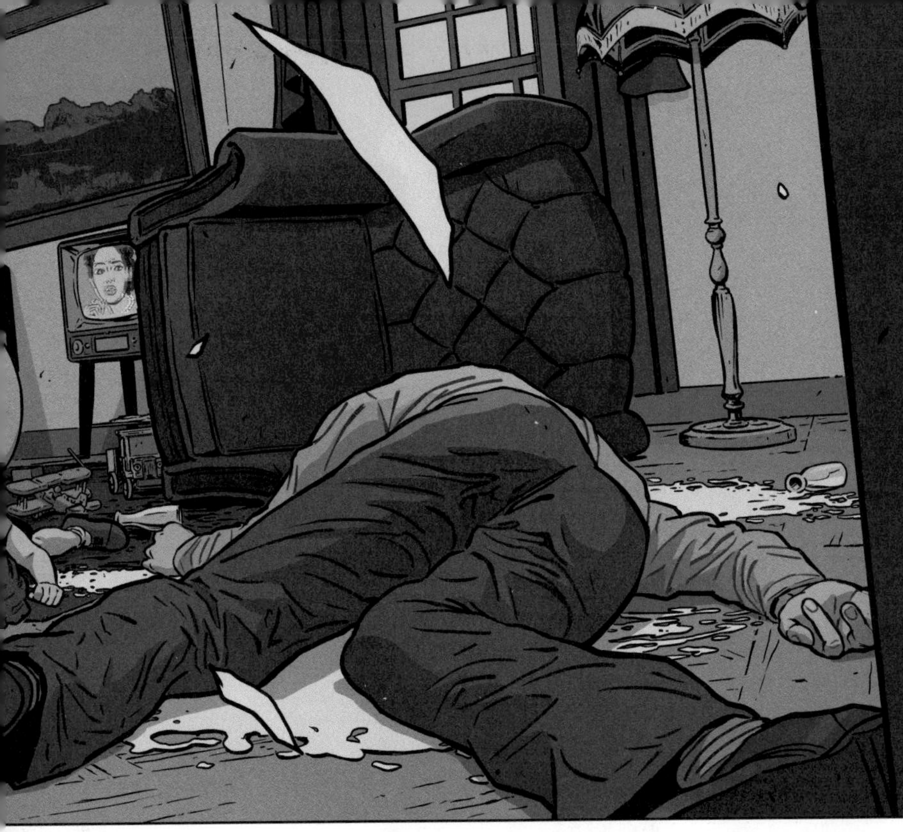

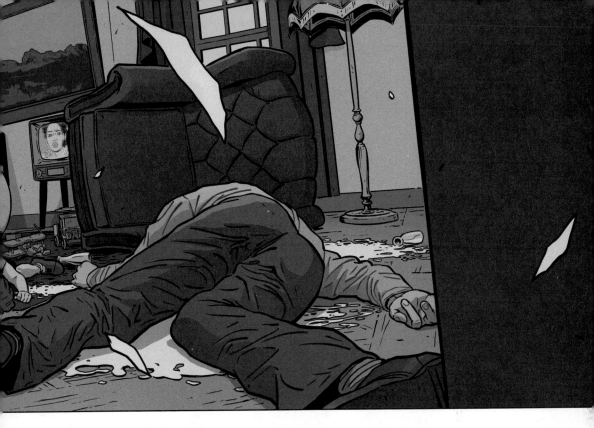

ARS PART ONE

SPECIAL THANKS TO
DAVID LORENZO RIVEIRO

FRANK QUITELY
COVER

JAMIE S. RICH
EDITOR

MOLLY MAHAN
ADDITONAL EDITS

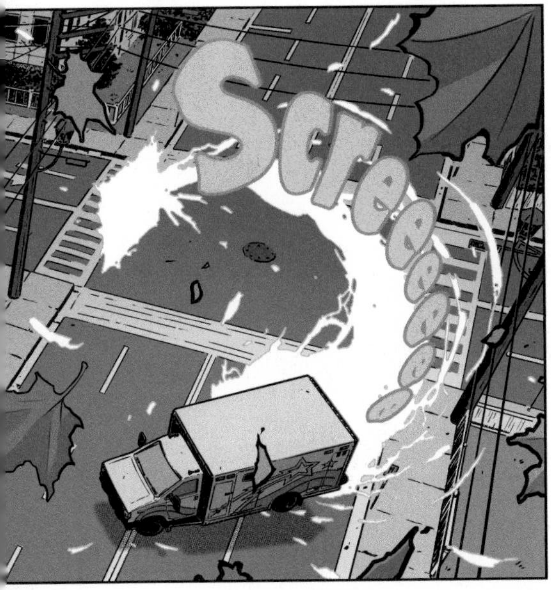
Screeeeee

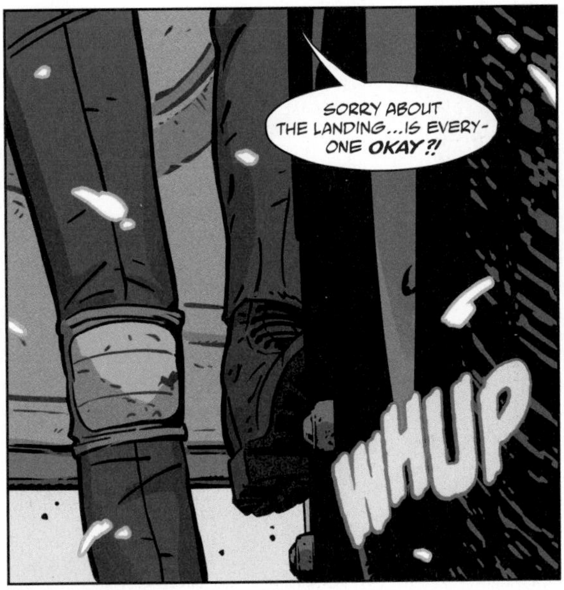
SORRY ABOUT THE LANDING...IS EVERY-ONE OKAY?!
WHUP

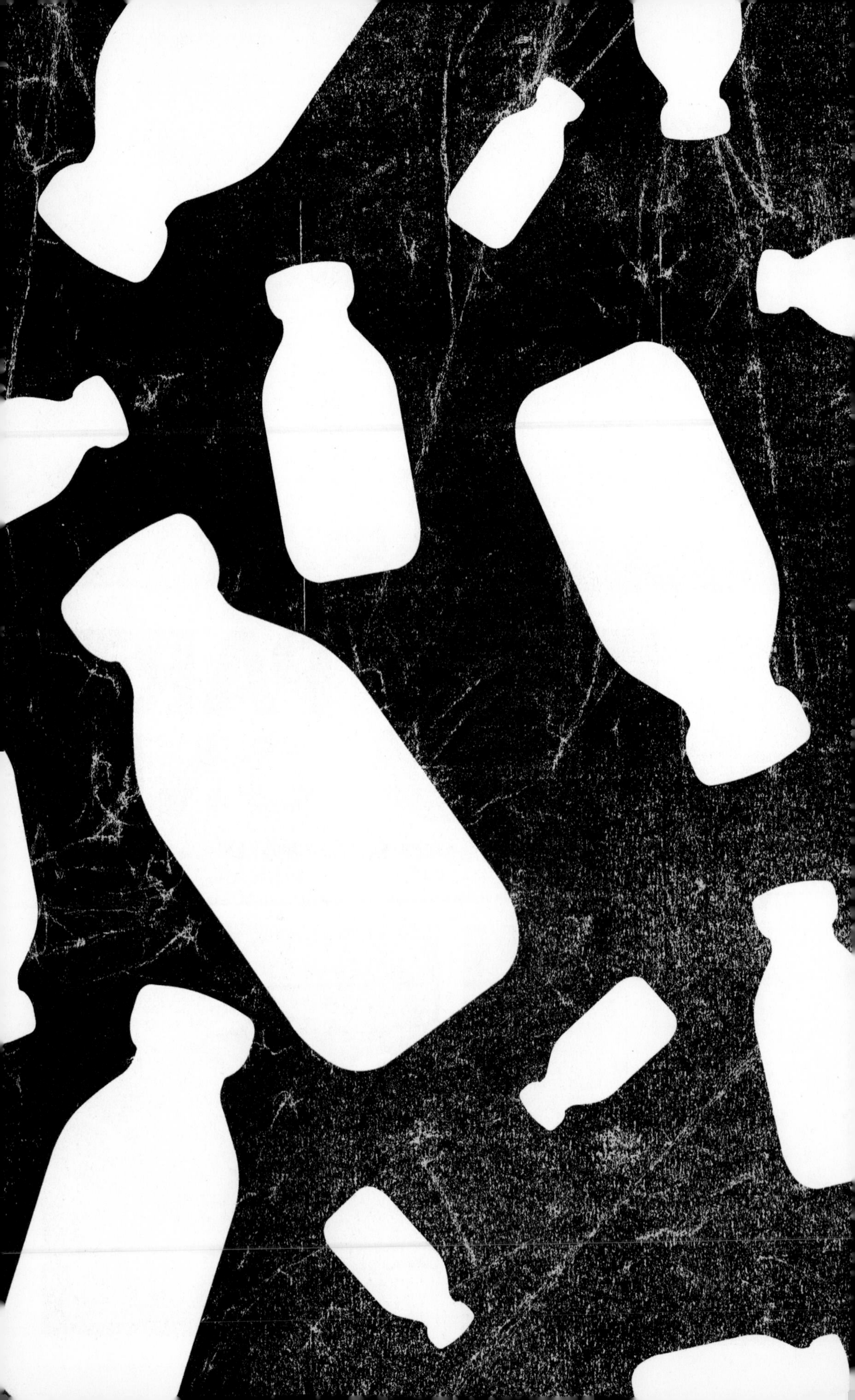

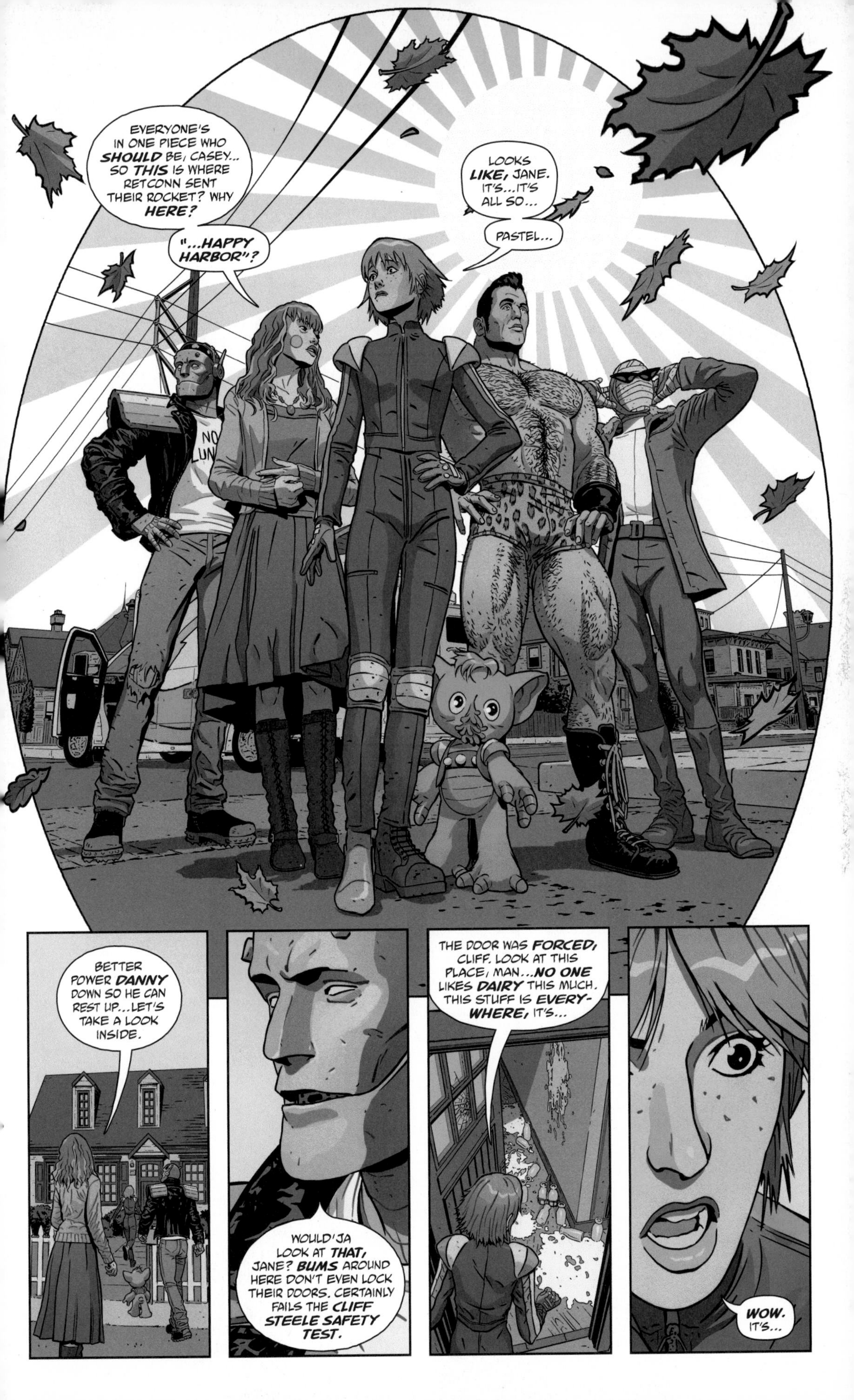
EVERYONE'S IN ONE PIECE WHO SHOULD BE, CASEY... SO THIS IS WHERE RETCONN SENT THEIR ROCKET? WHY HERE?
"...HAPPY HARBOR"?
LOOKS LIKE, JANE. IT'S...IT'S ALL SO...
PASTEL...
NO LUN
BETTER POWER DANNY DOWN SO HE CAN REST UP...LET'S TAKE A LOOK INSIDE.
WOULD'JA LOOK AT THAT, JANE? BUMS AROUND HERE DON'T EVEN LOCK THEIR DOORS. CERTAINLY FAILS THE CLIFF STEELE SAFETY TEST.
THE DOOR WAS FORCED, CLIFF. LOOK AT THIS PLACE, MAN...NO ONE LIKES DAIRY THIS MUCH. THIS STUFF IS EVERY-WHERE, IT'S...
WOW. IT'S...

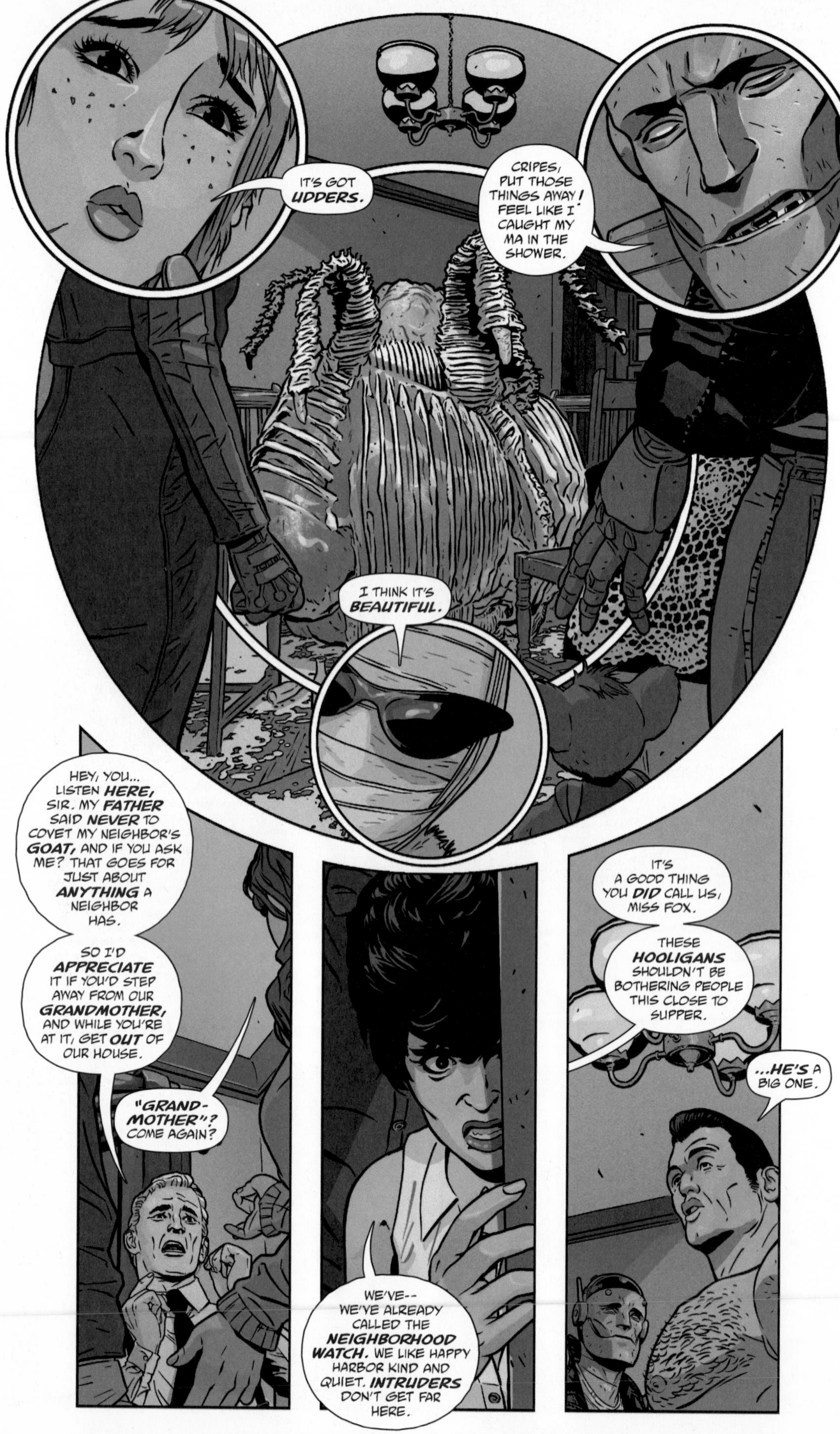
IT'S GOT UDDERS.
CRIPES, PUT THOSE THINGS AWAY! FEEL LIKE I CAUGHT MY MA IN THE SHOWER.
I THINK IT'S BEAUTIFUL.
HEY, YOU... LISTEN HERE, SIR. MY FATHER SAID NEVER TO COVET MY NEIGHBOR'S GOAT, AND IF YOU ASK ME? THAT GOES FOR JUST ABOUT ANYTHING A NEIGHBOR HAS.
SO I'D APPRECIATE IT IF YOU'D STEP AWAY FROM OUR GRANDMOTHER, AND WHILE YOU'RE AT IT, GET OUT OF OUR HOUSE.
"GRAND-MOTHER"? COME AGAIN?
WE'VE-- WE'VE ALREADY CALLED THE NEIGHBORHOOD WATCH. WE LIKE HAPPY HARBOR KIND AND QUIET. INTRUDERS DON'T GET FAR HERE.
IT'S A GOOD THING YOU DID CALL US, MISS FOX.
THESE HOOLIGANS SHOULDN'T BE BOTHERING PEOPLE THIS CLOSE TO SUPPER.
...HE'S A BIG ONE.

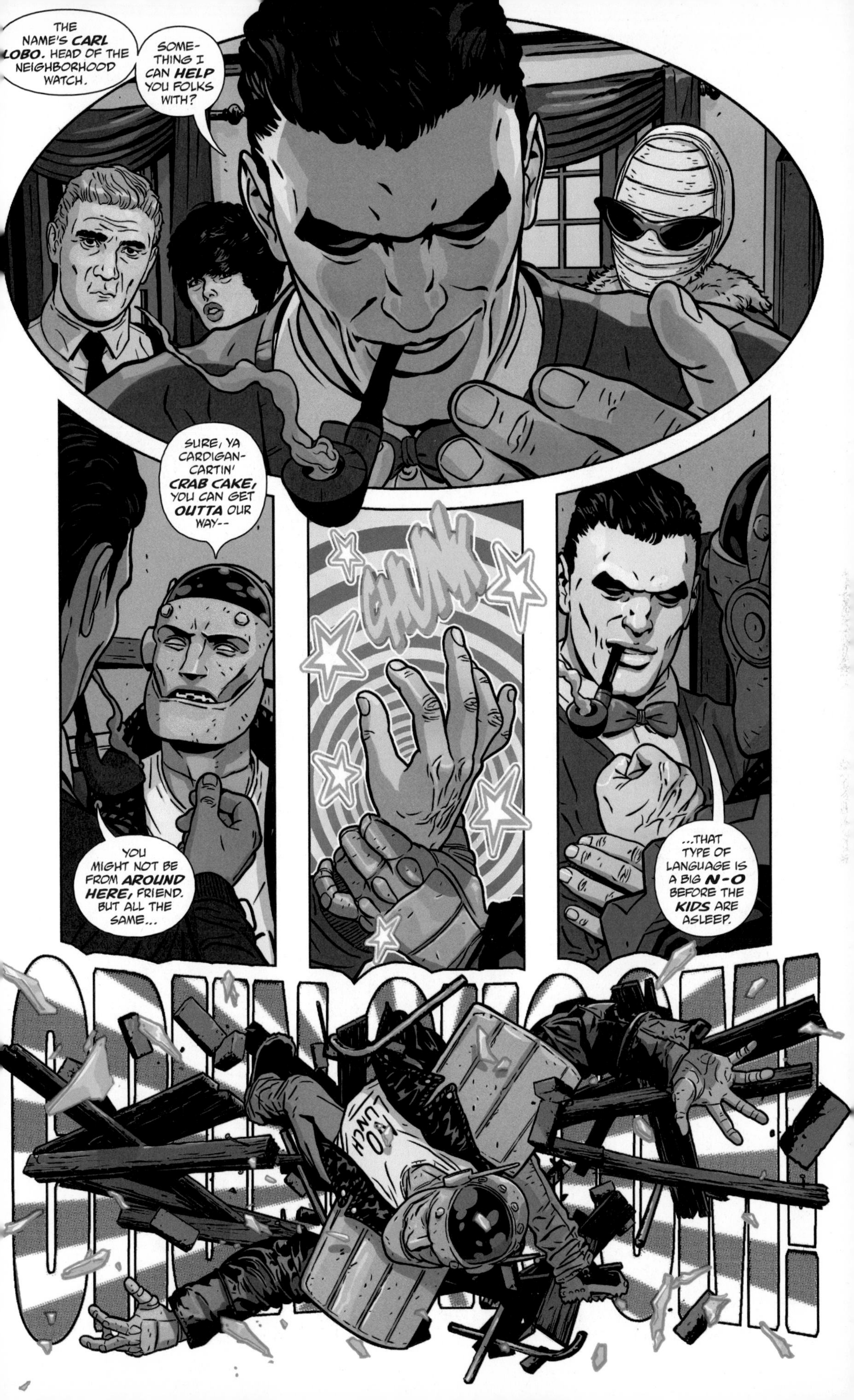
THE NAME'S **CARL LOBO.** HEAD OF THE NEIGHBORHOOD WATCH.
SOME-THING I CAN **HELP** YOU FOLKS WITH?
SURE, YA CARDIGAN-CARTIN' **CRAB CAKE,** YOU CAN GET **OUTTA** OUR WAY--
YOU MIGHT NOT BE FROM **AROUND HERE,** FRIEND. BUT ALL THE SAME...
CHUNK
...THAT TYPE OF LANGUAGE IS A BIG **N-O** BEFORE THE **KIDS** ARE ASLEEP.

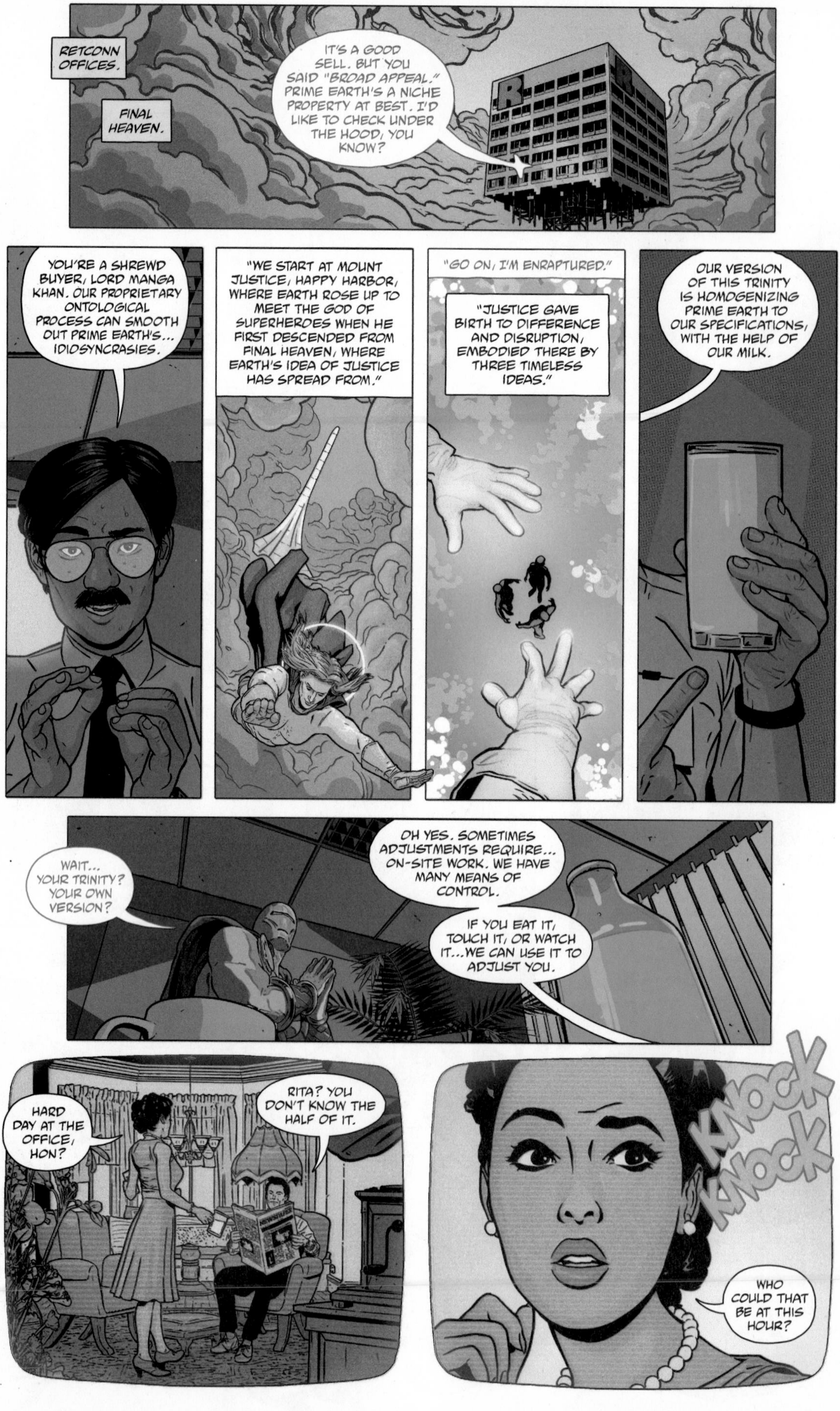
RETCONN OFFICES.
FINAL HEAVEN.
IT'S A GOOD SELL. BUT YOU SAID "BROAD APPEAL." PRIME EARTH'S A NICHE PROPERTY AT BEST. I'D LIKE TO CHECK UNDER THE HOOD, YOU KNOW?
YOU'RE A SHREWD BUYER, LORD MANGA KHAN. OUR PROPRIETARY ONTOLOGICAL PROCESS CAN SMOOTH OUT PRIME EARTH'S... IDIOSYNCRASIES.
"WE START AT MOUNT JUSTICE, HAPPY HARBOR, WHERE EARTH ROSE UP TO MEET THE GOD OF SUPERHEROES WHEN HE FIRST DESCENDED FROM FINAL HEAVEN, WHERE EARTH'S IDEA OF JUSTICE HAS SPREAD FROM."
"GO ON, I'M ENRAPTURED."
"JUSTICE GAVE BIRTH TO DIFFERENCE AND DISRUPTION, EMBODIED THERE BY THREE TIMELESS IDEAS."
OUR VERSION OF THIS TRINITY IS HOMOGENIZING PRIME EARTH TO OUR SPECIFICATIONS, WITH THE HELP OF OUR MILK.
WAIT... YOUR TRINITY? YOUR OWN VERSION?
OH YES. SOMETIMES ADJUSTMENTS REQUIRE... ON-SITE WORK. WE HAVE MANY MEANS OF CONTROL.
IF YOU EAT IT, TOUCH IT, OR WATCH IT...WE CAN USE IT TO ADJUST YOU.
HARD DAY AT THE OFFICE, HON?
RITA? YOU DON'T KNOW THE HALF OF IT.
KNOCK KNOCK
WHO COULD THAT BE AT THIS HOUR?

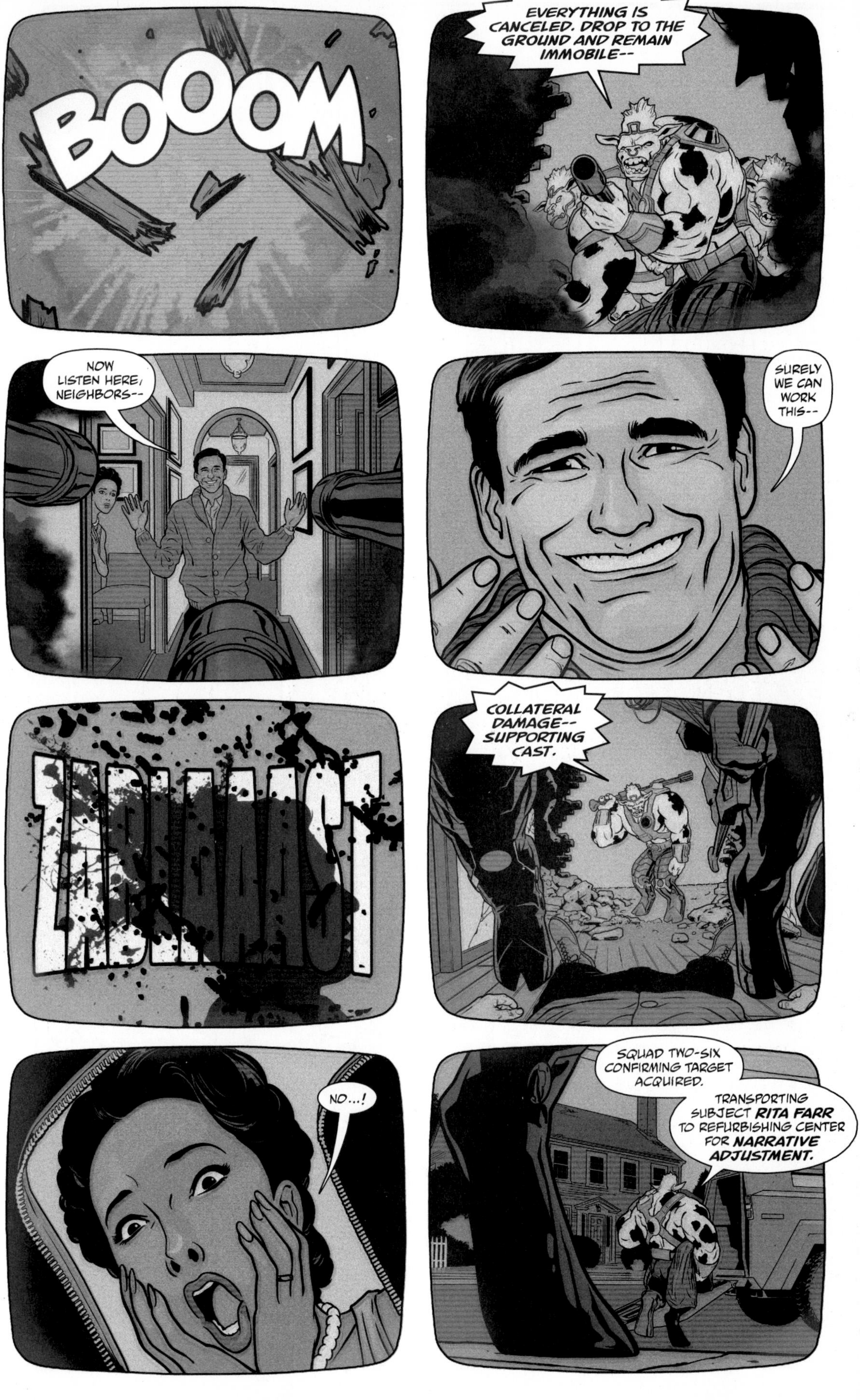
BOOOM
EVERYTHING IS CANCELED. DROP TO THE GROUND AND REMAIN IMMOBILE--
NOW LISTEN HERE, NEIGHBORS--
SURELY WE CAN WORK THIS--
COLLATERAL DAMAGE-- SUPPORTING CAST.
NO...!
SQUAD TWO-SIX CONFIRMING TARGET ACQUIRED.
TRANSPORTING SUBJECT RITA FARR TO REFURBISHING CENTER FOR NARRATIVE ADJUSTMENT.

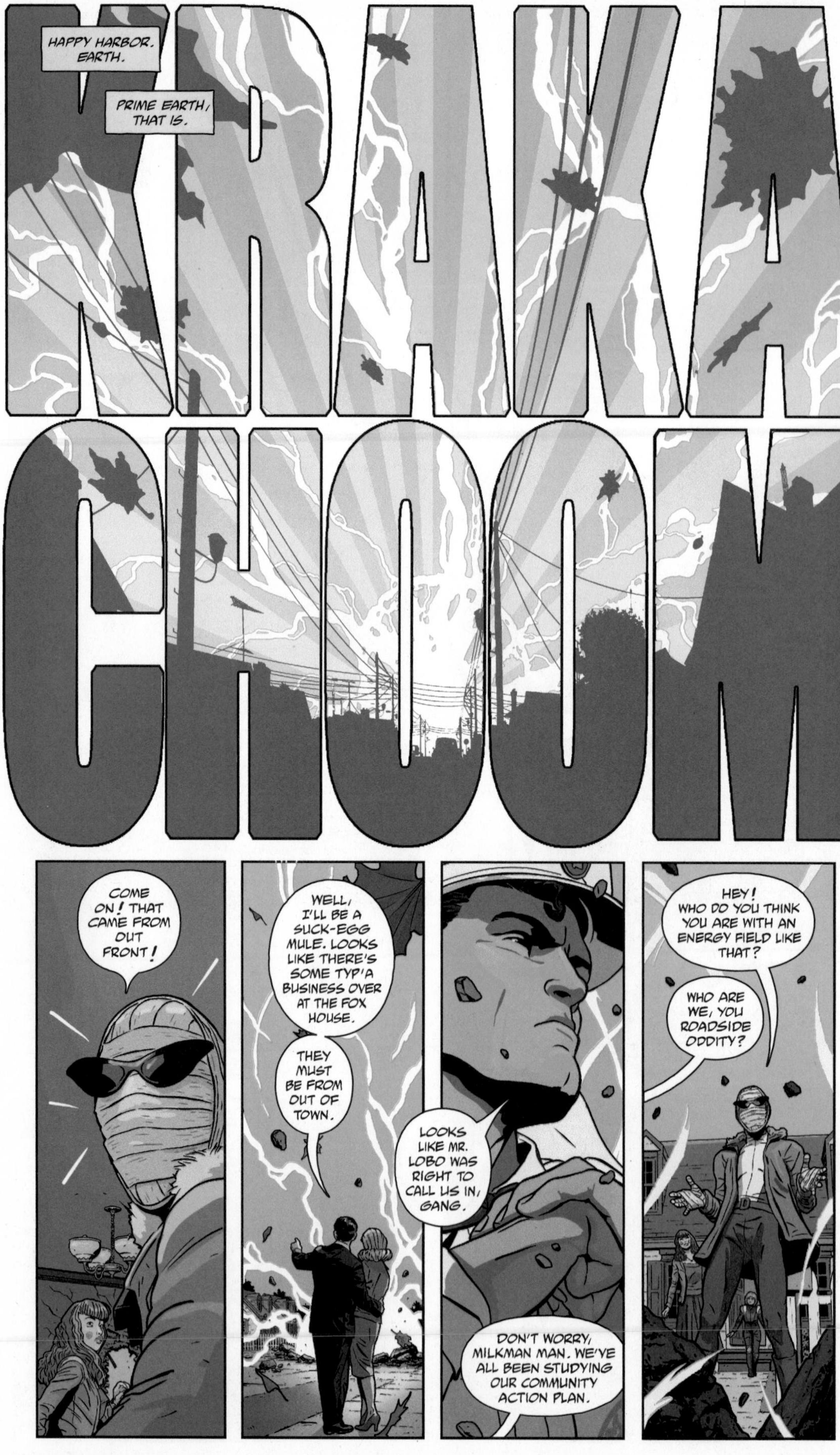
HAPPY HARBOR. EARTH.
PRIME EARTH, THAT IS.
KRAKA
CHOOM
COME ON! THAT CAME FROM OUT FRONT!
WELL, I'LL BE A SUCK-EGG MULE. LOOKS LIKE THERE'S SOME TYP'A BUSINESS OVER AT THE FOX HOUSE.
THEY MUST BE FROM OUT OF TOWN.
LOOKS LIKE MR. LOBO WAS RIGHT TO CALL US IN, GANG.
DON'T WORRY, MILKMAN MAN. WE'VE ALL BEEN STUDYING OUR COMMUNITY ACTION PLAN.
HEY! WHO DO YOU THINK YOU ARE WITH AN ENERGY FIELD LIKE THAT?
WHO ARE WE, YOU ROADSIDE ODDITY?

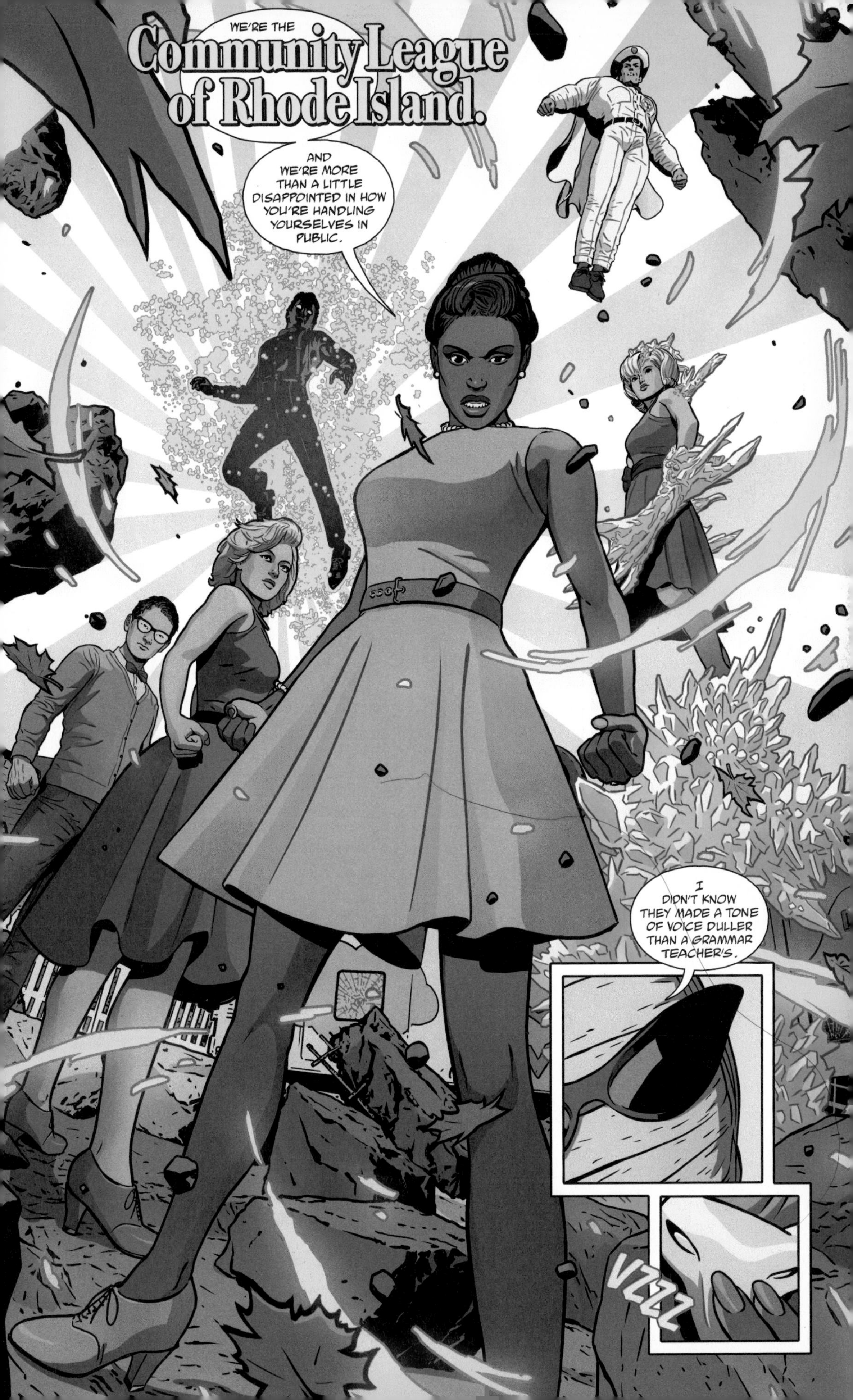
WE'RE THE Community League of Rhode Island.
AND WE'RE MORE THAN A LITTLE DISAPPOINTED IN HOW YOU'RE HANDLING YOURSELVES IN PUBLIC.
I DIDN'T KNOW THEY MADE A TONE OF VOICE DULLER THAN A GRAMMAR TEACHER'S.
VZZZ

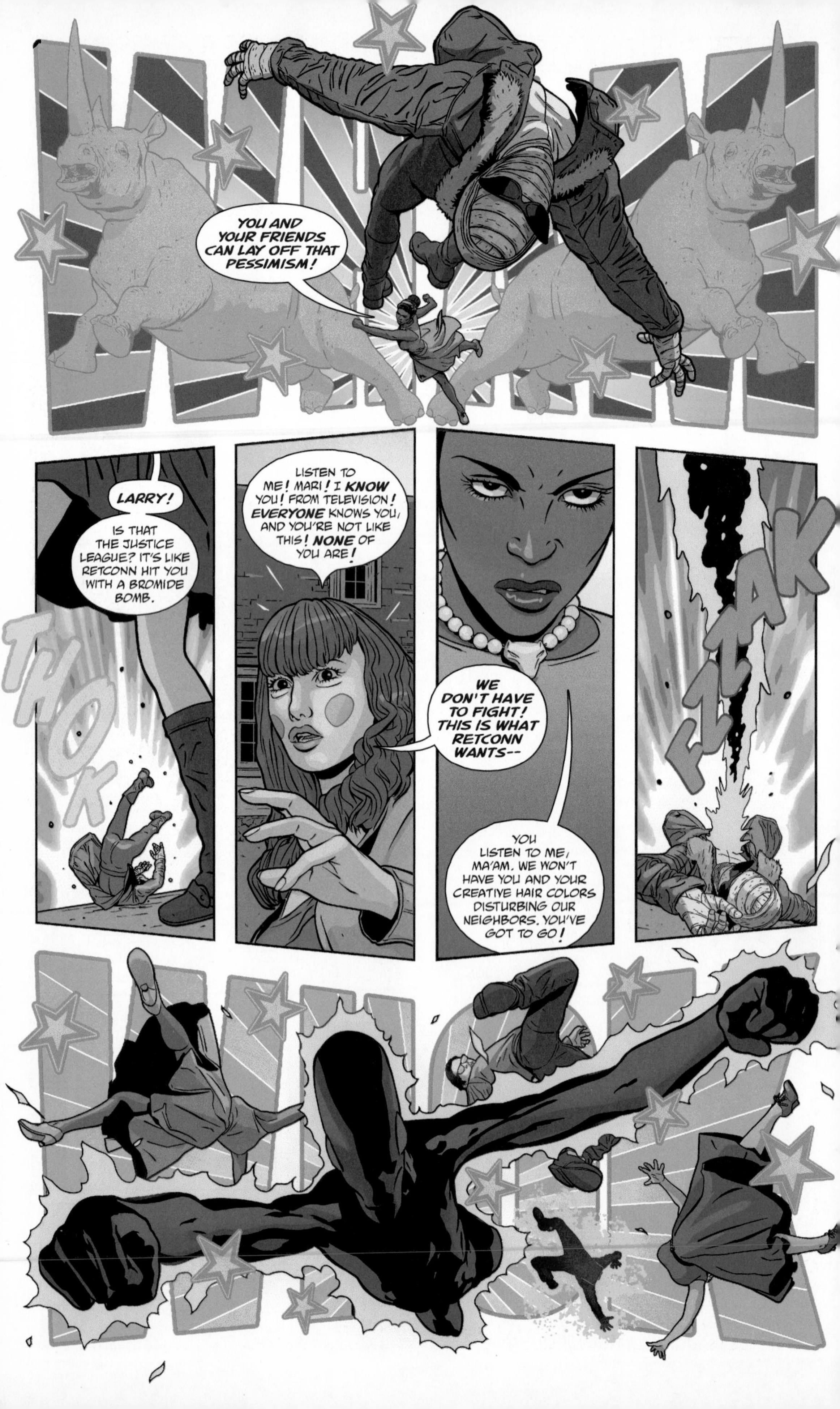
YOU AND YOUR FRIENDS CAN LAY OFF THAT PESSIMISM!
LARRY!
IS THAT THE JUSTICE LEAGUE? IT'S LIKE RETCONN HIT YOU WITH A BROMIDE BOMB.
THOK
LISTEN TO ME! MARI! I KNOW YOU! FROM TELEVISION! EVERYONE KNOWS YOU, AND YOU'RE NOT LIKE THIS! NONE OF YOU ARE!
WE DON'T HAVE TO FIGHT! THIS IS WHAT RETCONN WANTS--
YOU LISTEN TO ME, MA'AM. WE WON'T HAVE YOU AND YOUR CREATIVE HAIR COLORS DISTURBING OUR NEIGHBORS. YOU'VE GOT TO GO!
FZZAK

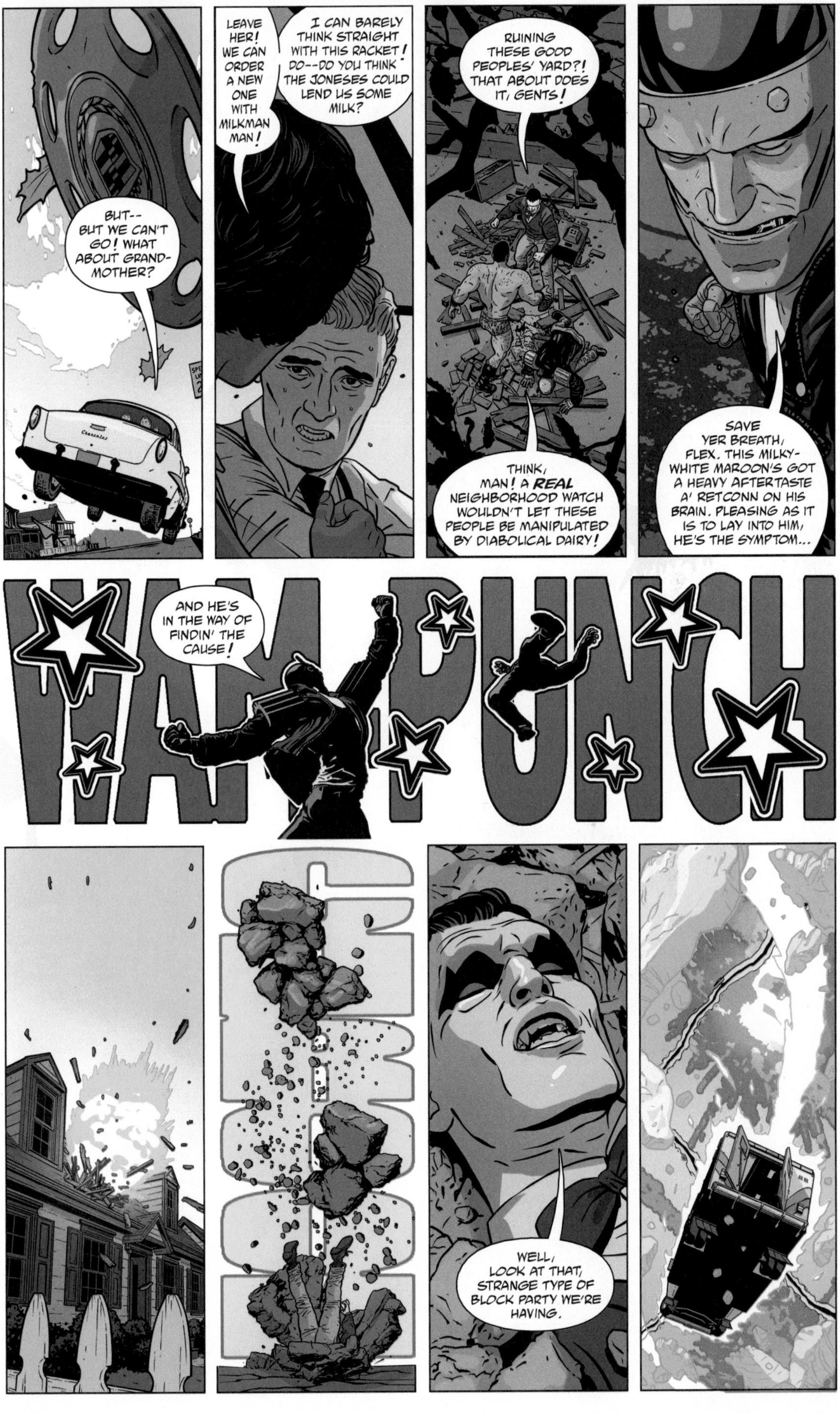

BUT-- BUT WE CAN'T GO! WHAT ABOUT GRAND-MOTHER?
LEAVE HER! WE CAN ORDER A NEW ONE WITH MILKMAN MAN!
I CAN BARELY THINK STRAIGHT WITH THIS RACKET! DO--DO YOU THINK THE JONESES COULD LEND US SOME MILK?
RUINING THESE GOOD PEOPLES' YARD?! THAT ABOUT DOES IT, GENTS!
THINK, MAN! A REAL NEIGHBORHOOD WATCH WOULDN'T LET THESE PEOPLE BE MANIPULATED BY DIABOLICAL DAIRY!
SAVE YER BREATH, FLEX. THIS MILKY-WHITE MAROON'S GOT A HEAVY AFTERTASTE A' RETCONN ON HIS BRAIN. PLEASING AS IT IS TO LAY INTO HIM, HE'S THE SYMPTOM...
AND HE'S IN THE WAY OF FINDIN' THE CAUSE!
PUNCH
WELL, LOOK AT THAT, STRANGE TYPE OF BLOCK PARTY WE'RE HAVING.

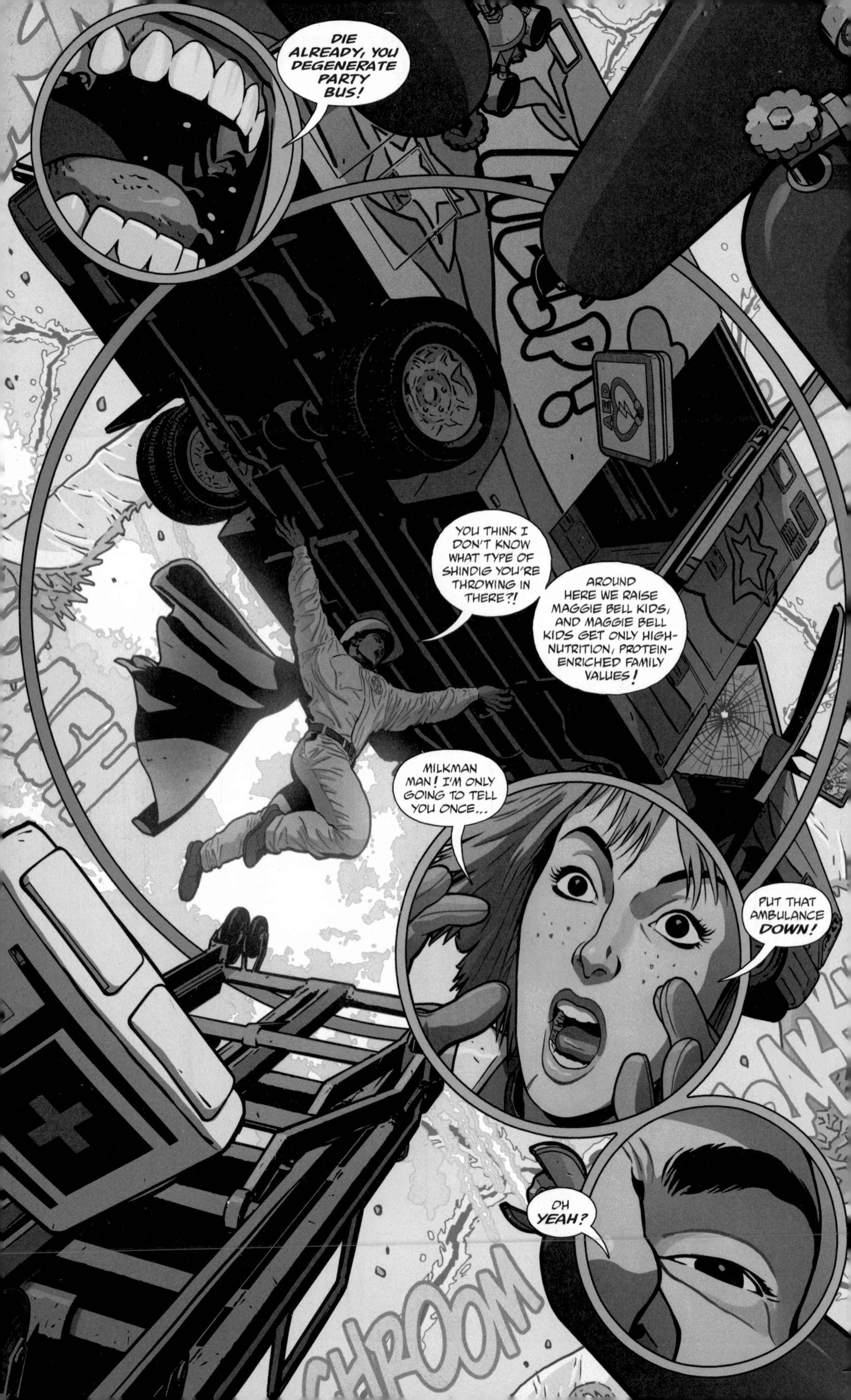
DIE ALREADY, YOU DEGENERATE PARTY BUS!
YOU THINK I DON'T KNOW WHAT TYPE OF SHINDIG YOU'RE THROWING IN THERE?!
AROUND HERE WE RAISE MAGGIE BELL KIDS, AND MAGGIE BELL KIDS GET ONLY HIGH-NUTRITION, PROTEIN-ENRICHED FAMILY VALUES!
MILKMAN MAN! I'M ONLY GOING TO TELL YOU ONCE...
PUT THAT AMBULANCE DOWN!
OH YEAH?
CHROOM

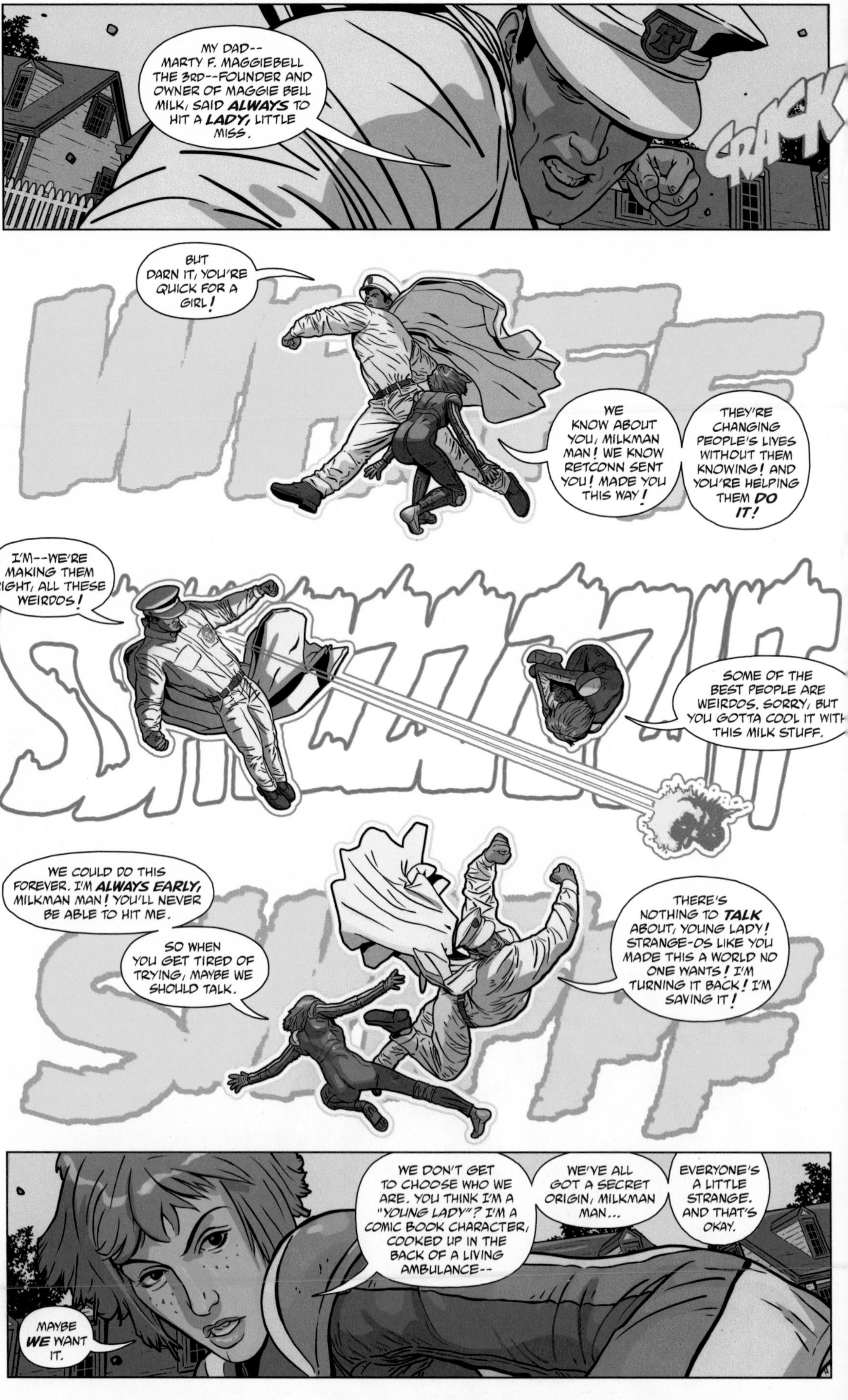

MY DAD-- MARTY F. MAGGIEBELL THE 3RD--FOUNDER AND OWNER OF MAGGIE BELL MILK, SAID ALWAYS TO HIT A LADY, LITTLE MISS.
CRACK
BUT DARN IT, YOU'RE QUICK FOR A GIRL!
WE KNOW ABOUT YOU, MILKMAN MAN! WE KNOW RETCONN SENT YOU! MADE YOU THIS WAY!
THEY'RE CHANGING PEOPLE'S LIVES WITHOUT THEM KNOWING! AND YOU'RE HELPING THEM DO IT!
I'M--WE'RE MAKING THEM RIGHT, ALL THESE WEIRDOS!
SOME OF THE BEST PEOPLE ARE WEIRDOS. SORRY, BUT YOU GOTTA COOL IT WITH THIS MILK STUFF.
WE COULD DO THIS FOREVER. I'M ALWAYS EARLY, MILKMAN MAN! YOU'LL NEVER BE ABLE TO HIT ME.
SO WHEN YOU GET TIRED OF TRYING, MAYBE WE SHOULD TALK.
THERE'S NOTHING TO TALK ABOUT, YOUNG LADY! STRANGE-OS LIKE YOU MADE THIS A WORLD NO ONE WANTS! I'M TURNING IT BACK! I'M SAVING IT!
MAYBE WE WANT IT.
WE DON'T GET TO CHOOSE WHO WE ARE. YOU THINK I'M A "YOUNG LADY"? I'M A COMIC BOOK CHARACTER, COOKED UP IN THE BACK OF A LIVING AMBULANCE--
WE'VE ALL GOT A SECRET ORIGIN, MILKMAN MAN...
EVERYONE'S A LITTLE STRANGE. AND THAT'S OKAY.

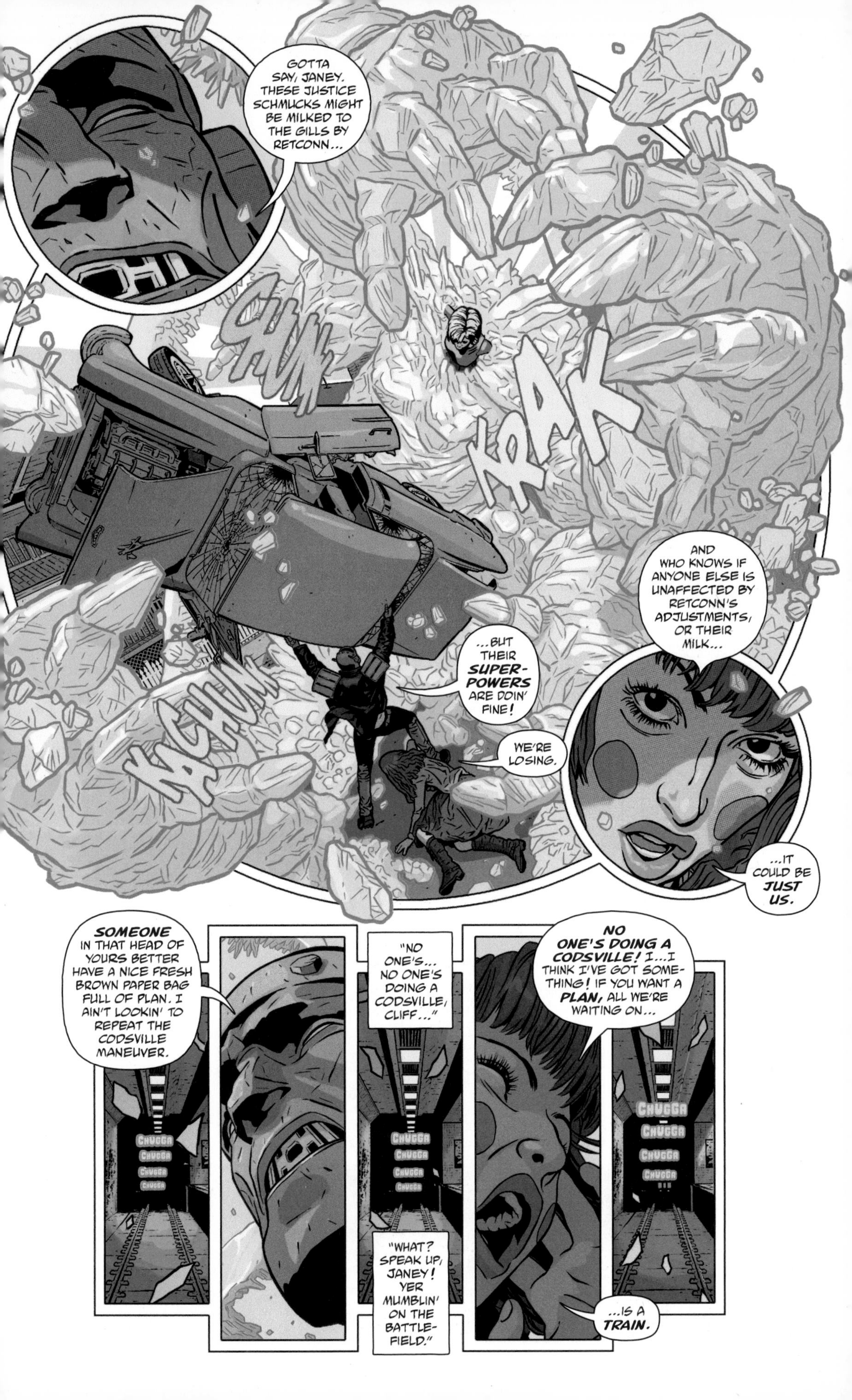
GOTTA SAY, JANEY. THESE JUSTICE SCHMUCKS MIGHT BE MILKED TO THE GILLS BY RETCONN...
CHUNK
KRAK
...BUT THEIR **SUPER-POWERS** ARE DOIN' FINE!
KACHUNK
WE'RE LOSING.
AND WHO KNOWS IF ANYONE ELSE IS UNAFFECTED BY RETCONN'S ADJUSTMENTS, OR THEIR MILK...
...IT COULD BE **JUST US.**
SOMEONE IN THAT HEAD OF YOURS BETTER HAVE A NICE FRESH BROWN PAPER BAG FULL OF PLAN. I AIN'T LOOKIN' TO REPEAT THE CODSVILLE MANEUVER.
CHUGGA CHUGGA CHUGGA CHUGGA
"NO ONE'S... NO ONE'S DOING A CODSVILLE, CLIFF..."
CHUGGA CHUGGA CHUGGA CHUGGA
"WHAT? SPEAK UP, JANEY! YER MUMBLIN' ON THE BATTLE-FIELD."
NO ONE'S DOING A CODSVILLE! I...I THINK I'VE GOT SOME-THING! IF YOU WANT A **PLAN,** ALL WE'RE WAITING ON...
CHUGGA CHUGGA CHUGGA CHUGGA
...IS A **TRAIN.**

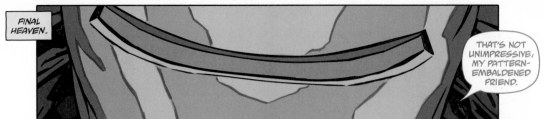

FINAL HEAVEN.

THAT'S NOT UNIMPRESSIVE, MY PATTERN-EMBALDENED FRIEND.

THAT IS RETCONN BRAND ICONOGRAPHY.

I KNOW IT'S GAUCHER THAN ASKING A FORAGER FOR A MAP, BUT I HAVE TO KNOW. HOW DO YOU MAKE YOUR OWN SUPERHERO?

PLEASE, LORD MANGA KHAN. SUPERHEROES ARE JUST LIKE ANYTHING ELSE. ALL YOU NEED ARE THE SCHEMATICS.

CLiK

AND THE LATE GOD OF SUPER-HEROES IS THE SCHEMATIC. WE OWN HIS AUTOPSY RIGHTS.

"THERE IS A LINEAGE OF JUSTICE, AN EVOLUTIONARY TREE LEADING BACK TO AHL, THE GOD OF SUPERHEROES.

"IDEAS BRANCH OFF FROM THE TREE. THEY'RE PERMUTATIONS, EXPRESSED AS MATHEMATICAL FORMULAS. BATMAN AND WONDER WOMAN'S ARE SOME OF THE MOST PRIMAL, MOST PURE.

"WITH THE RIGHT ADJUSTMENTS TO THEIR FORMULA, IT'S SIMPLE TO ALTER AND BROADEN THEIR APPEAL.

"SUPERMAN, HOWEVER, WAS MORE RESISTANT. HIS SYMBOLIC LINEAGE IS A DIRECT LINE FROM THE GOD OF SUPERHEROES. WE TRIED REPEATEDLY, BUT HIS FORMULA COULD NOT BE ADJUSTED."

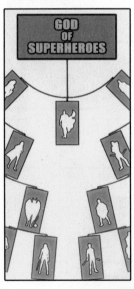
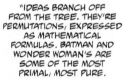

GOD OF SUPERHEROES

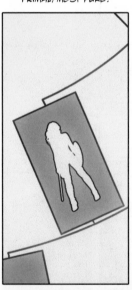

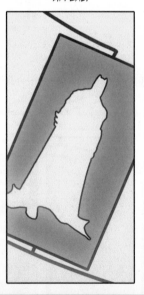

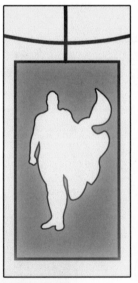

BUT IT COULD BE COPIED...SO WE MADE SOMETHING FROM NOTHING, INJECTED IT WITH OUR NARRATIVE, AND FIRED IT AT EARTH.

OUR BRANDED SUPERMAN. MILKMAN MAN.

...AND WHERE WOULD ONE GO ABOUT GETTING NOTHING?

HAPPY HARBOR.

CHUGGACHUGGA CHUGGACHUGGA

HERE WE GO.

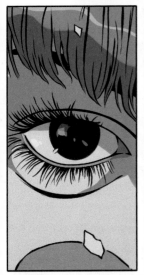

Screeeech
Screeeech

GOOD TO SEE YOU. IT'S BEEN A WHILE.

IT'S GOOD TO SEE ME?

NOT THAT I'M COMPLAINING, BUT I'M PRETTY SURE IT'S A WAR OUT THERE. I MAKE PAINTINGS SIZZLE. SO WHY ME?

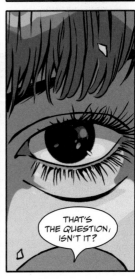

THAT'S THE QUESTION, ISN'T IT?

"NOW THAT WE'RE IN CONTROL, I'VE BEEN THINKING ABOUT YOU. AND I THINK YOU'VE BEEN HOLDING BACK.

"SOMETHING ABOUT WHAT CASEY SAID. SHE'S A COMIC BOOK CHARACTER, A PIECE OF ART. SO MAYBE...MAYBE EVERYONE IS, SOMEWHERE.

"I KNOW YOU'VE ONLY BEEN ABLE TO PSYCHICALLY ACTIVATE YOUR OWN ART. THAT WAS BEFORE WE WERE BALANCED.

"BECAUSE THE *TRUTH* IS..."

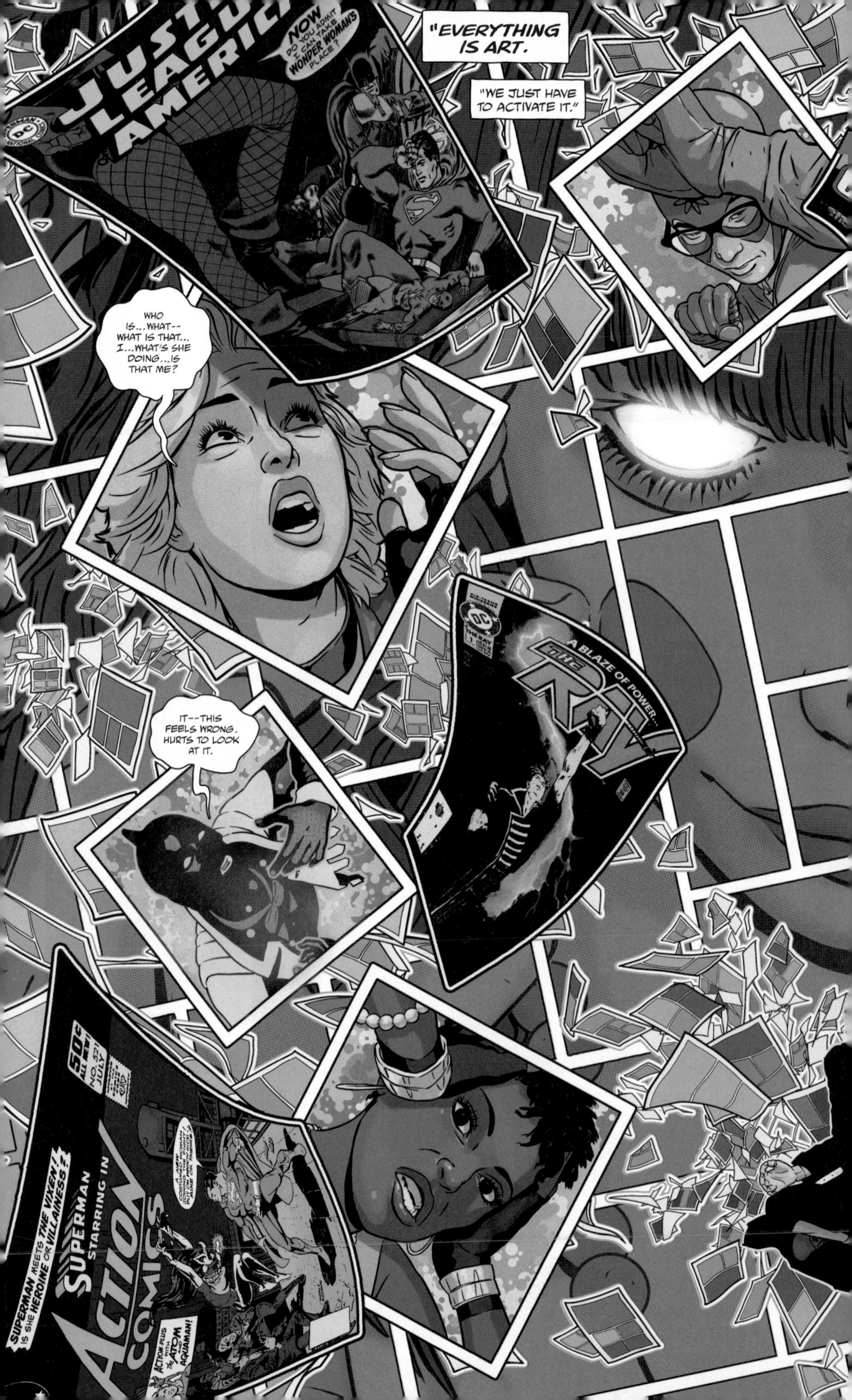
"EVERYTHING IS ART.
"WE JUST HAVE TO ACTIVATE IT."
JUSTICE LEAGUE OF AMERICA
NOW DO YOU ADMIT I CAN TAKE WONDER WOMAN'S PLACE?
WHO IS...WHAT-- WHAT IS THAT... I...WHAT'S SHE DOING...IS THAT ME?
IT--THIS FEELS WRONG. HURTS TO LOOK AT IT.
A BLAZE OF POWER...
THE RAY
SUPERMAN MEETS THE VIXEN! IS SHE HEROINE OR VILLAINESS?
SUPERMAN STARRING IN ACTION COMICS
ACTION PLUS THE ATOM AND AQUAMAN!

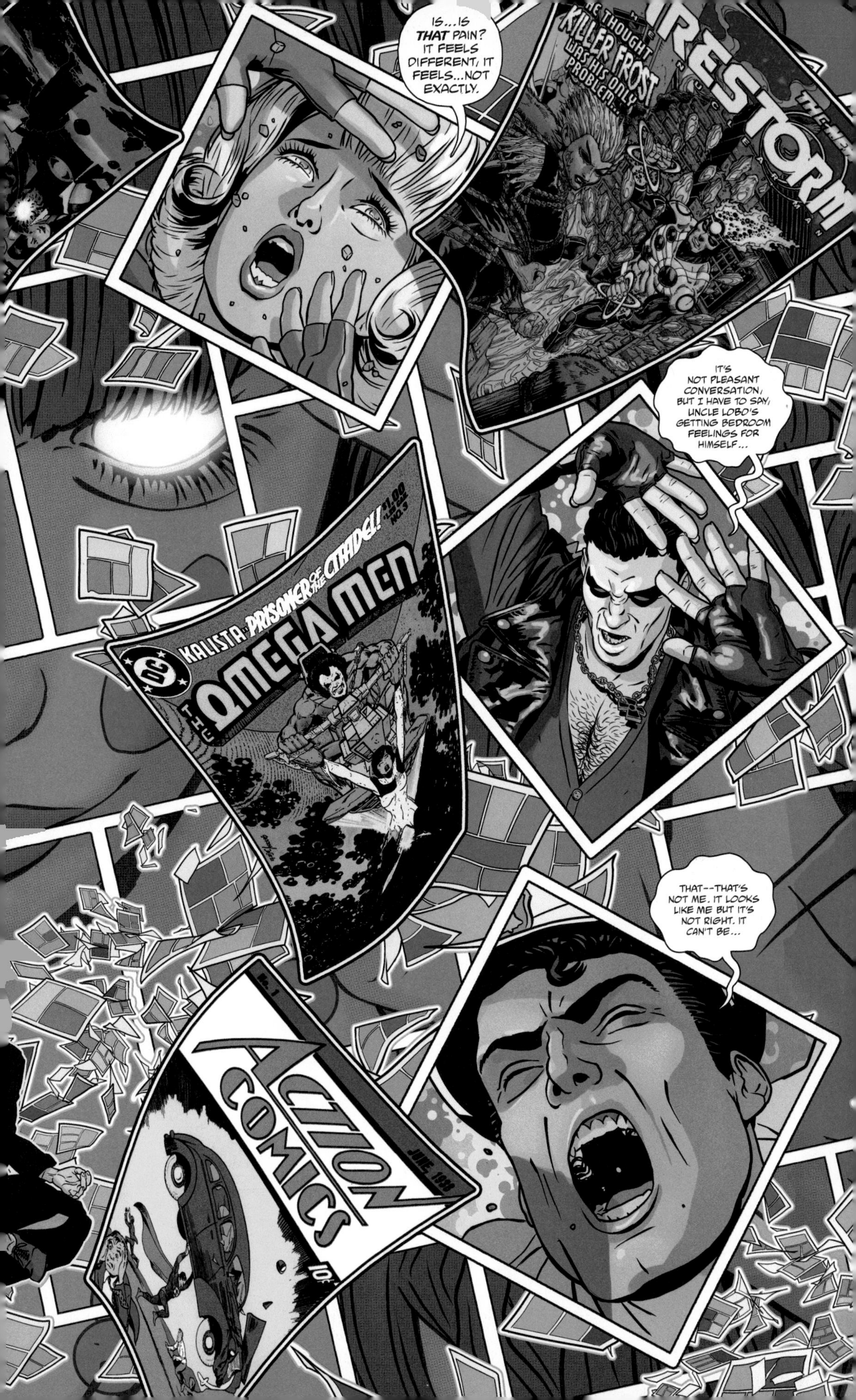
IS...IS THAT PAIN? IT FEELS DIFFERENT, IT FEELS...NOT EXACTLY.
KILLER FROST WAS HIS ONLY PROBLEM...
FIRESTORM
IT'S NOT PLEASANT CONVERSATION, BUT I HAVE TO SAY, UNCLE LOBO'S GETTING BEDROOM FEELINGS FOR HIMSELF...
KALISTA...PRISONER OF THE CITADEL!
$1.00
NO. 3
THE OMEGA MEN
THAT--THAT'S NOT ME. IT LOOKS LIKE ME BUT IT'S NOT RIGHT. IT CAN'T BE...
ACTION COMICS
JUNE, 1938
10¢

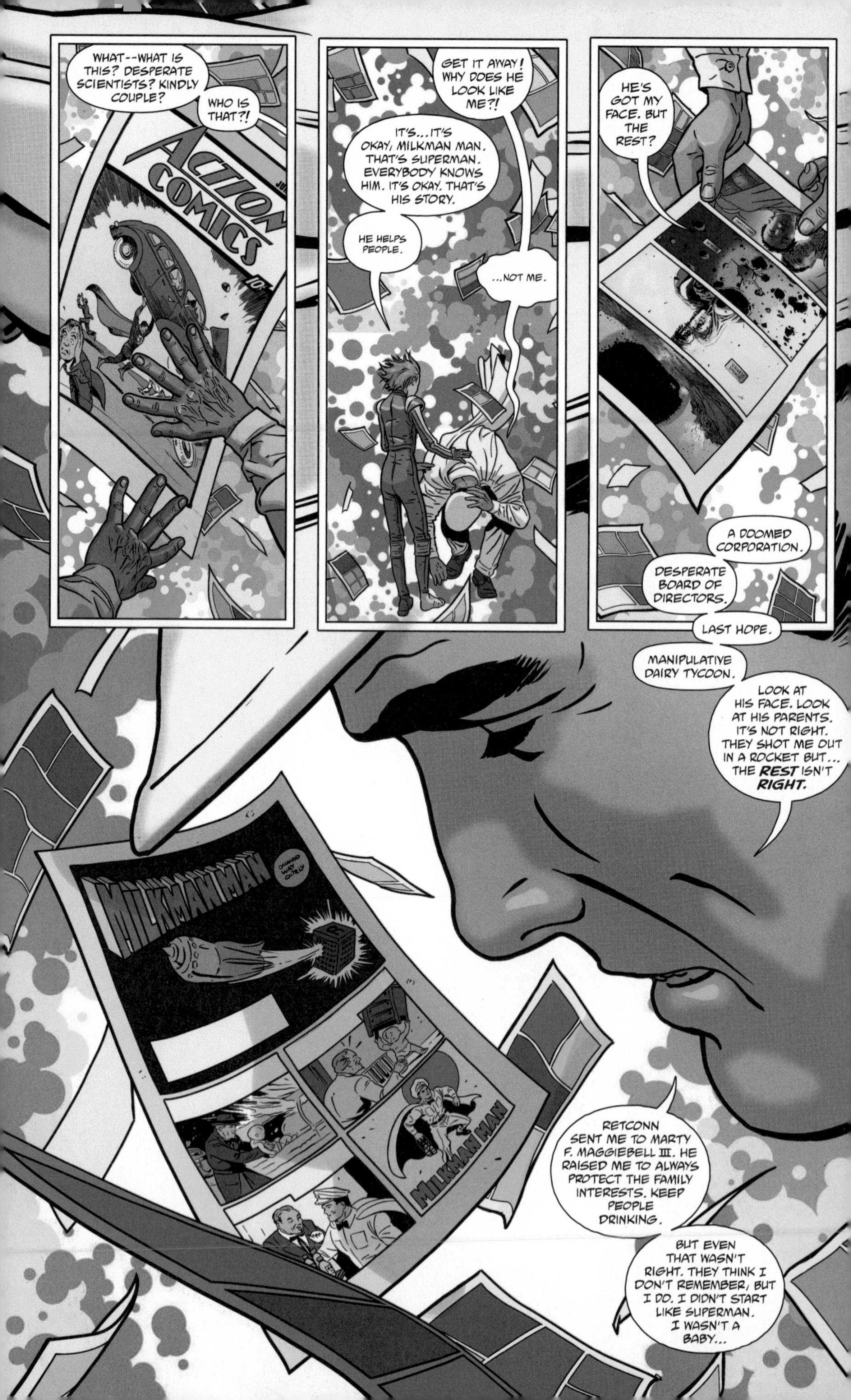

WHAT--WHAT IS THIS? DESPERATE SCIENTISTS? KINDLY COUPLE?
WHO IS THAT?!
ACTION COMICS
GET IT AWAY! WHY DOES HE LOOK LIKE ME?!
IT'S... IT'S OKAY, MILKMAN MAN. THAT'S SUPERMAN. EVERYBODY KNOWS HIM. IT'S OKAY. THAT'S HIS STORY.
HE HELPS PEOPLE.
...NOT ME.
HE'S GOT MY FACE. BUT THE REST?
A DOOMED CORPORATION.
DESPERATE BOARD OF DIRECTORS.
LAST HOPE.
MANIPULATIVE DAIRY TYCOON.
LOOK AT HIS FACE. LOOK AT HIS PARENTS. IT'S NOT RIGHT. THEY SHOT ME OUT IN A ROCKET BUT... THE REST ISN'T RIGHT.
MILKMAN MAN
MILKMAN MAN
RETCONN SENT ME TO MARTY F. MAGGIEBELL III. HE RAISED ME TO ALWAYS PROTECT THE FAMILY INTERESTS. KEEP PEOPLE DRINKING.
BUT EVEN THAT WASN'T RIGHT. THEY THINK I DON'T REMEMBER, BUT I DO. I DIDN'T START LIKE SUPERMAN. I WASN'T A BABY...

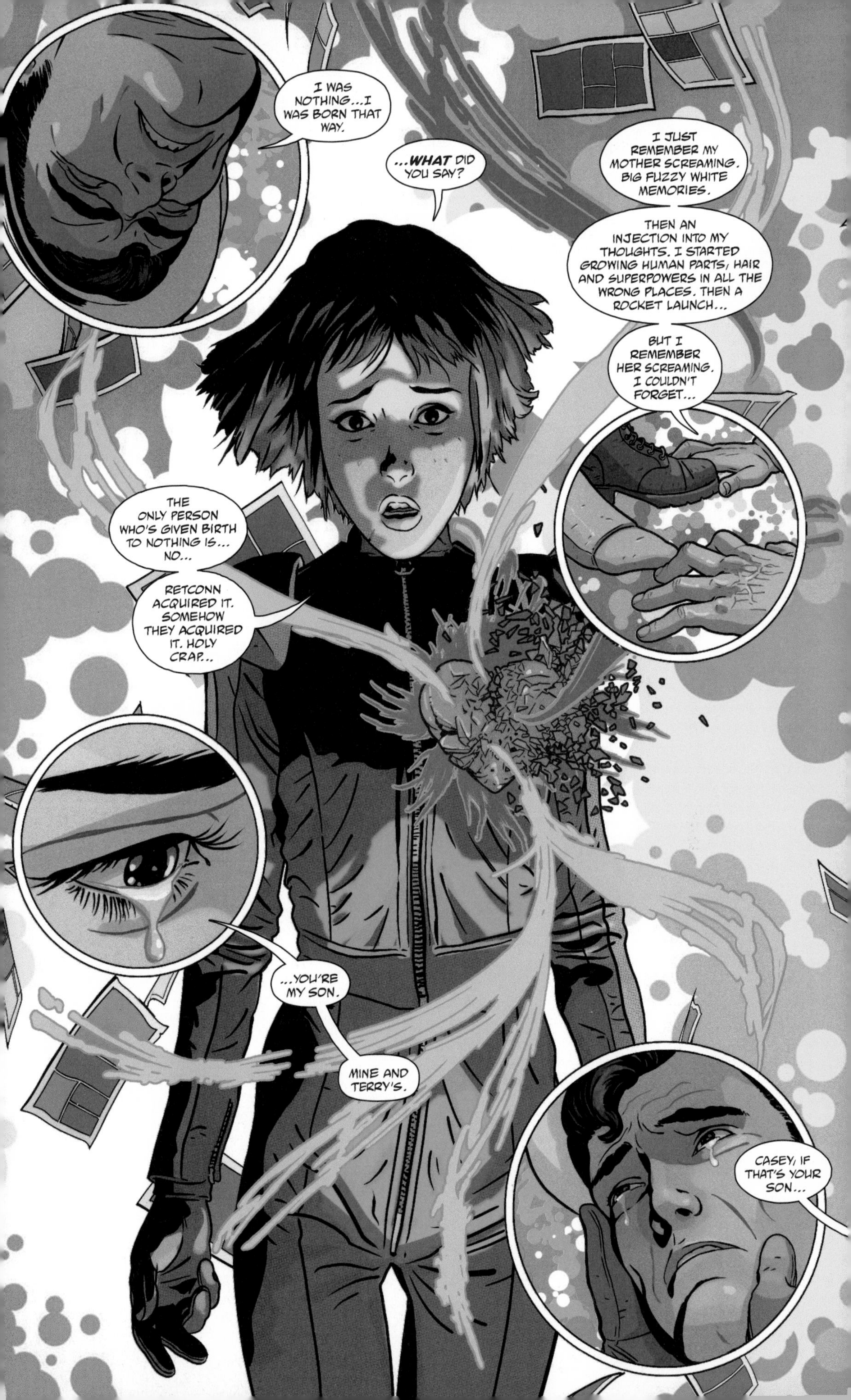
I WAS NOTHING...I WAS BORN THAT WAY.
...WHAT DID YOU SAY?
I JUST REMEMBER MY MOTHER SCREAMING. BIG FUZZY WHITE MEMORIES.
THEN AN INJECTION INTO MY THOUGHTS. I STARTED GROWING HUMAN PARTS, HAIR AND SUPERPOWERS IN ALL THE WRONG PLACES. THEN A ROCKET LAUNCH...
BUT I REMEMBER HER SCREAMING. I COULDN'T FORGET...
THE ONLY PERSON WHO'S GIVEN BIRTH TO NOTHING IS... NO...
RETCONN ACQUIRED IT. SOMEHOW THEY ACQUIRED IT. HOLY CRAP...
...YOU'RE MY SON.
MINE AND TERRY'S.
CASEY, IF THAT'S YOUR SON...

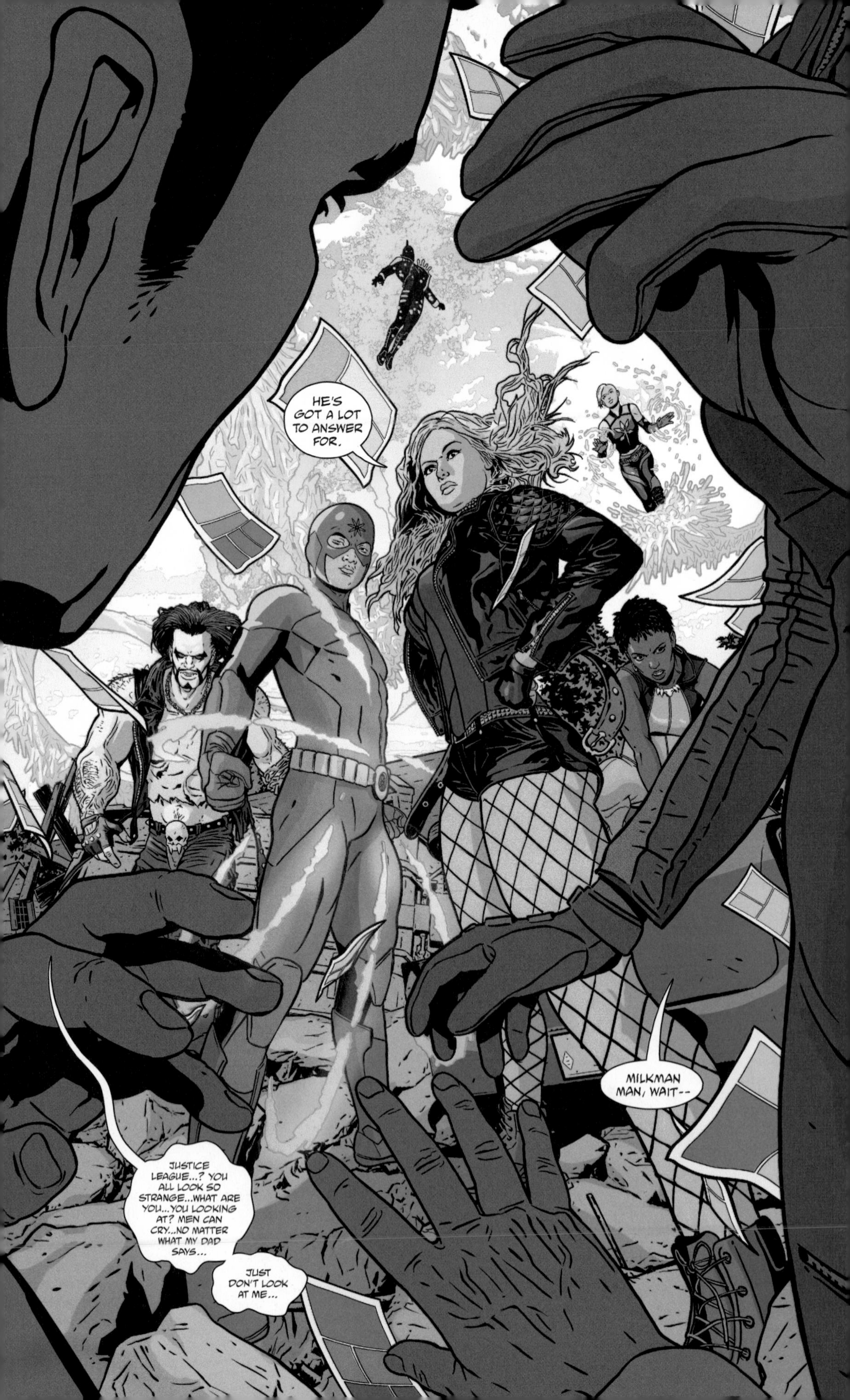
HE'S GOT A LOT TO ANSWER FOR.
MILKMAN MAN, WAIT--
JUSTICE LEAGUE...? YOU ALL LOOK SO STRANGE...WHAT ARE YOU...YOU LOOKING AT? MEN CAN CRY...NO MATTER WHAT MY DAD SAYS...
JUST DON'T LOOK AT ME...

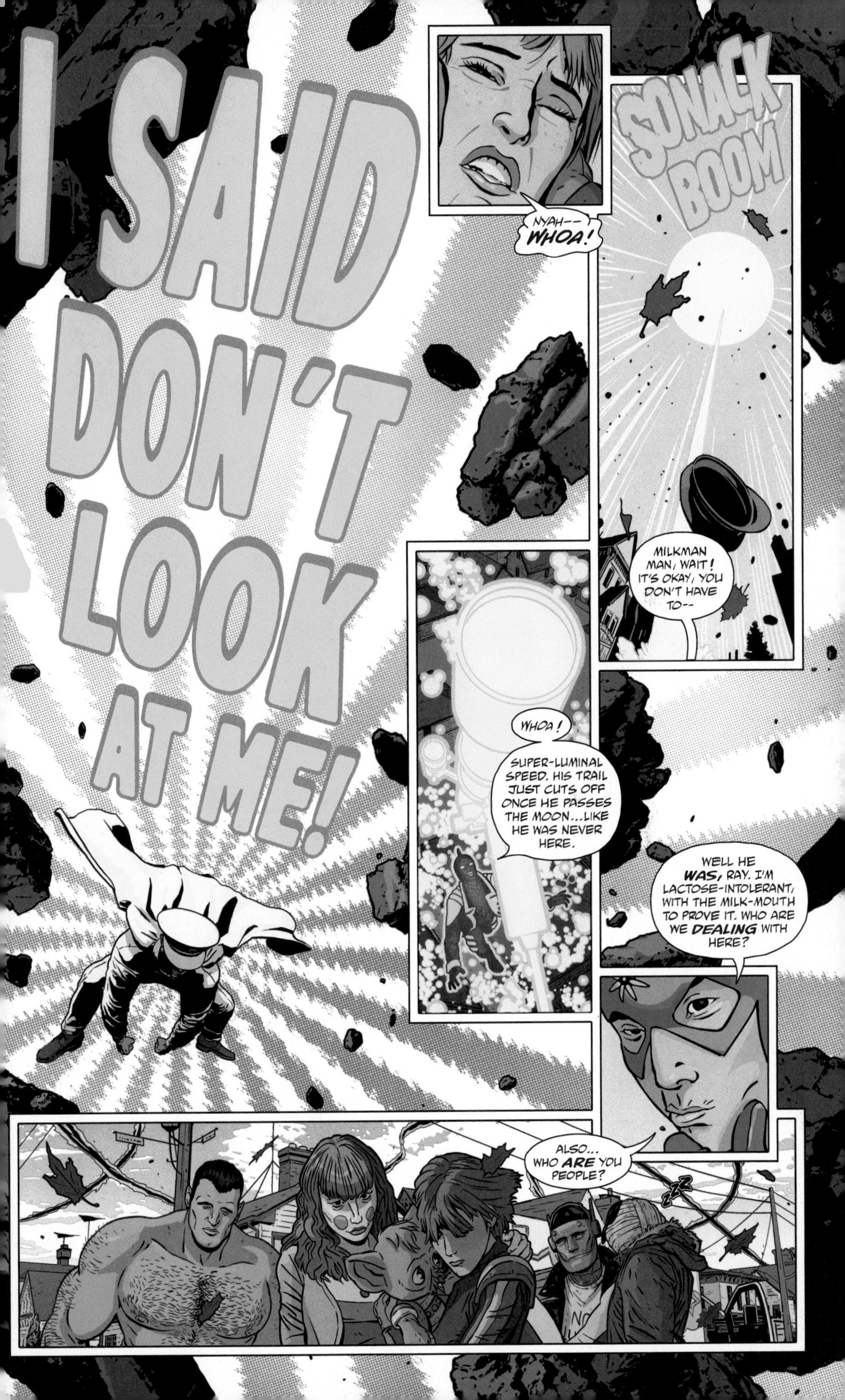
I SAID DON'T LOOK AT ME!
NYAH-- WHOA!
SONACK BOOM
MILKMAN MAN, WAIT! IT'S OKAY, YOU DON'T HAVE TO--
WHOA!
SUPER-LUMINAL SPEED. HIS TRAIL JUST CUTS OFF ONCE HE PASSES THE MOON...LIKE HE WAS NEVER HERE.
WELL HE WAS, RAY. I'M LACTOSE-INTOLERANT, WITH THE MILK-MOUTH TO PROVE IT. WHO ARE WE DEALING WITH HERE?
ALSO... WHO ARE YOU PEOPLE?

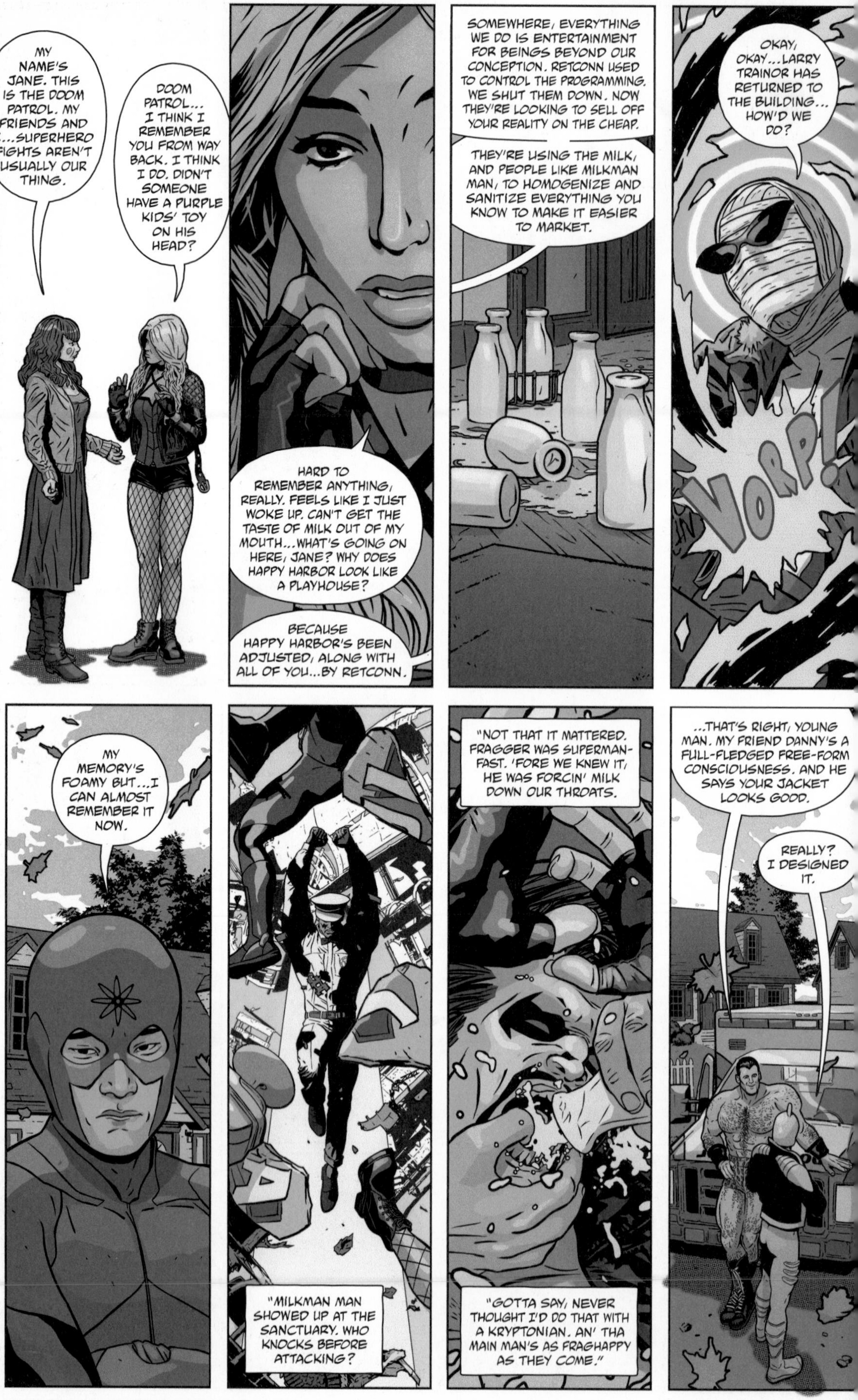
MY NAME'S JANE. THIS IS THE DOOM PATROL. MY FRIENDS AND I...SUPERHERO FIGHTS AREN'T USUALLY OUR THING.
DOOM PATROL... I THINK I REMEMBER YOU FROM WAY BACK. I THINK I DO. DIDN'T SOMEONE HAVE A PURPLE KIDS' TOY ON HIS HEAD?
HARD TO REMEMBER ANYTHING, REALLY. FEELS LIKE I JUST WOKE UP. CAN'T GET THE TASTE OF MILK OUT OF MY MOUTH...WHAT'S GOING ON HERE, JANE? WHY DOES HAPPY HARBOR LOOK LIKE A PLAYHOUSE?
BECAUSE HAPPY HARBOR'S BEEN ADJUSTED, ALONG WITH ALL OF YOU...BY RETCONN.
SOMEWHERE, EVERYTHING WE DO IS ENTERTAINMENT FOR BEINGS BEYOND OUR CONCEPTION. RETCONN USED TO CONTROL THE PROGRAMMING. WE SHUT THEM DOWN. NOW THEY'RE LOOKING TO SELL OFF YOUR REALITY ON THE CHEAP.
THEY'RE USING THE MILK, AND PEOPLE LIKE MILKMAN MAN, TO HOMOGENIZE AND SANITIZE EVERYTHING YOU KNOW TO MAKE IT EASIER TO MARKET.
OKAY, OKAY...LARRY TRAINOR HAS RETURNED TO THE BUILDING... HOW'D WE DO?
VORP!
MY MEMORY'S FOAMY BUT...I CAN ALMOST REMEMBER IT NOW.
"MILKMAN MAN SHOWED UP AT THE SANCTUARY. WHO KNOCKS BEFORE ATTACKING?
"NOT THAT IT MATTERED. FRAGGER WAS SUPERMAN-FAST. 'FORE WE KNEW IT, HE WAS FORCIN' MILK DOWN OUR THROATS.
"GOTTA SAY, NEVER THOUGHT I'D DO THAT WITH A KRYPTONIAN. AN' THA MAIN MAN'S AS FRAGHAPPY AS THEY COME."
...THAT'S RIGHT, YOUNG MAN. MY FRIEND DANNY'S A FULL-FLEDGED FREE-FORM CONSCIOUSNESS. AND HE SAYS YOUR JACKET LOOKS GOOD.
REALLY? I DESIGNED IT.

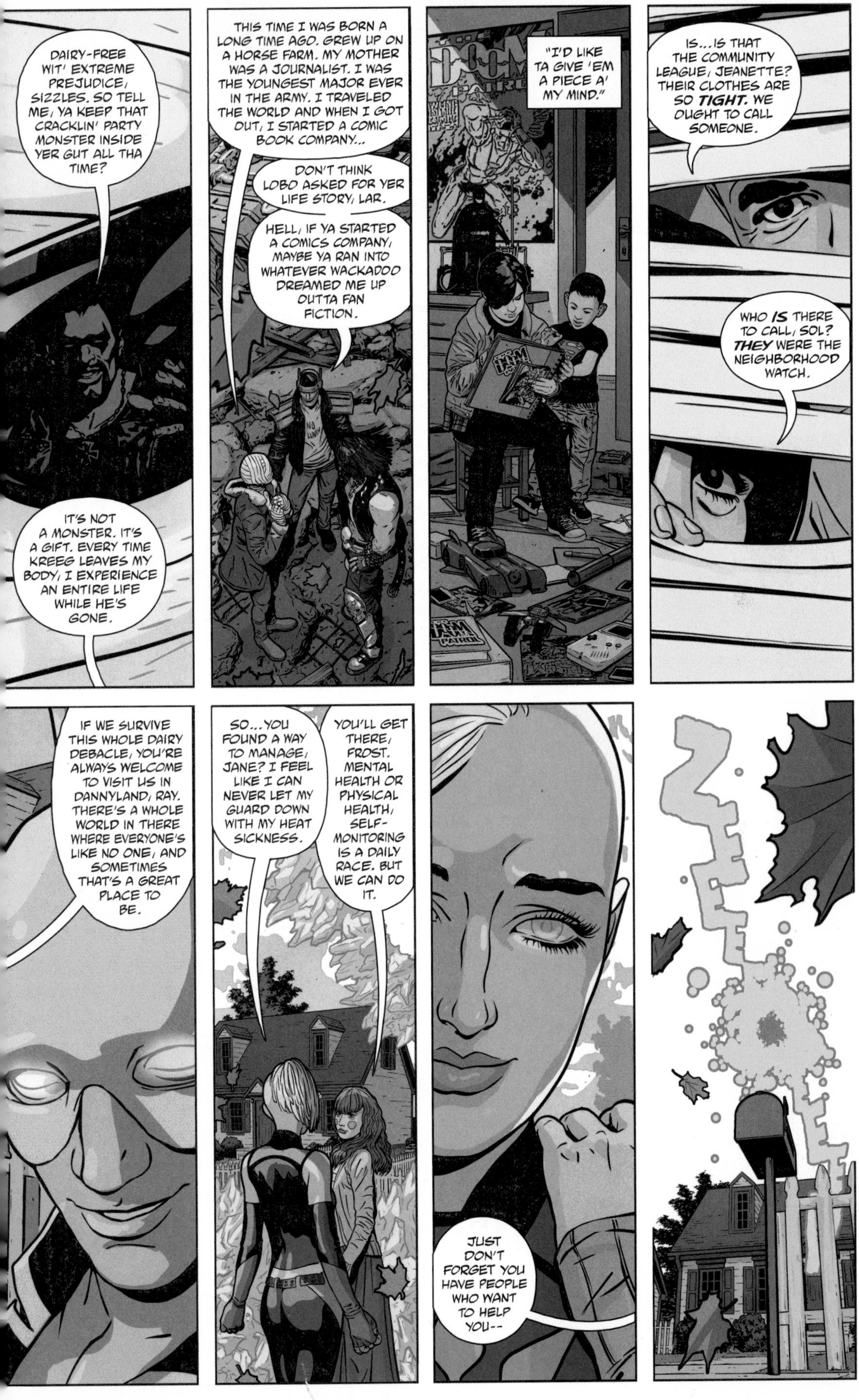
DAIRY-FREE WIT' EXTREME PREJUDICE, SIZZLES. SO TELL ME, YA KEEP THAT CRACKLIN' PARTY MONSTER INSIDE YER GUT ALL THA TIME?
IT'S NOT A MONSTER. IT'S A GIFT. EVERY TIME KREEG LEAVES MY BODY, I EXPERIENCE AN ENTIRE LIFE WHILE HE'S GONE.
THIS TIME I WAS BORN A LONG TIME AGO. GREW UP ON A HORSE FARM. MY MOTHER WAS A JOURNALIST. I WAS THE YOUNGEST MAJOR EVER IN THE ARMY. I TRAVELED THE WORLD AND WHEN I GOT OUT, I STARTED A COMIC BOOK COMPANY...
DON'T THINK LOBO ASKED FOR YER LIFE STORY, LAR.
HELL, IF YA STARTED A COMICS COMPANY, MAYBE YA RAN INTO WHATEVER WACKADOO DREAMED ME UP OUTTA FAN FICTION.
"I'D LIKE TA GIVE 'EM A PIECE A' MY MIND."
IS...IS THAT THE COMMUNITY LEAGUE, JEANETTE? THEIR CLOTHES ARE SO TIGHT. WE OUGHT TO CALL SOMEONE.
WHO IS THERE TO CALL, SOL? THEY WERE THE NEIGHBORHOOD WATCH.
IF WE SURVIVE THIS WHOLE DAIRY DEBACLE, YOU'RE ALWAYS WELCOME TO VISIT US IN DANNYLAND, RAY. THERE'S A WHOLE WORLD IN THERE WHERE EVERYONE'S LIKE NO ONE, AND SOMETIMES THAT'S A GREAT PLACE TO BE.
SO...YOU FOUND A WAY TO MANAGE, JANE? I FEEL LIKE I CAN NEVER LET MY GUARD DOWN WITH MY HEAT SICKNESS.
YOU'LL GET THERE, FROST. MENTAL HEALTH OR PHYSICAL HEALTH, SELF-MONITORING IS A DAILY RACE. BUT WE CAN DO IT.
JUST DON'T FORGET YOU HAVE PEOPLE WHO WANT TO HELP YOU--
ZEEEEEE

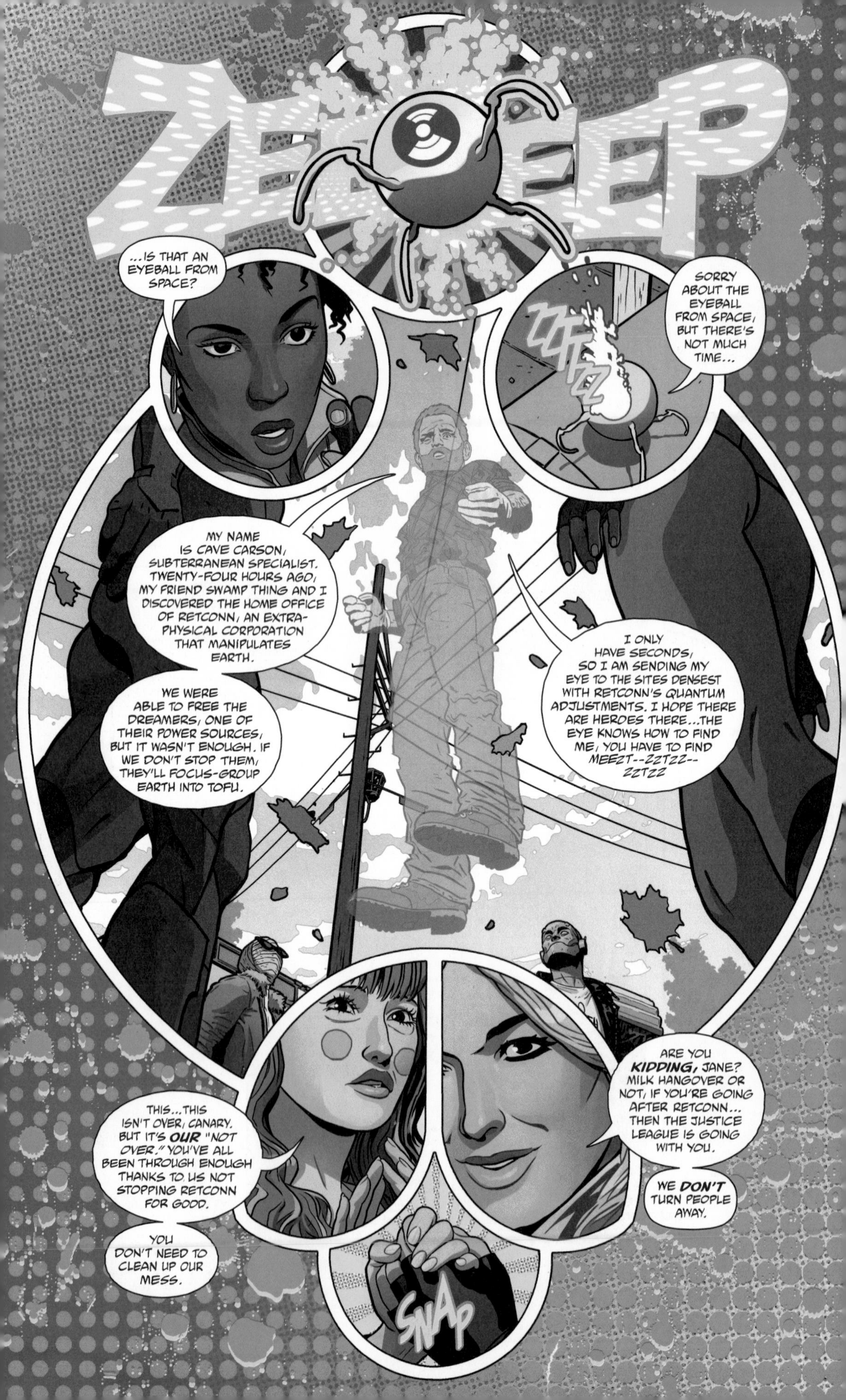
ZEEEEP
...IS THAT AN EYEBALL FROM SPACE?
SORRY ABOUT THE EYEBALL FROM SPACE, BUT THERE'S NOT MUCH TIME...
ZZFFZZ
MY NAME IS CAVE CARSON, SUBTERRANEAN SPECIALIST. TWENTY-FOUR HOURS AGO, MY FRIEND SWAMP THING AND I DISCOVERED THE HOME OFFICE OF RETCONN, AN EXTRA-PHYSICAL CORPORATION THAT MANIPULATES EARTH.
WE WERE ABLE TO FREE THE DREAMERS, ONE OF THEIR POWER SOURCES, BUT IT WASN'T ENOUGH. IF WE DON'T STOP THEM, THEY'LL FOCUS-GROUP EARTH INTO TOFU.
I ONLY HAVE SECONDS, SO I AM SENDING MY EYE TO THE SITES DENSEST WITH RETCONN'S QUANTUM ADJUSTMENTS. I HOPE THERE ARE HEROES THERE...THE EYE KNOWS HOW TO FIND ME, YOU HAVE TO FIND MEEZT--ZZTZZ--ZZTZZ
THIS...THIS ISN'T OVER, CANARY. BUT IT'S **OUR** "NOT OVER." YOU'VE ALL BEEN THROUGH ENOUGH THANKS TO US NOT STOPPING RETCONN FOR GOOD.
YOU DON'T NEED TO CLEAN UP OUR MESS.
ARE YOU **KIDDING,** JANE? MILK HANGOVER OR NOT, IF YOU'RE GOING AFTER RETCONN... THEN THE JUSTICE LEAGUE IS GOING WITH YOU.
WE **DON'T** TURN PEOPLE AWAY.
SNAP

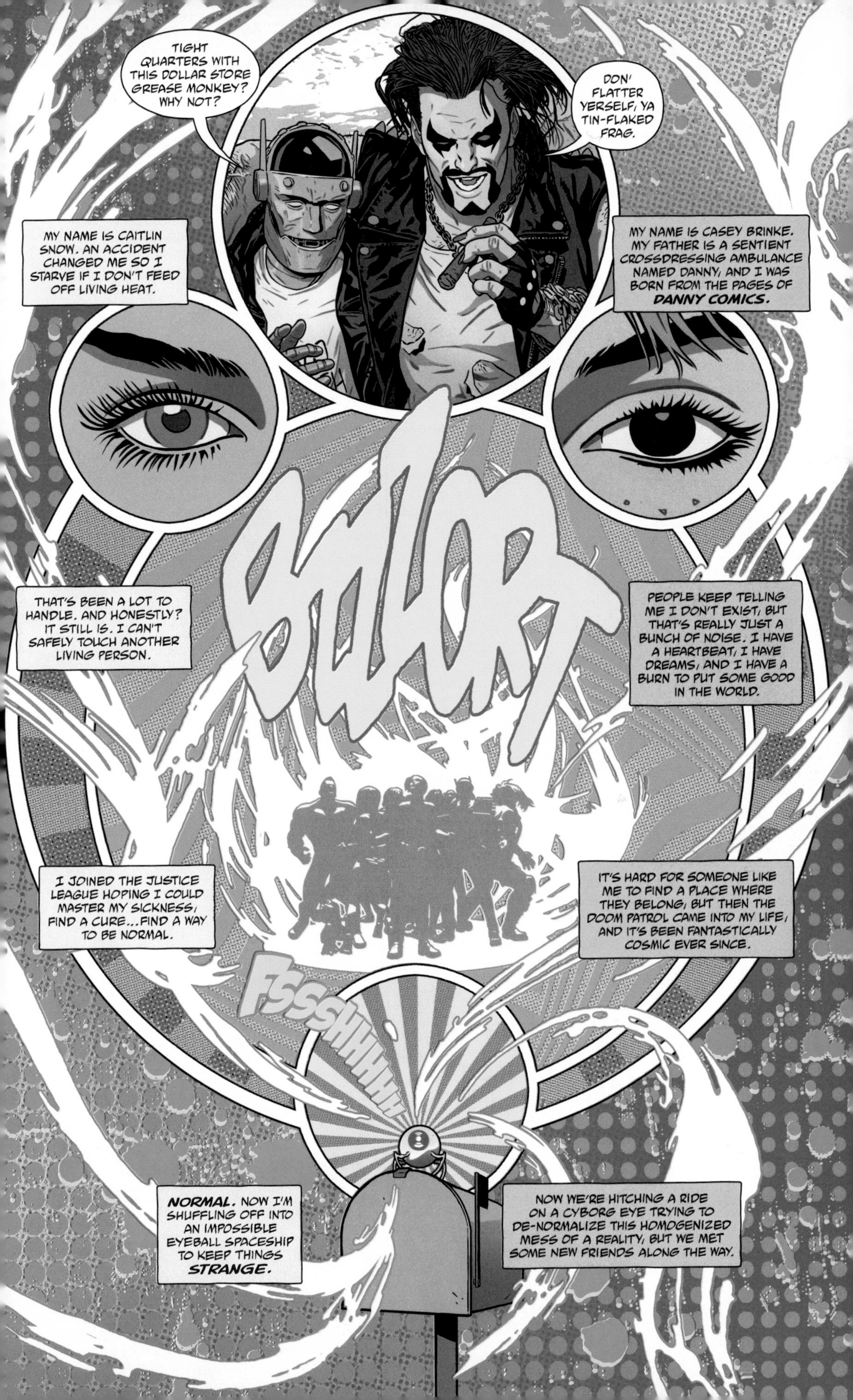
TIGHT QUARTERS WITH THIS DOLLAR STORE GREASE MONKEY? WHY NOT?
DON' FLATTER YERSELF, YA TIN-FLAKED FRAG.
MY NAME IS CAITLIN SNOW. AN ACCIDENT CHANGED ME SO I STARVE IF I DON'T FEED OFF LIVING HEAT.
MY NAME IS CASEY BRINKE. MY FATHER IS A SENTIENT CROSSDRESSING AMBULANCE NAMED DANNY, AND I WAS BORN FROM THE PAGES OF DANNY COMICS.
SPLORT
THAT'S BEEN A LOT TO HANDLE. AND HONESTLY? IT STILL IS. I CAN'T SAFELY TOUCH ANOTHER LIVING PERSON.
PEOPLE KEEP TELLING ME I DON'T EXIST, BUT THAT'S REALLY JUST A BUNCH OF NOISE. I HAVE A HEARTBEAT, I HAVE DREAMS, AND I HAVE A BURN TO PUT SOME GOOD IN THE WORLD.
I JOINED THE JUSTICE LEAGUE HOPING I COULD MASTER MY SICKNESS, FIND A CURE...FIND A WAY TO BE NORMAL.
IT'S HARD FOR SOMEONE LIKE ME TO FIND A PLACE WHERE THEY BELONG, BUT THEN THE DOOM PATROL CAME INTO MY LIFE, AND IT'S BEEN FANTASTICALLY COSMIC EVER SINCE.
FSSSHHHHH
NORMAL. NOW I'M SHUFFLING OFF INTO AN IMPOSSIBLE EYEBALL SPACESHIP TO KEEP THINGS STRANGE.
NOW WE'RE HITCHING A RIDE ON A CYBORG EYE TRYING TO DE-NORMALIZE THIS HOMOGENIZED MESS OF A REALITY, BUT WE MET SOME NEW FRIENDS ALONG THE WAY.

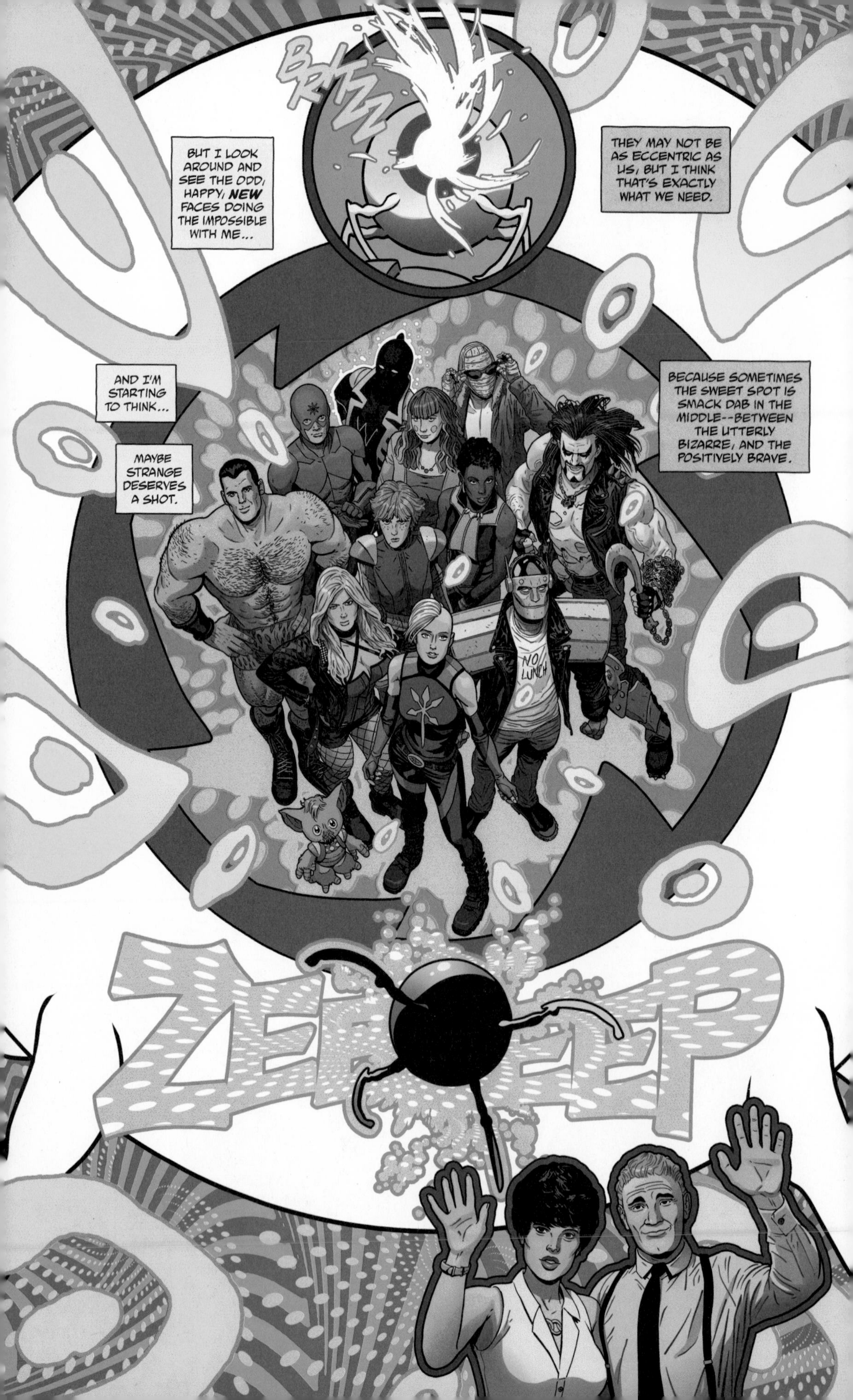

BRTZZZ
BUT I LOOK AROUND AND SEE THE ODD, HAPPY, **NEW** FACES DOING THE IMPOSSIBLE WITH ME...
THEY MAY NOT BE AS ECCENTRIC AS US, BUT I THINK THAT'S EXACTLY WHAT WE NEED.
AND I'M STARTING TO THINK...
MAYBE STRANGE DESERVES A SHOT.
BECAUSE SOMETIMES THE SWEET SPOT IS SMACK DAB IN THE MIDDLE--BETWEEN THE UTTERLY BIZARRE, AND THE POSITIVELY BRAVE.
NO LUNCH

Perhaps the strangest creation of George Sumner, the Formless Girl debuted in "The Birth of the Formless Girl" in 1956's ASTOUNDING TALES #32. Originally conceived as a "horror superhero," Sumner was forced by his editors to fit the character of Caroline Sharp into the increasingly popular science fiction superhero mold. Still, Caroline Sharp would never stray too far from Sumner's original idea, a monster movie heroine struggling to maintain her humanity.

"The Birth of the Formless Girl," ASTOUNDING TALES #32. Story and art by George Sumner. 1956.

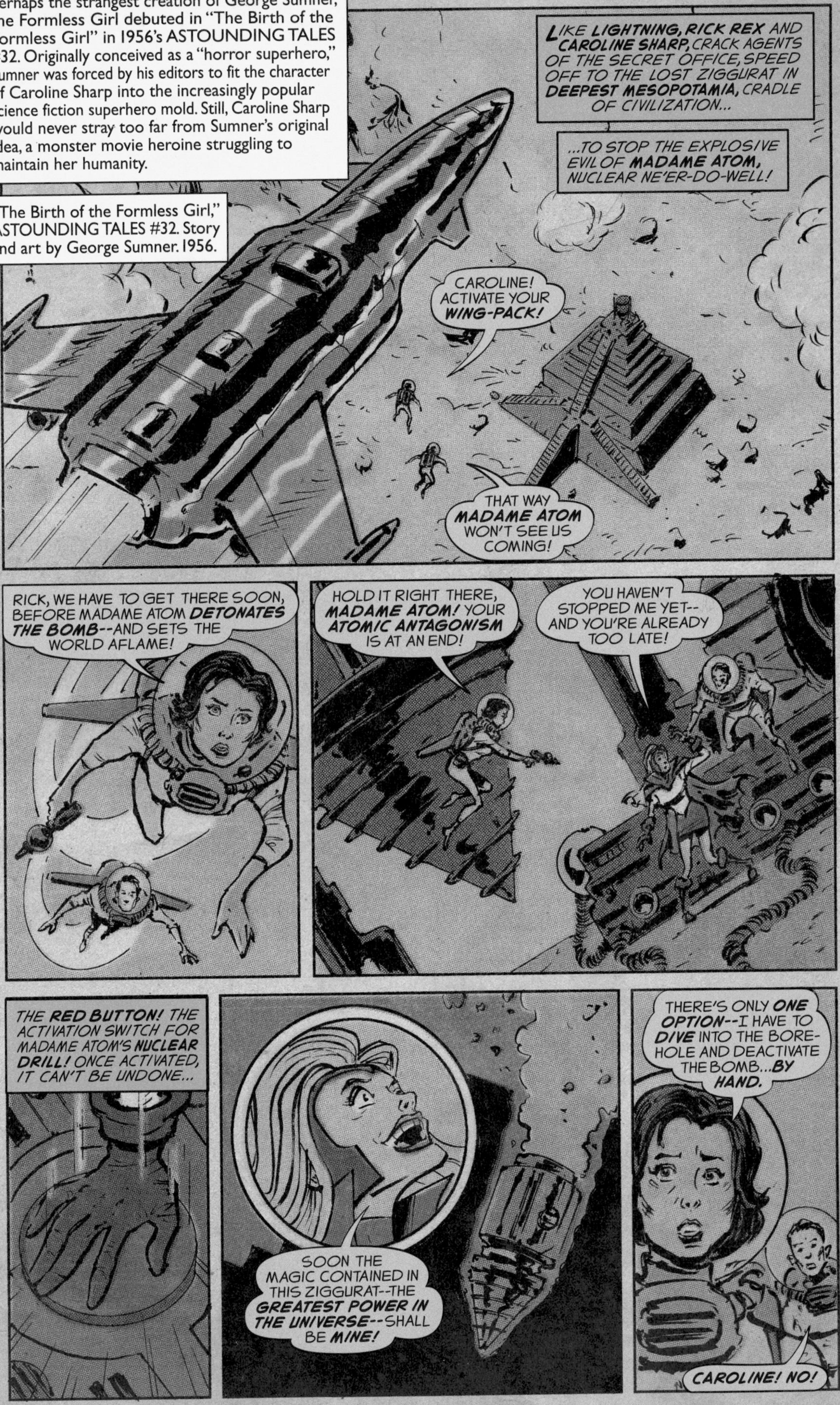

LIKE LIGHTNING, RICK REX AND CAROLINE SHARP, CRACK AGENTS OF THE SECRET OFFICE, SPEED OFF TO THE LOST ZIGGURAT IN DEEPEST MESOPOTAMIA, CRADLE OF CIVILIZATION...
...TO STOP THE EXPLOSIVE EVIL OF MADAME ATOM, NUCLEAR NE'ER-DO-WELL!
CAROLINE! ACTIVATE YOUR WING-PACK!
THAT WAY MADAME ATOM WON'T SEE US COMING!
RICK, WE HAVE TO GET THERE SOON, BEFORE MADAME ATOM DETONATES THE BOMB--AND SETS THE WORLD AFLAME!
HOLD IT RIGHT THERE, MADAME ATOM! YOUR ATOMIC ANTAGONISM IS AT AN END!
YOU HAVEN'T STOPPED ME YET--AND YOU'RE ALREADY TOO LATE!
THE RED BUTTON! THE ACTIVATION SWITCH FOR MADAME ATOM'S NUCLEAR DRILL! ONCE ACTIVATED, IT CAN'T BE UNDONE...
SOON THE MAGIC CONTAINED IN THIS ZIGGURAT--THE GREATEST POWER IN THE UNIVERSE--SHALL BE MINE!
THERE'S ONLY ONE OPTION--I HAVE TO DIVE INTO THE BORE-HOLE AND DEACTIVATE THE BOMB...BY HAND.
CAROLINE! NO!

BUT AGENT SHARP WON'T BE STOPPED! USING ONLY HER WING-PACK'S JET BOOSTERS TO CONTROL HER DESCENT, CAROLINE GOES AFTER THE NUCLEAR DRILL, LEAVING RICK ALONE TO HANDLE MADAME ATOM!

I'M RUNNING LOW ON TIME. BUT I CAN'T LET THE PRESSURE GET TO ME! ONE WRONG MOVE AND--

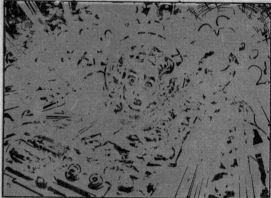

BAH-WHUM!

NO! THAT POWER WAS SUPPOSED TO BE MINE!

BUT WHAT'S THAT EMERGING FROM THE BOREHOLE? COULD IT BE...

...CAROLINE?!

RICK...YOU HAVE TO HELP ME!

WHAT HAVE I BECOME?!

MAGDALENE VISAGGIO: SCRIPT • SONNY LIEW: ART & COLOR • TODD KLEIN: LETTERS • JAMIE S. RICH: EDITS

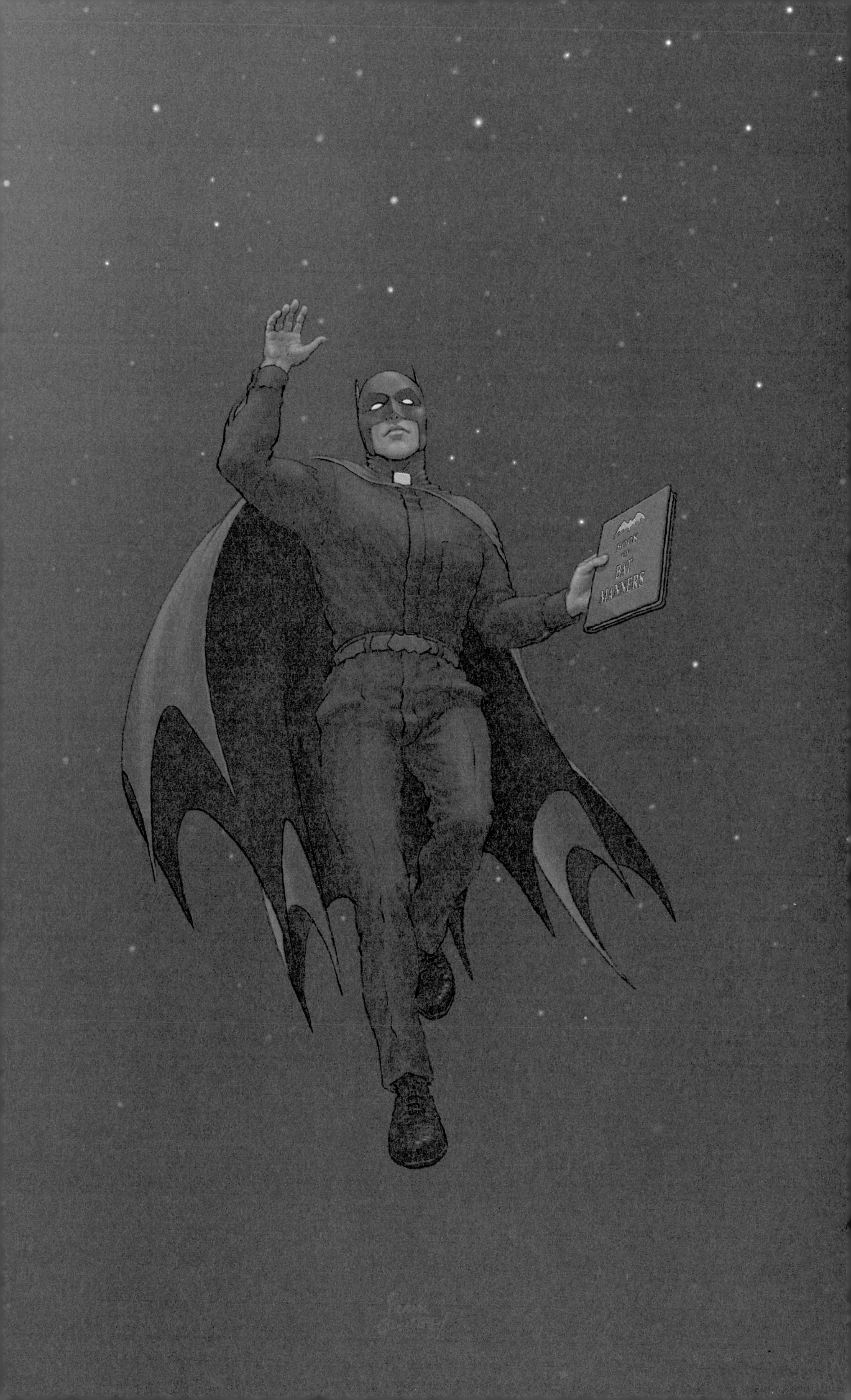
BOOK OF BAT MANNERS

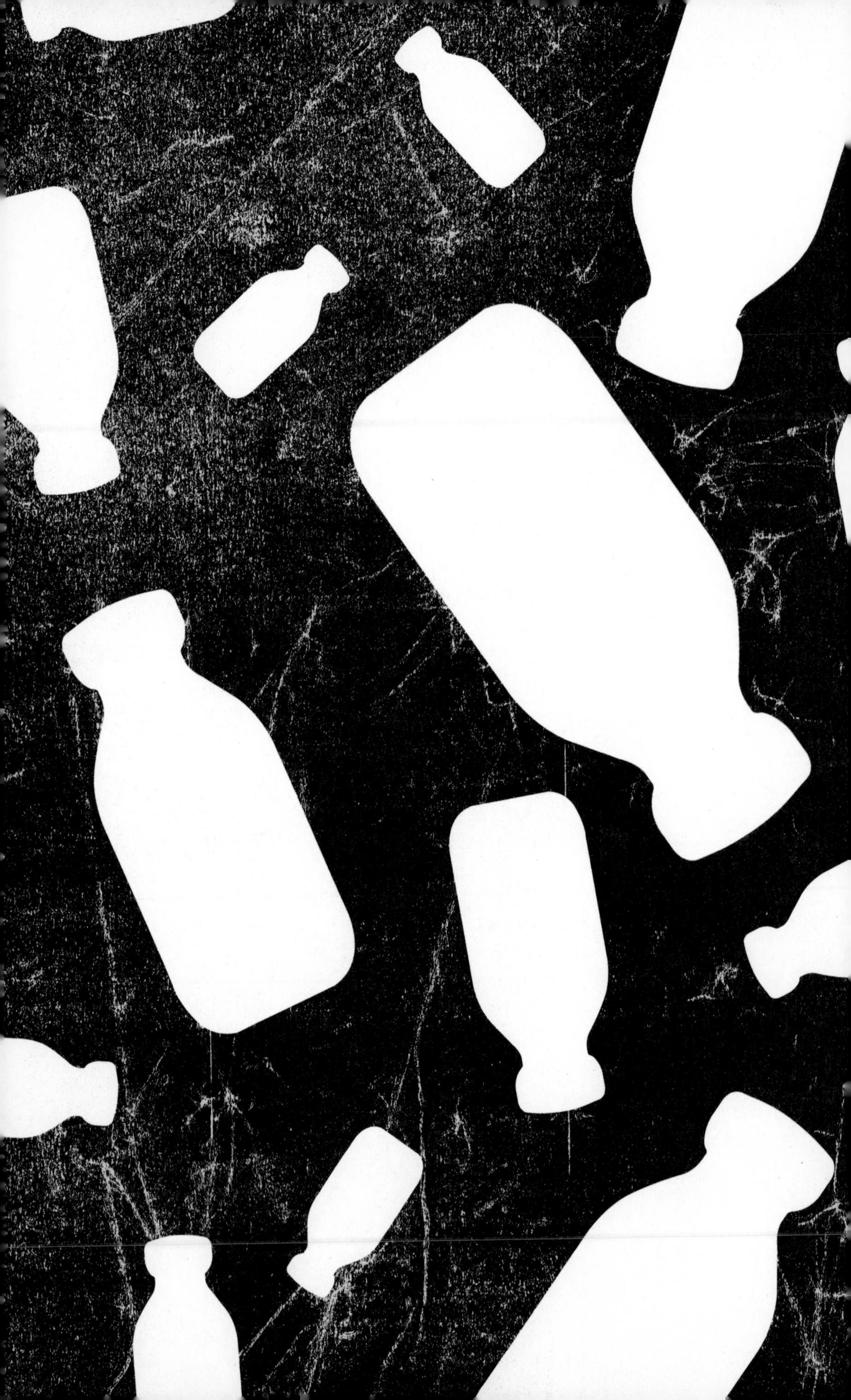

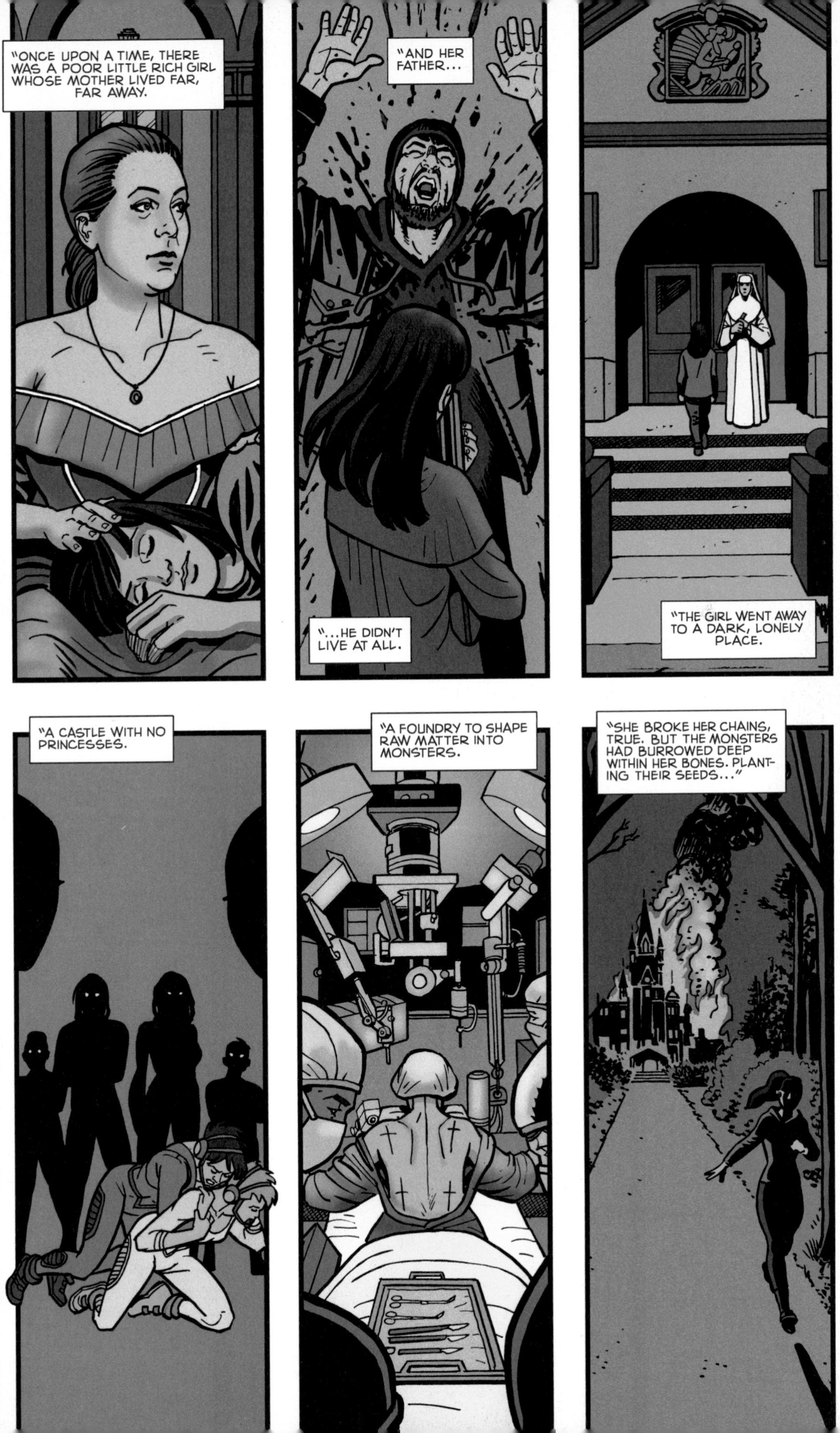
"ONCE UPON A TIME, THERE WAS A POOR LITTLE RICH GIRL WHOSE MOTHER LIVED FAR, FAR AWAY.
"AND HER FATHER...
"...HE DIDN'T LIVE AT ALL.
"THE GIRL WENT AWAY TO A DARK, LONELY PLACE.
"A CASTLE WITH NO PRINCESSES.
"A FOUNDRY TO SHAPE RAW MATTER INTO MONSTERS.
"SHE BROKE HER CHAINS, TRUE. BUT THE MONSTERS HAD BURROWED DEEP WITHIN HER BONES. PLANTING THEIR SEEDS..."

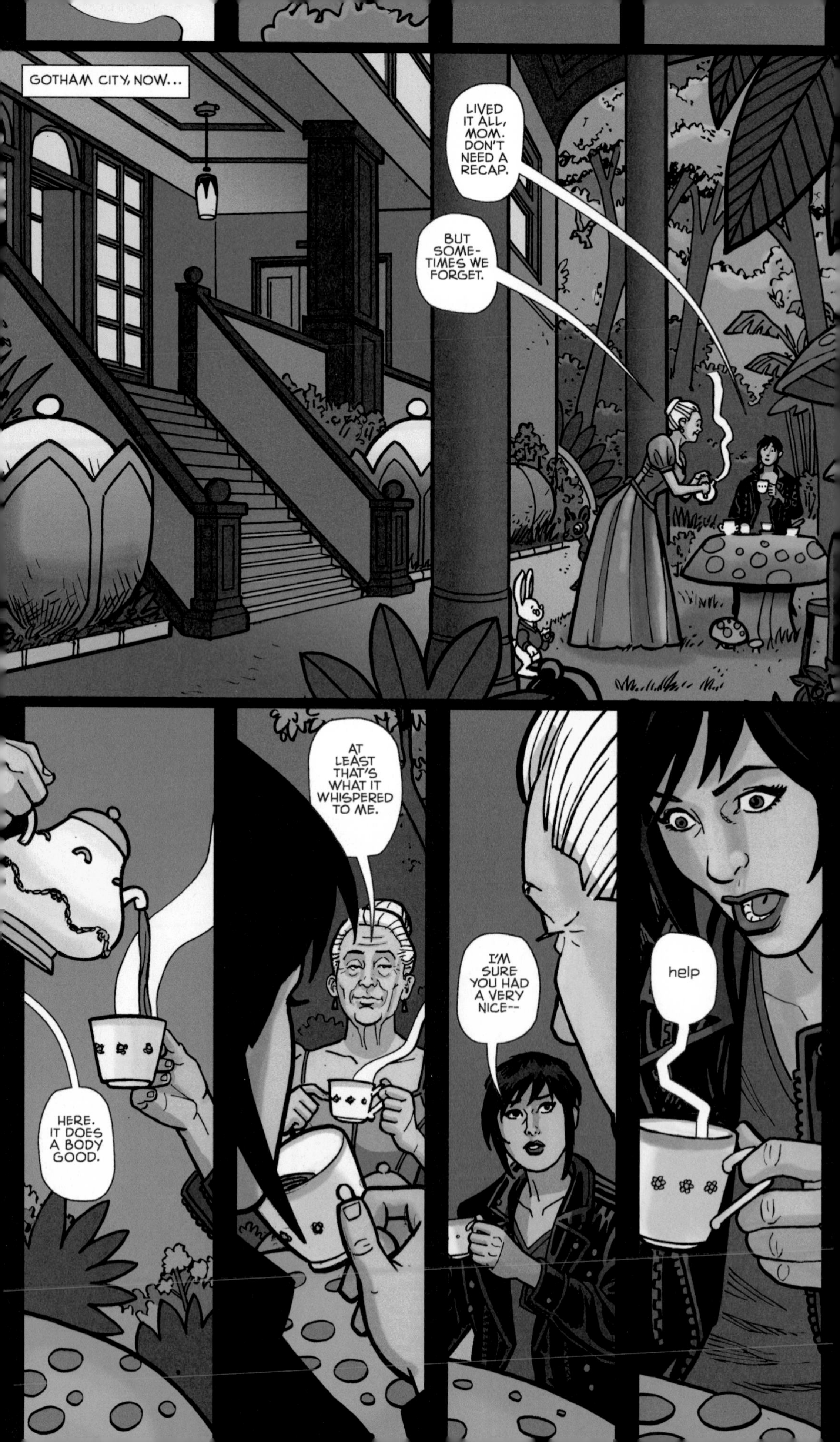
GOTHAM CITY, NOW...
LIVED IT ALL, MOM. DON'T NEED A RECAP.
BUT SOME-TIMES WE FORGET.
HERE. IT DOES A BODY GOOD.
AT LEAST THAT'S WHAT IT WHISPERED TO ME.
I'M SURE YOU HAD A VERY NICE--
help

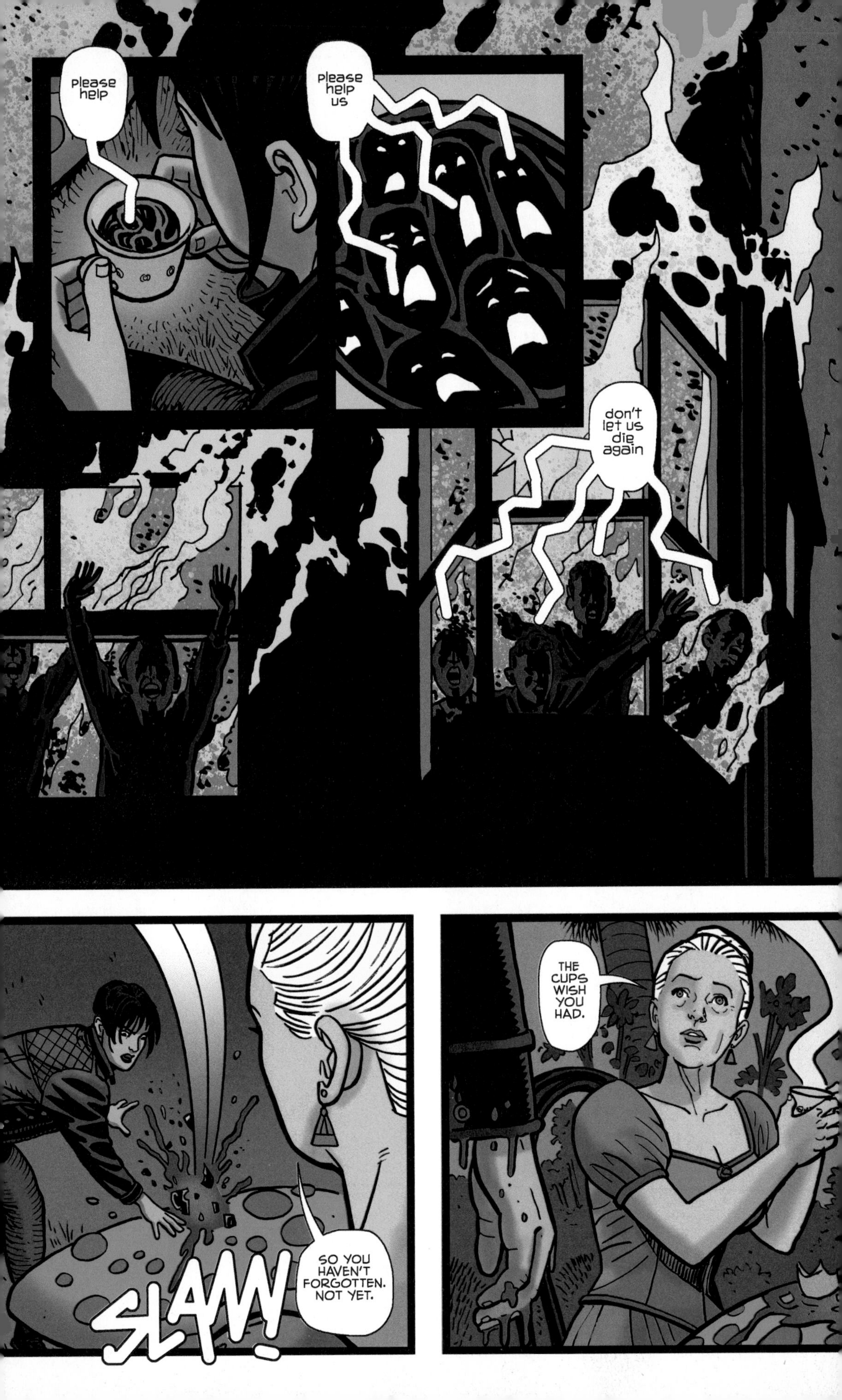
please help
please help us
don't let us die again
SLAM!
SO YOU HAVEN'T FORGOTTEN. NOT YET.
THE CUPS WISH YOU HAD.

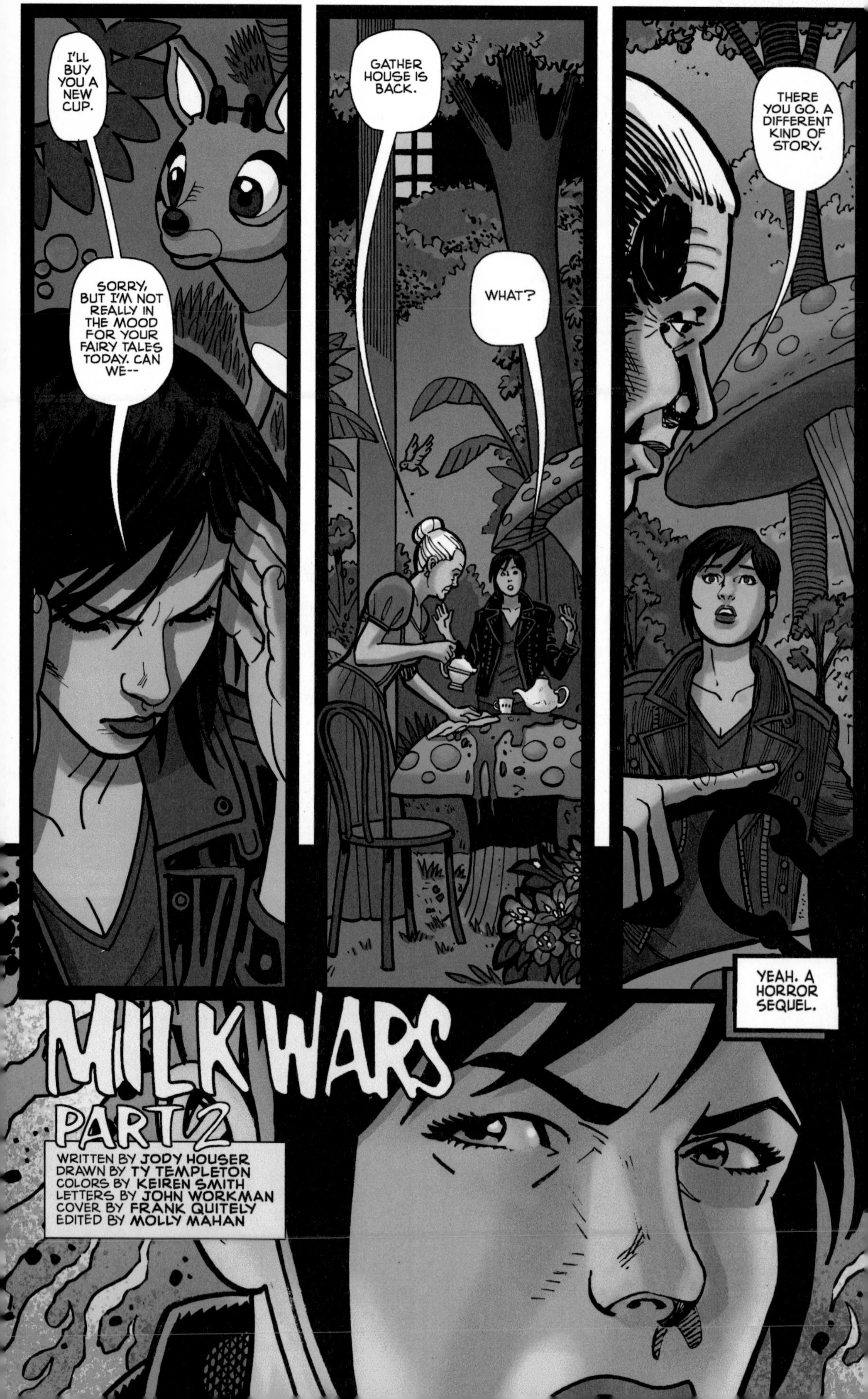

I'LL BUY YOU A NEW CUP.
SORRY, BUT I'M NOT REALLY IN THE MOOD FOR YOUR FAIRY TALES TODAY. CAN WE--
GATHER HOUSE IS BACK.
WHAT?
THERE YOU GO. A DIFFERENT KIND OF STORY.
YEAH. A HORROR SEQUEL.
MILK WARS
PART 2
WRITTEN BY JODY HOUSER
DRAWN BY TY TEMPLETON
COLORS BY KEIREN SMITH
LETTERS BY JOHN WORKMAN
COVER BY FRANK QUITELY
EDITED BY MOLLY MAHAN

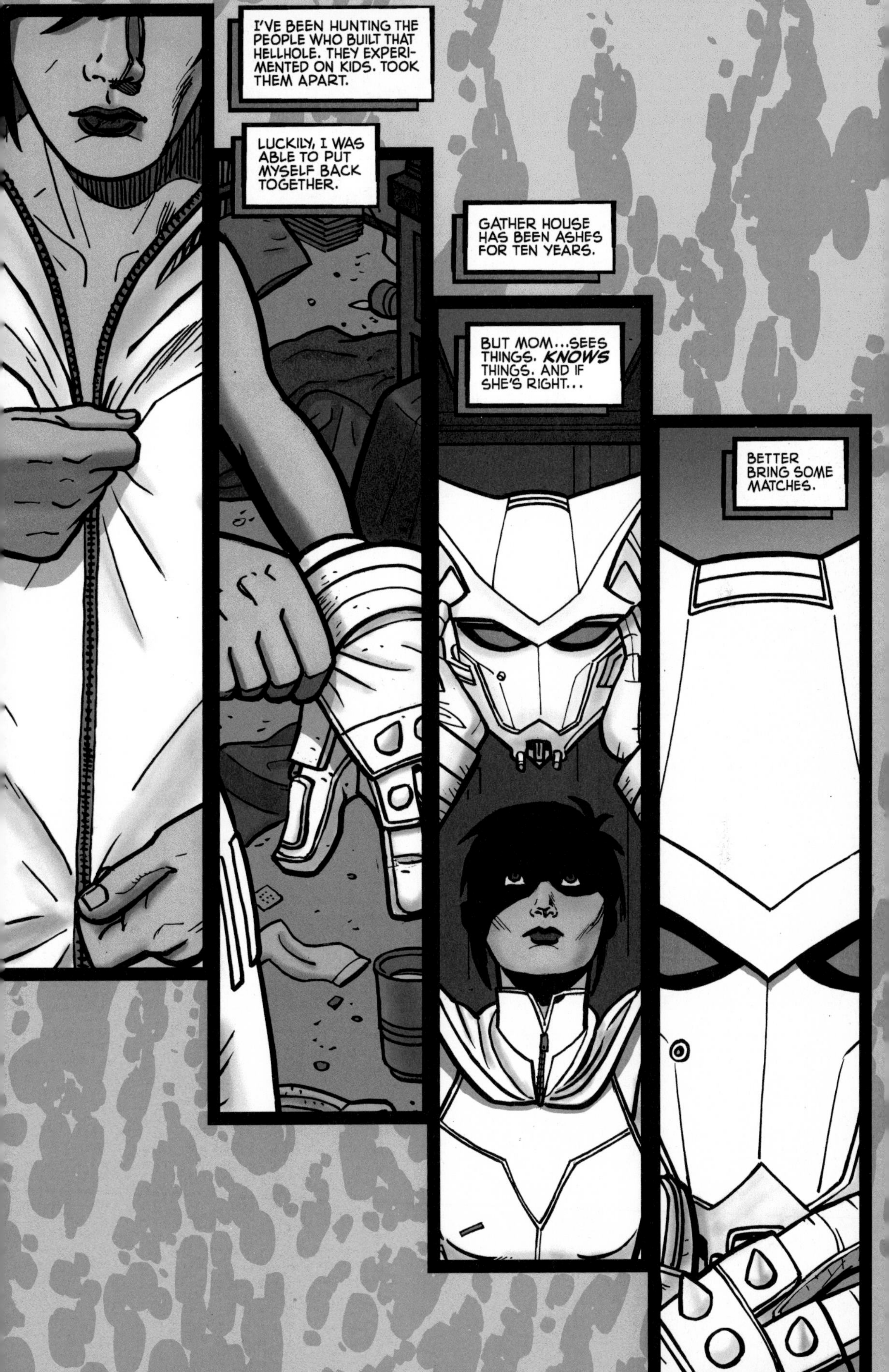
I'VE BEEN HUNTING THE PEOPLE WHO BUILT THAT HELLHOLE. THEY EXPERIMENTED ON KIDS. TOOK THEM APART.
LUCKILY, I WAS ABLE TO PUT MYSELF BACK TOGETHER.
GATHER HOUSE HAS BEEN ASHES FOR TEN YEARS.
BUT MOM...SEES THINGS. KNOWS THINGS. AND IF SHE'S RIGHT...
BETTER BRING SOME MATCHES.

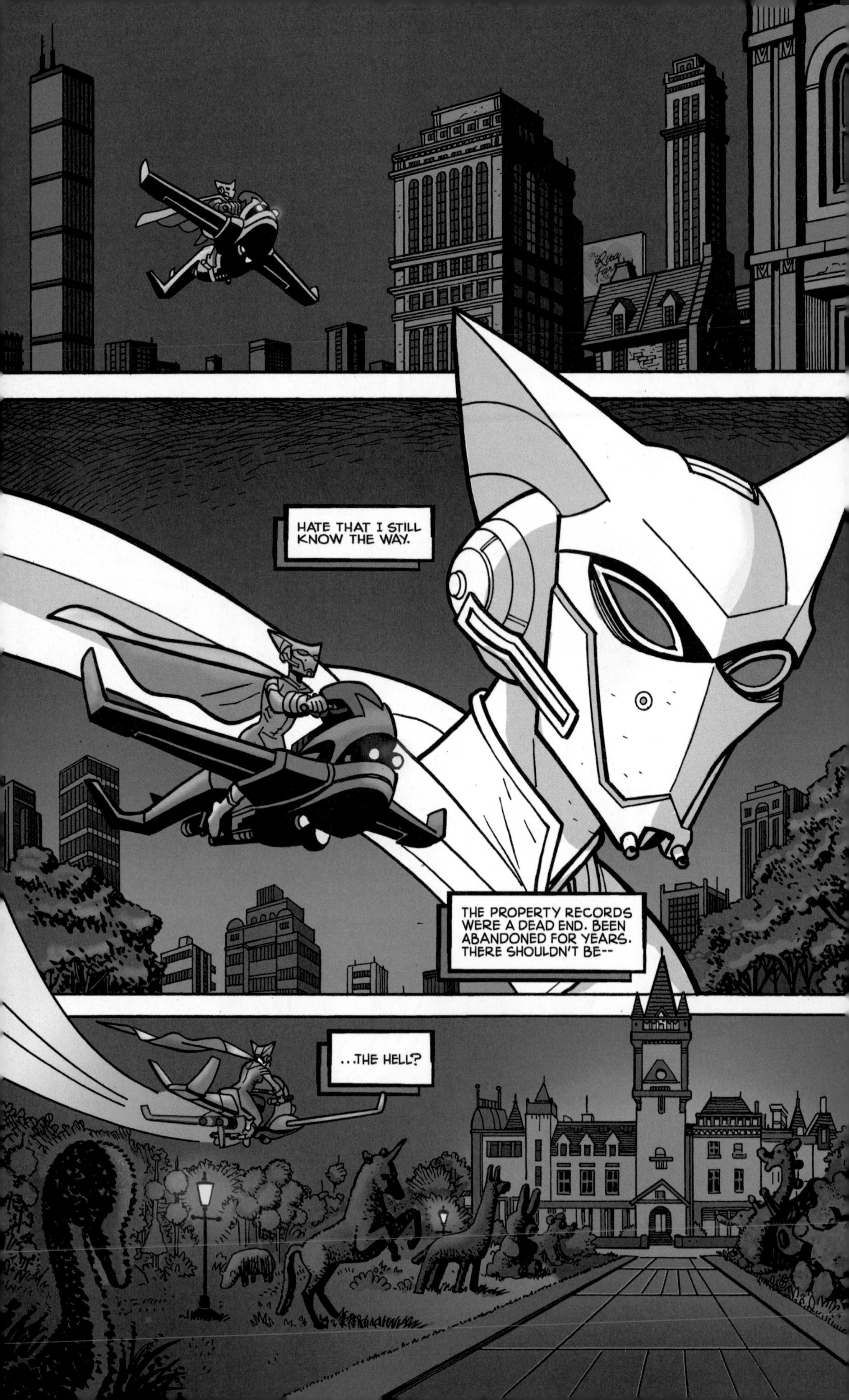
HATE THAT I STILL KNOW THE WAY.
THE PROPERTY RECORDS WERE A DEAD END. BEEN ABANDONED FOR YEARS. THERE SHOULDN'T BE--
...THE HELL?

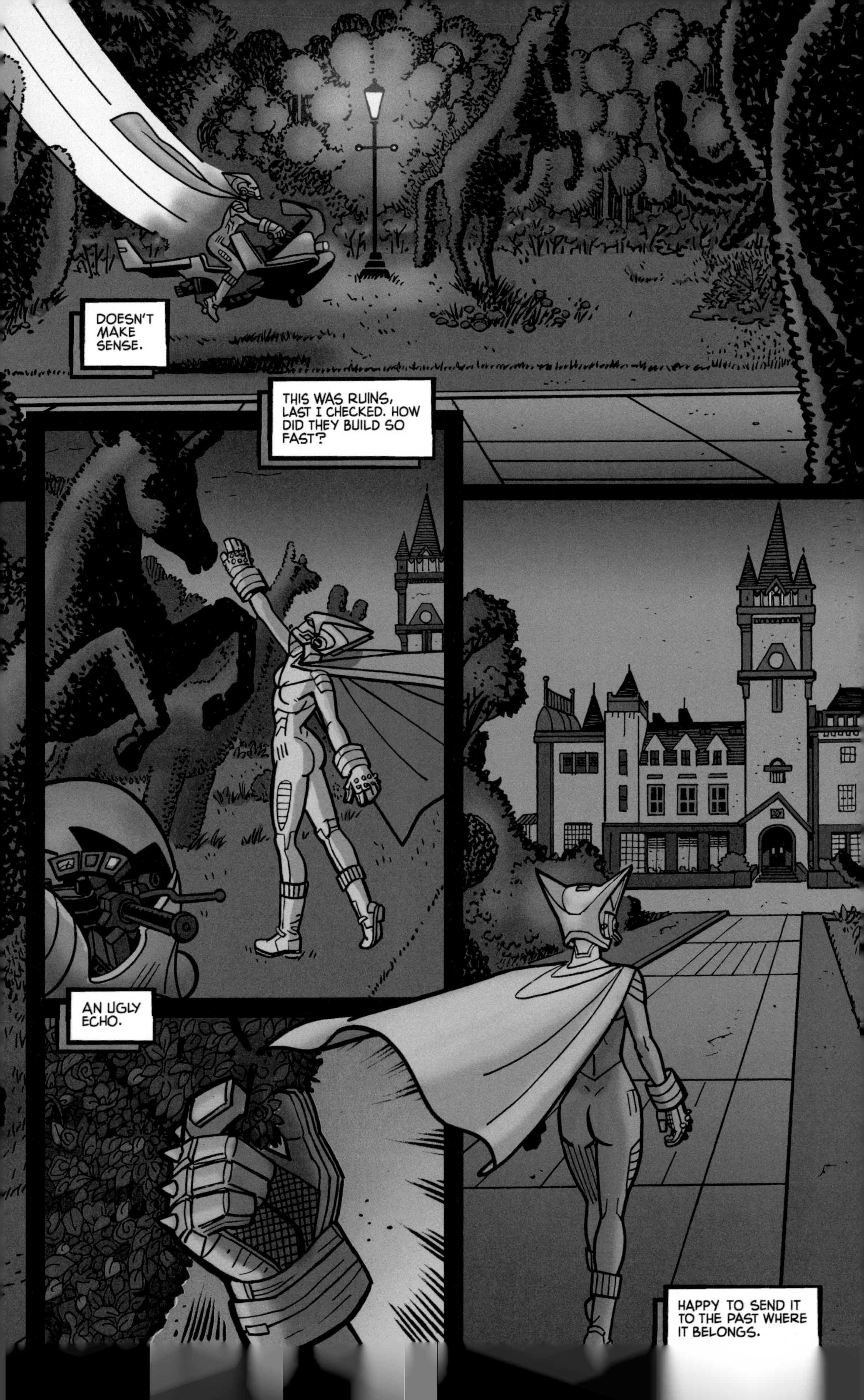
DOESN'T MAKE SENSE.
THIS WAS RUINS, LAST I CHECKED. HOW DID THEY BUILD SO FAST?
AN UGLY ECHO.
HAPPY TO SEND IT TO THE PAST WHERE IT BELONGS.

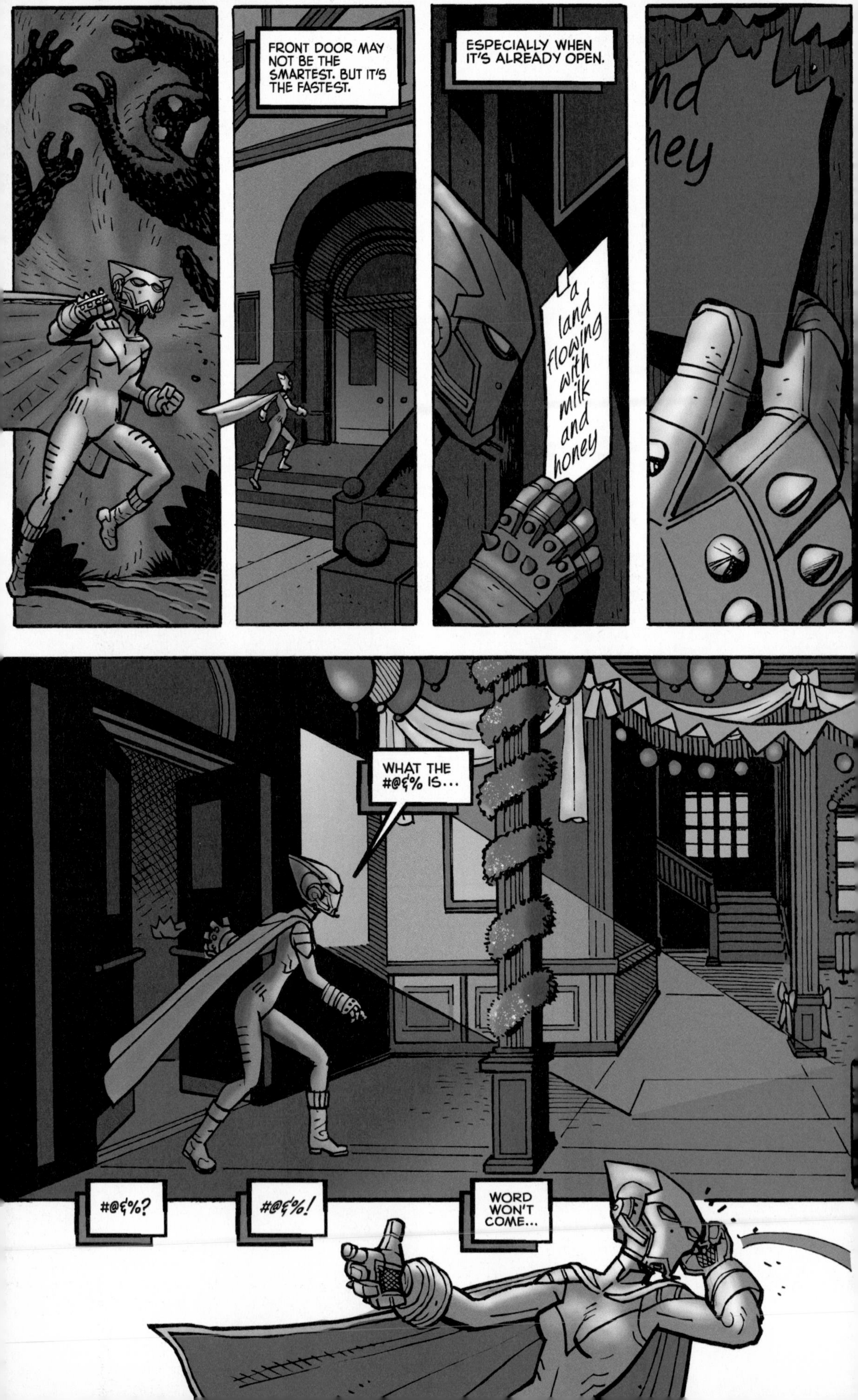
FRONT DOOR MAY NOT BE THE SMARTEST. BUT IT'S THE FASTEST.
ESPECIALLY WHEN IT'S ALREADY OPEN.
a land flowing with milk and honey
WHAT THE #@ξ% IS...
#@ξ%?
#@ξ%!
WORD WON'T COME...

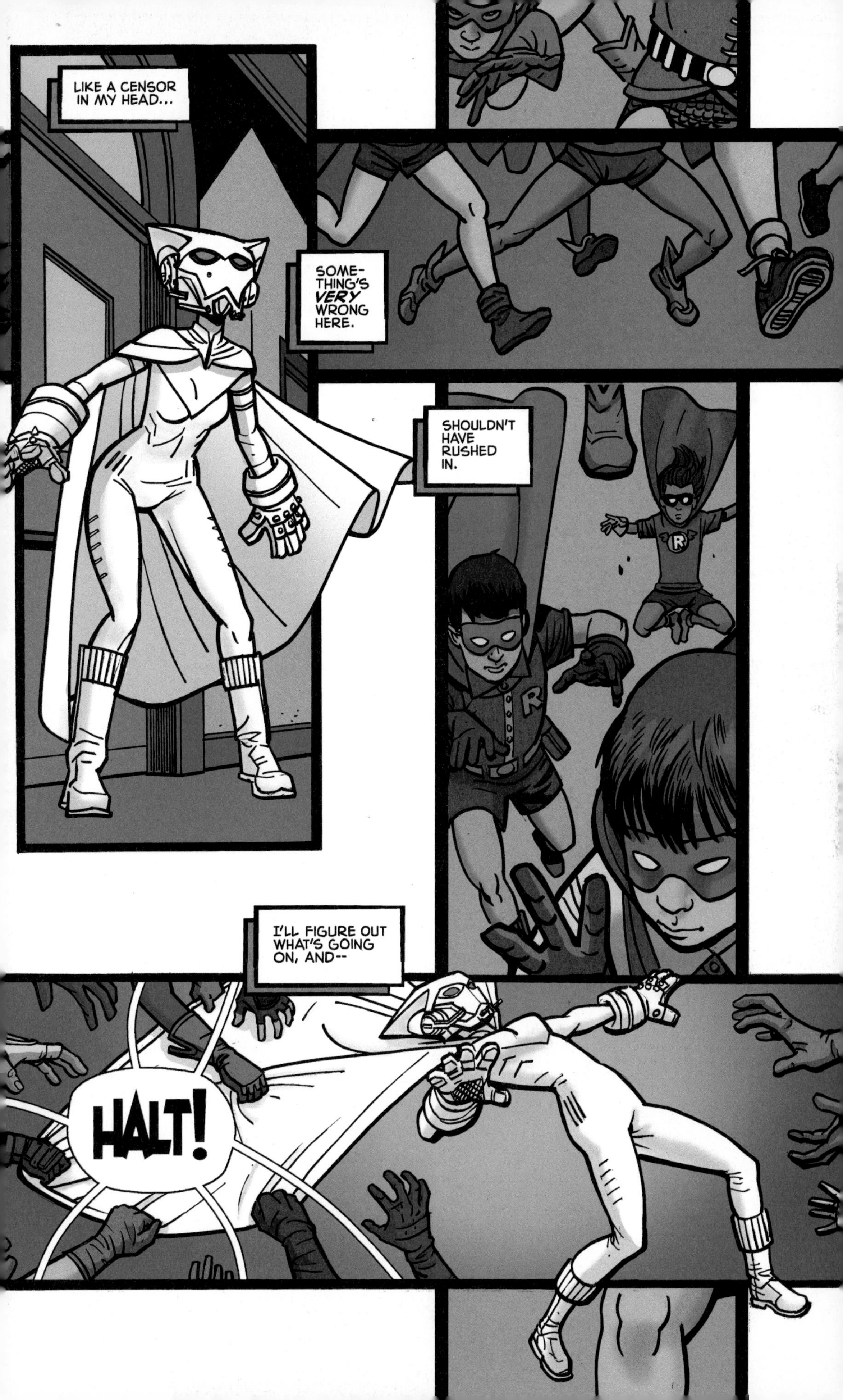
LIKE A CENSOR IN MY HEAD...
SOME-THING'S *VERY* WRONG HERE.
SHOULDN'T HAVE RUSHED IN.
I'LL FIGURE OUT WHAT'S GOING ON, AND--
HALT!

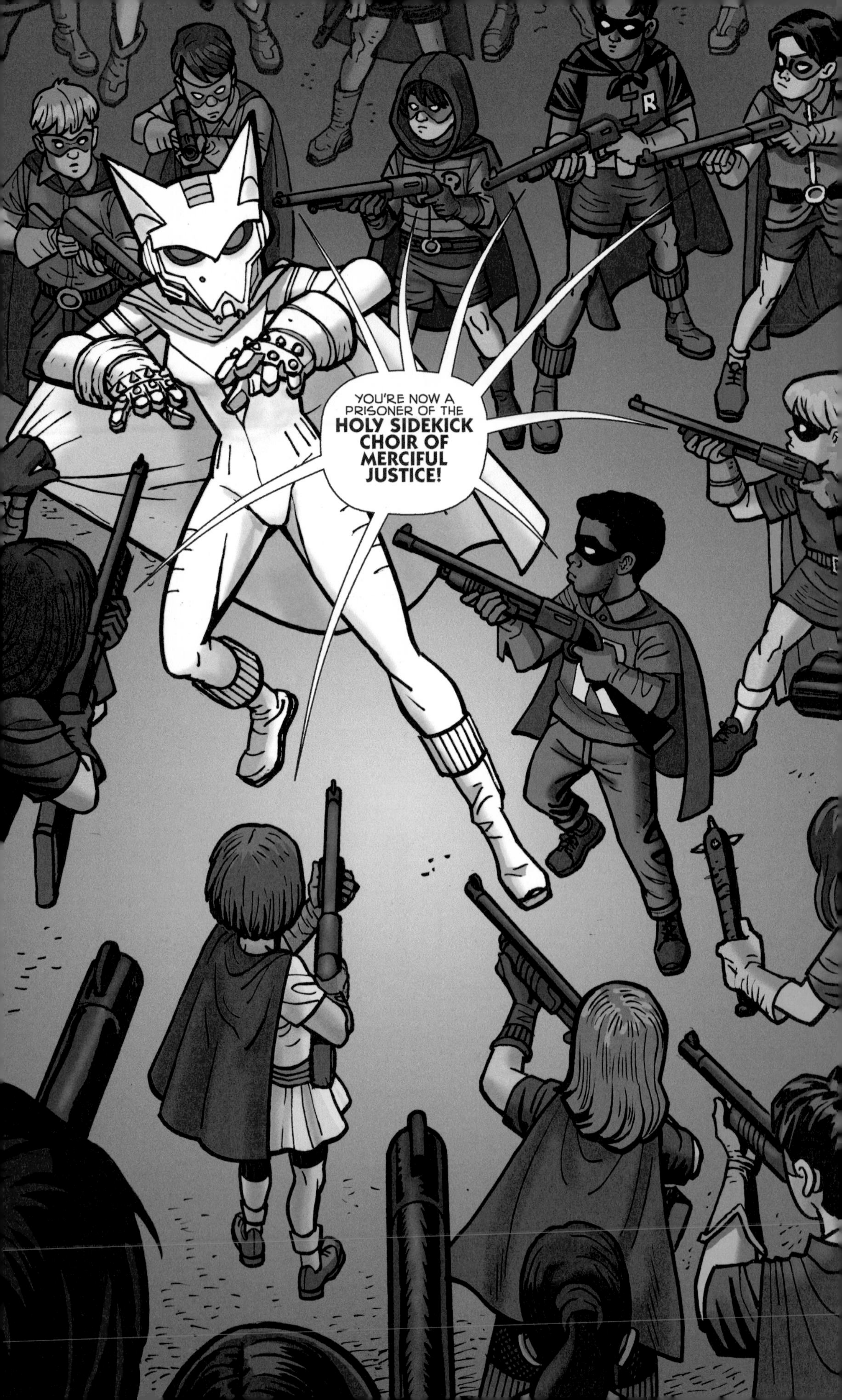
YOU'RE NOW A PRISONER OF THE HOLY SIDEKICK CHOIR OF MERCIFUL JUSTICE!

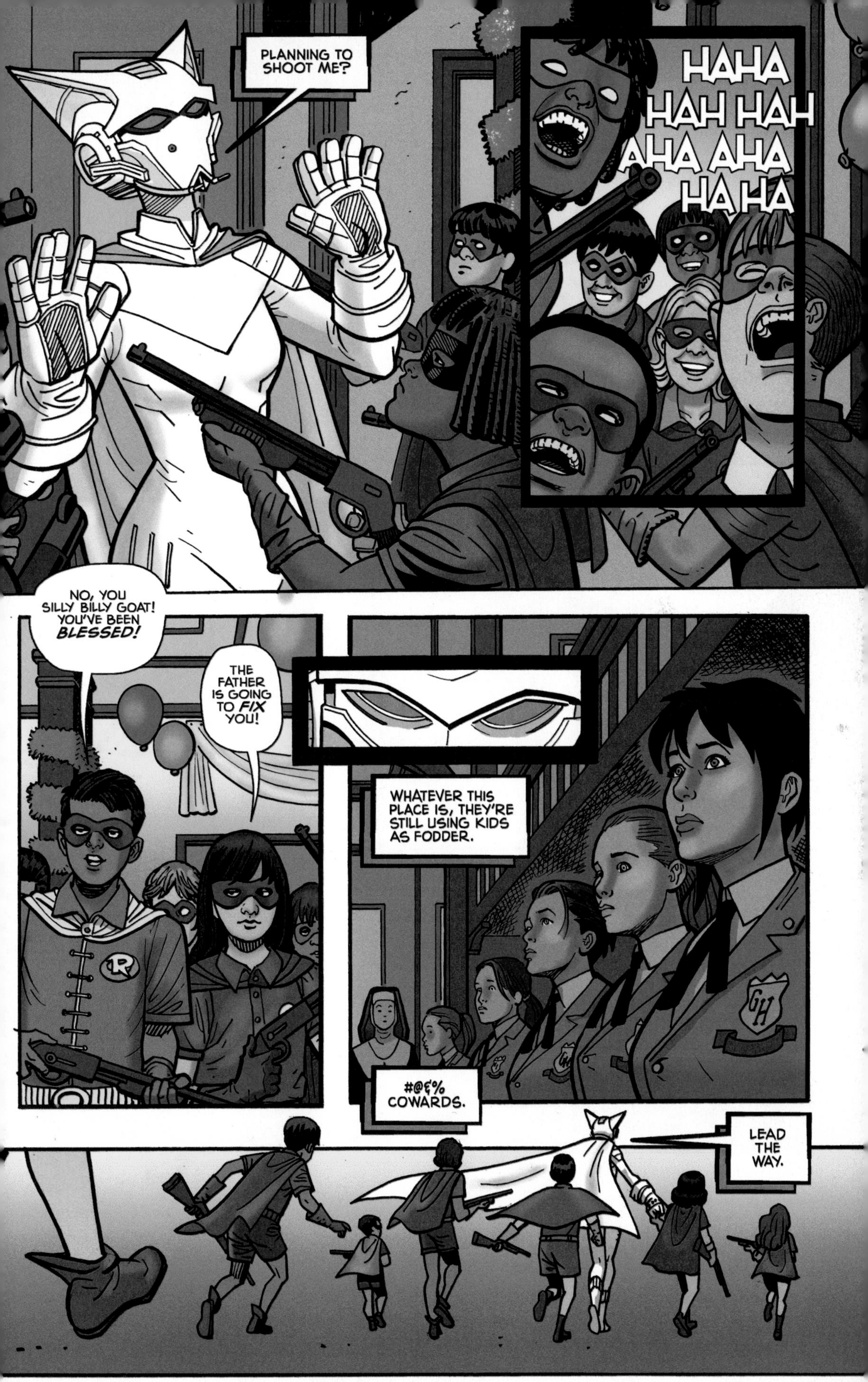
PLANNING TO SHOOT ME?
HAHA HAH HAH AHA AHA HA HA
NO, YOU SILLY BILLY GOAT! YOU'VE BEEN *BLESSED!*
THE FATHER IS GOING TO *FIX* YOU!
WHATEVER THIS PLACE IS, THEY'RE STILL USING KIDS AS FODDER.
#@&% COWARDS.
LEAD THE WAY.

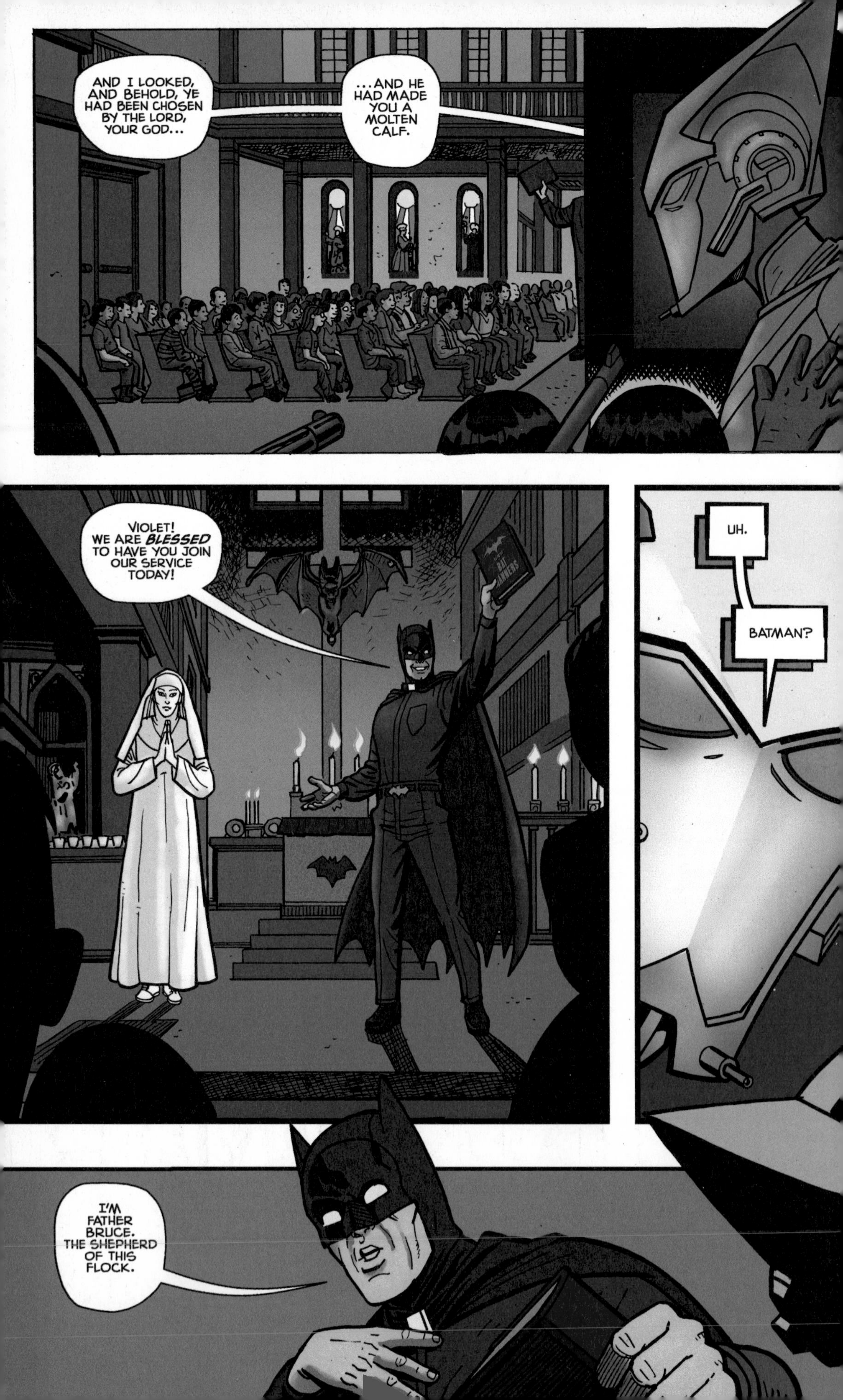
AND I LOOKED, AND BEHOLD, YE HAD BEEN CHOSEN BY THE LORD, YOUR GOD...
...AND HE HAD MADE YOU A MOLTEN CALF.
VIOLET! WE ARE *BLESSED* TO HAVE YOU JOIN OUR SERVICE TODAY!
UH.
BATMAN?
I'M FATHER BRUCE. THE SHEPHERD OF THIS FLOCK.

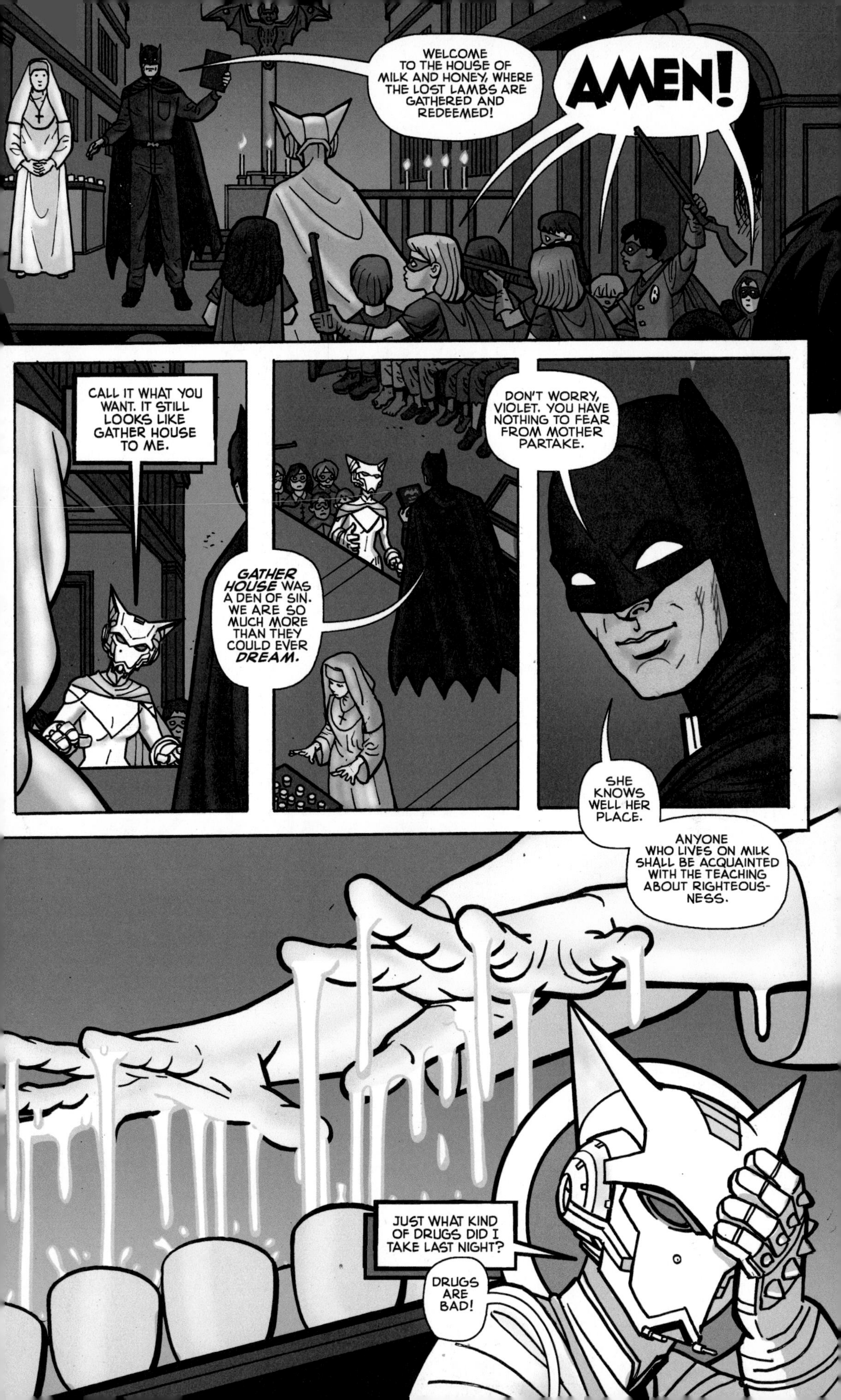
WELCOME TO THE HOUSE OF MILK AND HONEY, WHERE THE LOST LAMBS ARE GATHERED AND REDEEMED!
AMEN!
CALL IT WHAT YOU WANT. IT STILL LOOKS LIKE GATHER HOUSE TO ME.
GATHER HOUSE WAS A DEN OF SIN. WE ARE SO MUCH MORE THAN THEY COULD EVER DREAM.
DON'T WORRY, VIOLET. YOU HAVE NOTHING TO FEAR FROM MOTHER PARTAKE.
SHE KNOWS WELL HER PLACE.
ANYONE WHO LIVES ON MILK SHALL BE ACQUAINTED WITH THE TEACHING ABOUT RIGHTEOUS-NESS.
JUST WHAT KIND OF DRUGS DID I TAKE LAST NIGHT?
DRUGS ARE BAD!

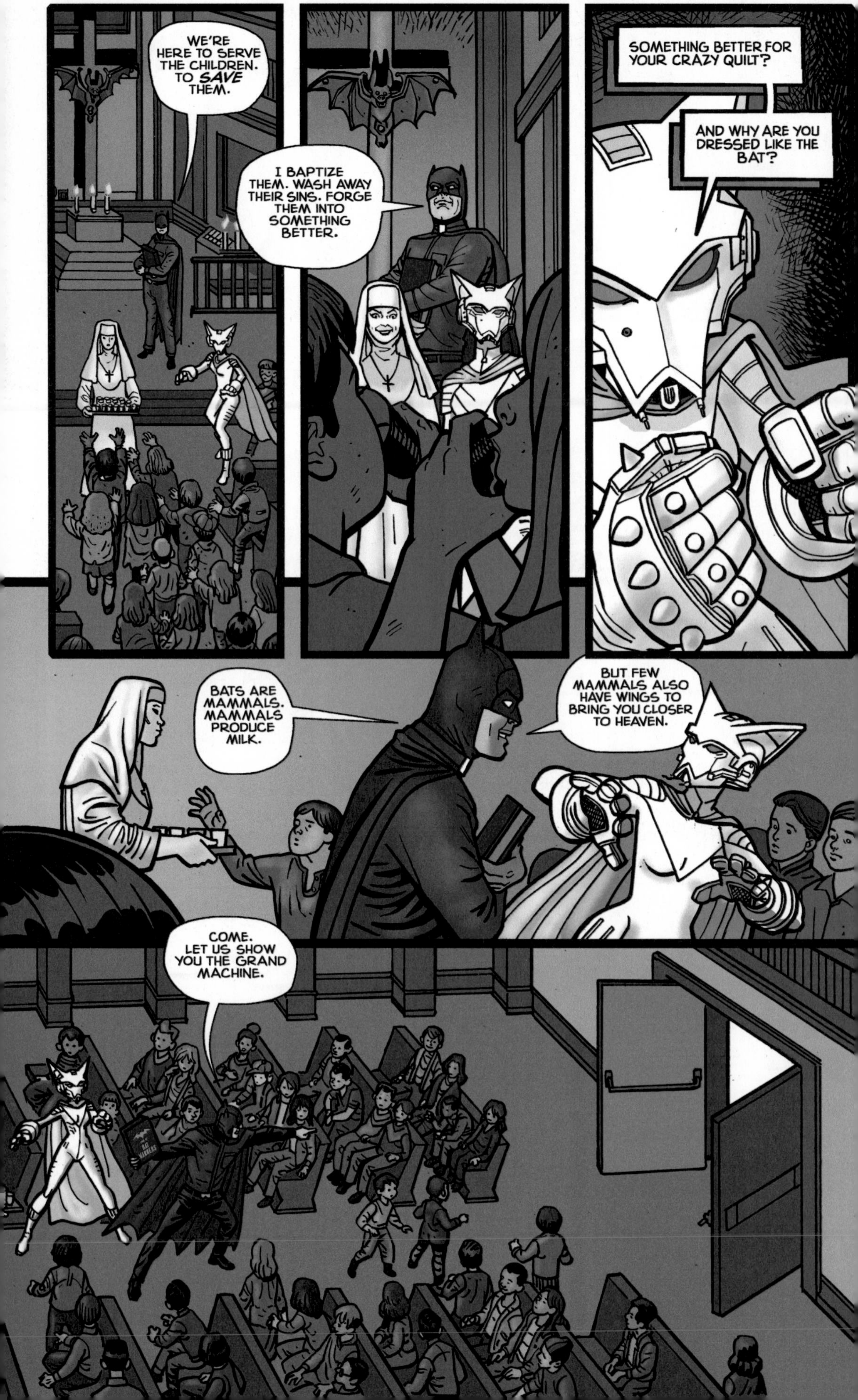
WE'RE HERE TO SERVE THE CHILDREN. TO SAVE THEM.
I BAPTIZE THEM. WASH AWAY THEIR SINS. FORGE THEM INTO SOMETHING BETTER.
SOMETHING BETTER FOR YOUR CRAZY QUILT?
AND WHY ARE YOU DRESSED LIKE THE BAT?
BATS ARE MAMMALS. MAMMALS PRODUCE MILK.
BUT FEW MAMMALS ALSO HAVE WINGS TO BRING YOU CLOSER TO HEAVEN.
COME. LET US SHOW YOU THE GRAND MACHINE.

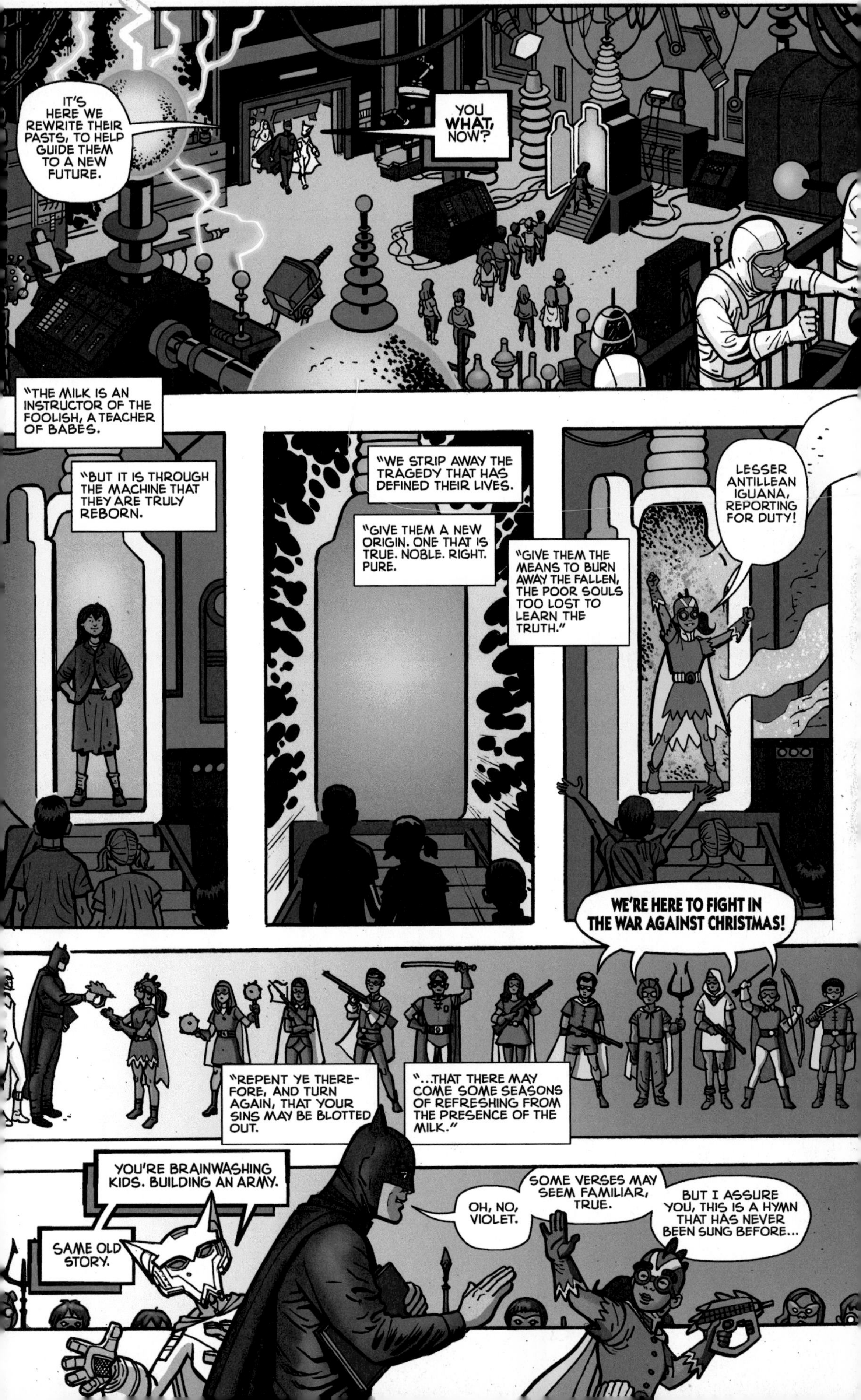

IT'S HERE WE REWRITE THEIR PASTS, TO HELP GUIDE THEM TO A NEW FUTURE.
YOU WHAT, NOW?
"THE MILK IS AN INSTRUCTOR OF THE FOOLISH, A TEACHER OF BABES.
"BUT IT IS THROUGH THE MACHINE THAT THEY ARE TRULY REBORN.
"WE STRIP AWAY THE TRAGEDY THAT HAS DEFINED THEIR LIVES.
"GIVE THEM A NEW ORIGIN. ONE THAT IS TRUE. NOBLE. RIGHT. PURE.
"GIVE THEM THE MEANS TO BURN AWAY THE FALLEN, THE POOR SOULS TOO LOST TO LEARN THE TRUTH."
LESSER ANTILLEAN IGUANA, REPORTING FOR DUTY!
WE'RE HERE TO FIGHT IN THE WAR AGAINST CHRISTMAS!
"REPENT YE THEREFORE, AND TURN AGAIN, THAT YOUR SINS MAY BE BLOTTED OUT.
"...THAT THERE MAY COME SOME SEASONS OF REFRESHING FROM THE PRESENCE OF THE MILK."
YOU'RE BRAINWASHING KIDS. BUILDING AN ARMY.
SAME OLD STORY.
OH, NO, VIOLET.
SOME VERSES MAY SEEM FAMILIAR, TRUE.
BUT I ASSURE YOU, THIS IS A HYMN THAT HAS NEVER BEEN SUNG BEFORE...

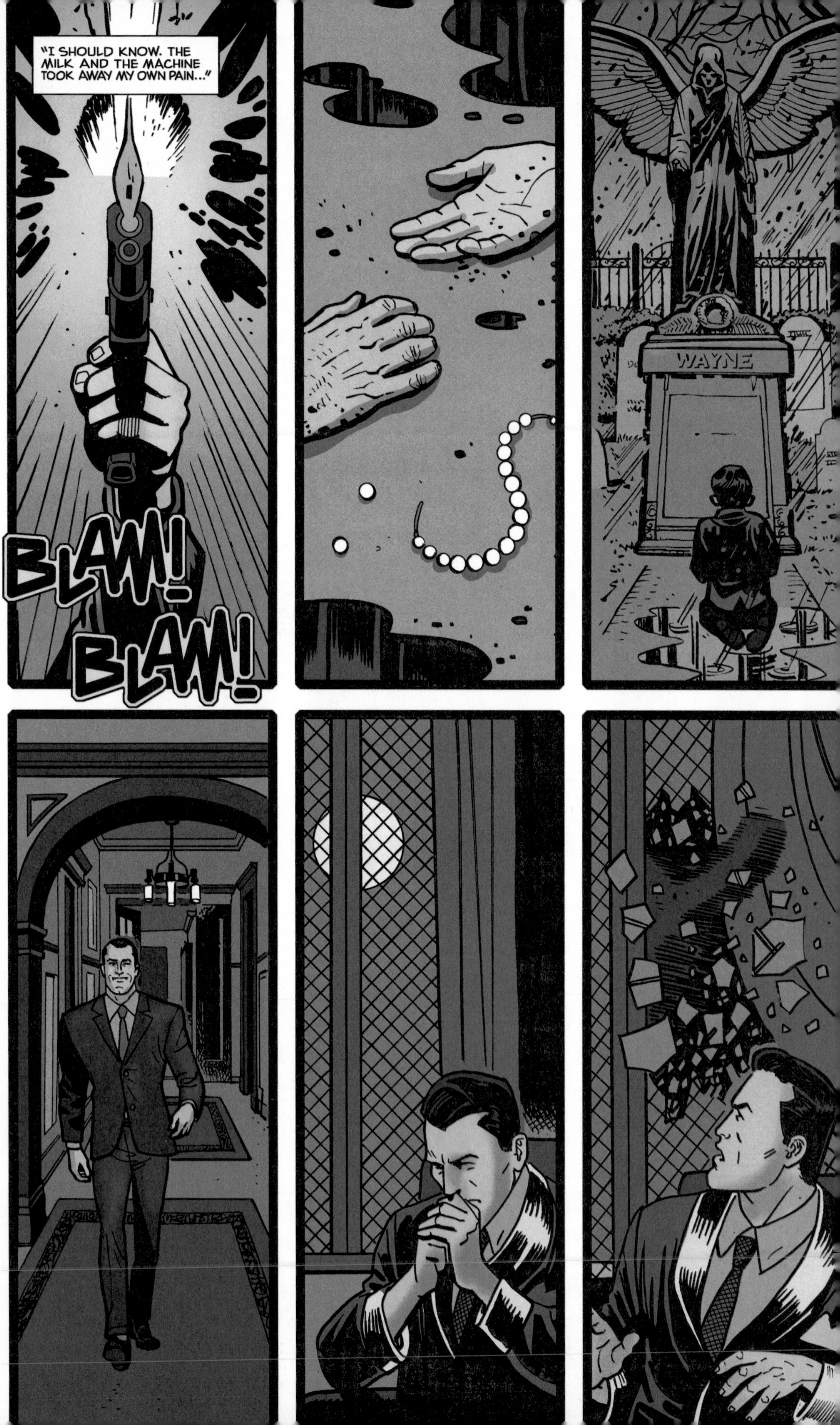
"I SHOULD KNOW. THE MILK AND THE MACHINE TOOK AWAY MY OWN PAIN..."
BLAM! BLAM!
WAYNE

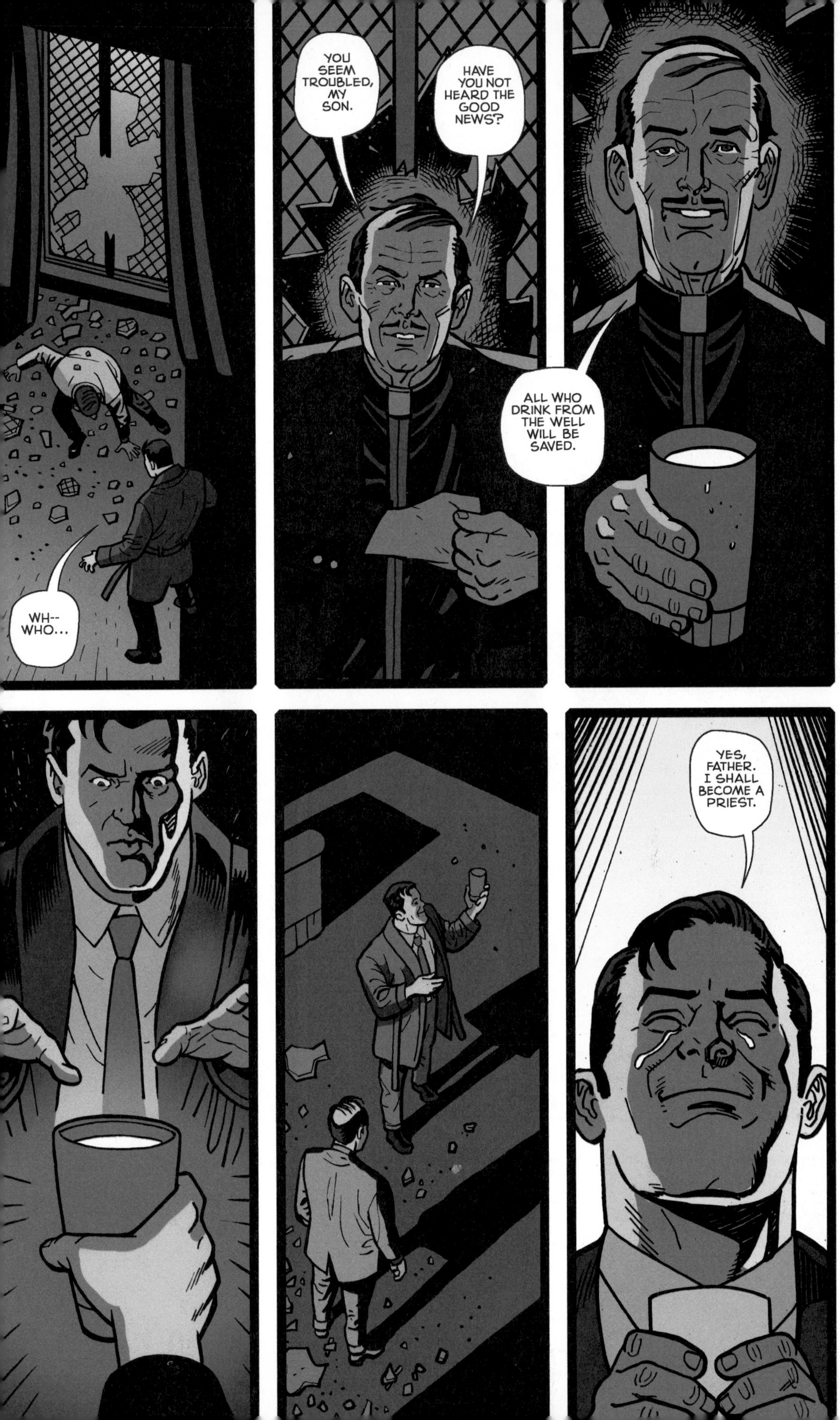
WH-- WHO...
YOU SEEM TROUBLED, MY SON.
HAVE YOU NOT HEARD THE GOOD NEWS?
ALL WHO DRINK FROM THE WELL WILL BE SAVED.
YES, FATHER. I SHALL BECOME A PRIEST.

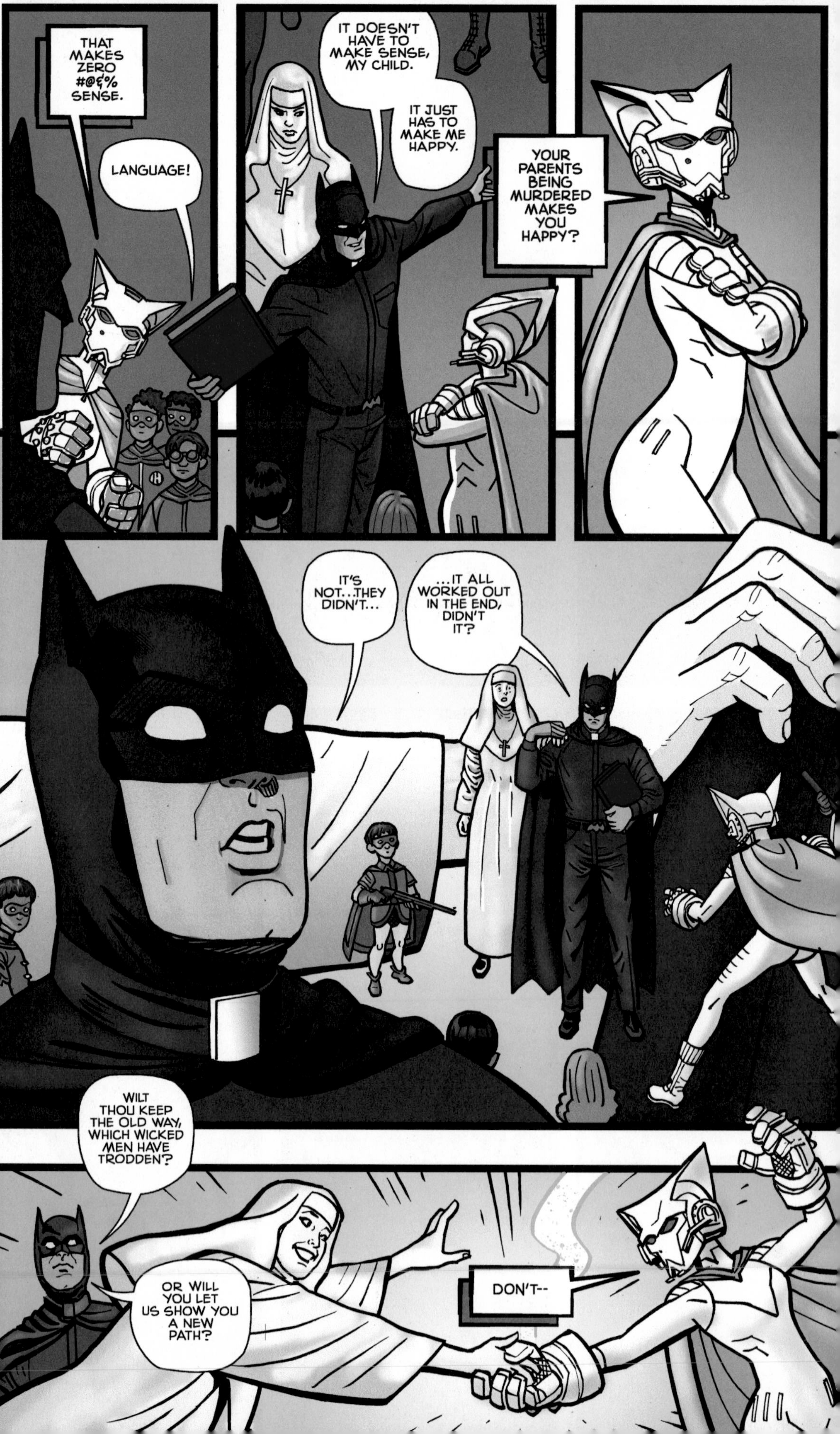
THAT MAKES ZERO #@&% SENSE.
LANGUAGE!
IT DOESN'T HAVE TO MAKE SENSE, MY CHILD.
IT JUST HAS TO MAKE ME HAPPY.
YOUR PARENTS BEING MURDERED MAKES YOU HAPPY?
IT'S NOT...THEY DIDN'T...
...IT ALL WORKED OUT IN THE END, DIDN'T IT?
WILT THOU KEEP THE OLD WAY, WHICH WICKED MEN HAVE TRODDEN?
OR WILL YOU LET US SHOW YOU A NEW PATH?
DON'T--

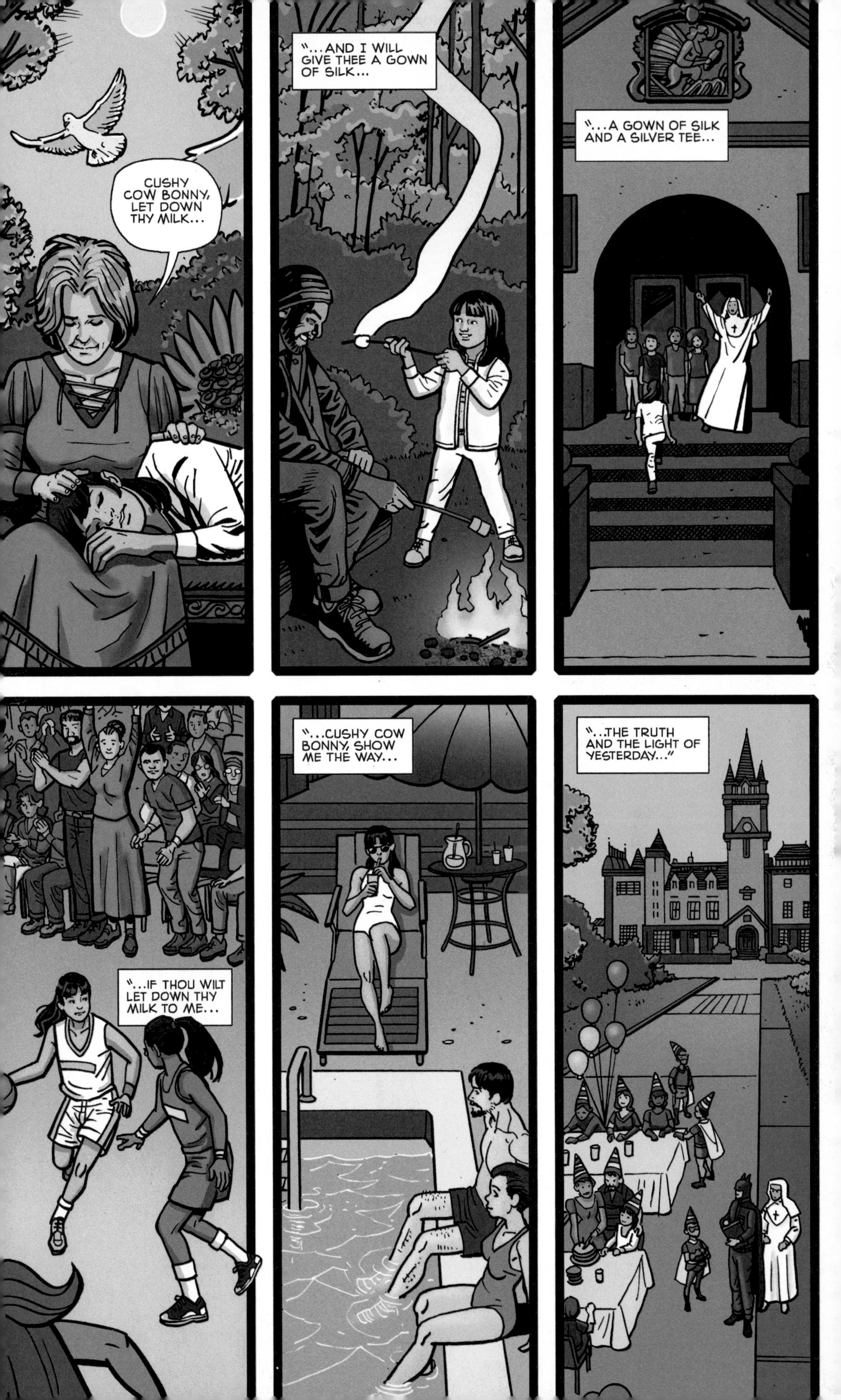
CUSHY COW BONNY, LET DOWN THY MILK...
"...AND I WILL GIVE THEE A GOWN OF SILK...
"...A GOWN OF SILK AND A SILVER TEE...
"...IF THOU WILT LET DOWN THY MILK TO ME...
"...CUSHY COW BONNY, SHOW ME THE WAY...
"...THE TRUTH AND THE LIGHT OF YESTERDAY..."

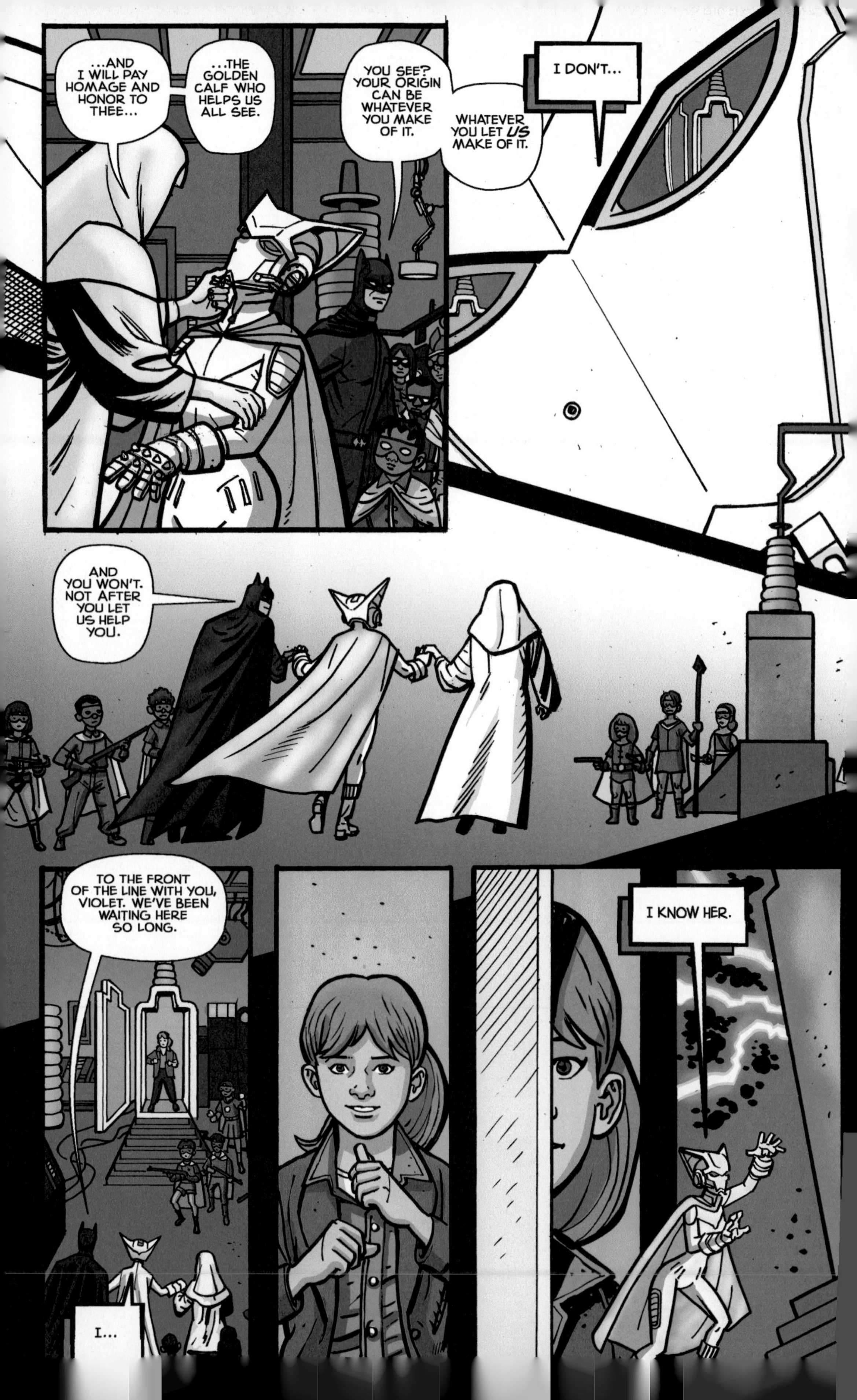

...AND I WILL PAY HOMAGE AND HONOR TO THEE...
...THE GOLDEN CALF WHO HELPS US ALL SEE.
YOU SEE? YOUR ORIGIN CAN BE WHATEVER YOU MAKE OF IT.
WHATEVER YOU LET *US* MAKE OF IT.
I DON'T...
AND YOU WON'T. NOT AFTER YOU LET US HELP YOU.
TO THE FRONT OF THE LINE WITH YOU, VIOLET. WE'VE BEEN WAITING HERE SO LONG.
I...
I KNOW HER.

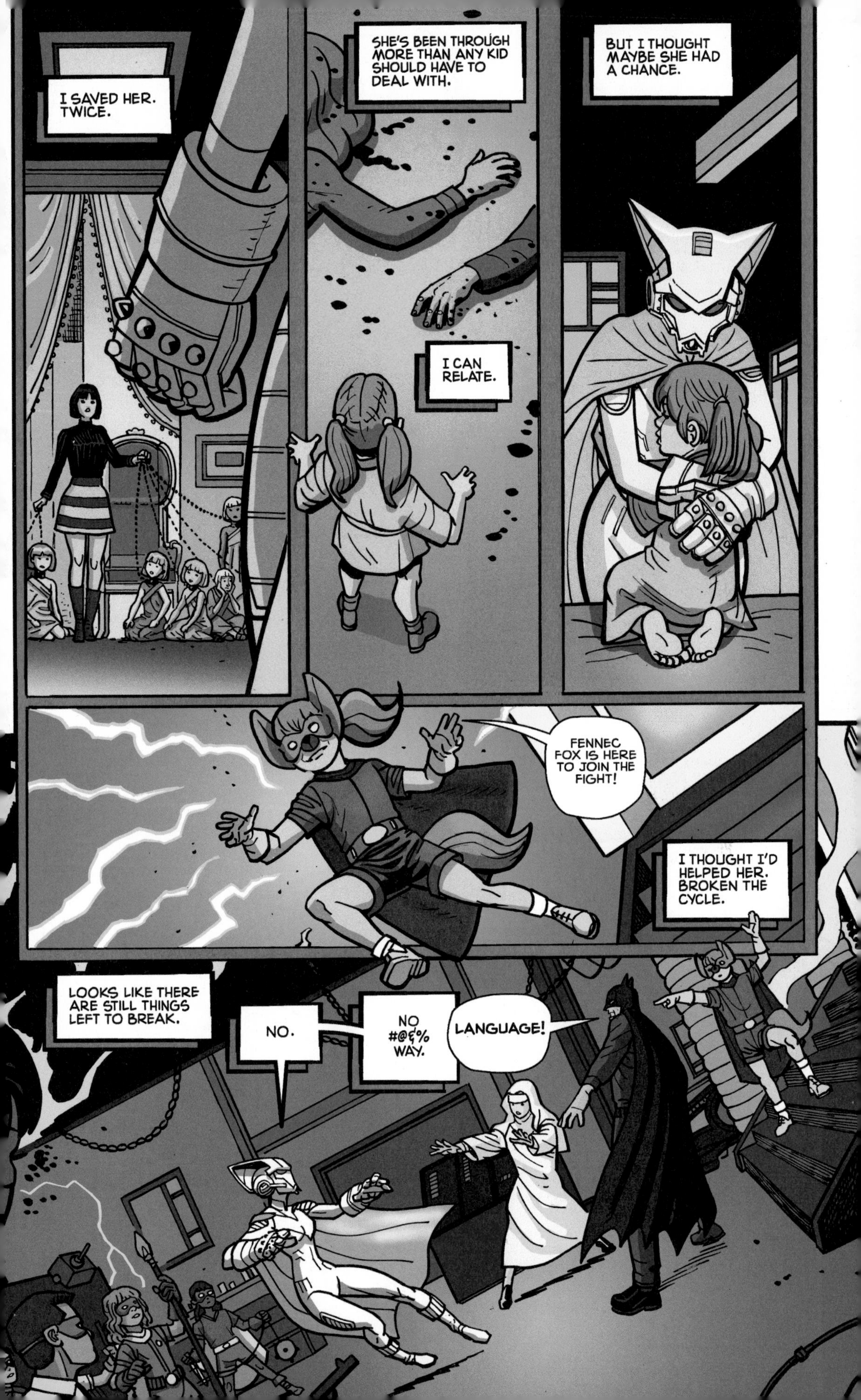
I SAVED HER. TWICE.
SHE'S BEEN THROUGH MORE THAN ANY KID SHOULD HAVE TO DEAL WITH.
I CAN RELATE.
BUT I THOUGHT MAYBE SHE HAD A CHANCE.
FENNEC FOX IS HERE TO JOIN THE FIGHT!
I THOUGHT I'D HELPED HER. BROKEN THE CYCLE.
LOOKS LIKE THERE ARE STILL THINGS LEFT TO BREAK.
NO.
NO #@&% WAY.
LANGUAGE!

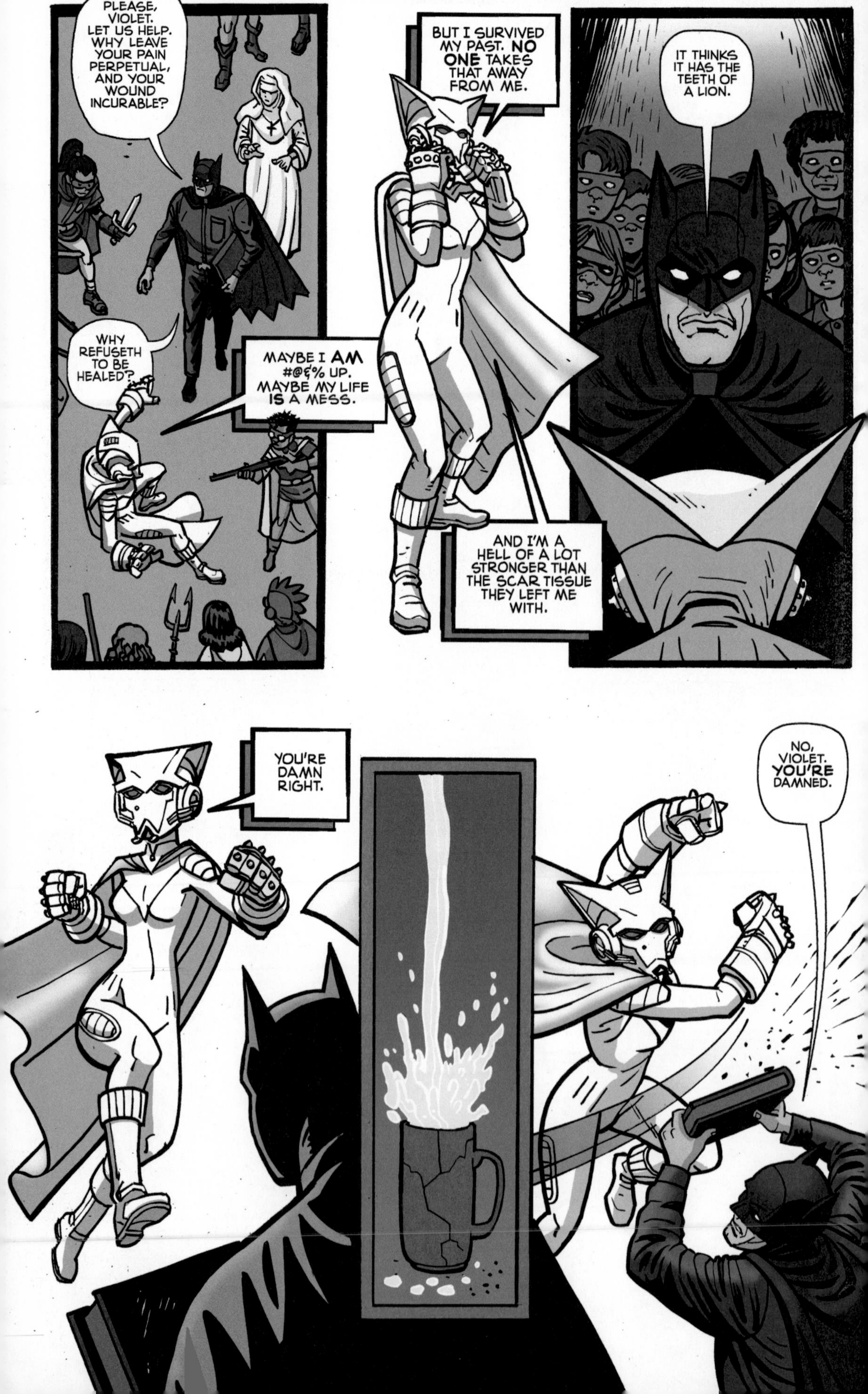
PLEASE, VIOLET. LET US HELP. WHY LEAVE YOUR PAIN PERPETUAL, AND YOUR WOUND INCURABLE?
WHY REFUSETH TO BE HEALED?
MAYBE I AM #@&% UP. MAYBE MY LIFE IS A MESS.
BUT I SURVIVED MY PAST. NO ONE TAKES THAT AWAY FROM ME.
AND I'M A HELL OF A LOT STRONGER THAN THE SCAR TISSUE THEY LEFT ME WITH.
IT THINKS IT HAS THE TEETH OF A LION.
YOU'RE DAMN RIGHT.
NO, VIOLET. YOU'RE DAMNED.

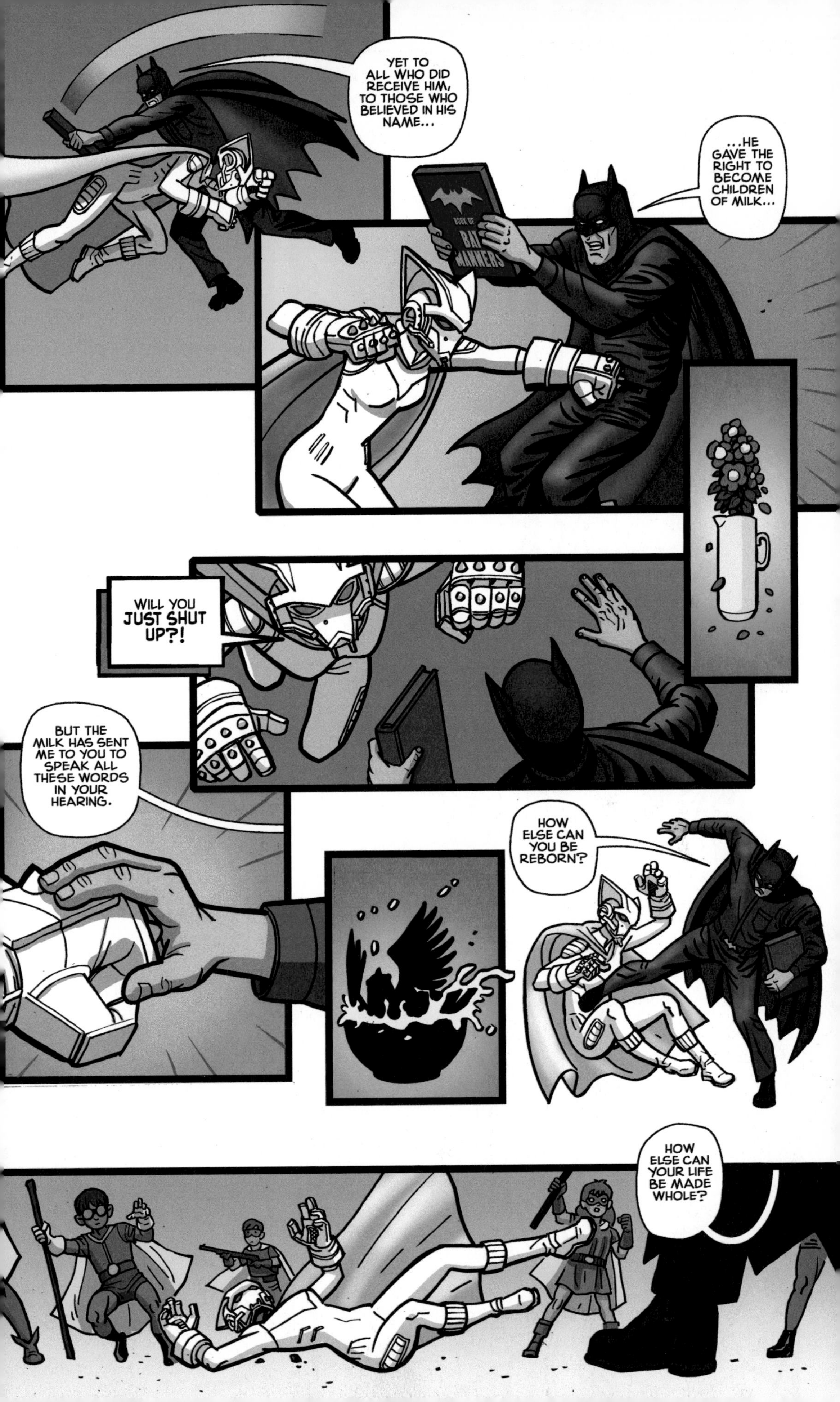

YET TO ALL WHO DID RECEIVE HIM, TO THOSE WHO BELIEVED IN HIS NAME...
...HE GAVE THE RIGHT TO BECOME CHILDREN OF MILK...
BOOK OF BAT MANNERS
WILL YOU JUST SHUT UP?!
BUT THE MILK HAS SENT ME TO YOU TO SPEAK ALL THESE WORDS IN YOUR HEARING.
HOW ELSE CAN YOU BE REBORN?
HOW ELSE CAN YOUR LIFE BE MADE WHOLE?

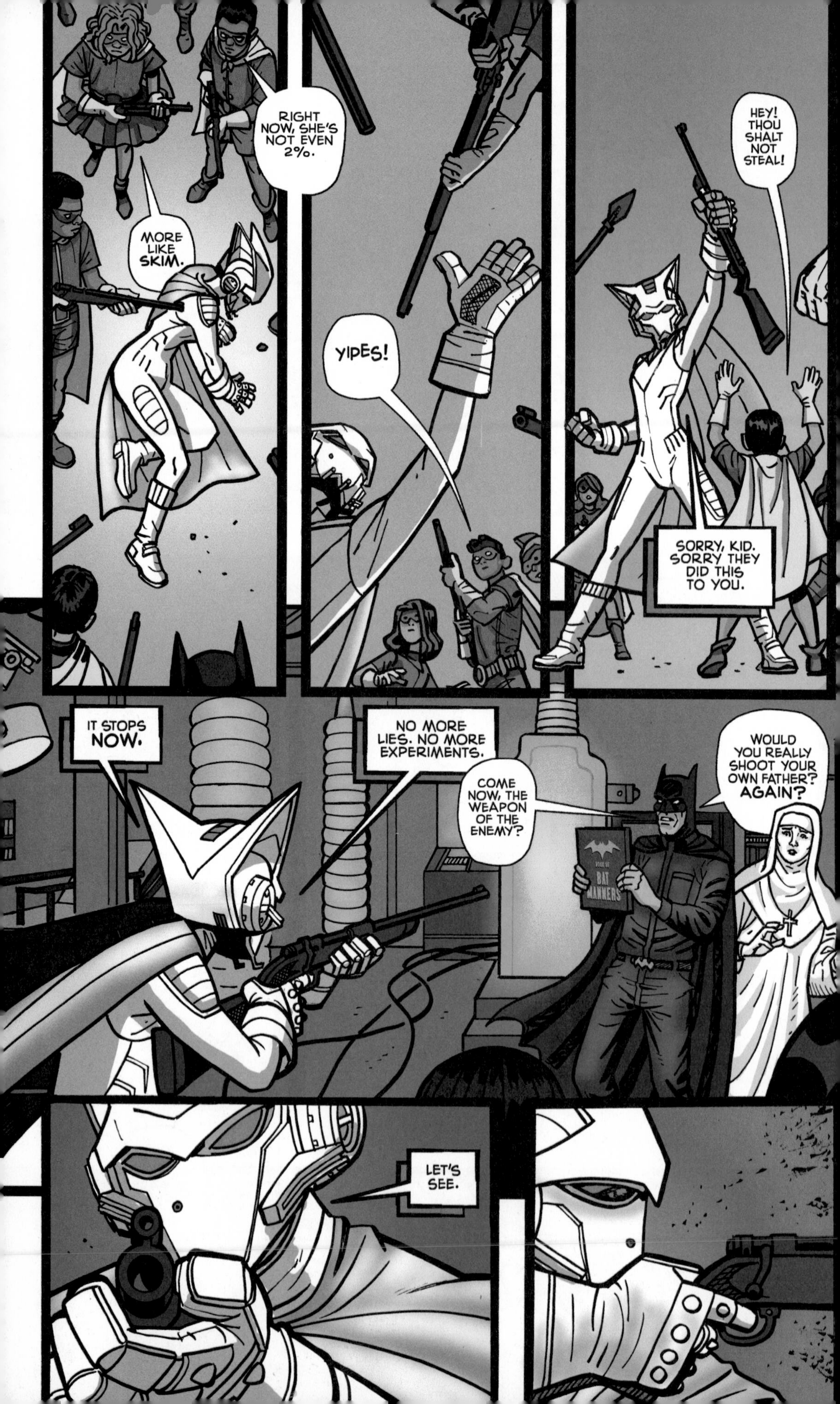

RIGHT NOW, SHE'S NOT EVEN 2%.
MORE LIKE SKIM.
YIPES!
HEY! THOU SHALT NOT STEAL!
SORRY, KID. SORRY THEY DID THIS TO YOU.
IT STOPS NOW.
NO MORE LIES. NO MORE EXPERIMENTS.
COME NOW, THE WEAPON OF THE ENEMY?
WOULD YOU REALLY SHOOT YOUR OWN FATHER? AGAIN?
LET'S SEE.

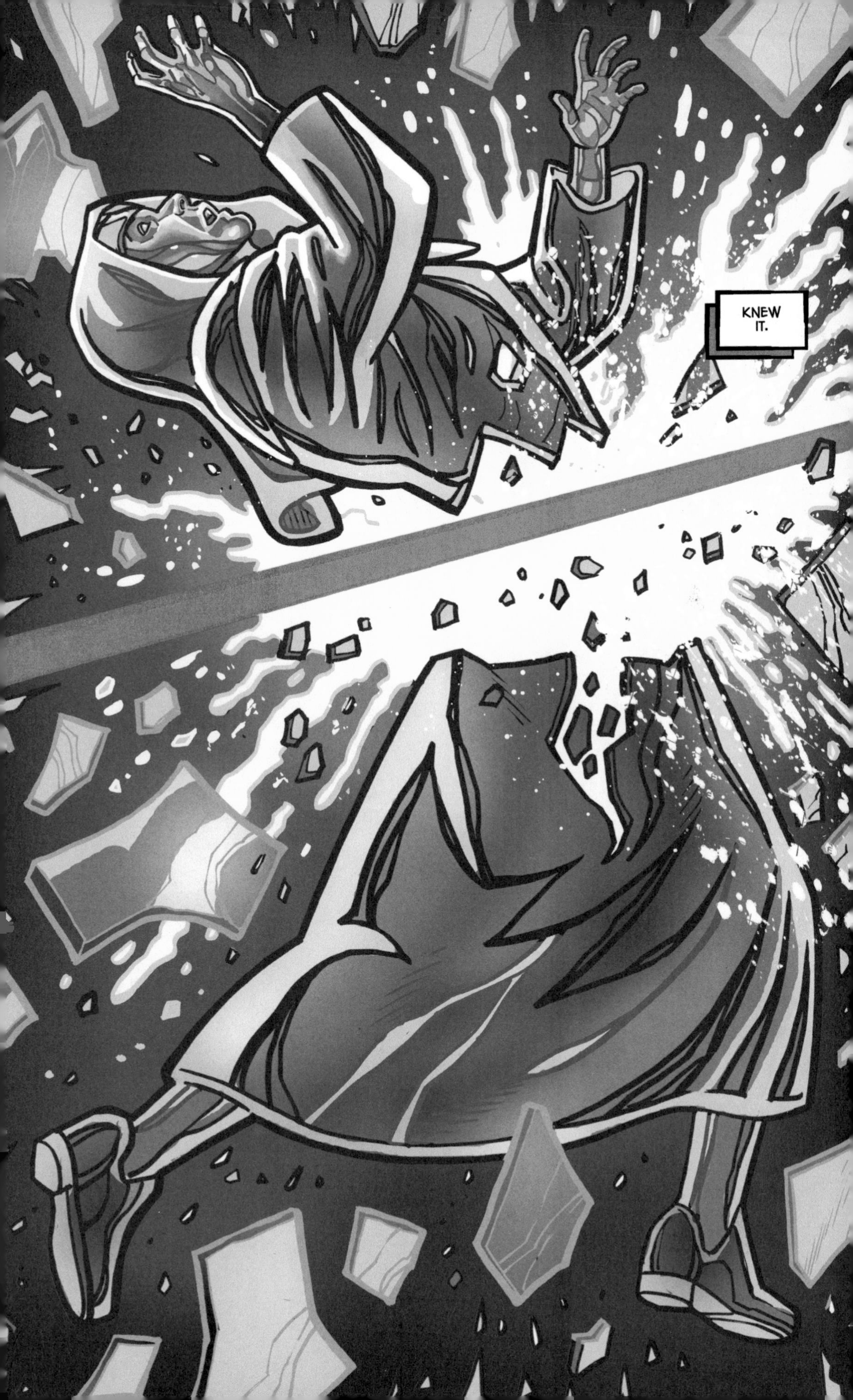
KNEW
IT.

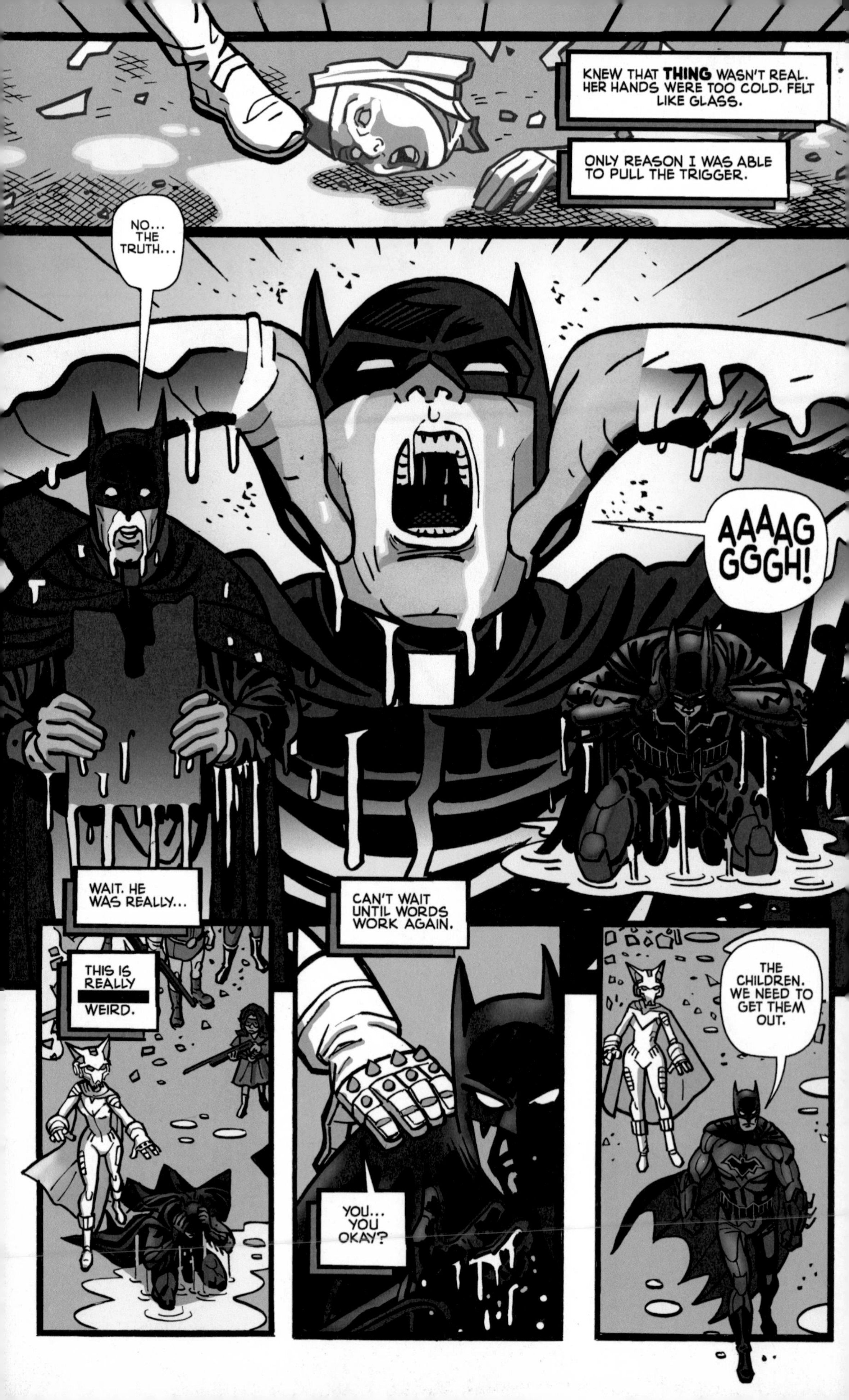
KNEW THAT **THING** WASN'T REAL. HER HANDS WERE TOO COLD. FELT LIKE GLASS.
ONLY REASON I WAS ABLE TO PULL THE TRIGGER.
NO... THE TRUTH...
AAAAGGGGH!
WAIT. HE WAS REALLY...
CAN'T WAIT UNTIL WORDS WORK AGAIN.
THIS IS REALLY [redacted] WEIRD.
YOU... YOU OKAY?
THE CHILDREN. WE NEED TO GET THEM OUT.

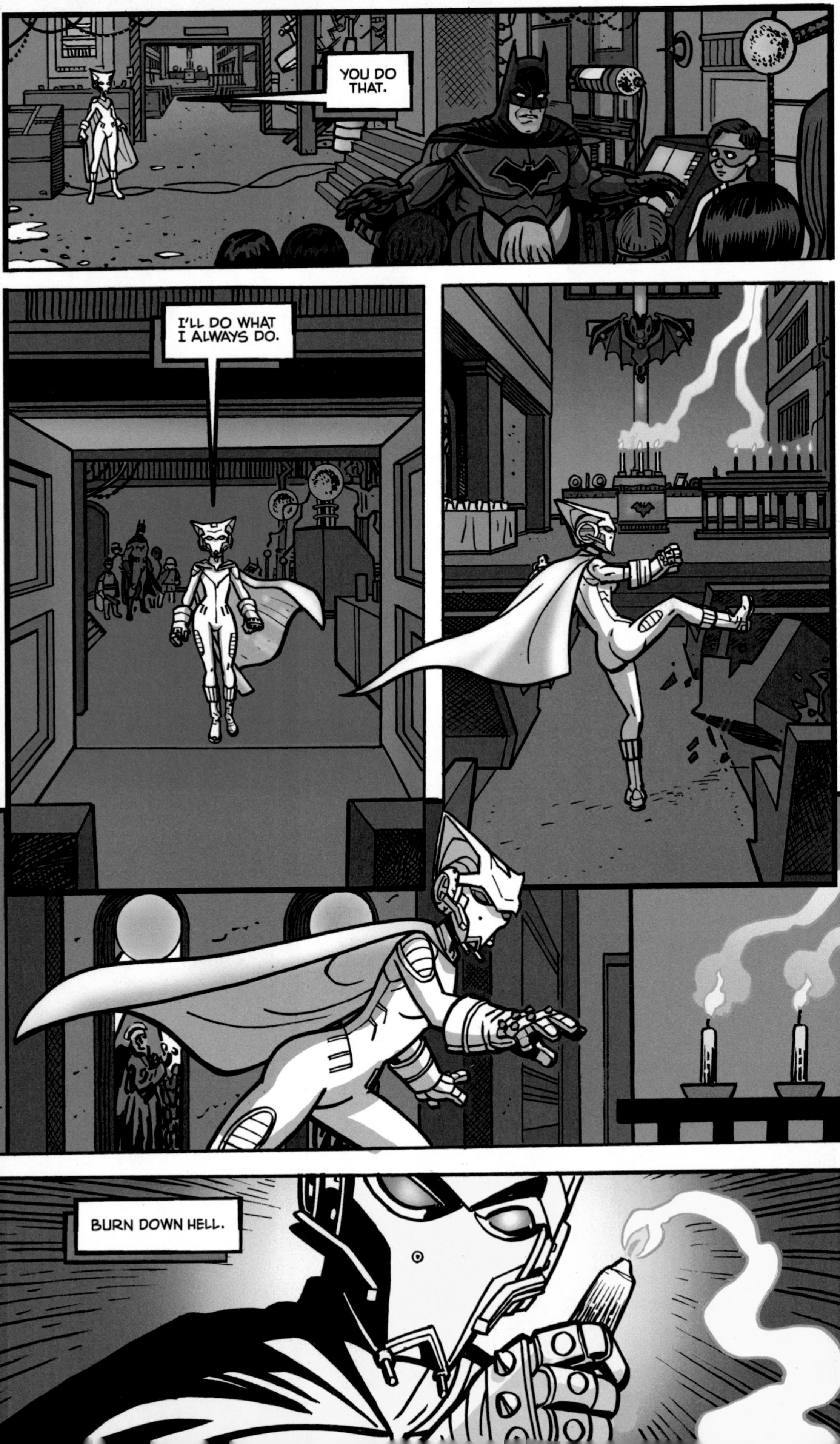
YOU DO THAT.
I'LL DO WHAT I ALWAYS DO.
BURN DOWN HELL.

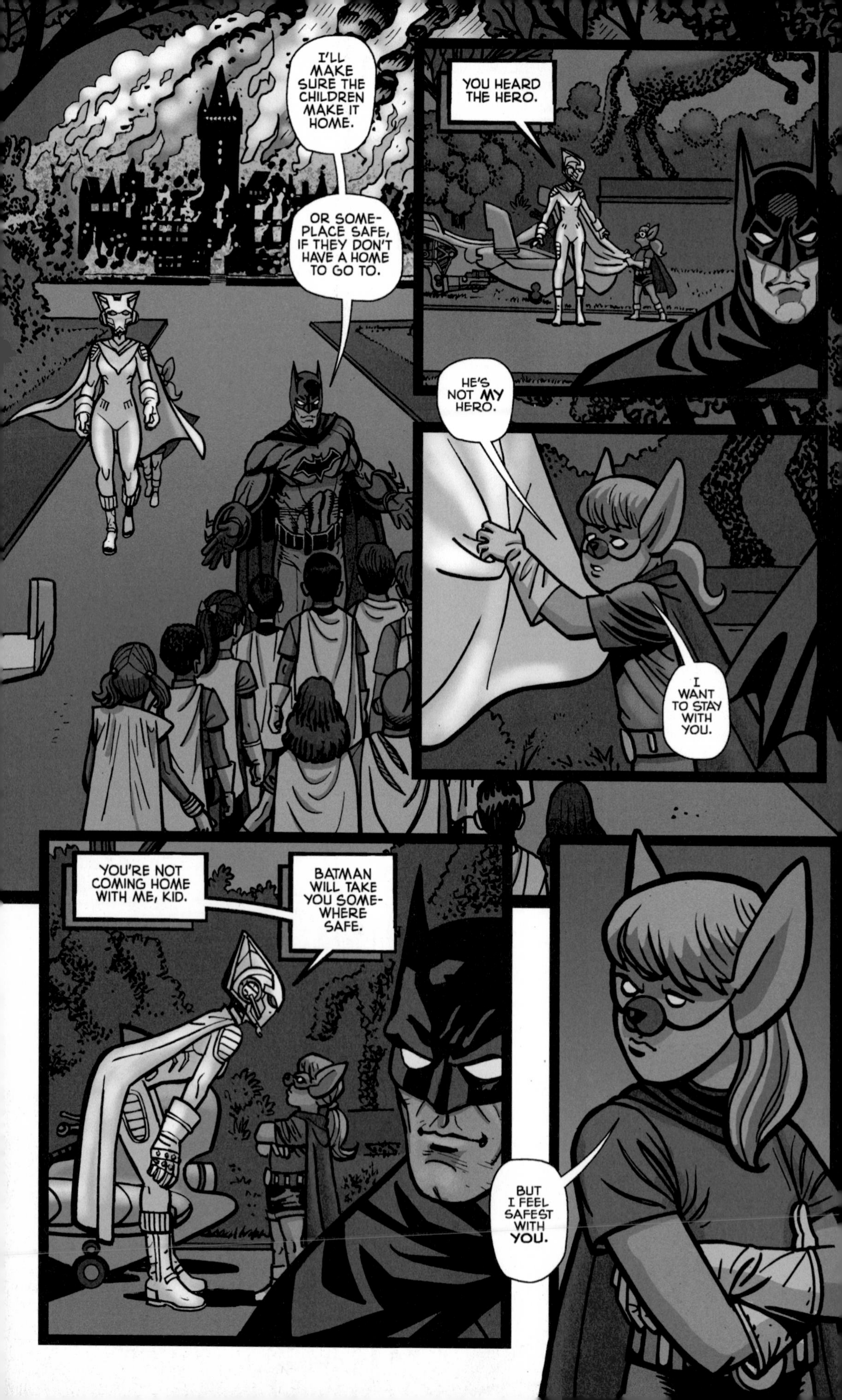
I'LL MAKE SURE THE CHILDREN MAKE IT HOME.
OR SOME-PLACE SAFE, IF THEY DON'T HAVE A HOME TO GO TO.
YOU HEARD THE HERO.
HE'S NOT MY HERO.
I WANT TO STAY WITH YOU.
YOU'RE NOT COMING HOME WITH ME, KID.
BATMAN WILL TAKE YOU SOME-WHERE SAFE.
BUT I FEEL SAFEST WITH YOU.

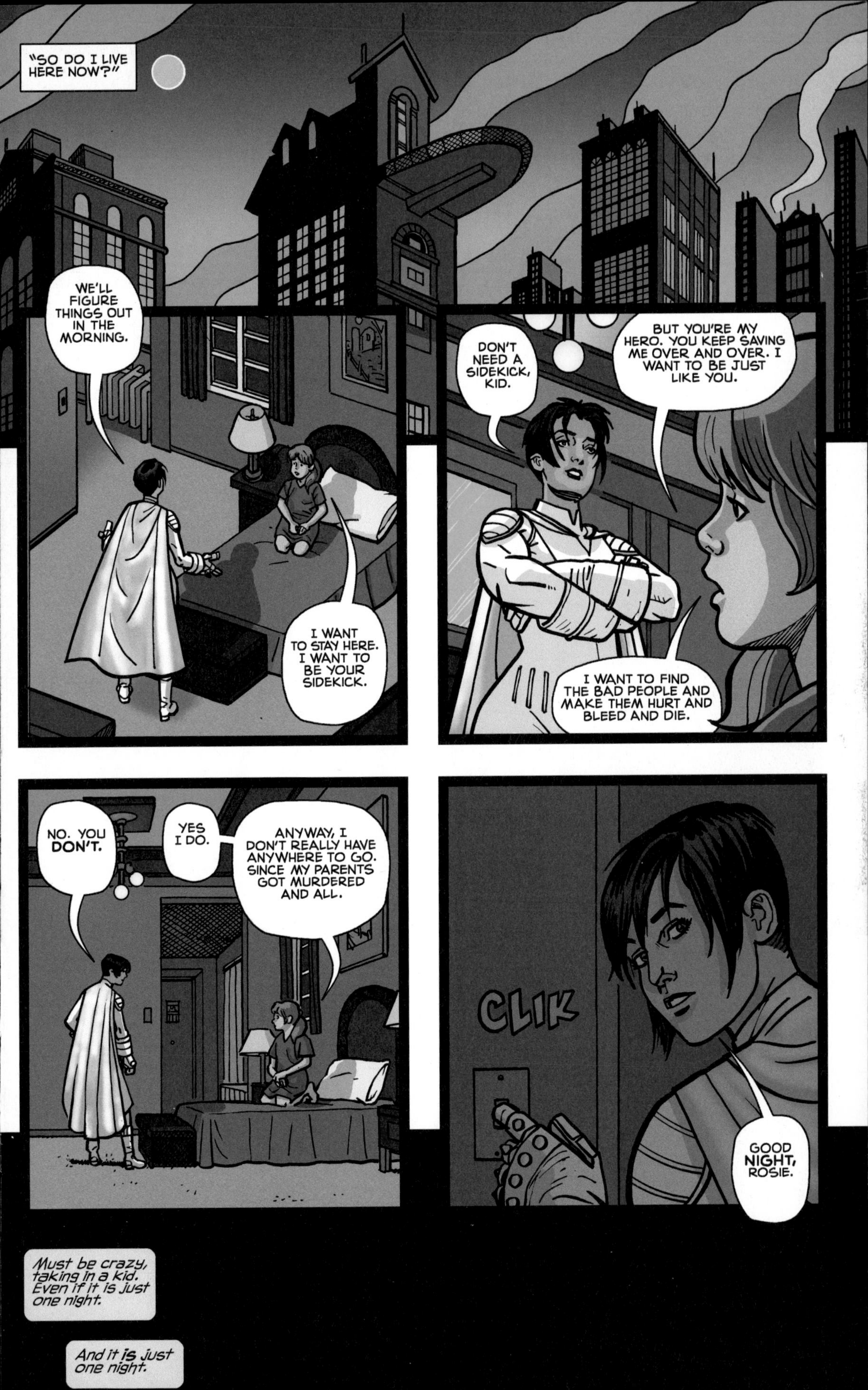
"SO DO I LIVE HERE NOW?"
WE'LL FIGURE THINGS OUT IN THE MORNING.
I WANT TO STAY HERE. I WANT TO BE YOUR SIDEKICK.
DON'T NEED A SIDEKICK, KID.
BUT YOU'RE MY HERO. YOU KEEP SAVING ME OVER AND OVER. I WANT TO BE JUST LIKE YOU.
I WANT TO FIND THE BAD PEOPLE AND MAKE THEM HURT AND BLEED AND DIE.
NO. YOU DON'T.
YES I DO.
ANYWAY, I DON'T REALLY HAVE ANYWHERE TO GO. SINCE MY PARENTS GOT MURDERED AND ALL.
CLIK
GOOD NIGHT, ROSIE.
Must be crazy, taking in a kid. Even if it is just one night.
And it is just one night.

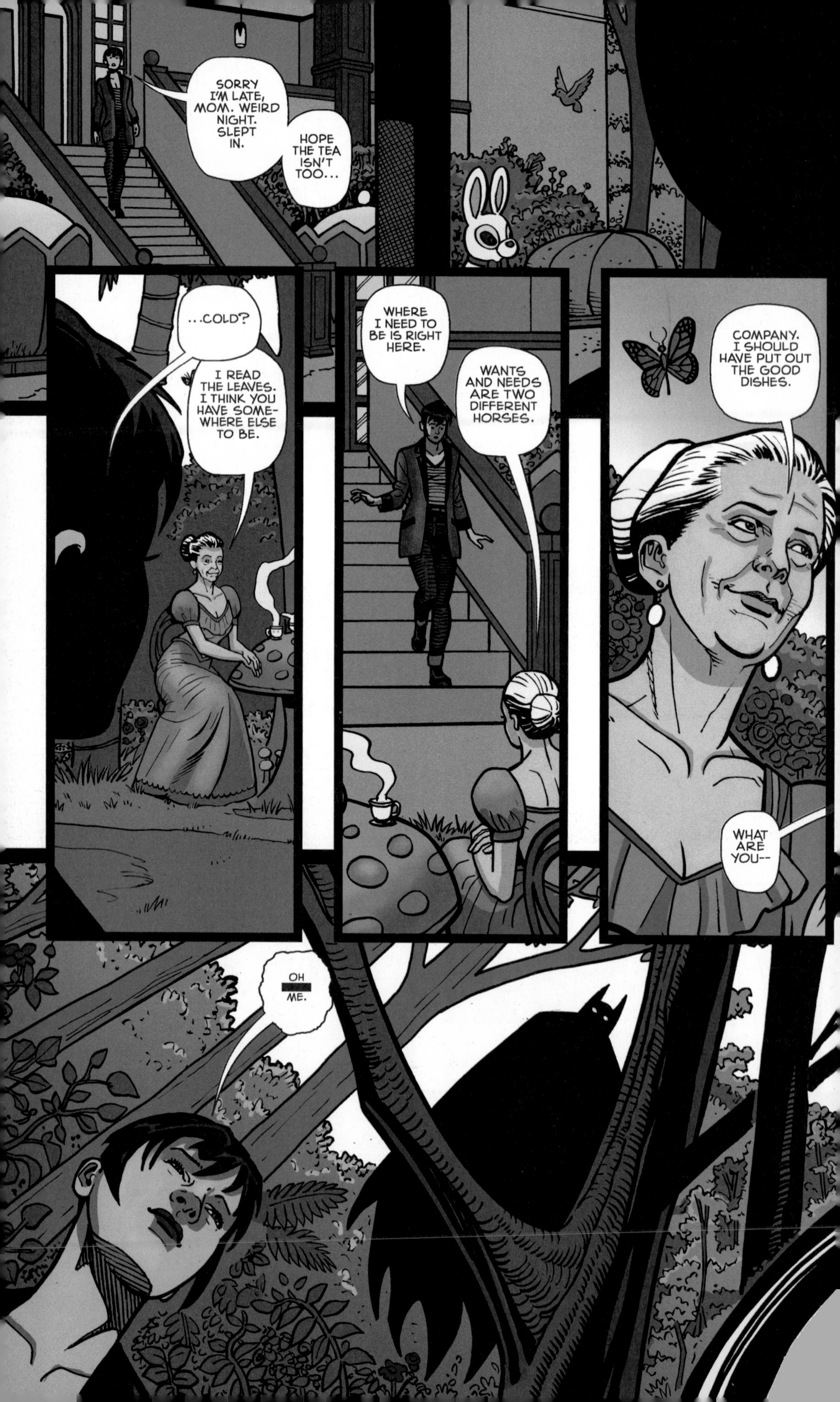
SORRY I'M LATE, MOM. WEIRD NIGHT. SLEPT IN.
HOPE THE TEA ISN'T TOO...
...COLD?
I READ THE LEAVES. I THINK YOU HAVE SOME-WHERE ELSE TO BE.
WHERE I NEED TO BE IS RIGHT HERE.
WANTS AND NEEDS ARE TWO DIFFERENT HORSES.
COMPANY. I SHOULD HAVE PUT OUT THE GOOD DISHES.
WHAT ARE YOU--
OH [redacted] ME.

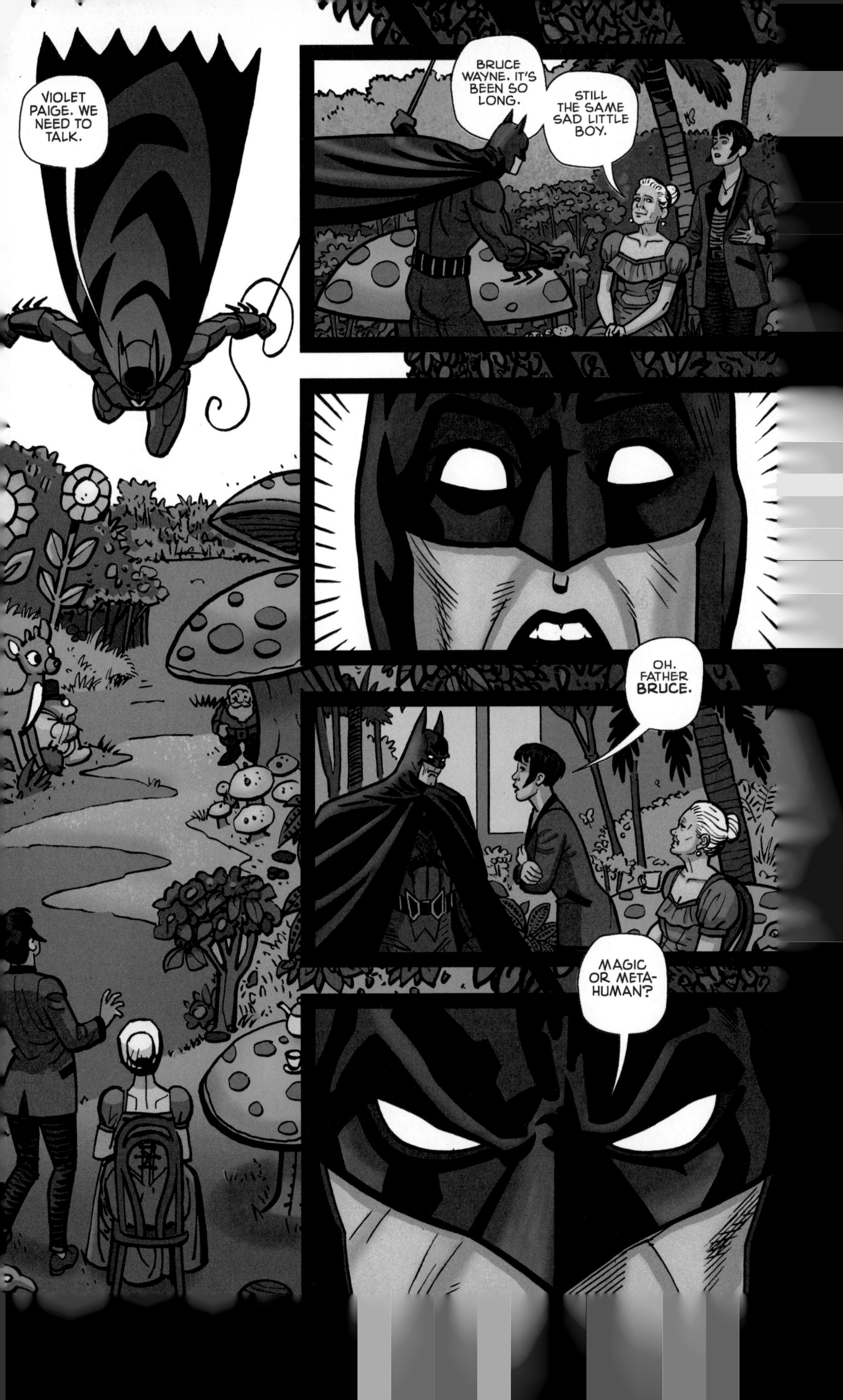
VIOLET PAIGE. WE NEED TO TALK.
BRUCE WAYNE. IT'S BEEN SO LONG.
STILL THE SAME SAD LITTLE BOY.
OH. FATHER BRUCE.
MAGIC OR META-HUMAN?

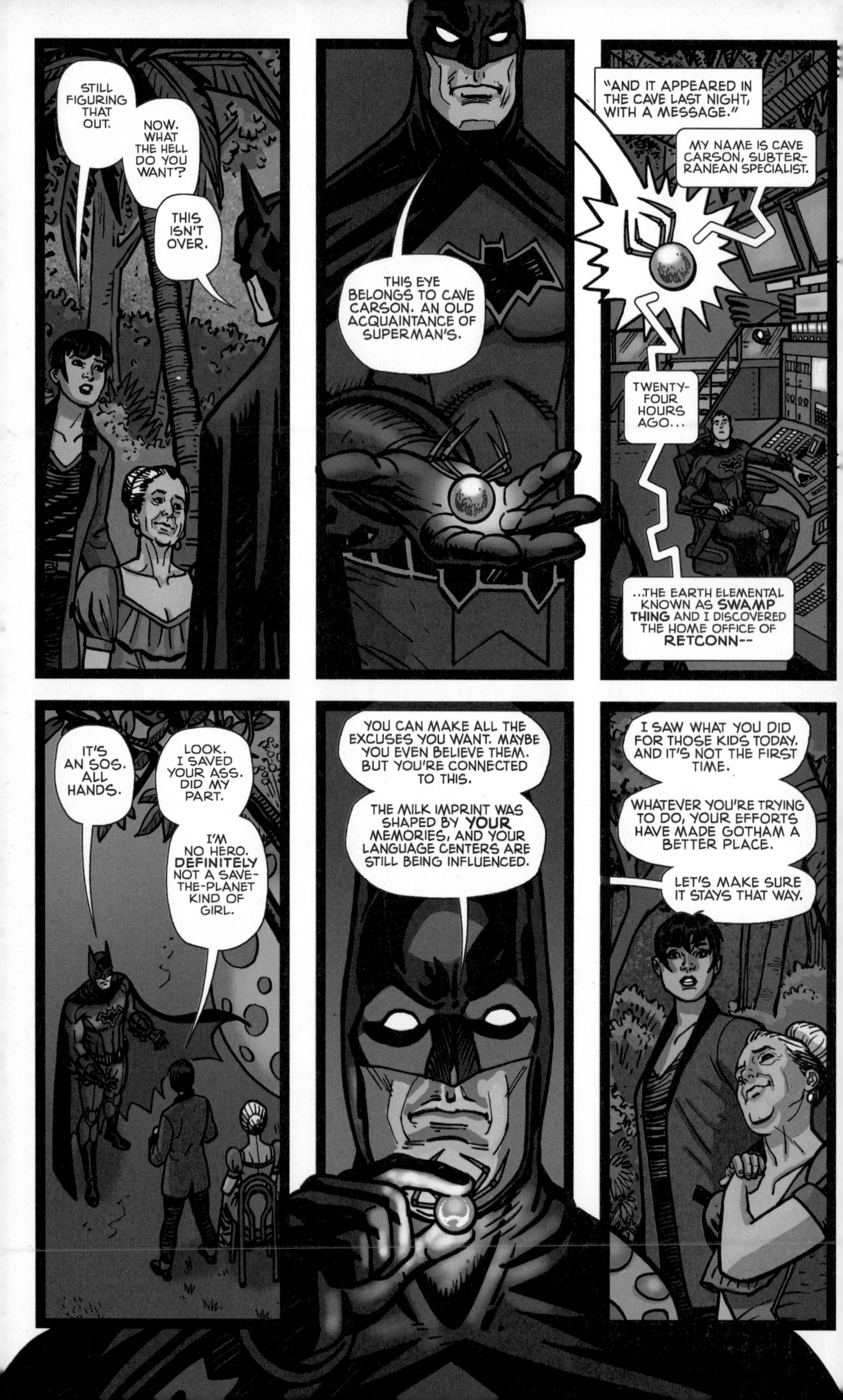

STILL FIGURING THAT OUT.
NOW. WHAT THE HELL DO YOU WANT?
THIS ISN'T OVER.
THIS EYE BELONGS TO CAVE CARSON. AN OLD ACQUAINTANCE OF SUPERMAN'S.
"AND IT APPEARED IN THE CAVE LAST NIGHT, WITH A MESSAGE."
MY NAME IS CAVE CARSON, SUBTERRANEAN SPECIALIST.
TWENTY-FOUR HOURS AGO...
...THE EARTH ELEMENTAL KNOWN AS SWAMP THING AND I DISCOVERED THE HOME OFFICE OF RETCONN--
IT'S AN SOS. ALL HANDS.
LOOK. I SAVED YOUR ASS. DID MY PART.
I'M NO HERO. DEFINITELY NOT A SAVE-THE-PLANET KIND OF GIRL.
YOU CAN MAKE ALL THE EXCUSES YOU WANT. MAYBE YOU EVEN BELIEVE THEM. BUT YOU'RE CONNECTED TO THIS.
THE MILK IMPRINT WAS SHAPED BY YOUR MEMORIES, AND YOUR LANGUAGE CENTERS ARE STILL BEING INFLUENCED.
I SAW WHAT YOU DID FOR THOSE KIDS TODAY. AND IT'S NOT THE FIRST TIME.
WHATEVER YOU'RE TRYING TO DO, YOUR EFFORTS HAVE MADE GOTHAM A BETTER PLACE.
LET'S MAKE SURE IT STAYS THAT WAY.

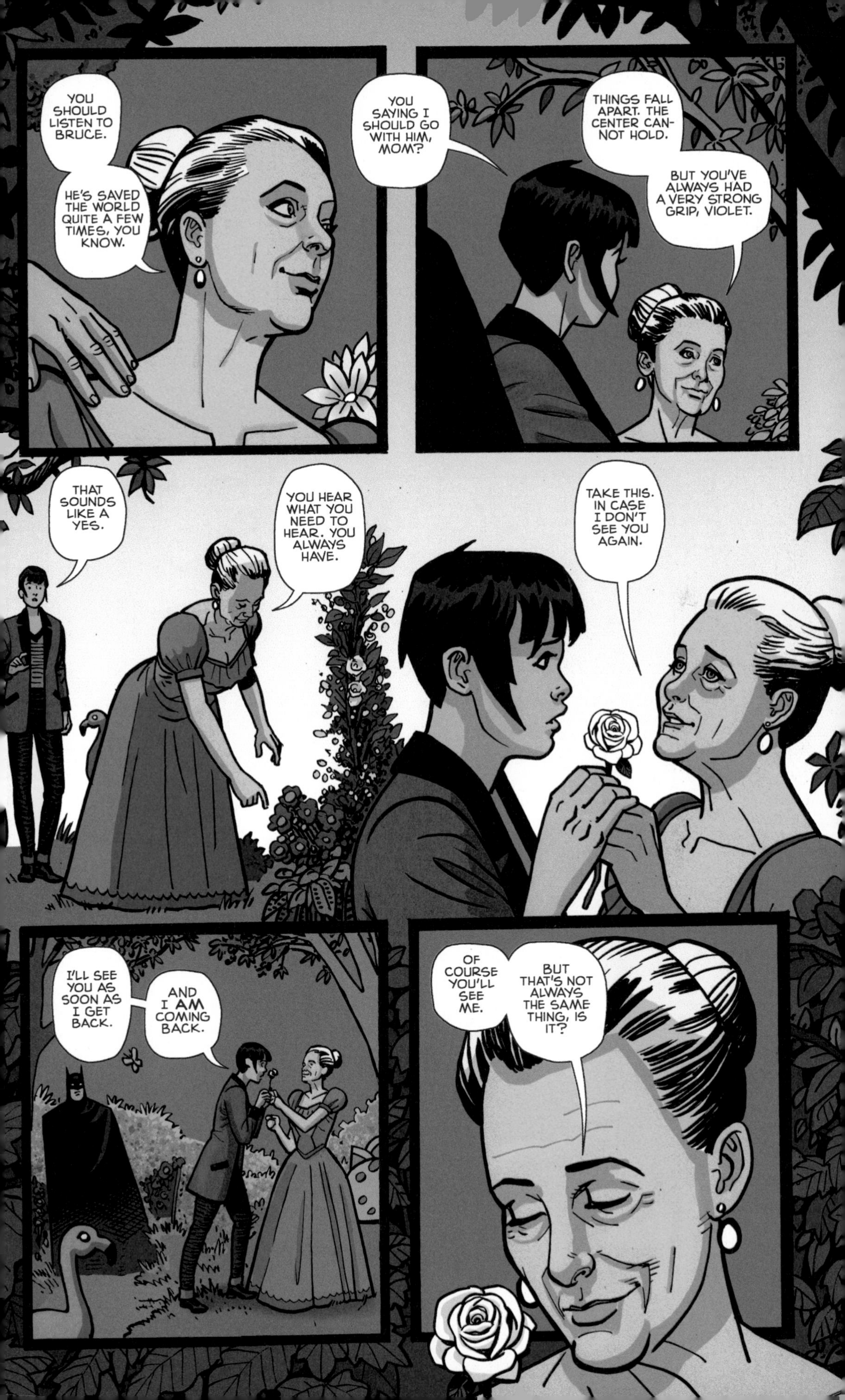
YOU SHOULD LISTEN TO BRUCE.
HE'S SAVED THE WORLD QUITE A FEW TIMES, YOU KNOW.
YOU SAYING I SHOULD GO WITH HIM, MOM?
THINGS FALL APART. THE CENTER CAN-NOT HOLD.
BUT YOU'VE ALWAYS HAD A VERY STRONG GRIP, VIOLET.
THAT SOUNDS LIKE A YES.
YOU HEAR WHAT YOU NEED TO HEAR. YOU ALWAYS HAVE.
TAKE THIS. IN CASE I DON'T SEE YOU AGAIN.
I'LL SEE YOU AS SOON AS I GET BACK.
AND I AM COMING BACK.
OF COURSE YOU'LL SEE ME.
BUT THAT'S NOT ALWAYS THE SAME THING, IS IT?

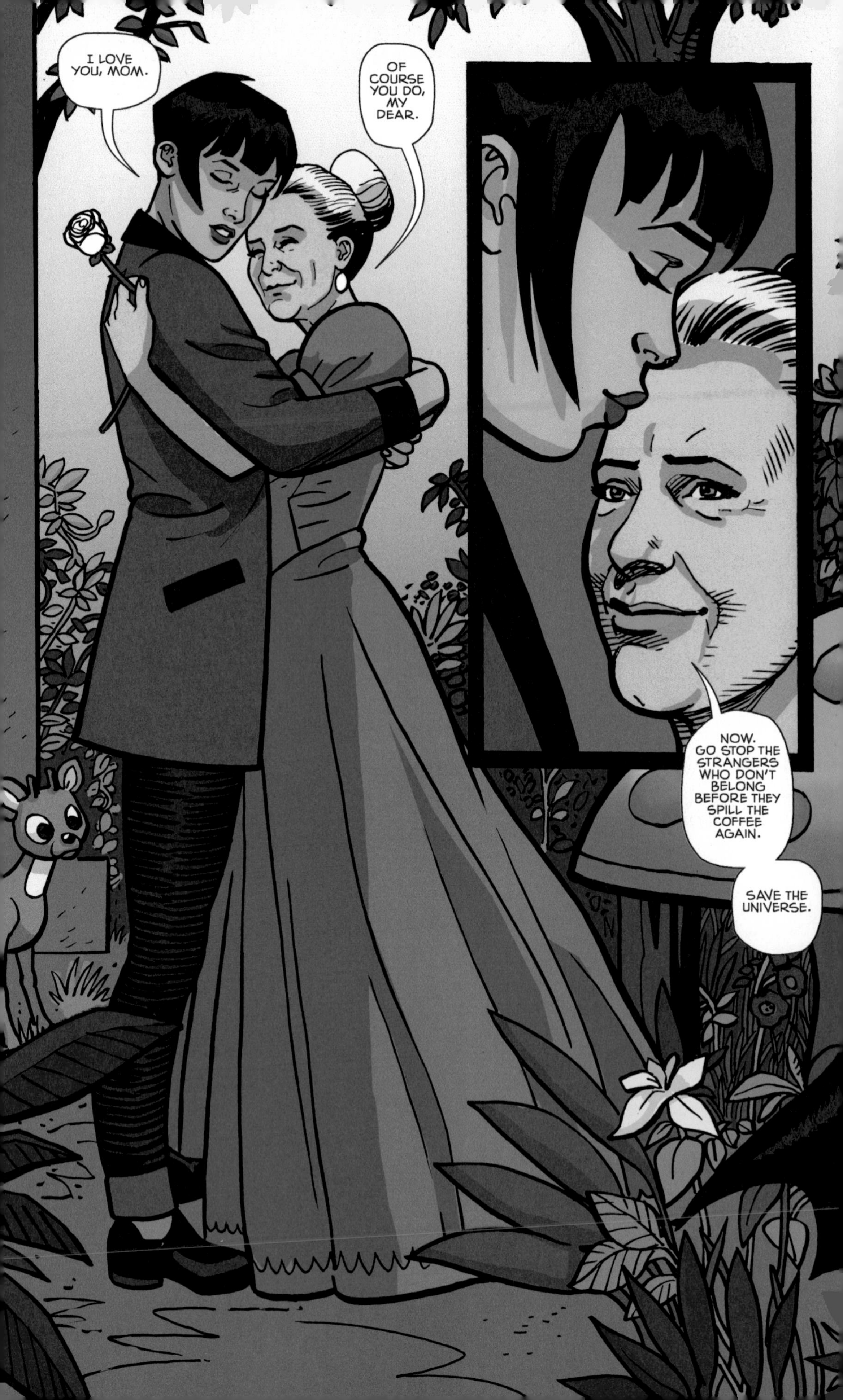
I LOVE YOU, MOM.
OF COURSE YOU DO, MY DEAR.
NOW. GO STOP THE STRANGERS WHO DON'T BELONG BEFORE THEY SPILL THE COFFEE AGAIN.
SAVE THE UNIVERSE.

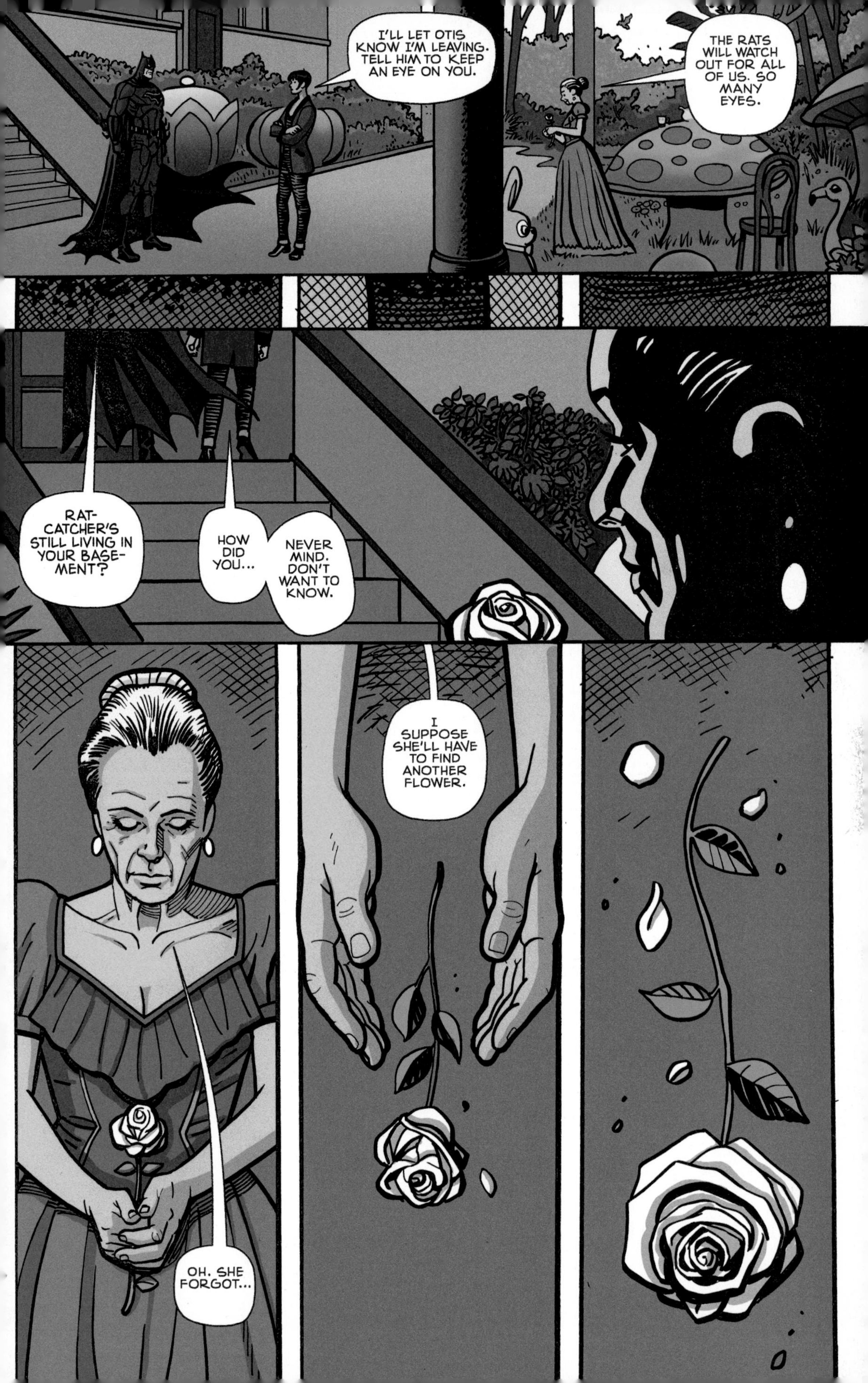
I'LL LET OTIS KNOW I'M LEAVING. TELL HIM TO KEEP AN EYE ON YOU.
THE RATS WILL WATCH OUT FOR ALL OF US. SO MANY EYES.
RAT-CATCHER'S STILL LIVING IN YOUR BASEMENT?
HOW DID YOU...
NEVER MIND. DON'T WANT TO KNOW.
OH. SHE FORGOT...
I SUPPOSE SHE'LL HAVE TO FIND ANOTHER FLOWER.

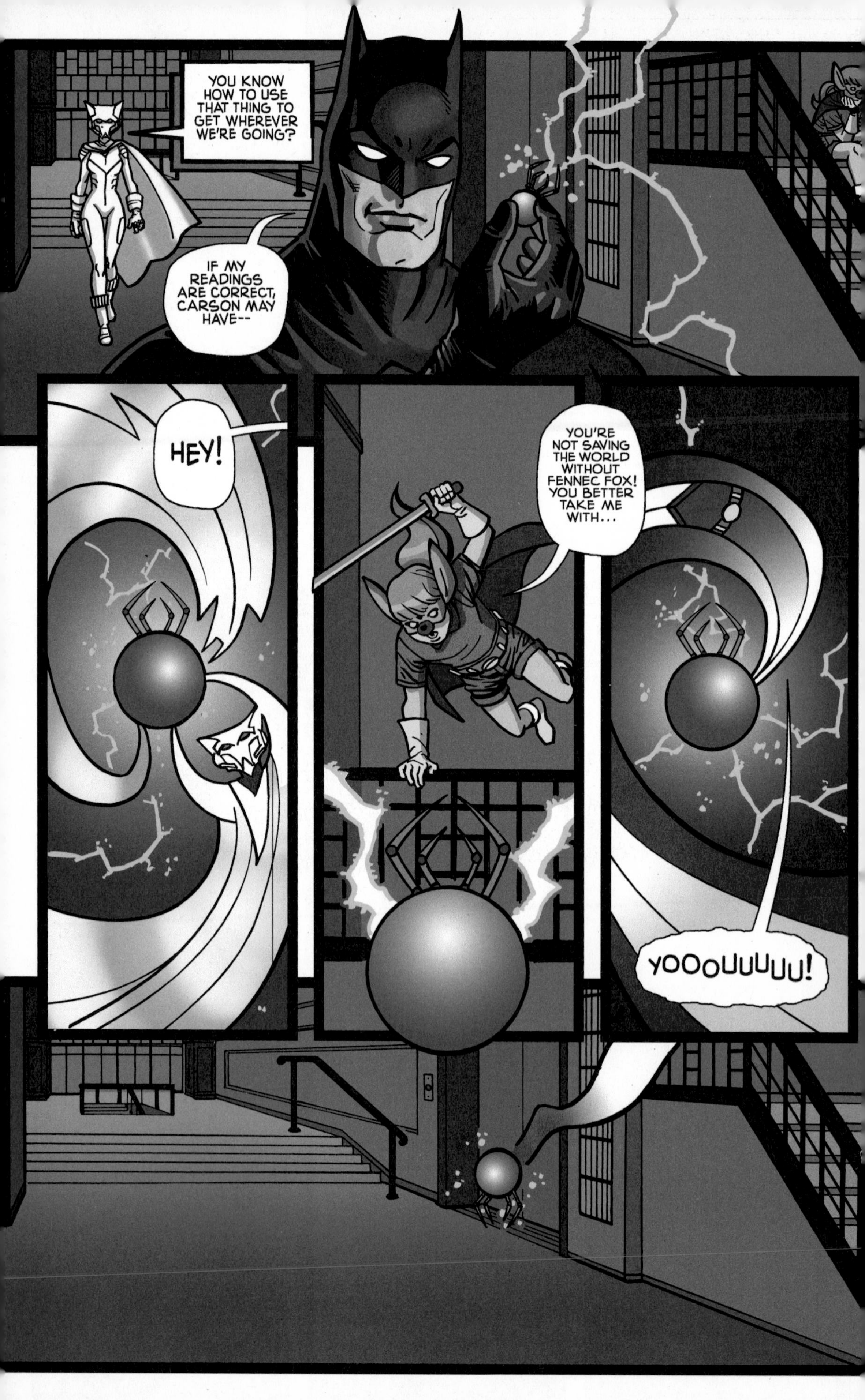
YOU KNOW HOW TO USE THAT THING TO GET WHEREVER WE'RE GOING?
IF MY READINGS ARE CORRECT, CARSON MAY HAVE--
HEY!
YOU'RE NOT SAVING THE WORLD WITHOUT FENNEC FOX! YOU BETTER TAKE ME WITH...
YOOOUUUUU!

By the early 1960s, ASTOUNDING TALES had been canceled, and "the Formless Girl" with it. But in 1981, the writer-artist team of Fred Hand and Garry Streicher brought the book back to life as ALPHA 13. Hand's version named Caroline Sharp "Chrysalis" for the first time, the leader of a team of super-powered misfits working for a secret governmental organization to stop Madame Atom's plan to plunge the world into anarchy. A book without clear-cut heroes and villains, ALPHA 13 pitted anarchism against exploitative authorities, and struggled to maintain an audience.

"Nevermore, Never Man," ALPHA 13 #27. Story by Fred Hand, art by Garry Streicher. 1983.

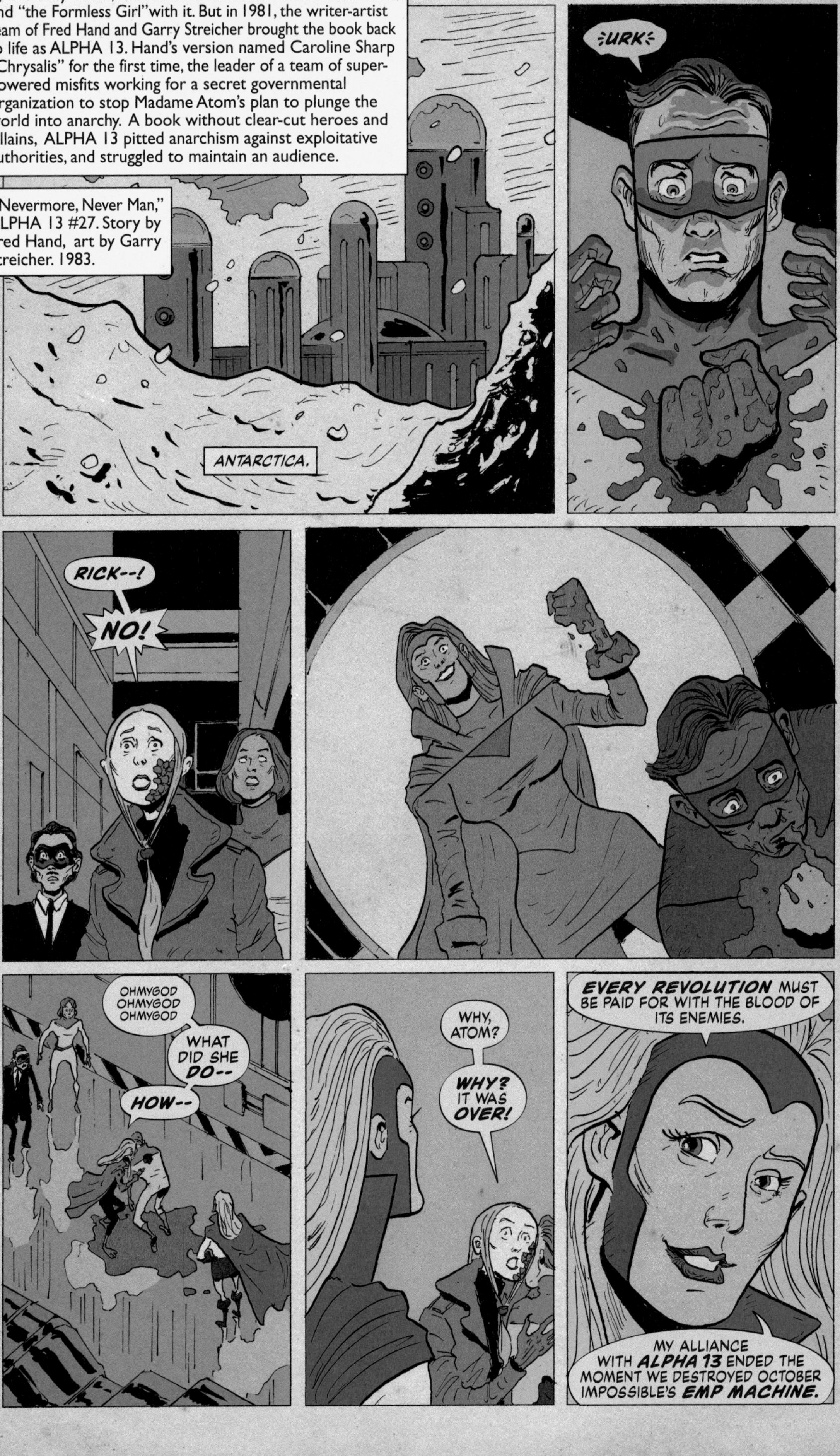
ANTARCTICA.
URK
RICK--!
NO!
OHMYGOD OHMYGOD OHMYGOD
WHAT DID SHE DO--
HOW--
WHY, ATOM?
WHY? IT WAS OVER!
EVERY REVOLUTION MUST BE PAID FOR WITH THE BLOOD OF ITS ENEMIES.
MY ALLIANCE WITH ALPHA 13 ENDED THE MOMENT WE DESTROYED OCTOBER IMPOSSIBLE'S EMP MACHINE.

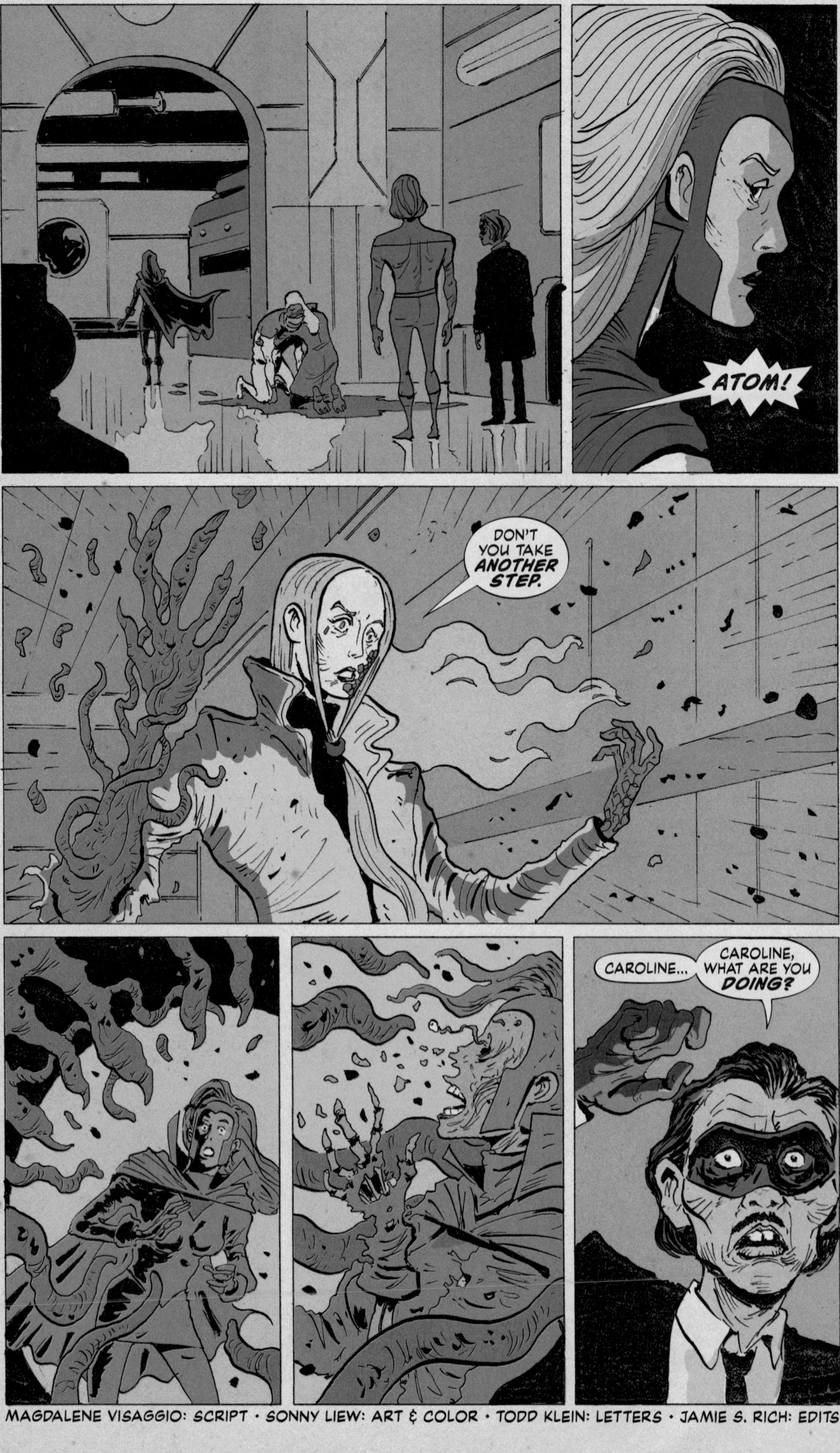
ATOM!
DON'T YOU TAKE ANOTHER STEP.
CAROLINE...
CAROLINE, WHAT ARE YOU DOING?

MAGDALENE VISAGGIO: SCRIPT • SONNY LIEW: ART & COLOR • TODD KLEIN: LETTERS • JAMIE S. RICH: EDITS

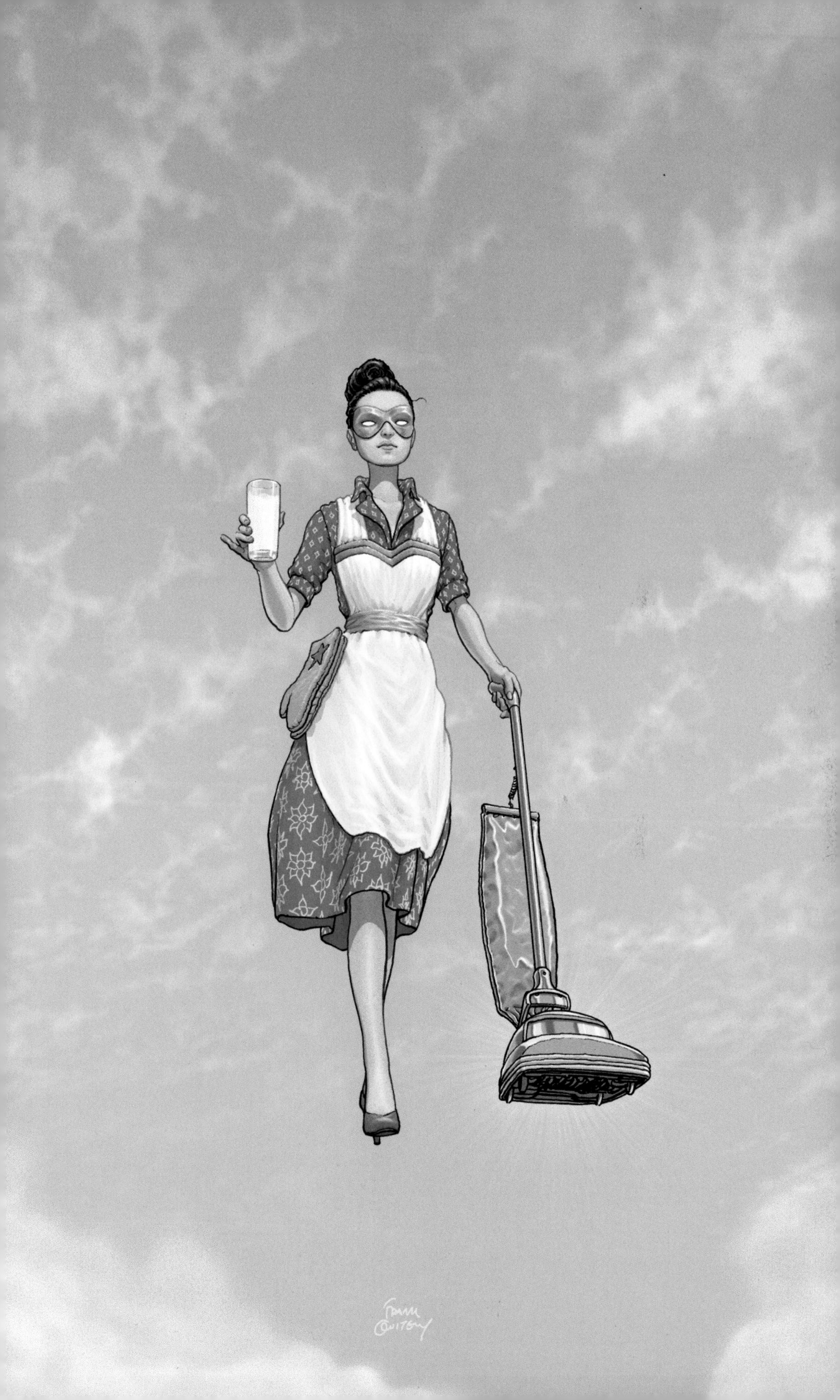

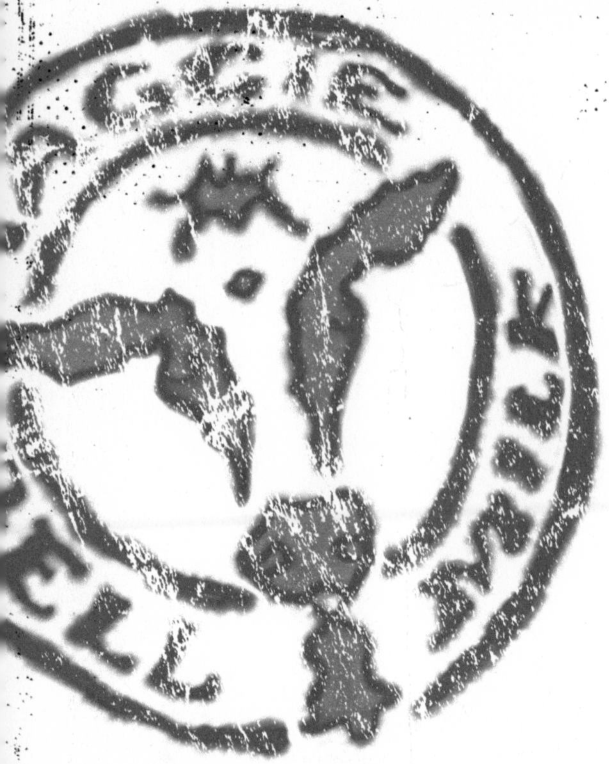
AGGIE
ELL
MILK

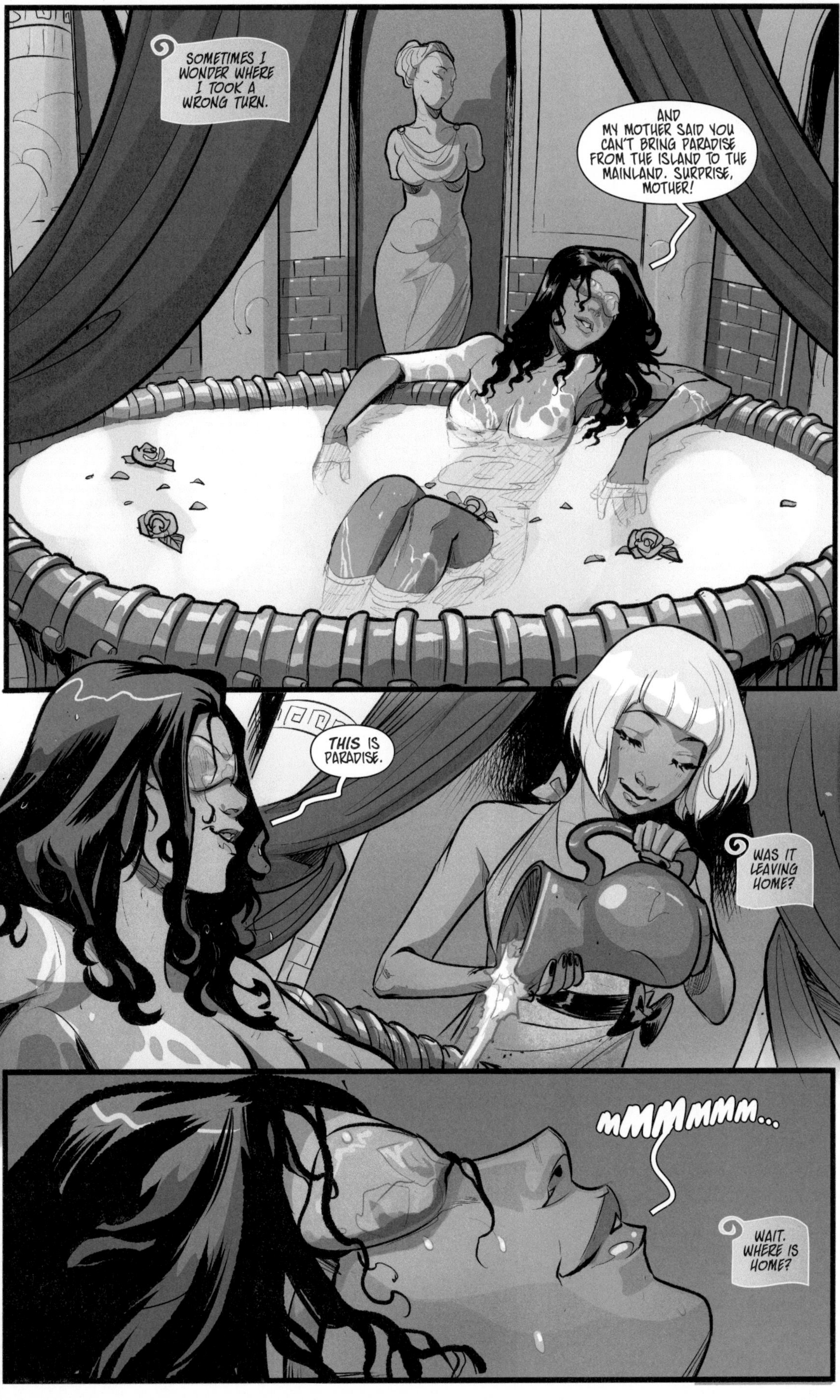
SOMETIMES I WONDER WHERE I TOOK A WRONG TURN.
AND MY MOTHER SAID YOU CAN'T BRING PARADISE FROM THE ISLAND TO THE MAINLAND. SURPRISE, MOTHER!
THIS IS PARADISE.
WAS IT LEAVING HOME?
mMMmmm...
WAIT. WHERE IS HOME?

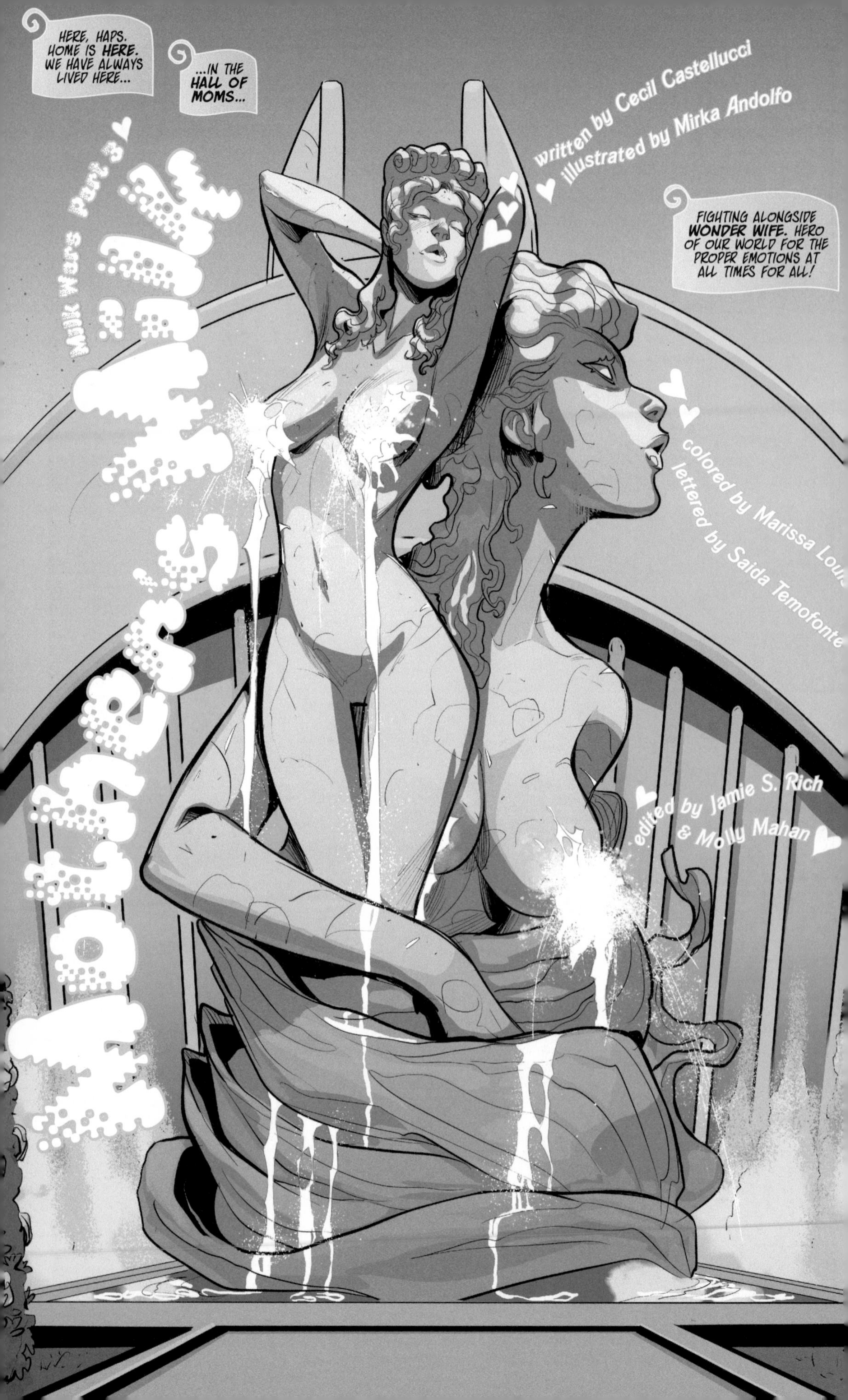
HERE, HAPS. HOME IS HERE. WE HAVE ALWAYS LIVED HERE...
...IN THE HALL OF MOMS...
FIGHTING ALONGSIDE WONDER WIFE. HERO OF OUR WORLD FOR THE PROPER EMOTIONS AT ALL TIMES FOR ALL!
Milk Wars Part 3
Mother's Milk
written by Cecil Castellucci
illustrated by Mirka Andolfo
colored by Marissa Lou
lettered by Saida Temofonte
edited by Jamie S. Rich & Molly Mahan

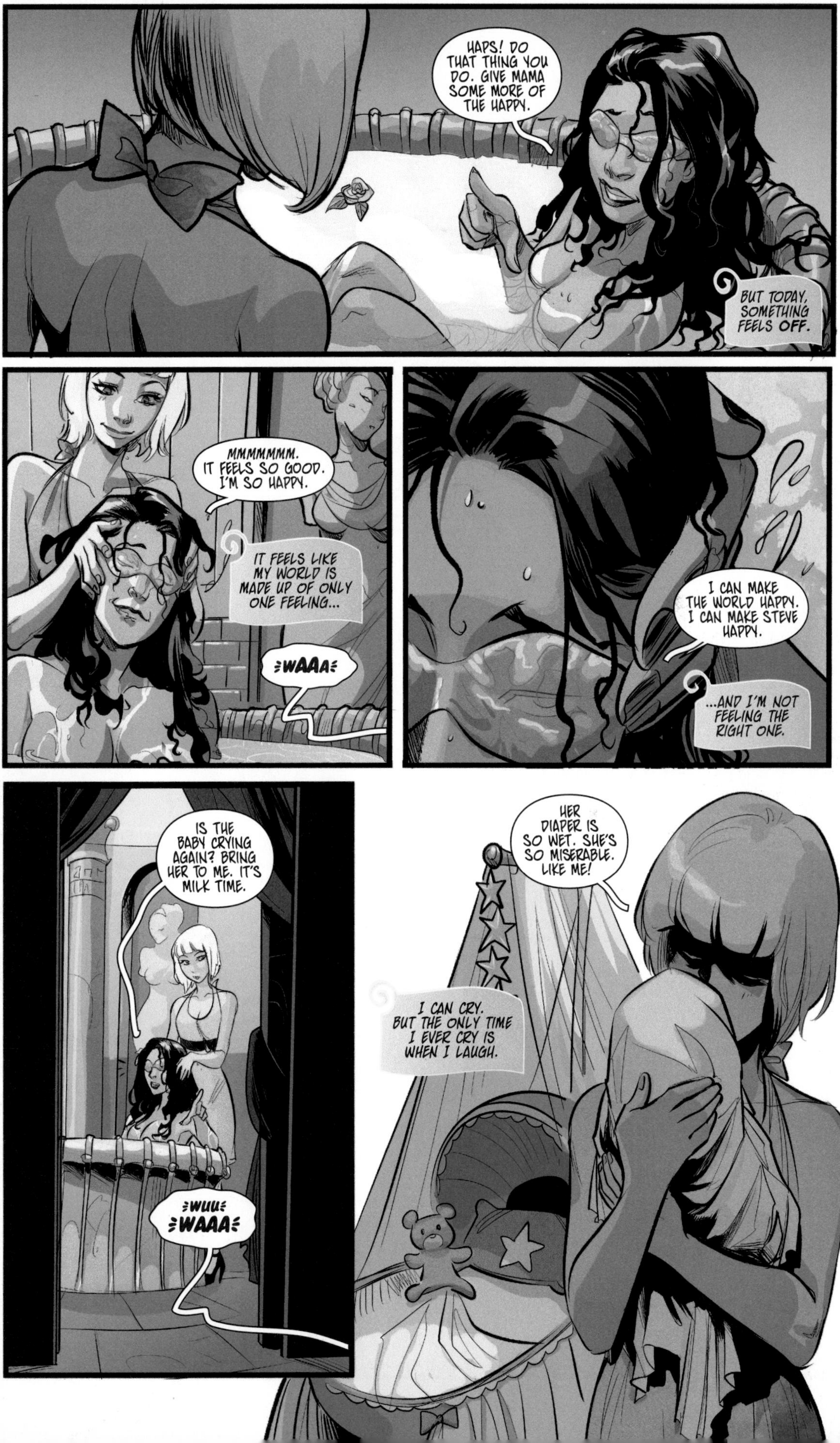
HAPS! DO THAT THING YOU DO. GIVE MAMA SOME MORE OF THE HAPPY.
BUT TODAY, SOMETHING FEELS OFF.
MMMMMMM. IT FEELS SO GOOD. I'M SO HAPPY.
IT FEELS LIKE MY WORLD IS MADE UP OF ONLY ONE FEELING...
WAAA
I CAN MAKE THE WORLD HAPPY. I CAN MAKE STEVE HAPPY.
...AND I'M NOT FEELING THE RIGHT ONE.
IS THE BABY CRYING AGAIN? BRING HER TO ME. IT'S MILK TIME.
WUU WAAA
HER DIAPER IS SO WET. SHE'S SO MISERABLE. LIKE ME!
I CAN CRY. BUT THE ONLY TIME I EVER CRY IS WHEN I LAUGH.

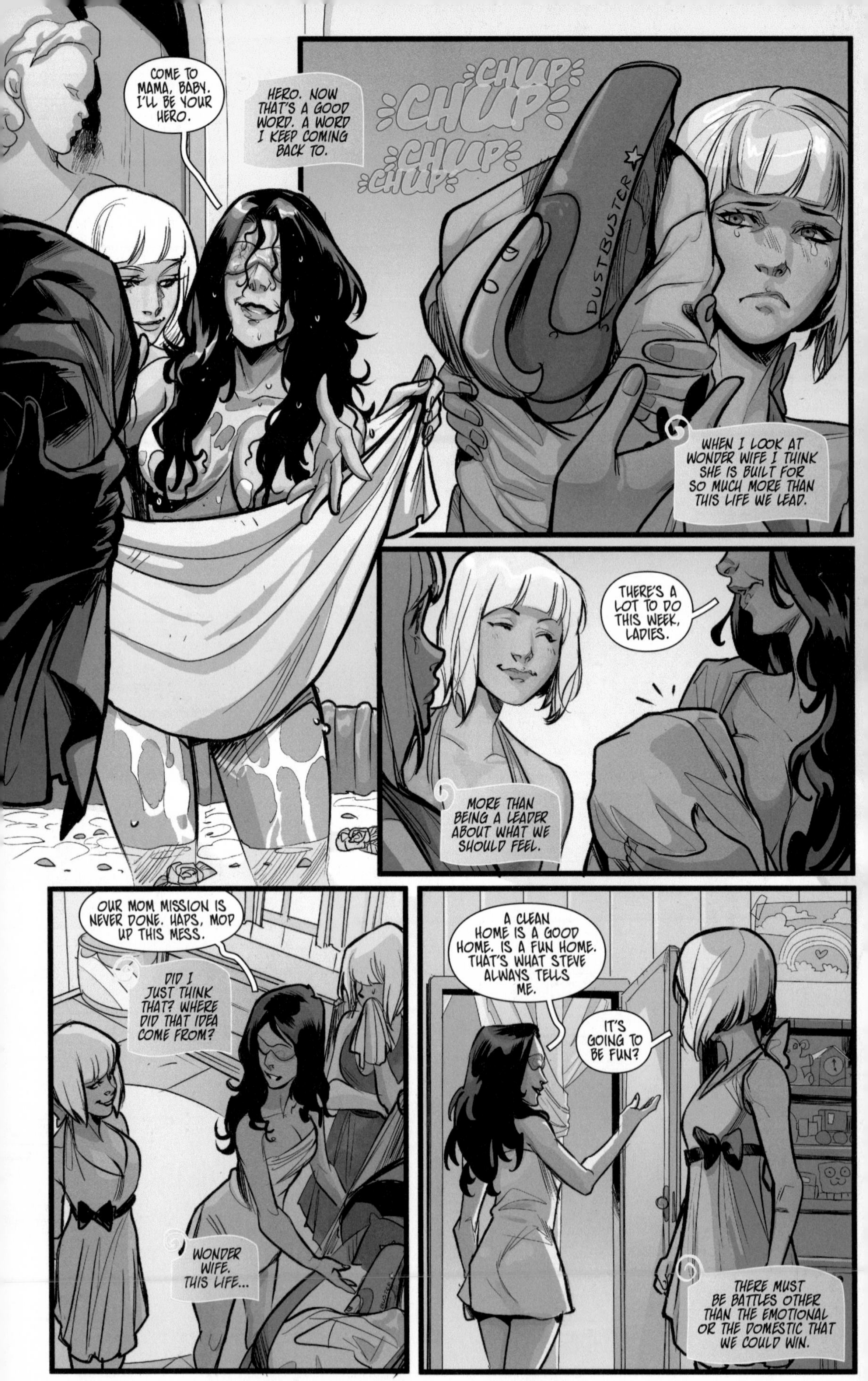

COME TO MAMA, BABY. I'LL BE YOUR HERO.
HERO. NOW THAT'S A GOOD WORD. A WORD I KEEP COMING BACK TO.
CHUP CHUP CHUP CHUP
DUSTBUSTER
WHEN I LOOK AT WONDER WIFE I THINK SHE IS BUILT FOR SO MUCH MORE THAN THIS LIFE WE LEAD.
THERE'S A LOT TO DO THIS WEEK, LADIES.
MORE THAN BEING A LEADER ABOUT WHAT WE SHOULD FEEL.
OUR MOM MISSION IS NEVER DONE. HAPS, MOP UP THIS MESS.
DID I JUST THINK THAT? WHERE DID THAT IDEA COME FROM?
WONDER WIFE. THIS LIFE...
A CLEAN HOME IS A GOOD HOME. IS A FUN HOME. THAT'S WHAT STEVE ALWAYS TELLS ME.
IT'S GOING TO BE FUN?
THERE MUST BE BATTLES OTHER THAN THE EMOTIONAL OR THE DOMESTIC THAT WE COULD WIN.

NOTHING IS EVER FUN! IT'S ALL SO SAD. SADNESS IS CRAWLING OUT OF MY SKIN!
YOU'RE GOING TO HURT YOURSELF WITH ALL THIS WEEPING YOU DO. I THINK IT'S BAD FOR WONDER WIFE.
I HAVE A FEELING WORMS LIVING INSIDE OF ME THAT AREN'T MINE.
FUN IS ALWAYS THE STATE THAT COMES OUT, BUT IT'S A LIE.
I HURT ALL THE TIME. YOU WOULDN'T UNDERSTAND BECAUSE YOU HOARD ALL THE HAPPINESS.
YOU CAN HAVE SOME, BLUE. YOU JUST HAVE TO SEE THE GLASS AS HALF FULL.
OR MAYBE I COULD SEE THE GLASS DIFFERENTLY, MAYBE IT'S NOT THERE AT ALL?
IF I HAVE TO BE IN CHARGE OF HAPPY, THEN GETTING RID OF BLUE WILL MAKE ME HAPPY.
WE HAVE A LOT OF HEROIC EMOTIONAL WORK TO DO. JOIN THE OTHERS AND EAT SOMETHING.
I KNOW! I'M USELESS, HAPS. OUR EMOTIONAL WORK JUST NEVER ENDS!
OUCH!
LYING GETS EASIER THE MORE YOU DO IT.
I HAVE TO REMEMBER, WONDER WIFE IS HERE FOR US ALL.

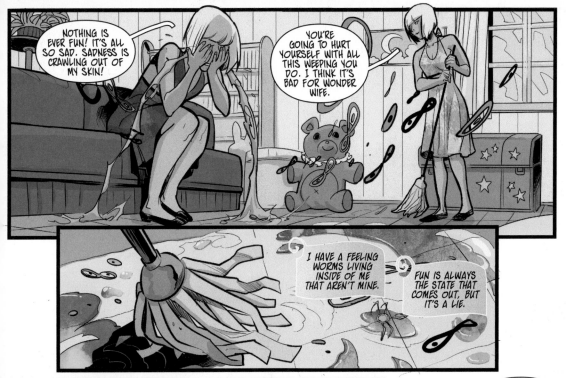

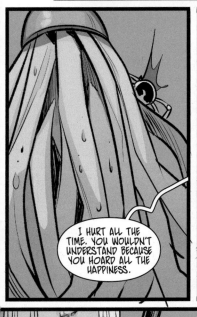

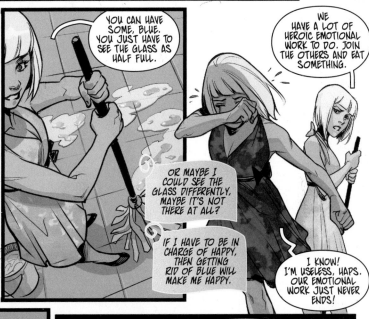

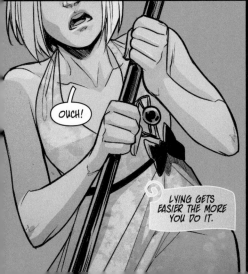

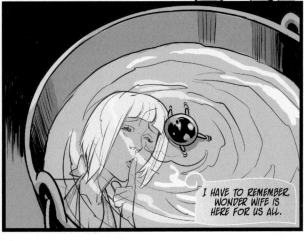

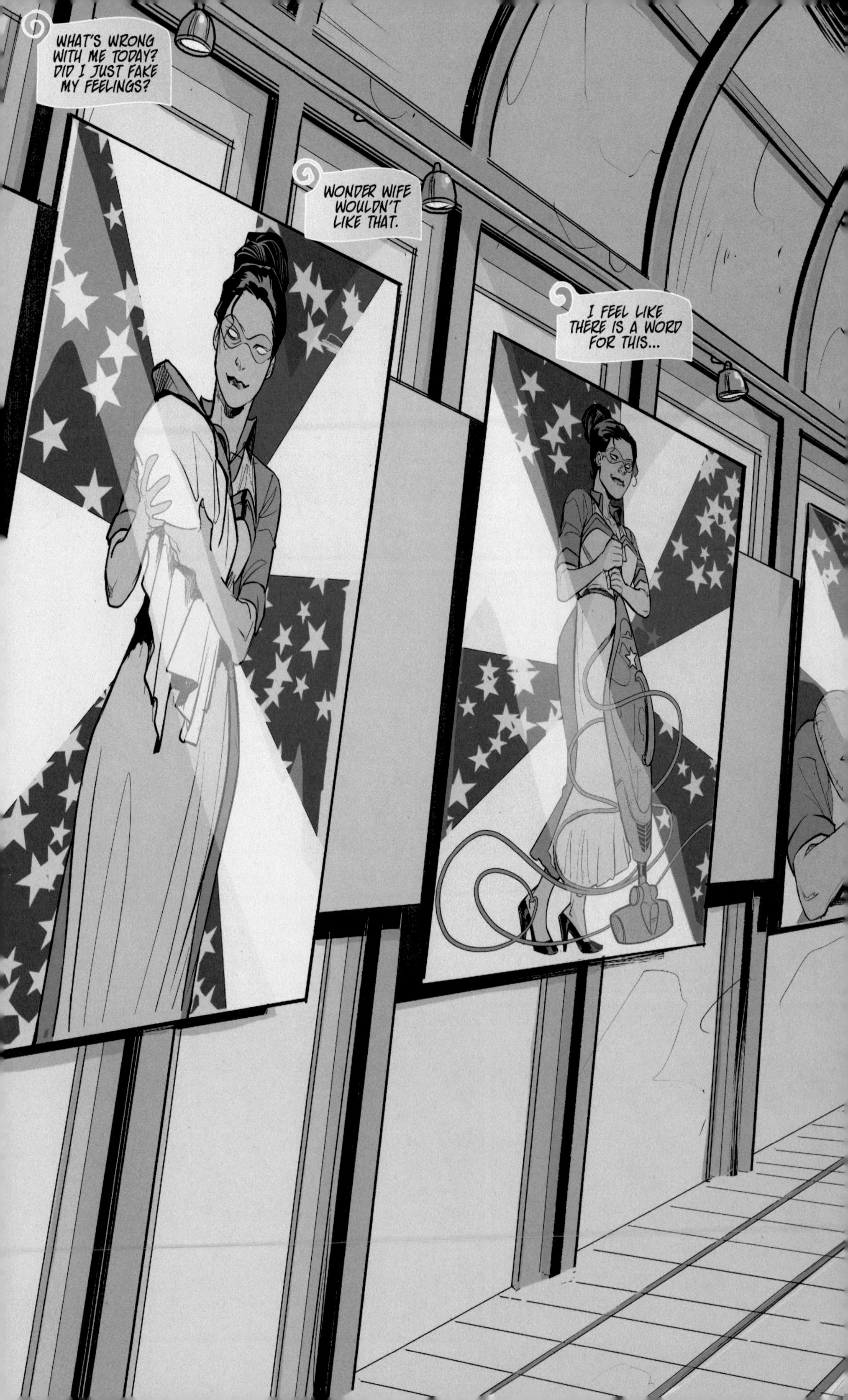
WHAT'S WRONG WITH ME TODAY? DID I JUST FAKE MY FEELINGS?
WONDER WIFE WOULDN'T LIKE THAT.
I FEEL LIKE THERE IS A WORD FOR THIS...

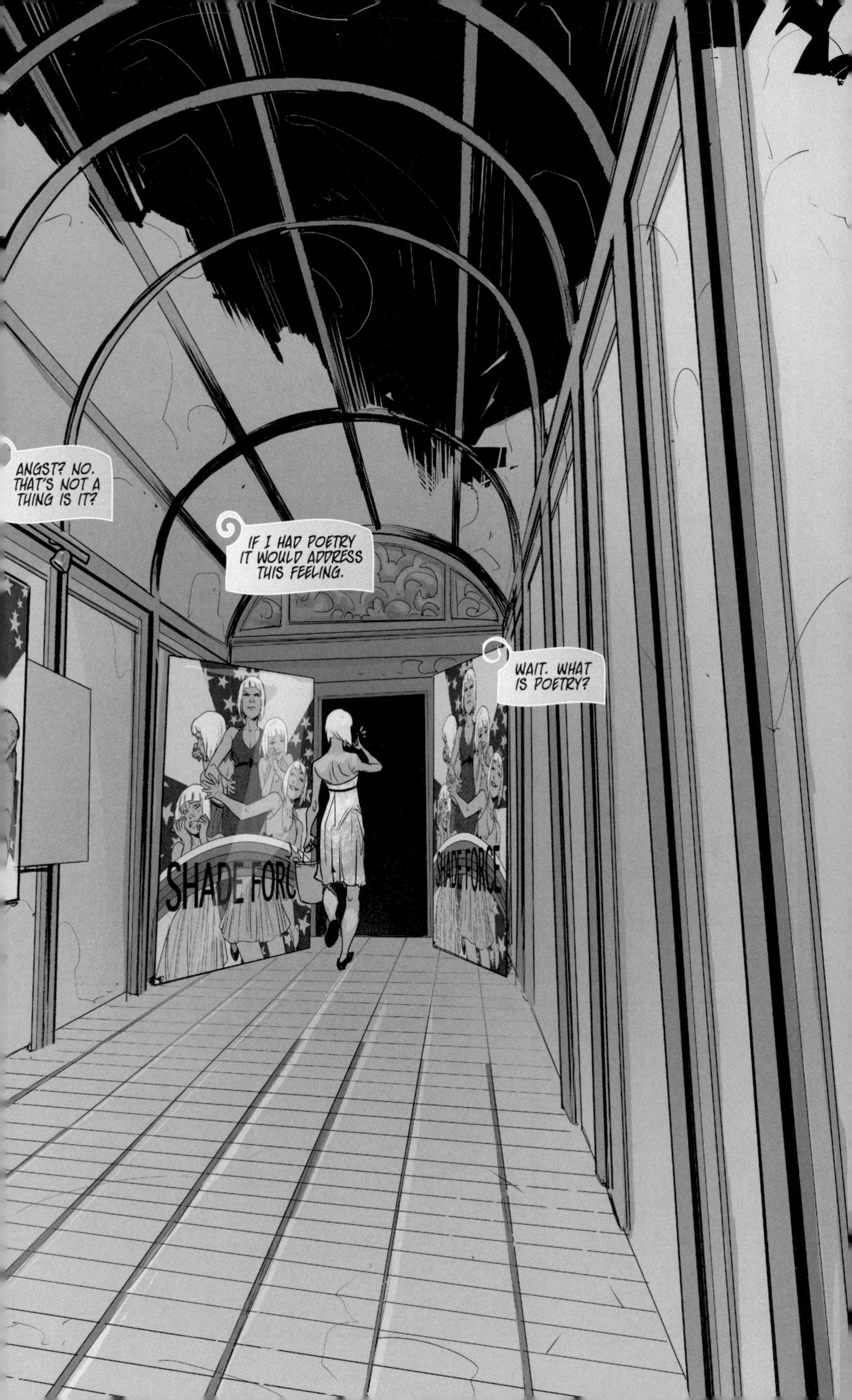
ANGST? NO. THAT'S NOT A THING IS IT?
IF I HAD POETRY IT WOULD ADDRESS THIS FEELING.
WAIT. WHAT IS POETRY?
SHADE FORC
SHADE FORCE

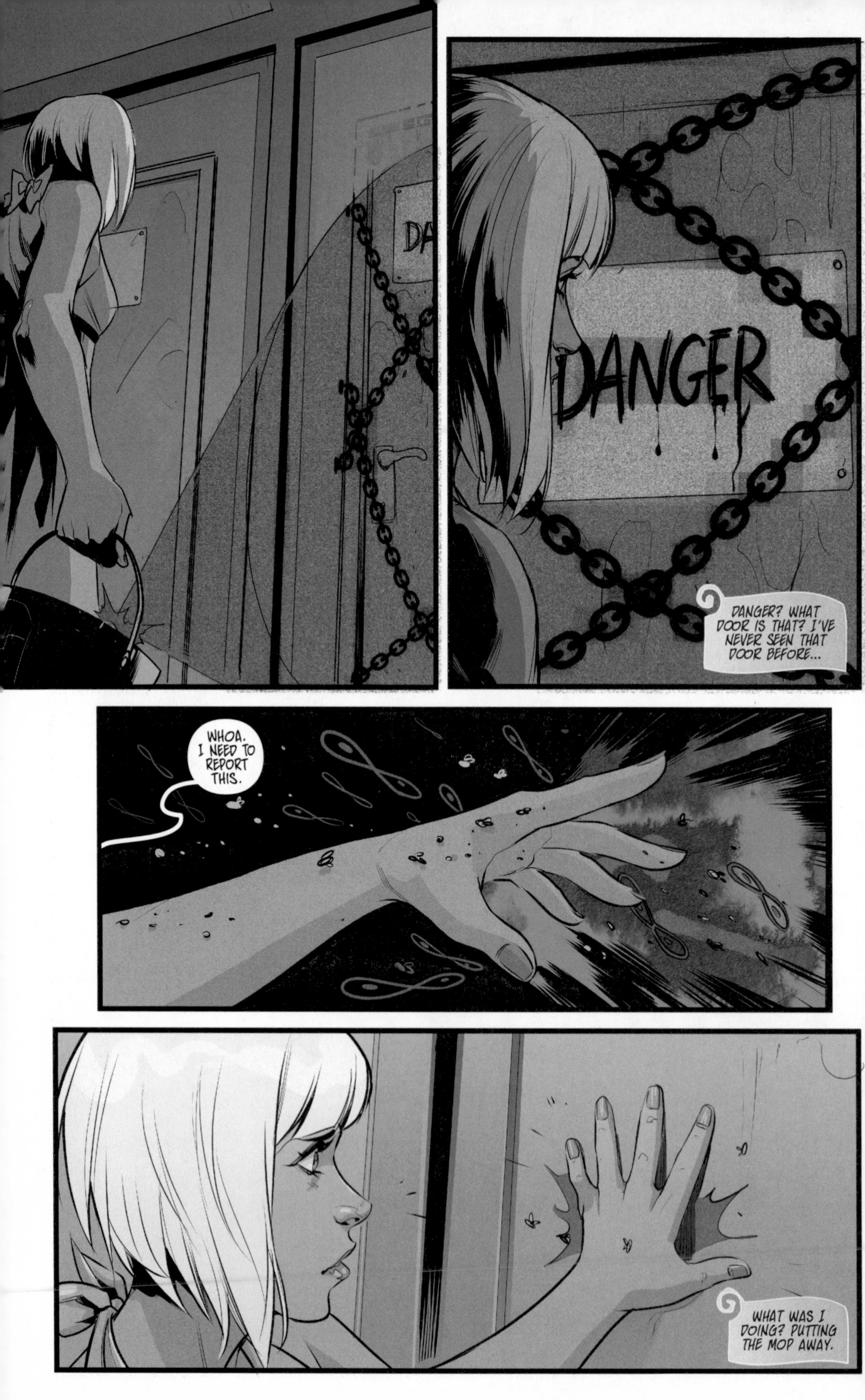
DANGER
DANGER? WHAT DOOR IS THAT? I'VE NEVER SEEN THAT DOOR BEFORE...
WHOA. I NEED TO REPORT THIS.
WHAT WAS I DOING? PUTTING THE MOP AWAY.

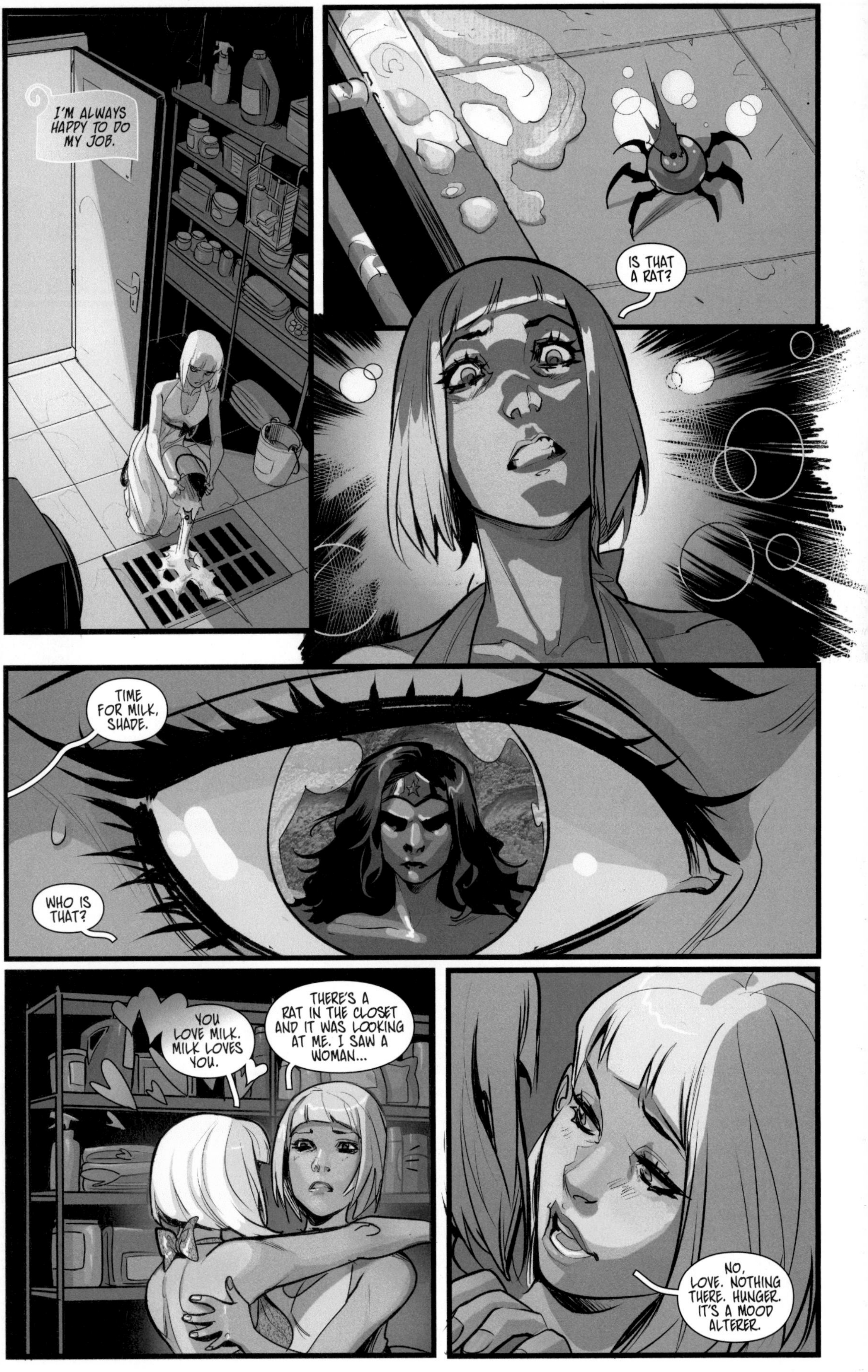
I'M ALWAYS HAPPY TO DO MY JOB.
IS THAT A RAT?
TIME FOR MILK, SHADE.
WHO IS THAT?
YOU LOVE MILK. MILK LOVES YOU.
THERE'S A RAT IN THE CLOSET AND IT WAS LOOKING AT ME. I SAW A WOMAN...
NO, LOVE. NOTHING THERE. HUNGER. IT'S A MOOD ALTERER.

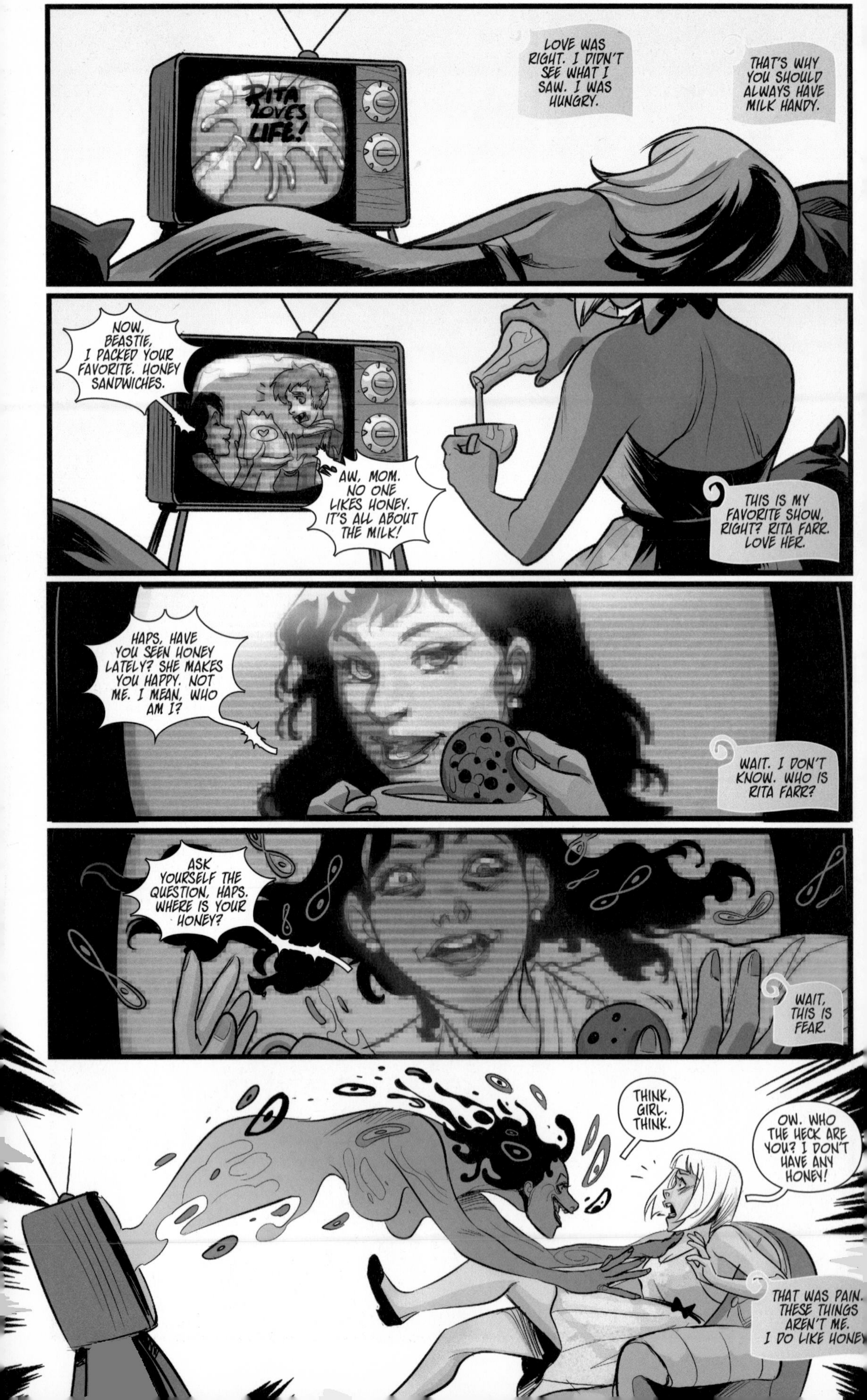

RITA LOVES LIFE!
LOVE WAS RIGHT. I DIDN'T SEE WHAT I SAW. I WAS HUNGRY.
THAT'S WHY YOU SHOULD ALWAYS HAVE MILK HANDY.
NOW, BEASTIE, I PACKED YOUR FAVORITE. HONEY SANDWICHES.
AW, MOM. NO ONE LIKES HONEY. IT'S ALL ABOUT THE MILK!
THIS IS MY FAVORITE SHOW, RIGHT? RITA FARR. LOVE HER.
HAPS, HAVE YOU SEEN HONEY LATELY? SHE MAKES YOU HAPPY. NOT ME. I MEAN, WHO AM I?
WAIT. I DON'T KNOW. WHO IS RITA FARR?
ASK YOURSELF THE QUESTION, HAPS. WHERE IS YOUR HONEY?
WAIT, THIS IS FEAR.
THINK, GIRL. THINK.
OW. WHO THE HECK ARE YOU? I DON'T HAVE ANY HONEY!
THAT WAS PAIN. THESE THINGS AREN'T ME. I DO LIKE HONEY

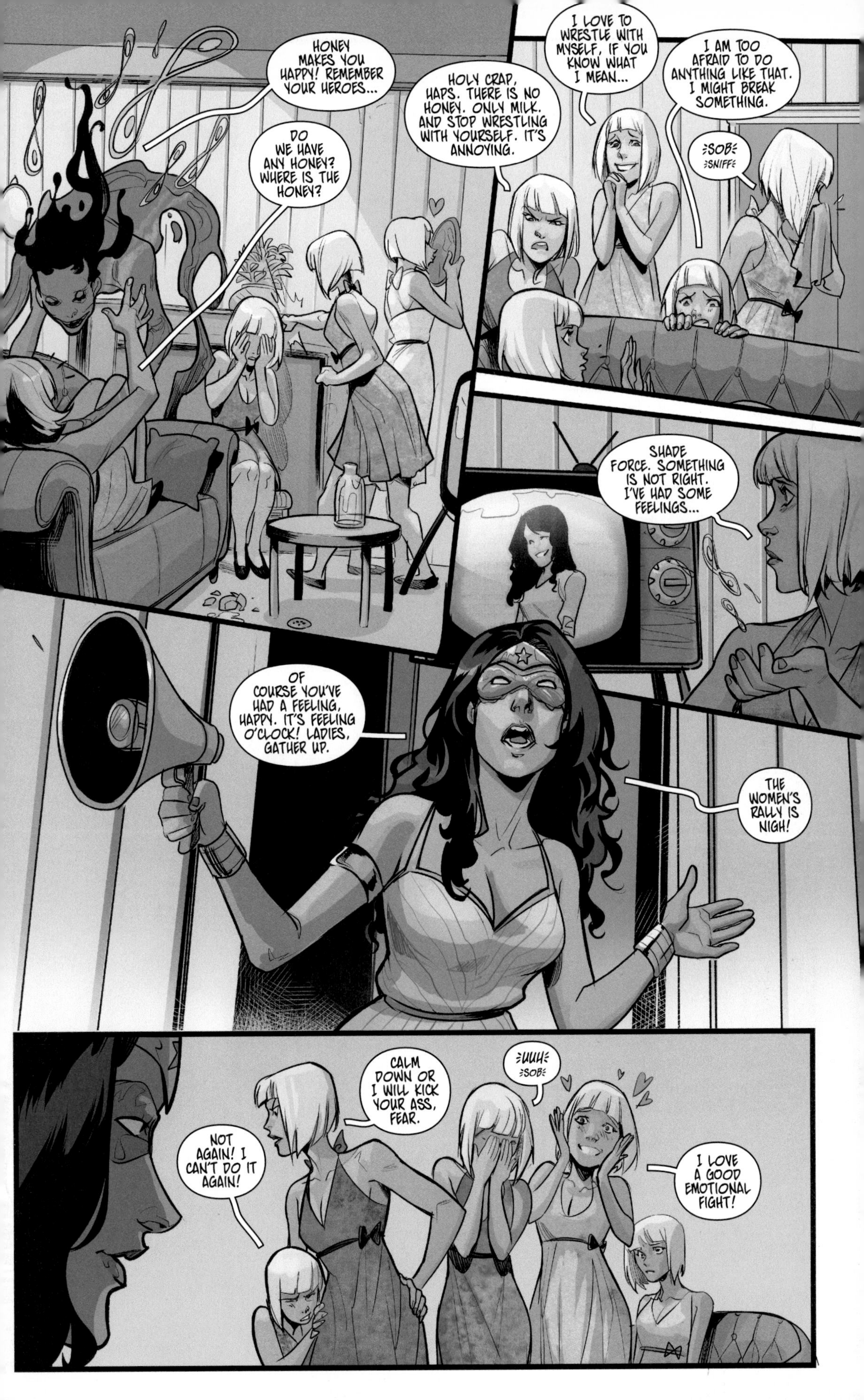
HONEY MAKES YOU HAPPY! REMEMBER YOUR HEROES...
DO WE HAVE ANY HONEY? WHERE IS THE HONEY?
HOLY CRAP, HAPS. THERE IS NO HONEY. ONLY MILK. AND STOP WRESTLING WITH YOURSELF. IT'S ANNOYING.
I LOVE TO WRESTLE WITH MYSELF, IF YOU KNOW WHAT I MEAN...
I AM TOO AFRAID TO DO ANYTHING LIKE THAT. I MIGHT BREAK SOMETHING.
SOB
SNIFF
SHADE FORCE. SOMETHING IS NOT RIGHT. I'VE HAD SOME FEELINGS...
OF COURSE YOU'VE HAD A FEELING, HAPPY. IT'S FEELING O'CLOCK! LADIES, GATHER UP.
THE WOMEN'S RALLY IS NIGH!
NOT AGAIN! I CAN'T DO IT AGAIN!
CALM DOWN OR I WILL KICK YOUR ASS, FEAR.
UUH
SOB
I LOVE A GOOD EMOTIONAL FIGHT!

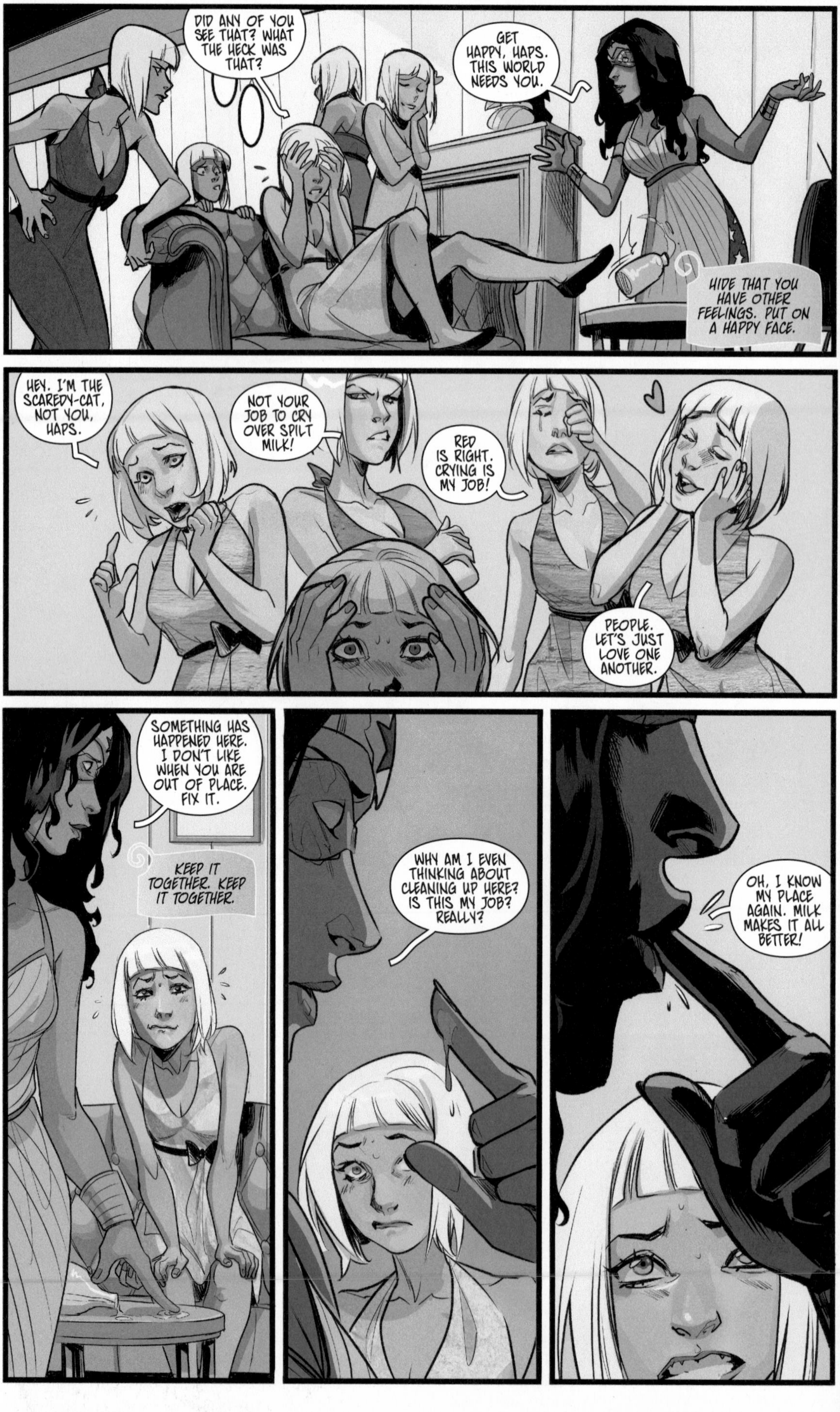
DID ANY OF YOU SEE THAT? WHAT THE HECK WAS THAT?
GET HAPPY, HAPS. THIS WORLD NEEDS YOU.
HIDE THAT YOU HAVE OTHER FEELINGS. PUT ON A HAPPY FACE.
HEY. I'M THE SCAREDY-CAT, NOT YOU, HAPS.
NOT YOUR JOB TO CRY OVER SPILT MILK!
RED IS RIGHT. CRYING IS MY JOB!
PEOPLE. LET'S JUST LOVE ONE ANOTHER.
SOMETHING HAS HAPPENED HERE. I DON'T LIKE WHEN YOU ARE OUT OF PLACE. FIX IT.
KEEP IT TOGETHER. KEEP IT TOGETHER.
WHY AM I EVEN THINKING ABOUT CLEANING UP HERE? IS THIS MY JOB? REALLY?
OH, I KNOW MY PLACE AGAIN. MILK MAKES IT ALL BETTER!

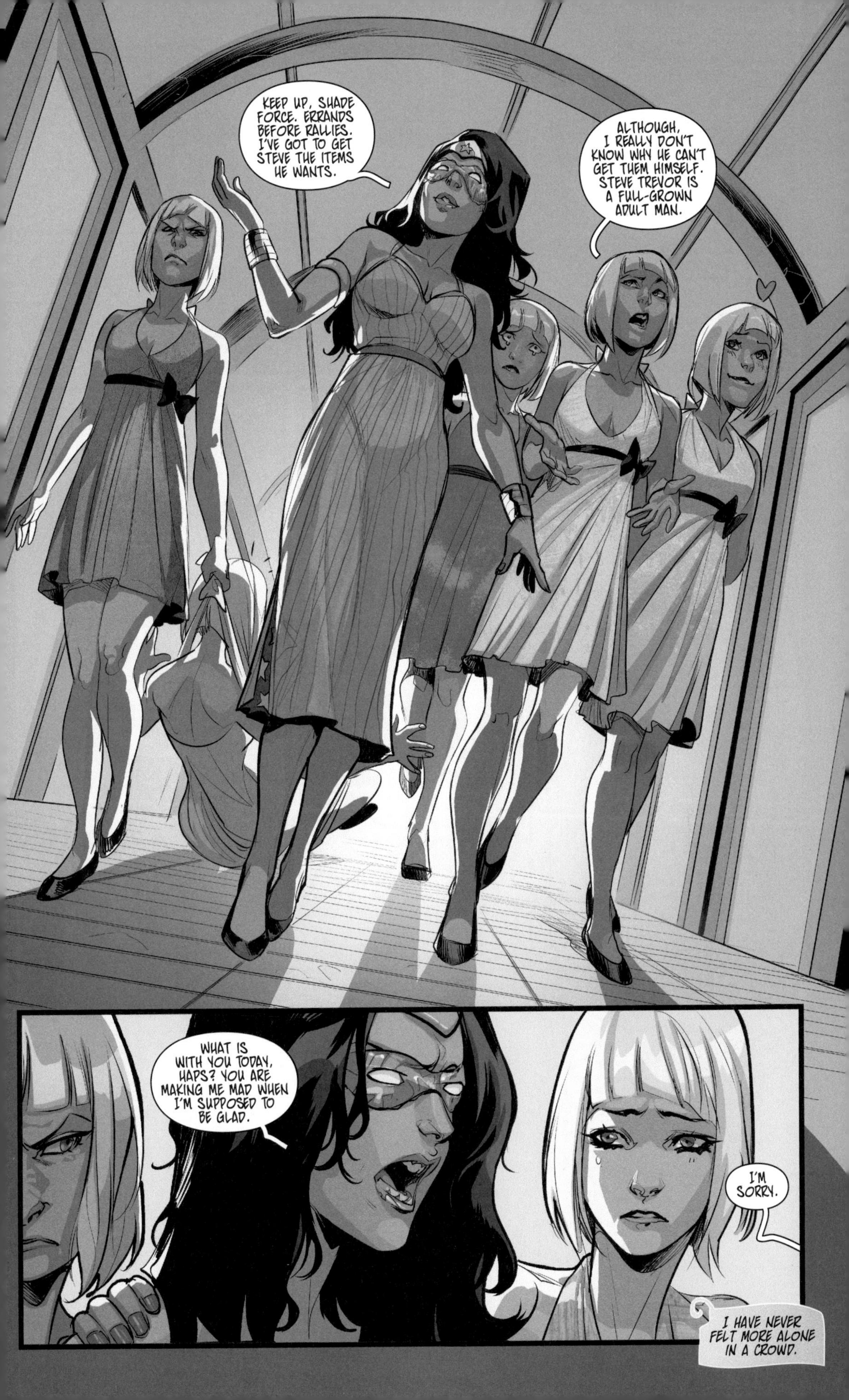
KEEP UP, SHADE FORCE. ERRANDS BEFORE RALLIES. I'VE GOT TO GET STEVE THE ITEMS HE WANTS.
ALTHOUGH, I REALLY DON'T KNOW WHY HE CAN'T GET THEM HIMSELF. STEVE TREVOR IS A FULL-GROWN ADULT MAN.
WHAT IS WITH YOU TODAY, HAPS? YOU ARE MAKING ME MAD WHEN I'M SUPPOSED TO BE GLAD.
I'M SORRY.
I HAVE NEVER FELT MORE ALONE IN A CROWD.

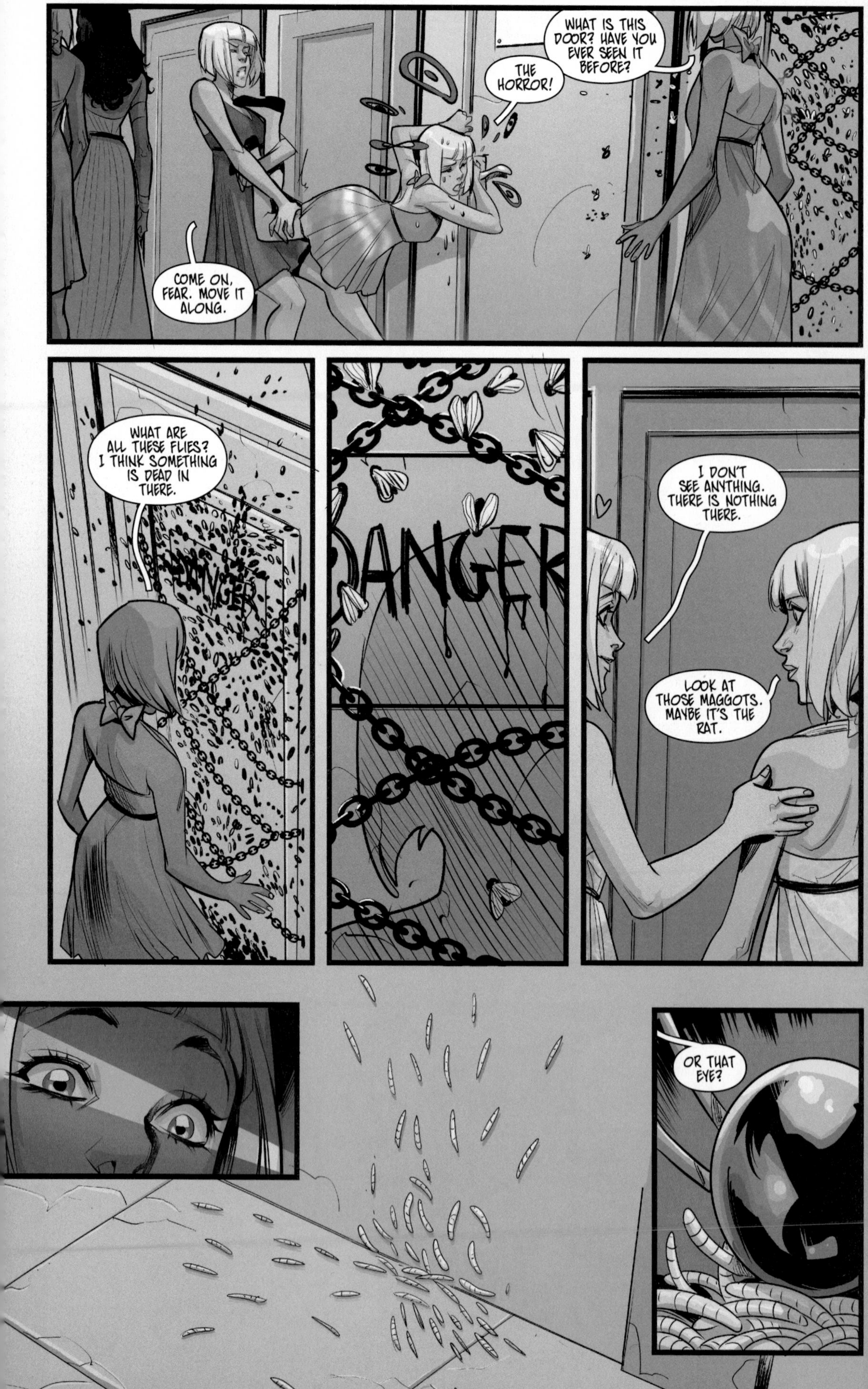
COME ON, FEAR. MOVE IT ALONG.
THE HORROR!
WHAT IS THIS DOOR? HAVE YOU EVER SEEN IT BEFORE?
WHAT ARE ALL THESE FLIES? I THINK SOMETHING IS DEAD IN THERE.
DANGER
I DON'T SEE ANYTHING. THERE IS NOTHING THERE.
LOOK AT THOSE MAGGOTS. MAYBE IT'S THE RAT.
OR THAT EYE?

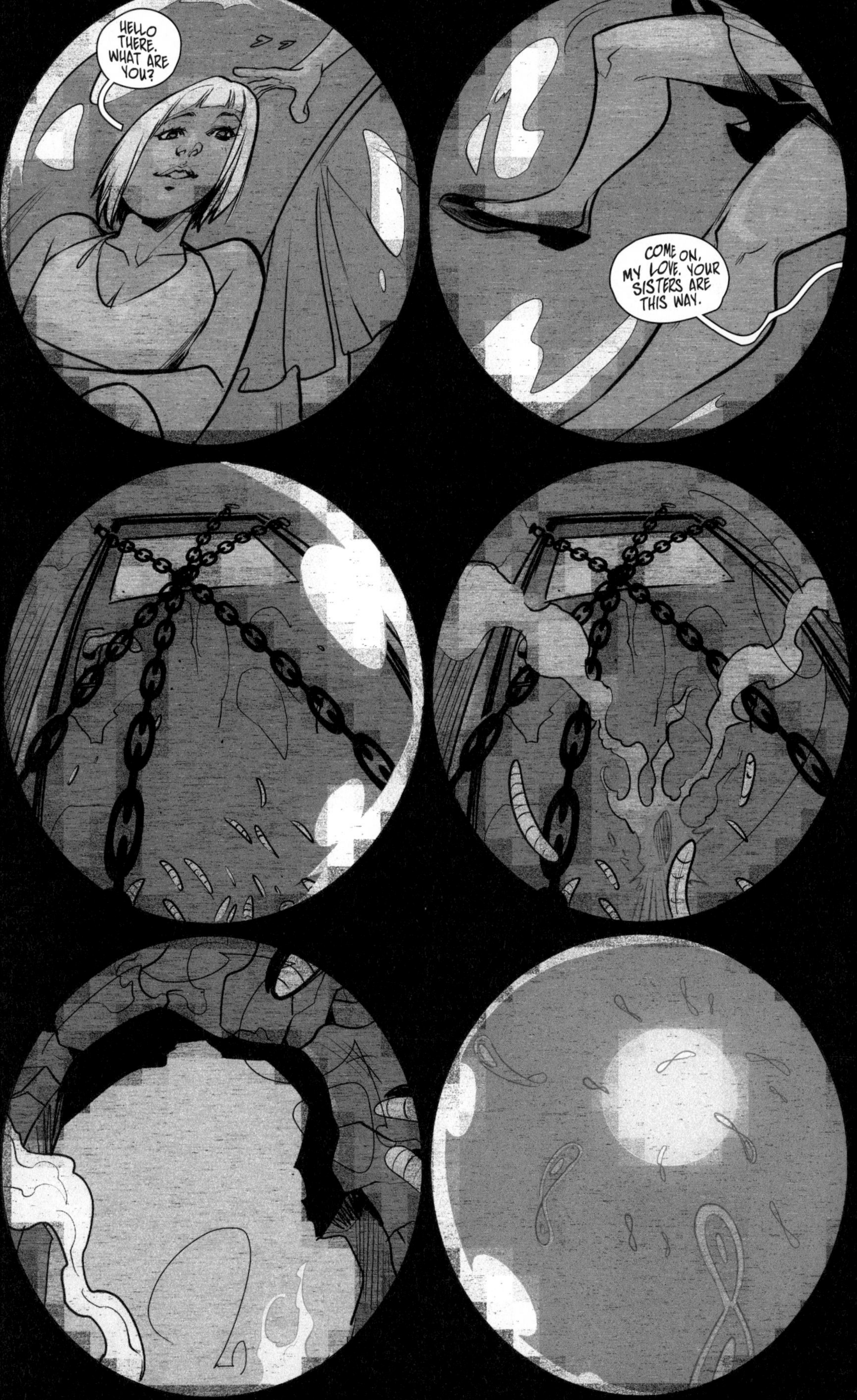
HELLO THERE. WHAT ARE YOU?
COME ON, MY LOVE. YOUR SISTERS ARE THIS WAY.

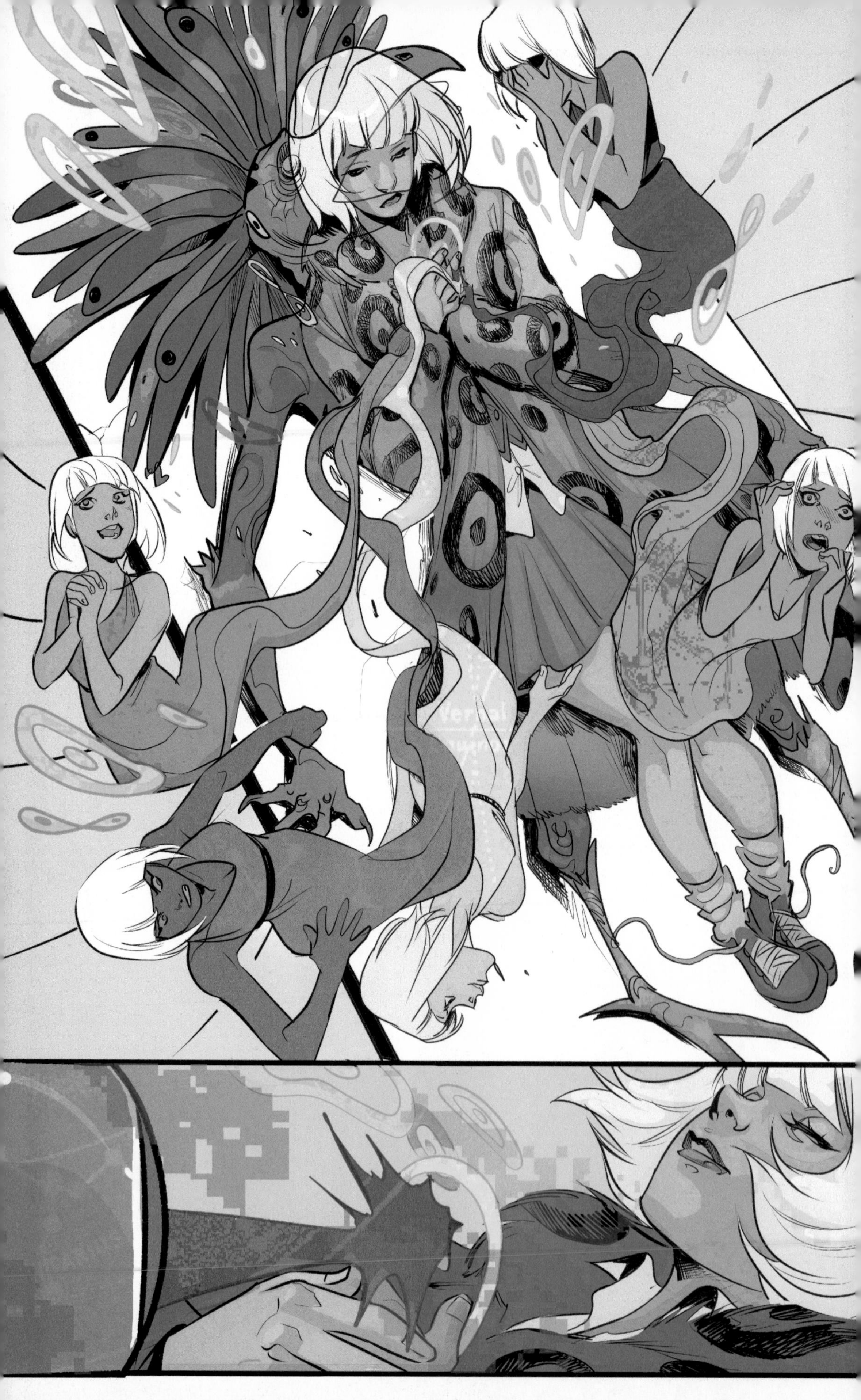

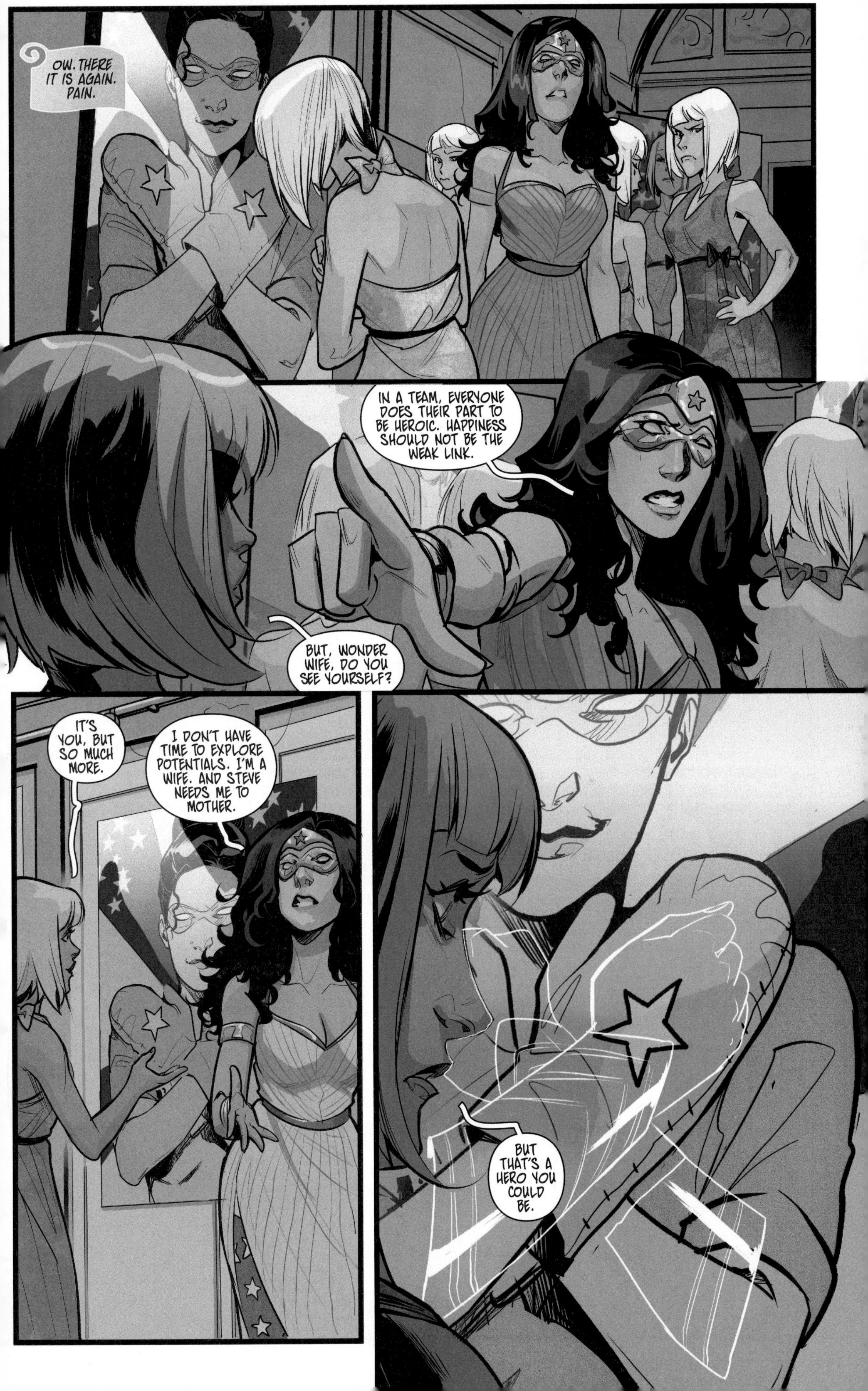
OW. THERE IT IS AGAIN. PAIN.
IN A TEAM, EVERYONE DOES THEIR PART TO BE HEROIC. HAPPINESS SHOULD NOT BE THE WEAK LINK.
BUT, WONDER WIFE, DO YOU SEE YOURSELF?
IT'S YOU, BUT SO MUCH MORE.
I DON'T HAVE TIME TO EXPLORE POTENTIALS. I'M A WIFE. AND STEVE NEEDS ME TO MOTHER.
BUT THAT'S A HERO YOU COULD BE.

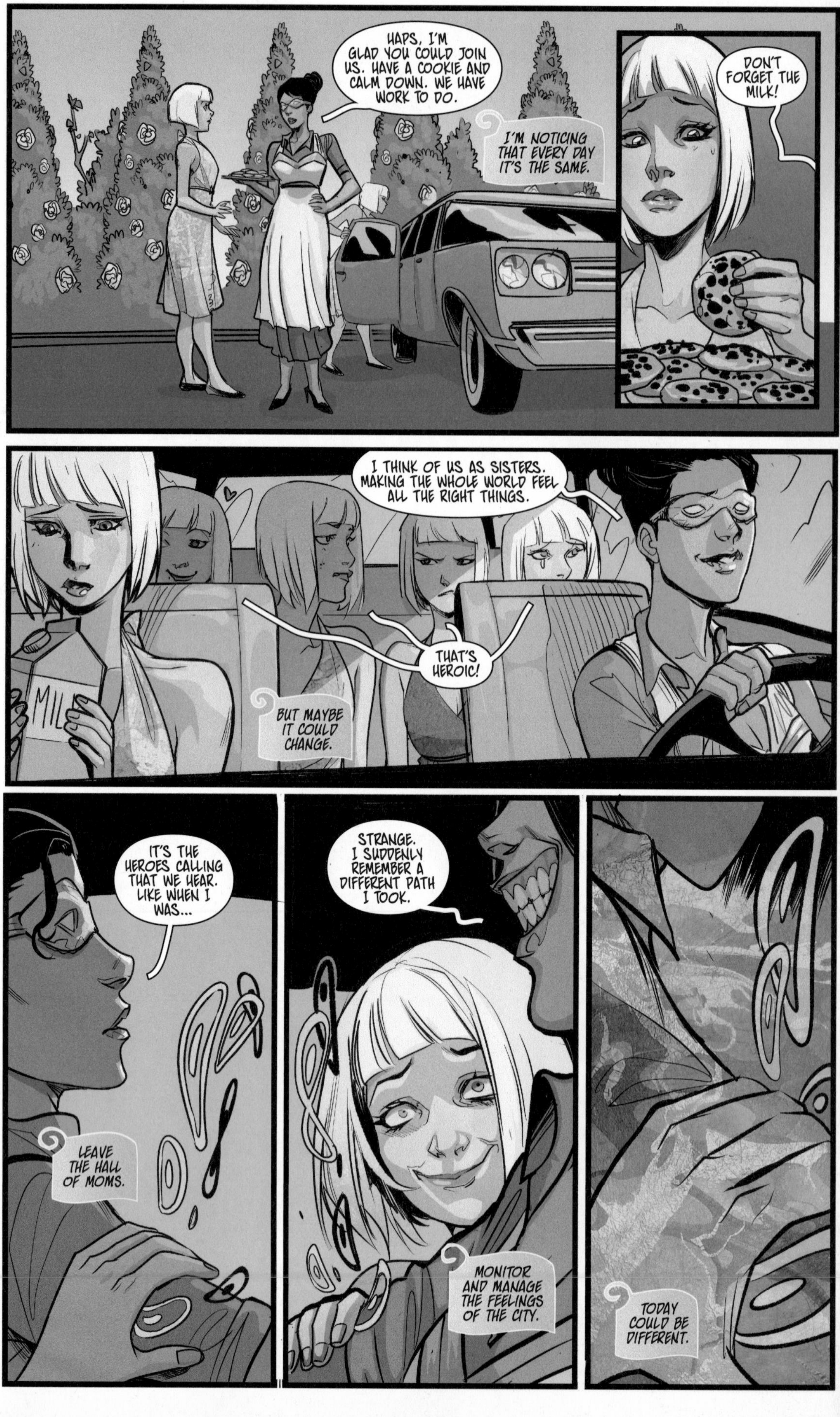
HAPS, I'M GLAD YOU COULD JOIN US. HAVE A COOKIE AND CALM DOWN. WE HAVE WORK TO DO.
I'M NOTICING THAT EVERY DAY IT'S THE SAME.
DON'T FORGET THE MILK!
I THINK OF US AS SISTERS. MAKING THE WHOLE WORLD FEEL ALL THE RIGHT THINGS.
THAT'S HEROIC!
BUT MAYBE IT COULD CHANGE.
MILK
IT'S THE HEROES CALLING THAT WE HEAR. LIKE WHEN I WAS...
LEAVE THE HALL OF MOMS.
STRANGE. I SUDDENLY REMEMBER A DIFFERENT PATH I TOOK.
MONITOR AND MANAGE THE FEELINGS OF THE CITY.
TODAY COULD BE DIFFERENT.

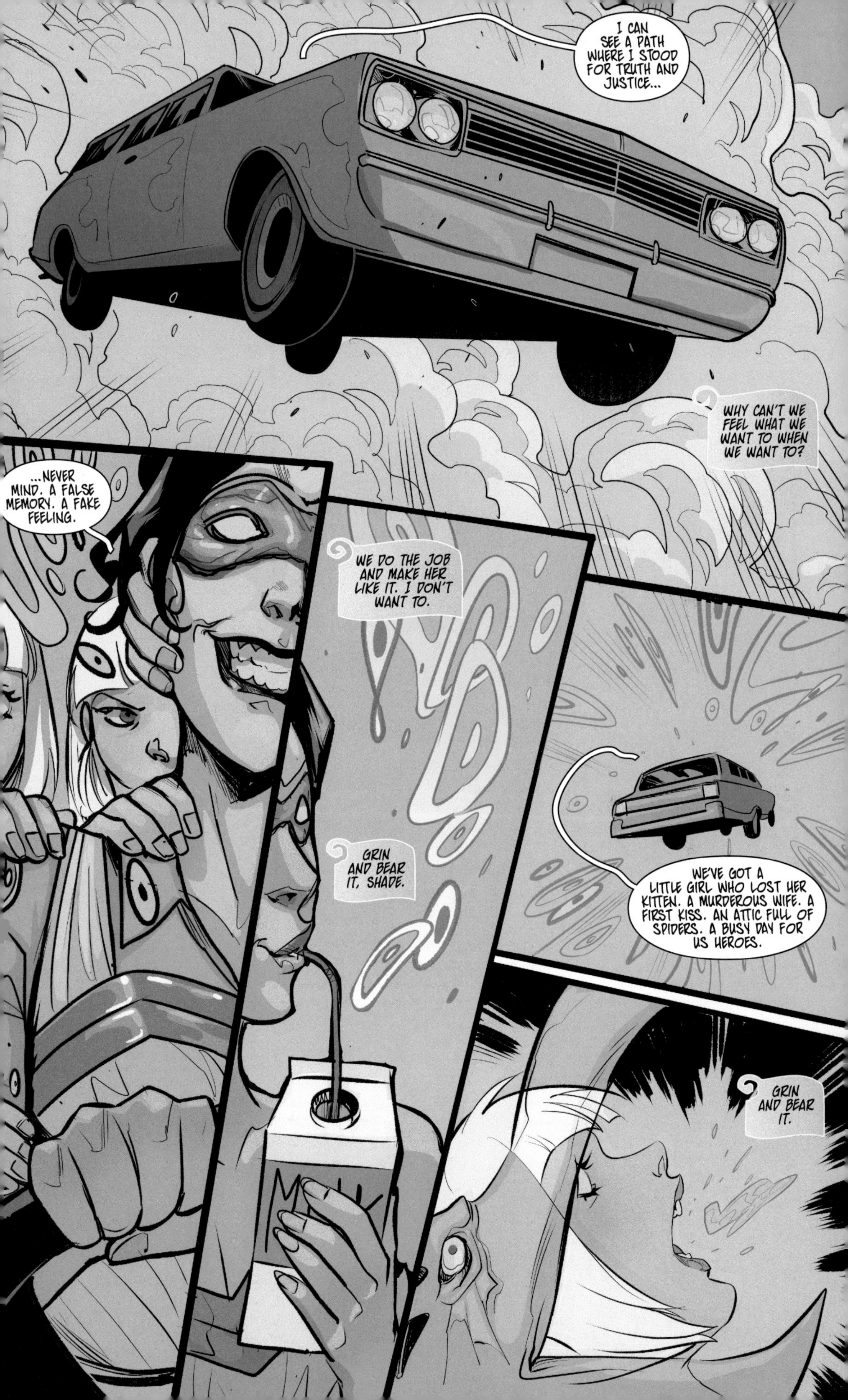
I CAN SEE A PATH WHERE I STOOD FOR TRUTH AND JUSTICE...
WHY CAN'T WE FEEL WHAT WE WANT TO WHEN WE WANT TO?
...NEVER MIND. A FALSE MEMORY. A FAKE FEELING.
WE DO THE JOB AND MAKE HER LIKE IT. I DON'T WANT TO.
GRIN AND BEAR IT, SHADE.
WE'VE GOT A LITTLE GIRL WHO LOST HER KITTEN. A MURDEROUS WIFE. A FIRST KISS. AN ATTIC FULL OF SPIDERS. A BUSY DAY FOR US HEROES.
GRIN AND BEAR IT.

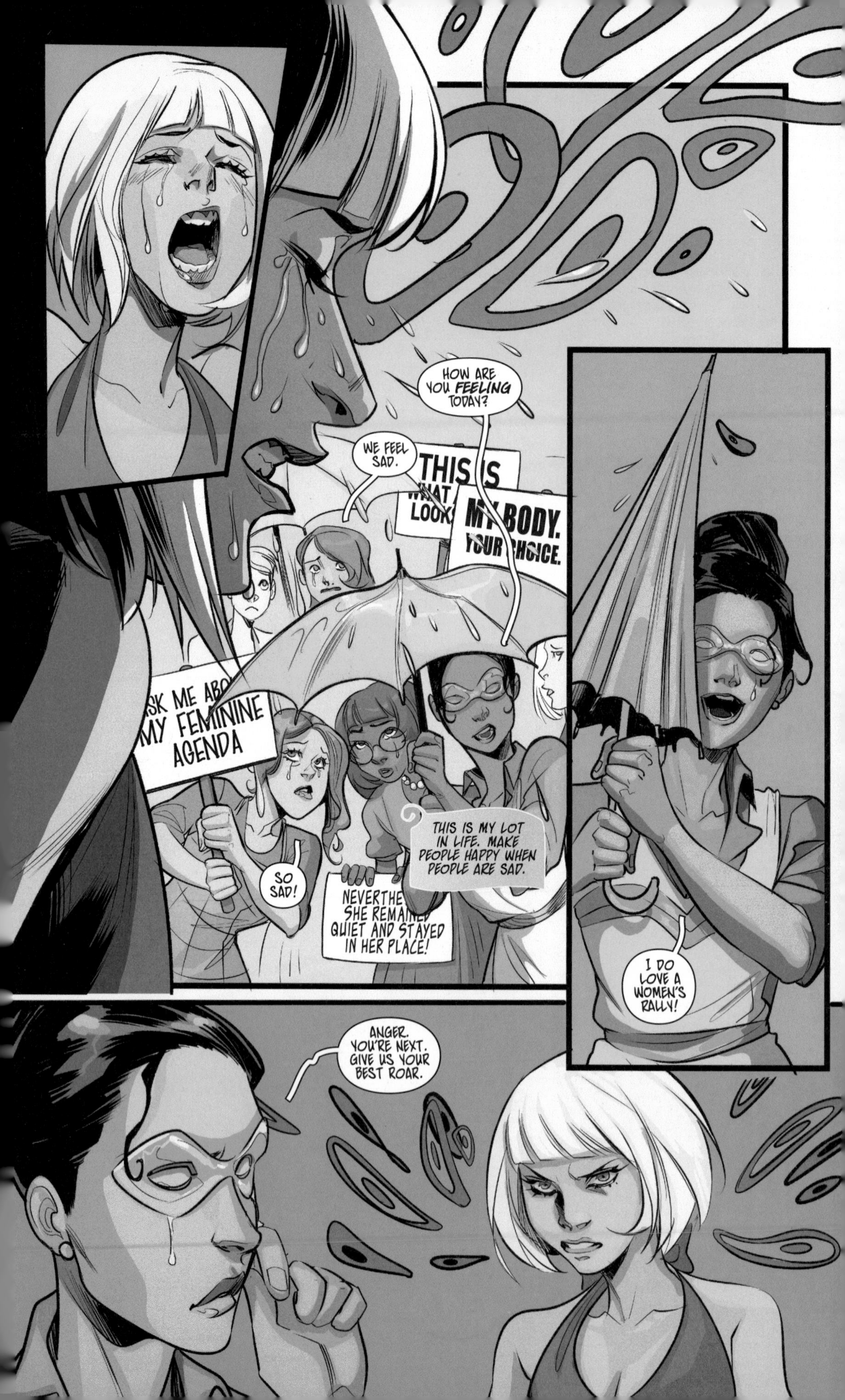
HOW ARE YOU FEELING TODAY?
WE FEEL SAD.
THIS IS
MY BODY. YOUR CHOICE.
MY FEMININE AGENDA
SO SAD!
THIS IS MY LOT IN LIFE. MAKE PEOPLE HAPPY WHEN PEOPLE ARE SAD.
SHE REMAINED QUIET AND STAYED IN HER PLACE!
I DO LOVE A WOMEN'S RALLY!
ANGER. YOU'RE NEXT. GIVE US YOUR BEST ROAR.

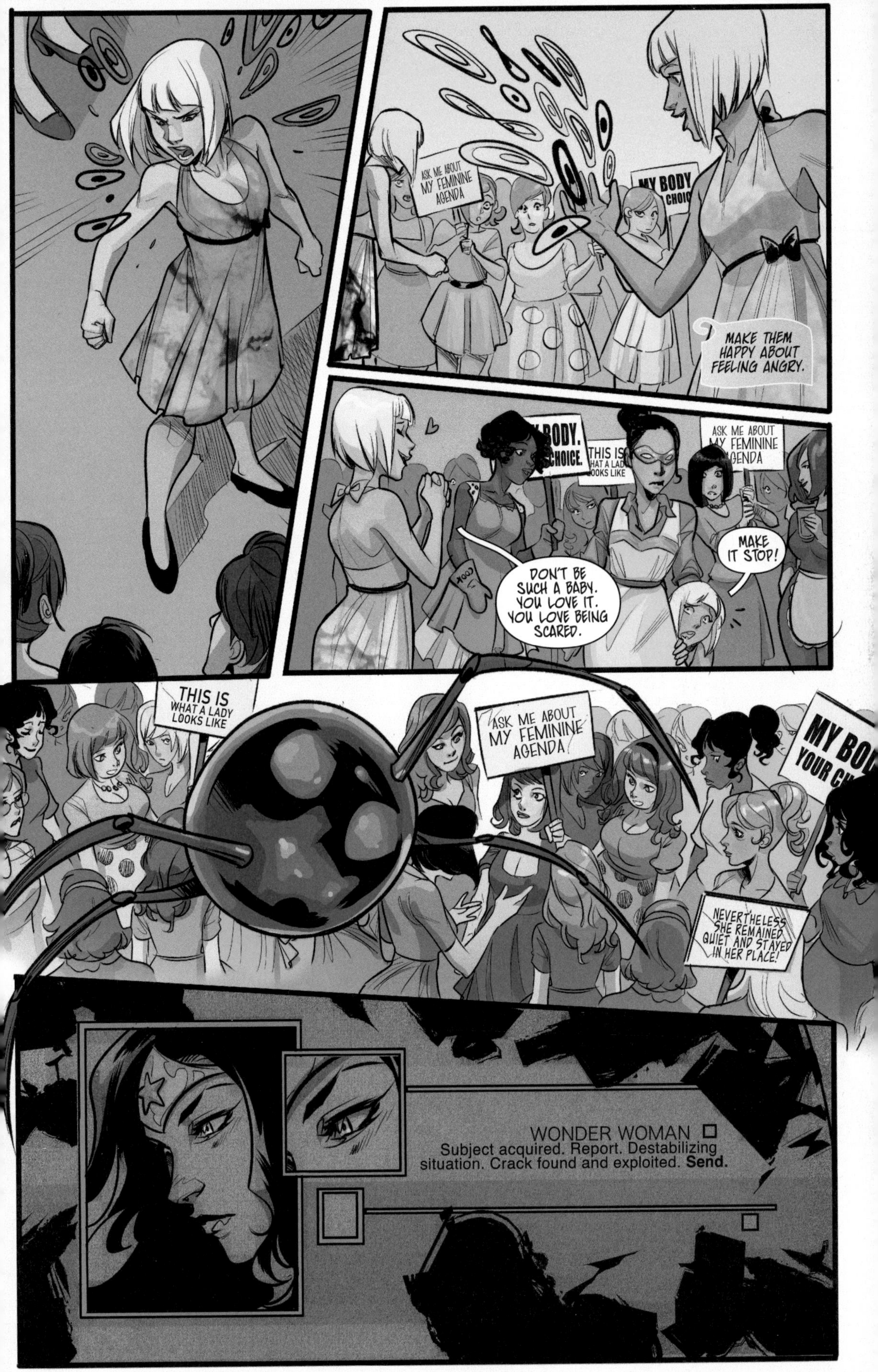
ASK ME ABOUT MY FEMININE AGENDA
MY BODY CHOIC
MAKE THEM HAPPY ABOUT FEELING ANGRY.
BODY. CHOICE.
THIS IS WHAT A LADY LOOKS LIKE
ASK ME ABOUT MY FEMININE AGENDA
DON'T BE SUCH A BABY. YOU LOVE IT. YOU LOVE BEING SCARED.
MAKE IT STOP!
THIS IS WHAT A LADY LOOKS LIKE
ASK ME ABOUT MY FEMININE AGENDA
MY BOD YOUR CH
NEVERTHELESS SHE REMAINED QUIET AND STAYED IN HER PLACE!
WONDER WOMAN
Subject acquired. Report. Destabilizing situation. Crack found and exploited. Send.

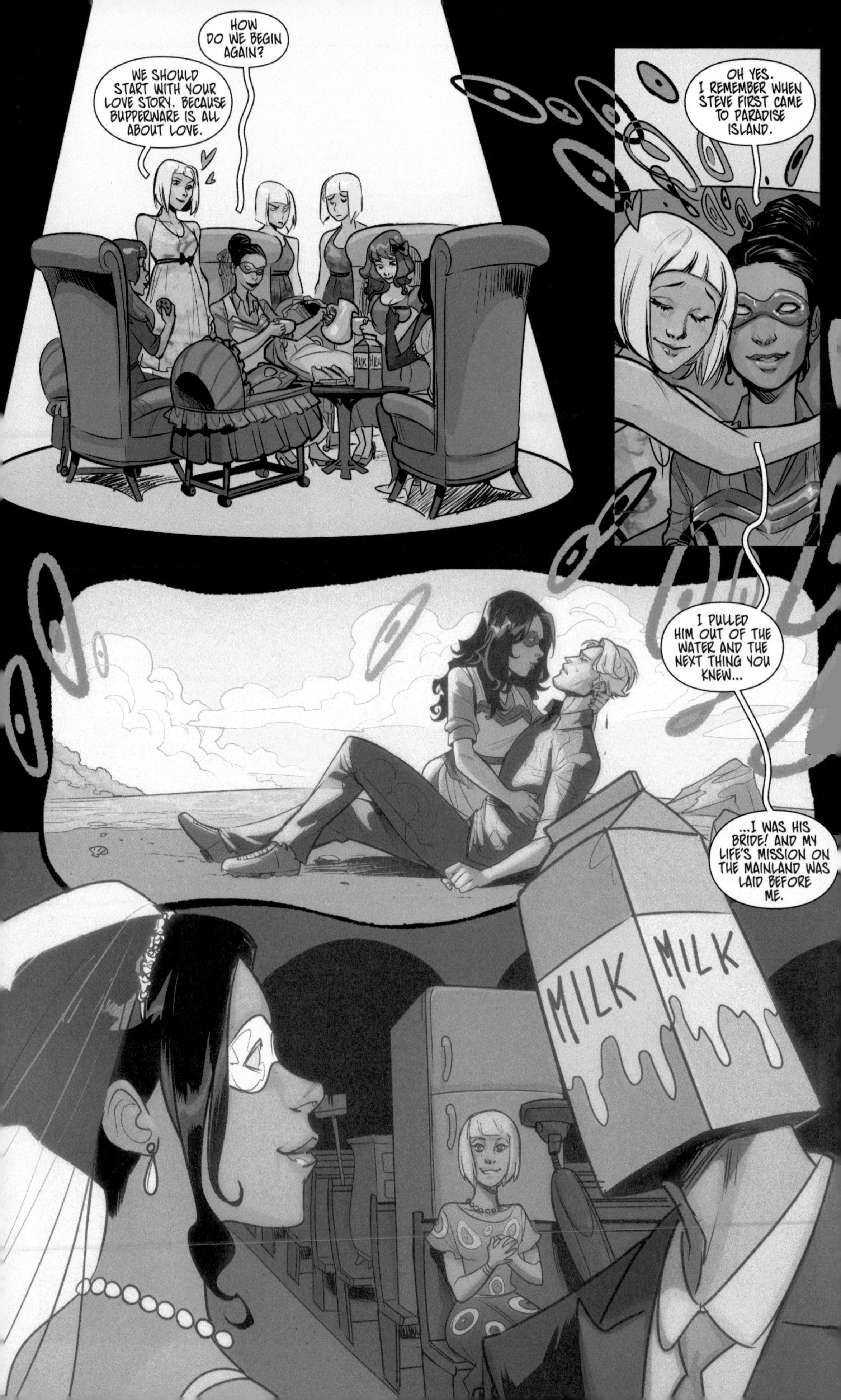
WE SHOULD START WITH YOUR LOVE STORY. BECAUSE BUPPERWARE IS ALL ABOUT LOVE.
HOW DO WE BEGIN AGAIN?
MILK
MILK
OH YES. I REMEMBER WHEN STEVE FIRST CAME TO PARADISE ISLAND.
I PULLED HIM OUT OF THE WATER AND THE NEXT THING YOU KNEW...
...I WAS HIS BRIDE! AND MY LIFE'S MISSION ON THE MAINLAND WAS LAID BEFORE ME.
MILK
MILK

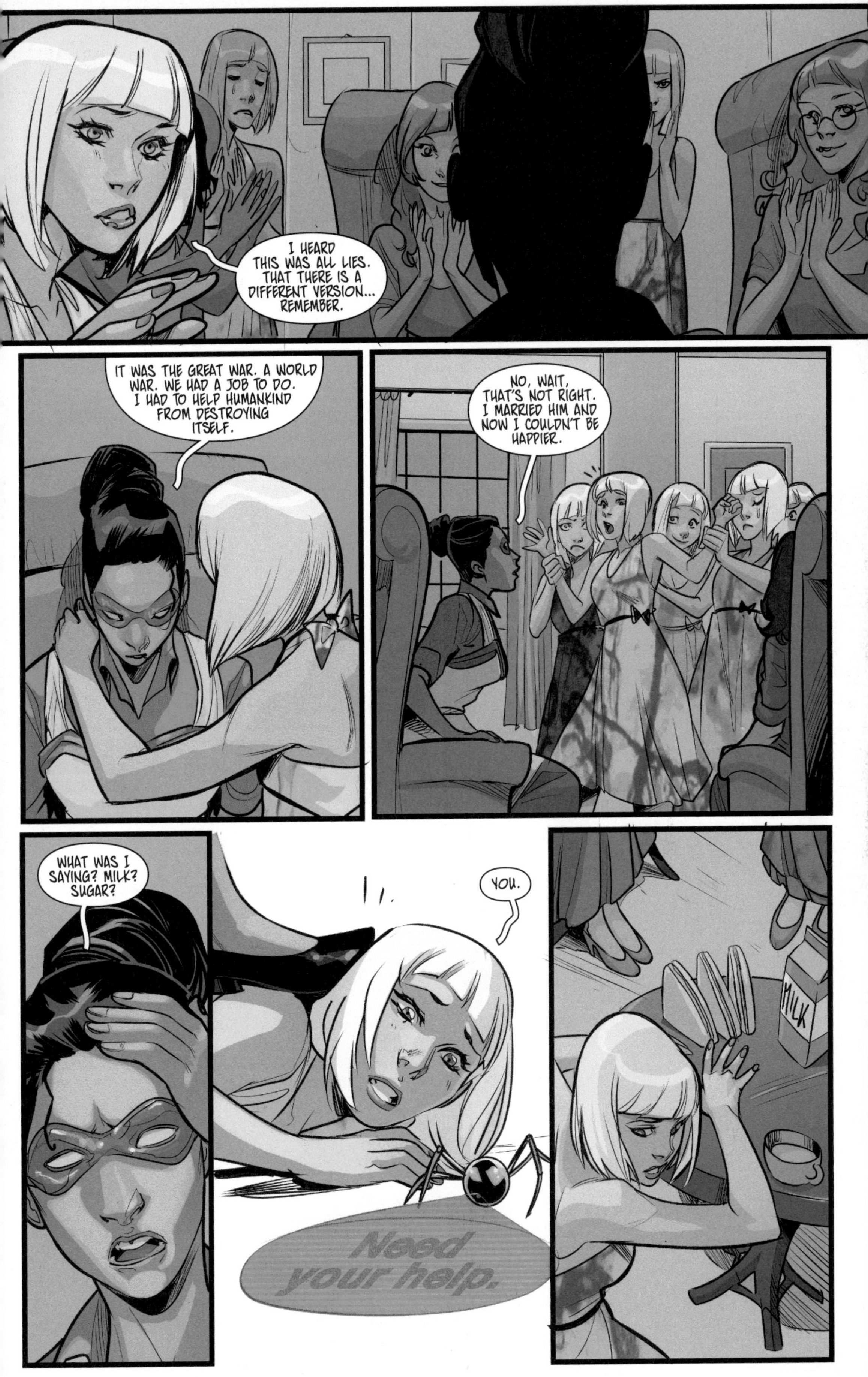

I HEARD THIS WAS ALL LIES. THAT THERE IS A DIFFERENT VERSION... REMEMBER.
IT WAS THE GREAT WAR. A WORLD WAR. WE HAD A JOB TO DO. I HAD TO HELP HUMANKIND FROM DESTROYING ITSELF.
NO, WAIT, THAT'S NOT RIGHT. I MARRIED HIM AND NOW I COULDN'T BE HAPPIER.
WHAT WAS I SAYING? MILK? SUGAR?
YOU.
Need your help.
MILK

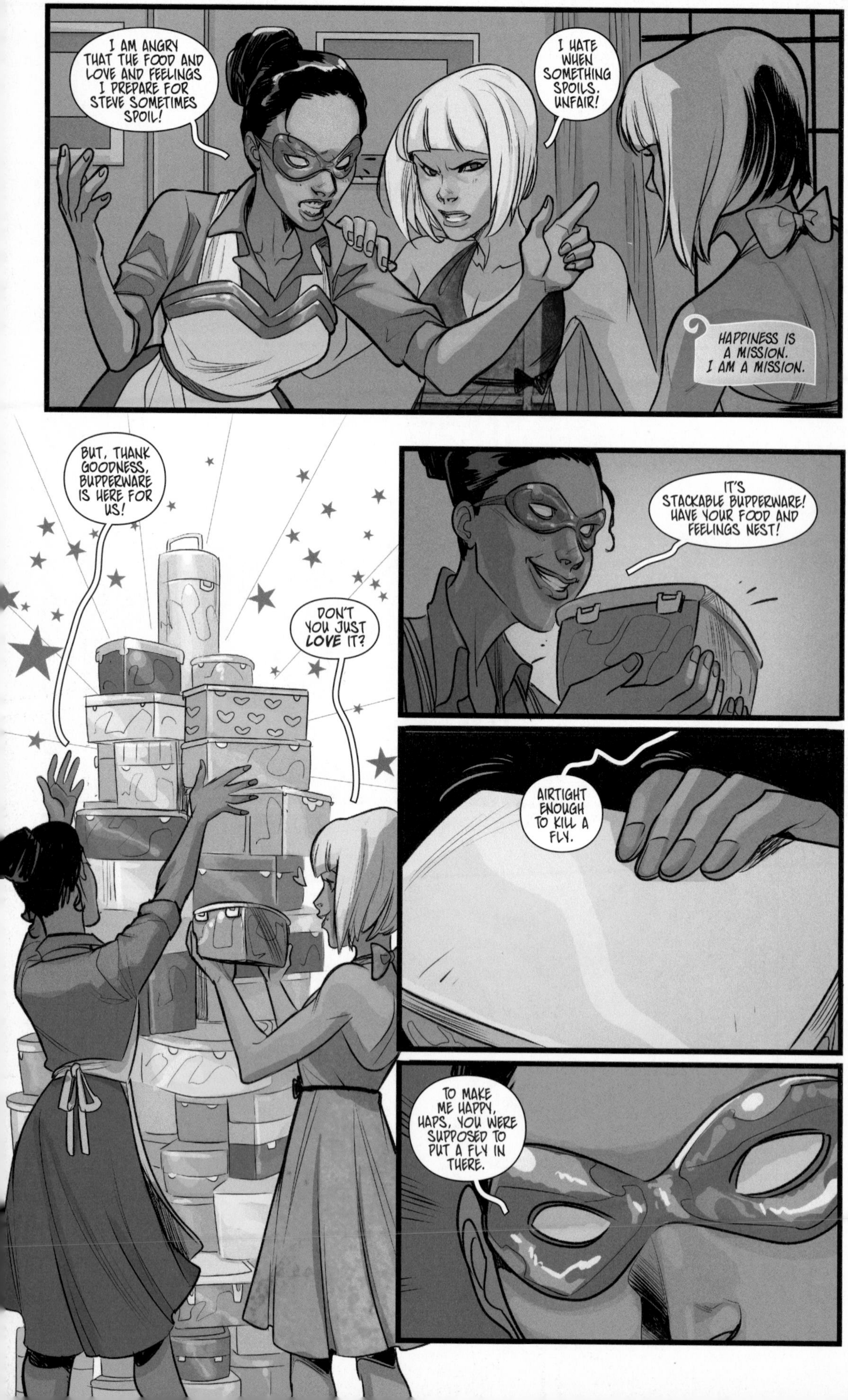
I AM ANGRY THAT THE FOOD AND LOVE AND FEELINGS I PREPARE FOR STEVE SOMETIMES SPOIL!
I HATE WHEN SOMETHING SPOILS. UNFAIR!
HAPPINESS IS A MISSION. I AM A MISSION.
BUT, THANK GOODNESS, BUPPERWARE IS HERE FOR US!
DON'T YOU JUST LOVE IT?
IT'S STACKABLE BUPPERWARE! HAVE YOUR FOOD AND FEELINGS NEST!
AIRTIGHT ENOUGH TO KILL A FLY.
TO MAKE ME HAPPY, HAPS, YOU WERE SUPPOSED TO PUT A FLY IN THERE.

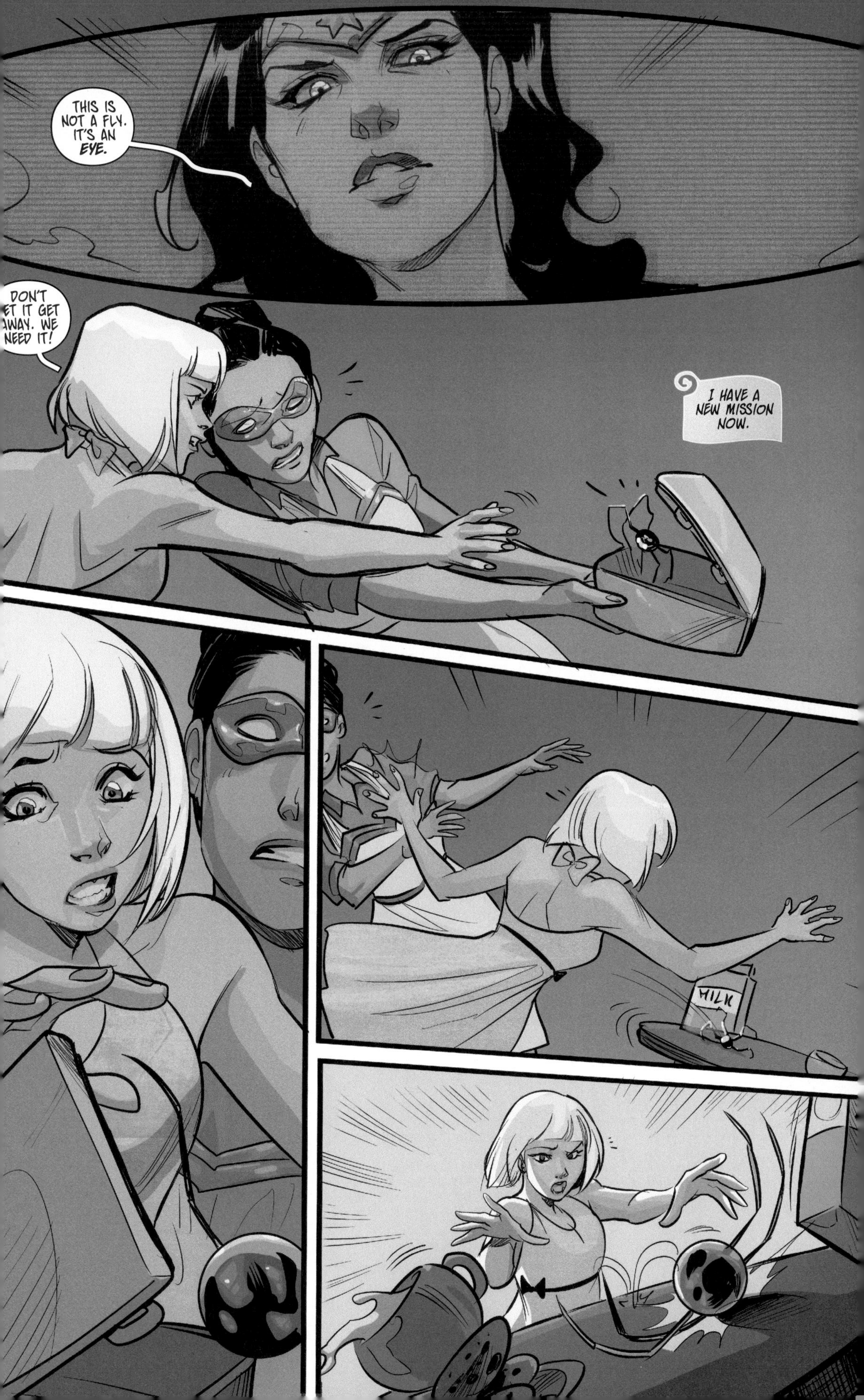
THIS IS NOT A FLY. IT'S AN EYE.
DON'T LET IT GET AWAY. WE NEED IT!
I HAVE A NEW MISSION NOW.
MILK

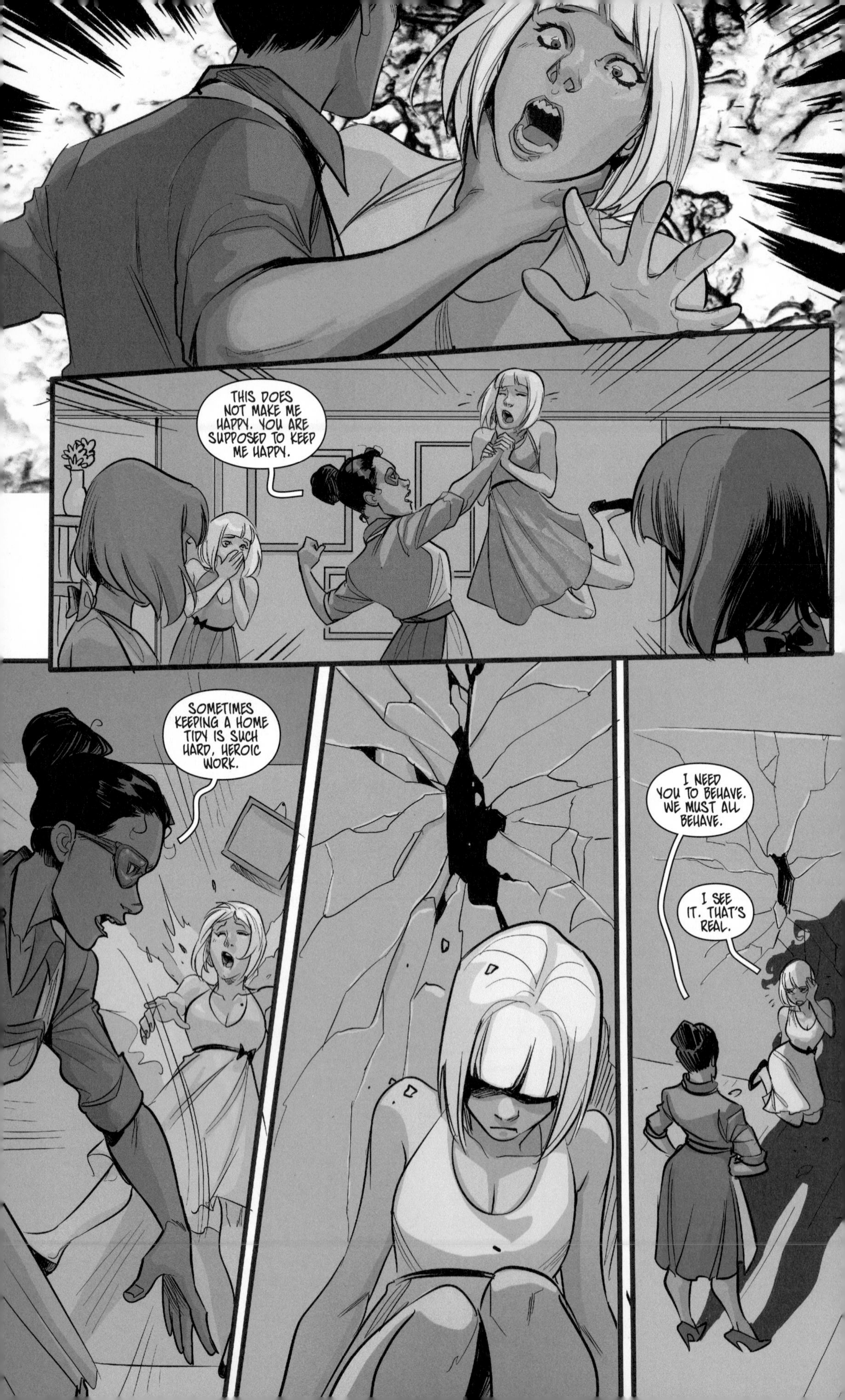
THIS DOES NOT MAKE ME HAPPY. YOU ARE SUPPOSED TO KEEP ME HAPPY.
SOMETIMES KEEPING A HOME TIDY IS SUCH HARD, HEROIC WORK.
I NEED YOU TO BEHAVE. WE MUST ALL BEHAVE.
I SEE IT. THAT'S REAL.

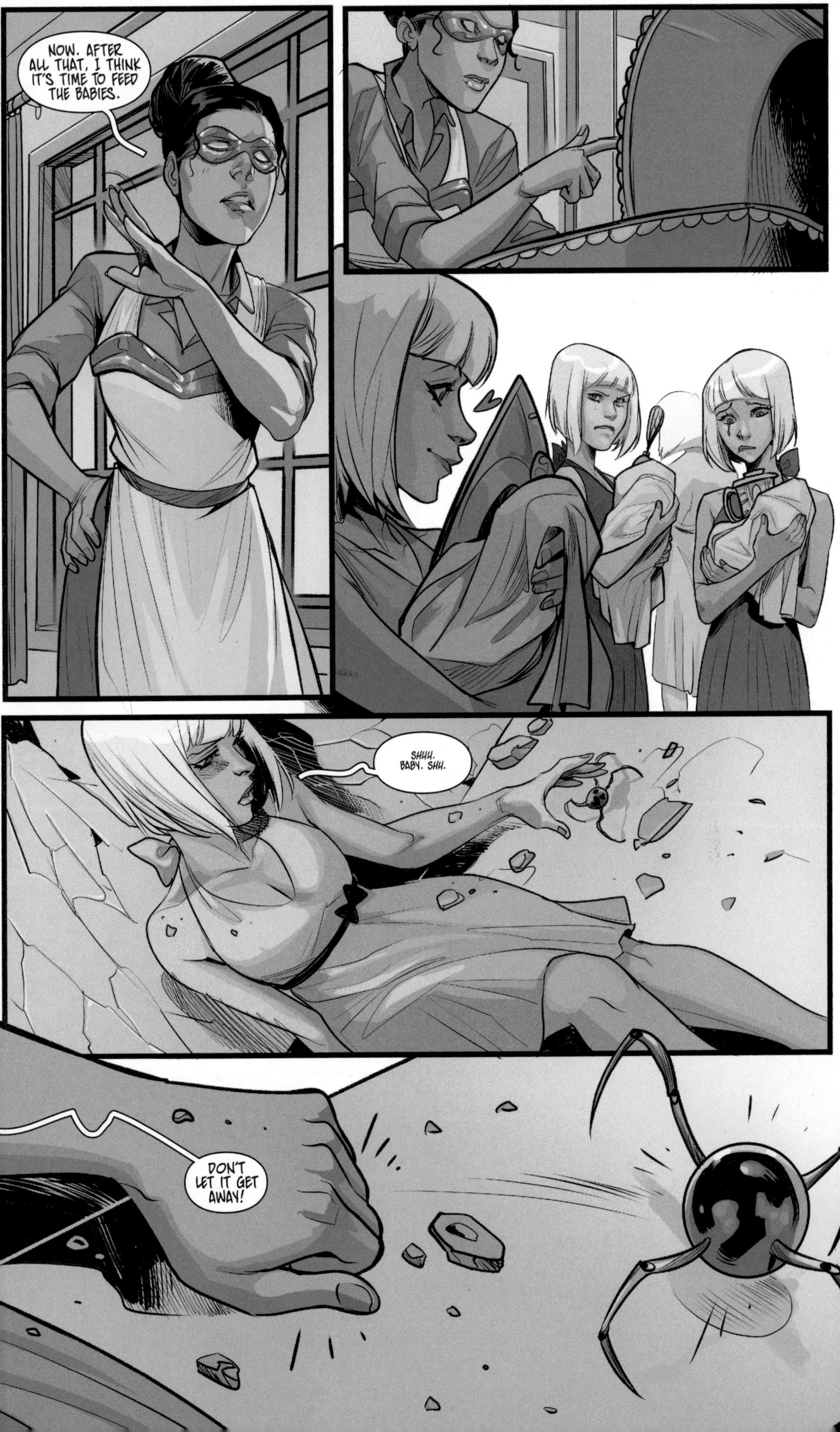
NOW. AFTER ALL THAT, I THINK IT'S TIME TO FEED THE BABIES.
SHUU. BABY. SHU.
DON'T LET IT GET AWAY!

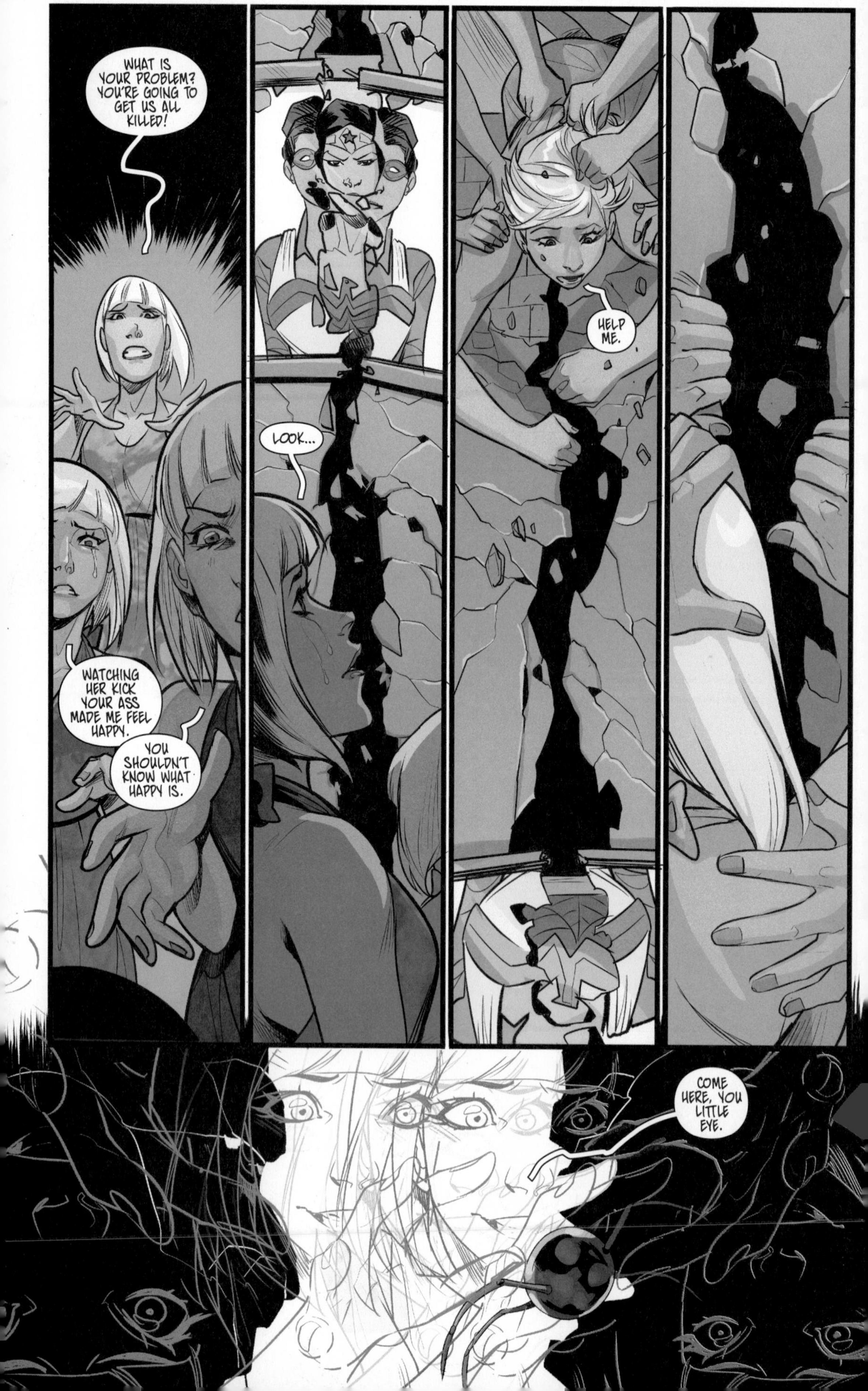
WHAT IS YOUR PROBLEM? YOU'RE GOING TO GET US ALL KILLED!
WATCHING HER KICK YOUR ASS MADE ME FEEL HAPPY.
YOU SHOULDN'T KNOW WHAT HAPPY IS.
LOOK...
HELP ME.
COME HERE, YOU LITTLE EYE.

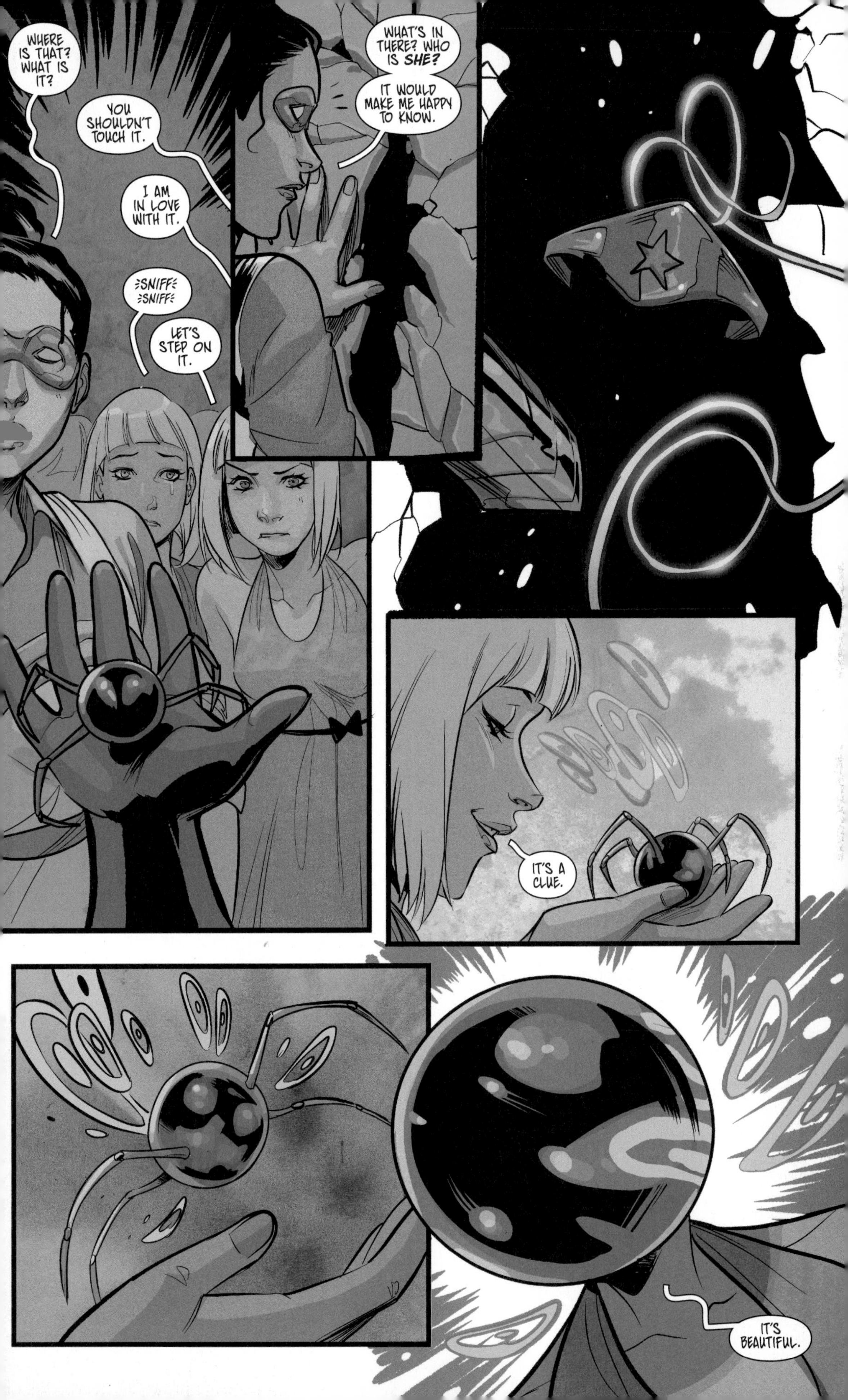
WHERE IS THAT? WHAT IS IT?
WHAT'S IN THERE? WHO IS SHE?
IT WOULD MAKE ME HAPPY TO KNOW.
YOU SHOULDN'T TOUCH IT.
I AM IN LOVE WITH IT.
SNIFF SNIFF
LET'S STEP ON IT.
IT'S A CLUE.
IT'S BEAUTIFUL.

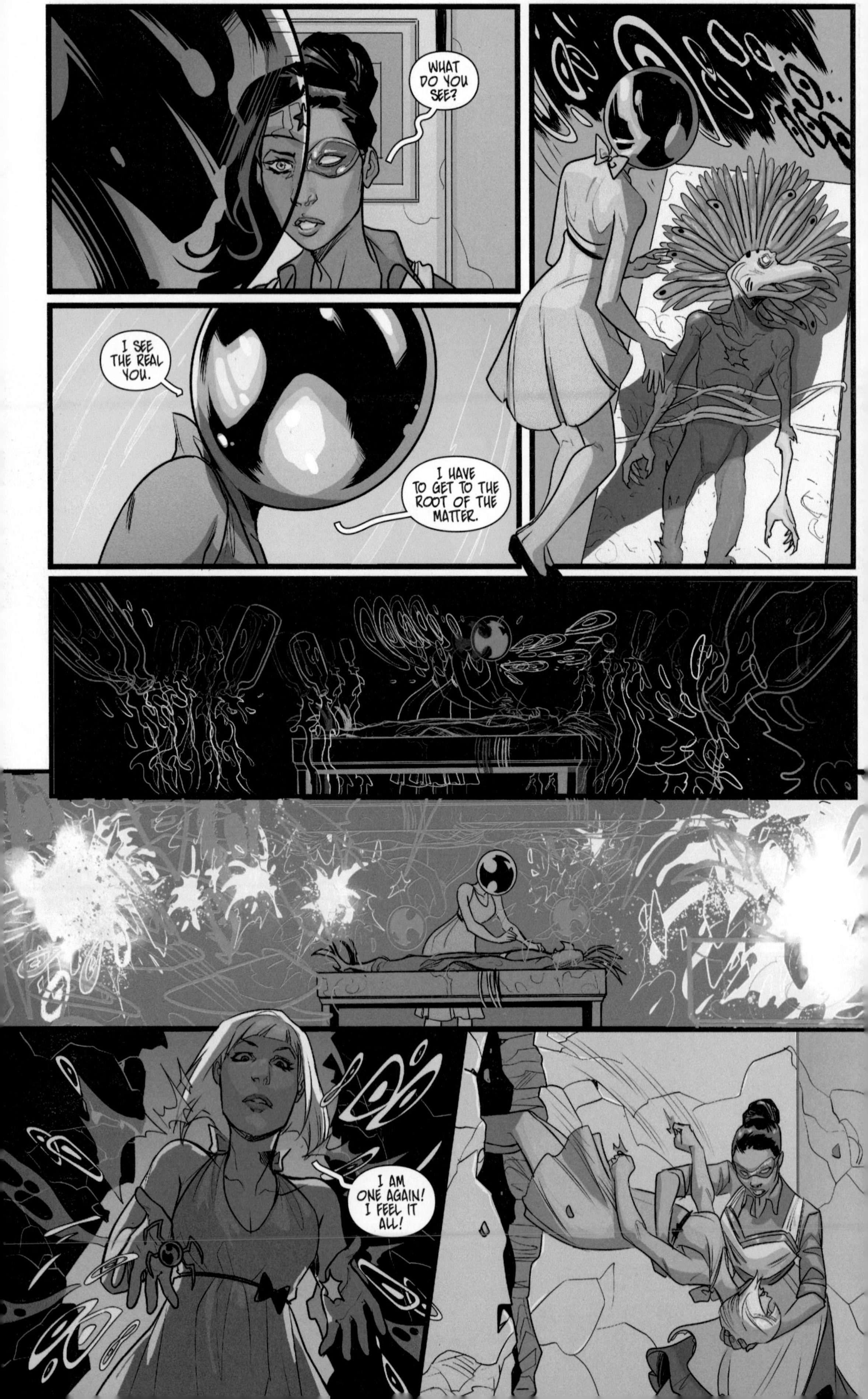
WHAT DO YOU SEE?
I SEE THE REAL YOU.
I HAVE TO GET TO THE ROOT OF THE MATTER.
I AM ONE AGAIN! I FEEL IT ALL!

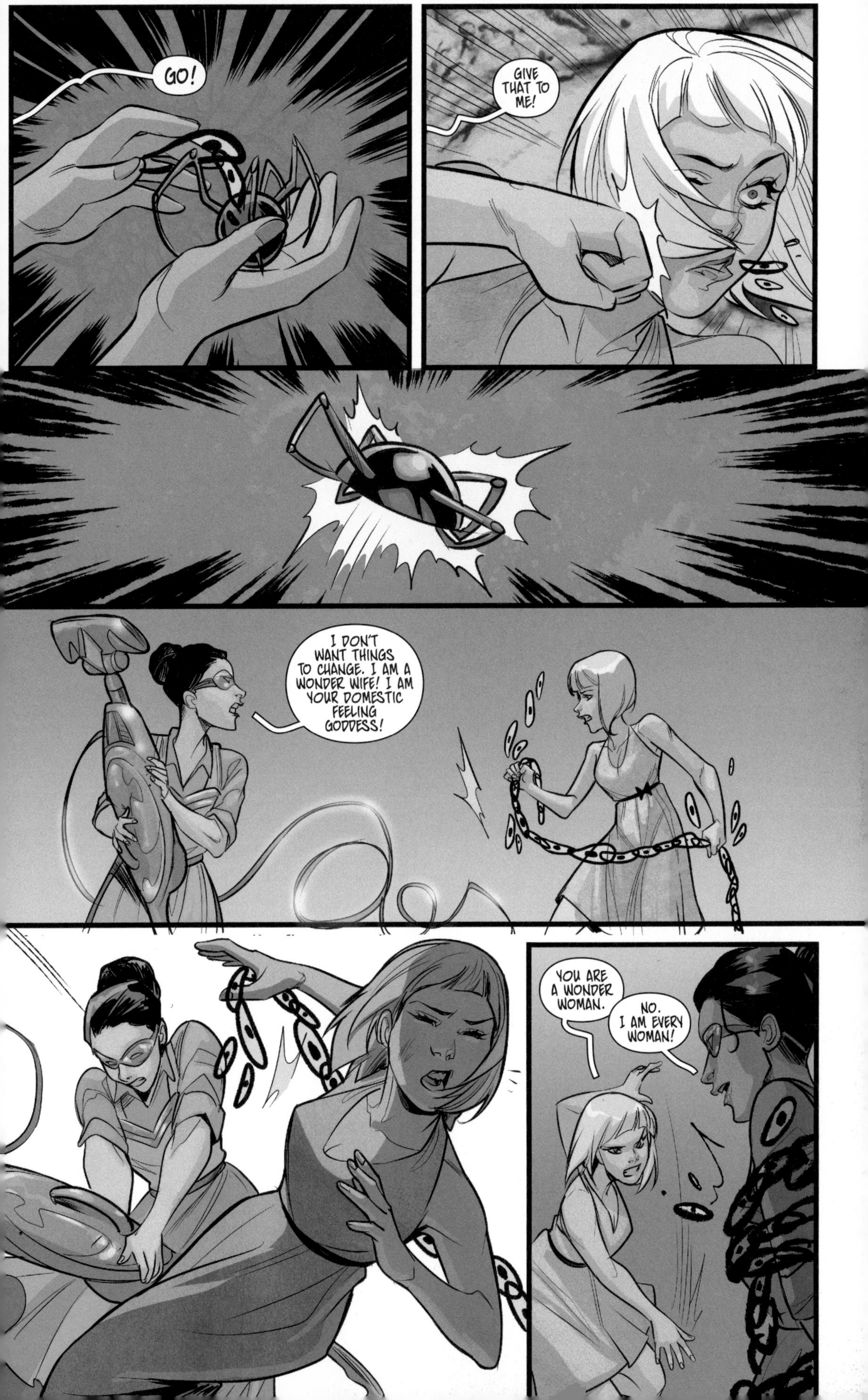
GO!
GIVE THAT TO ME!
I DON'T WANT THINGS TO CHANGE. I AM A WONDER WIFE! I AM YOUR DOMESTIC FEELING GODDESS!
YOU ARE A WONDER WOMAN.
NO. I AM EVERY WOMAN!

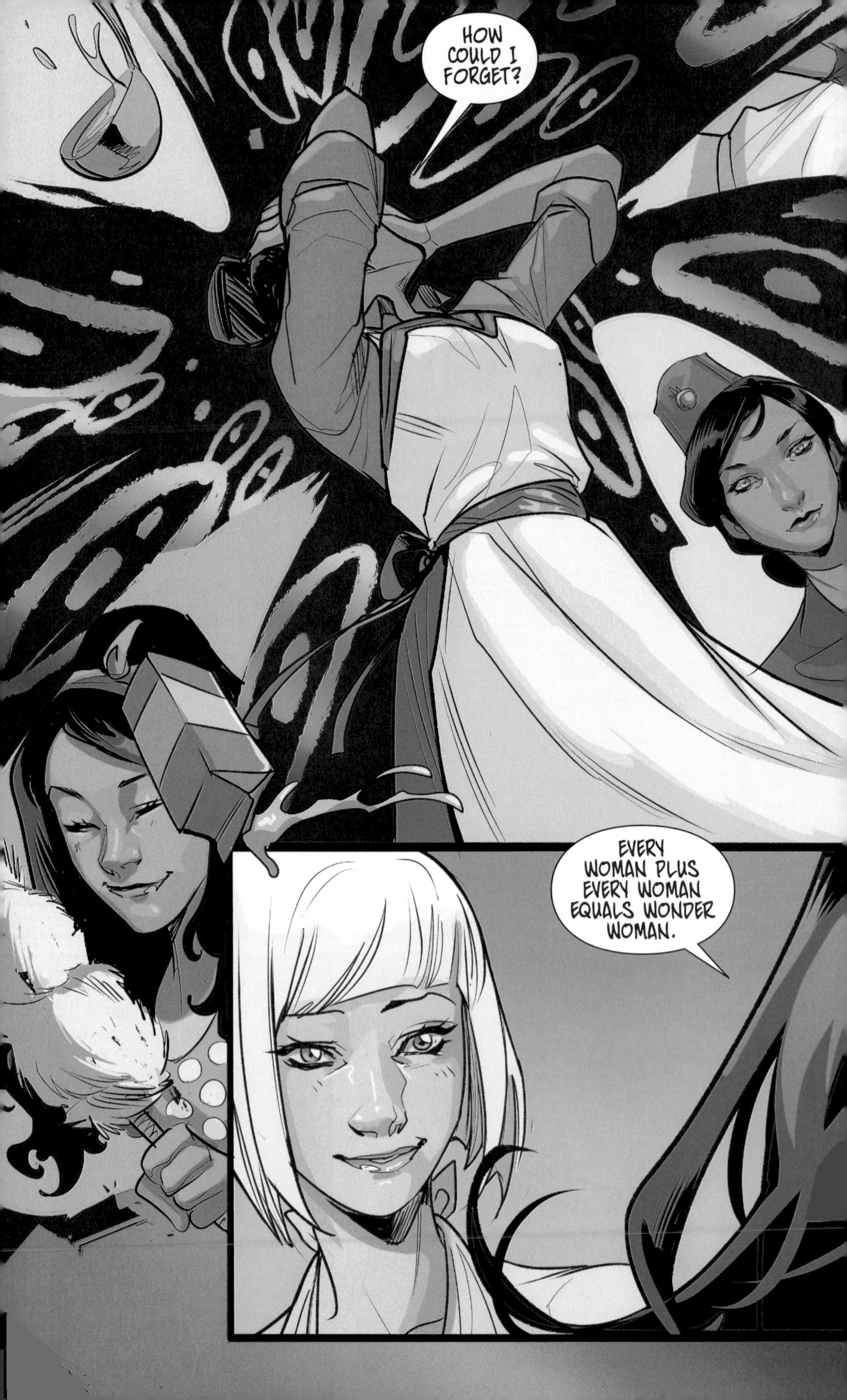
HOW COULD I FORGET?
EVERY WOMAN PLUS EVERY WOMAN EQUALS WONDER WOMAN.

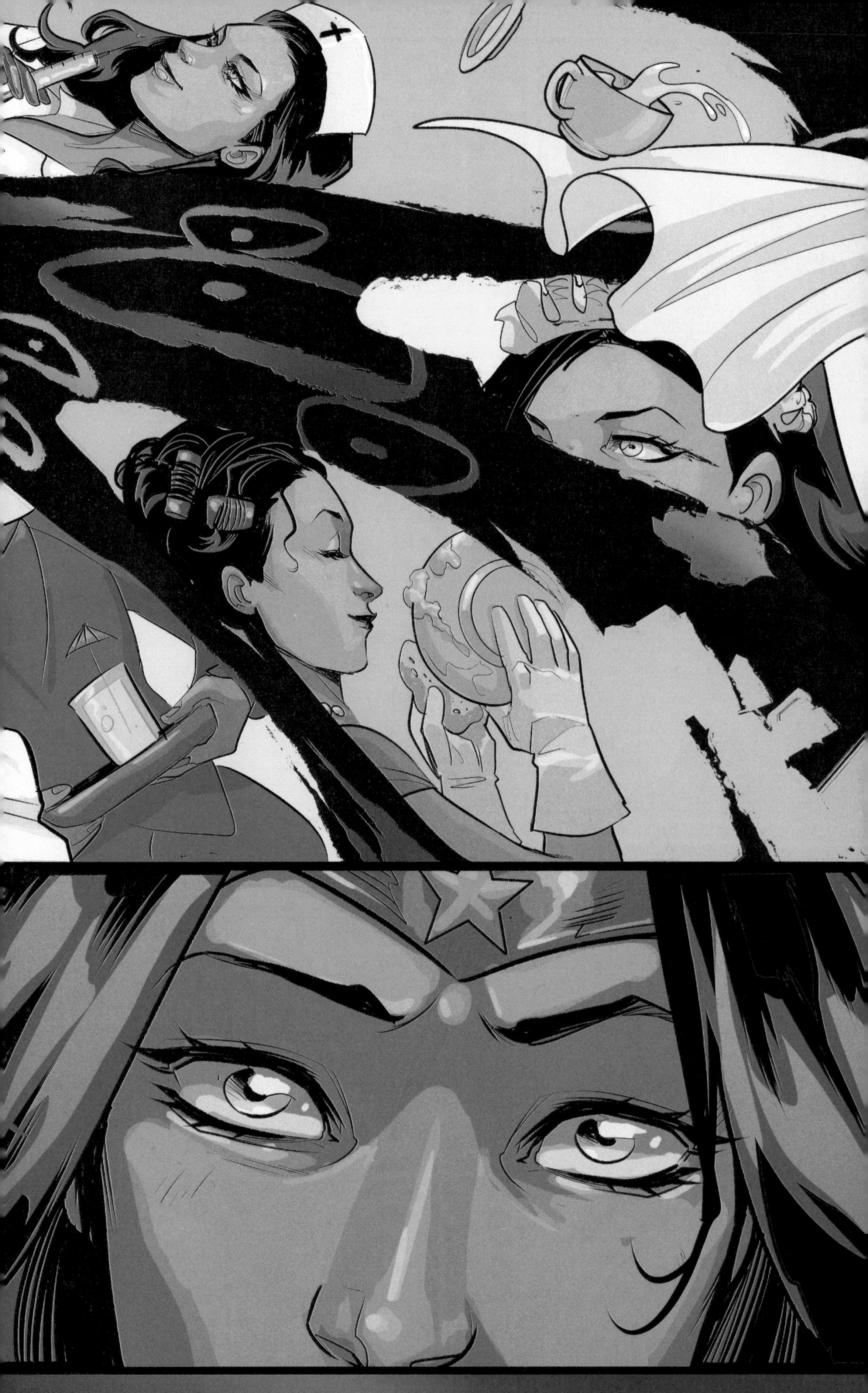

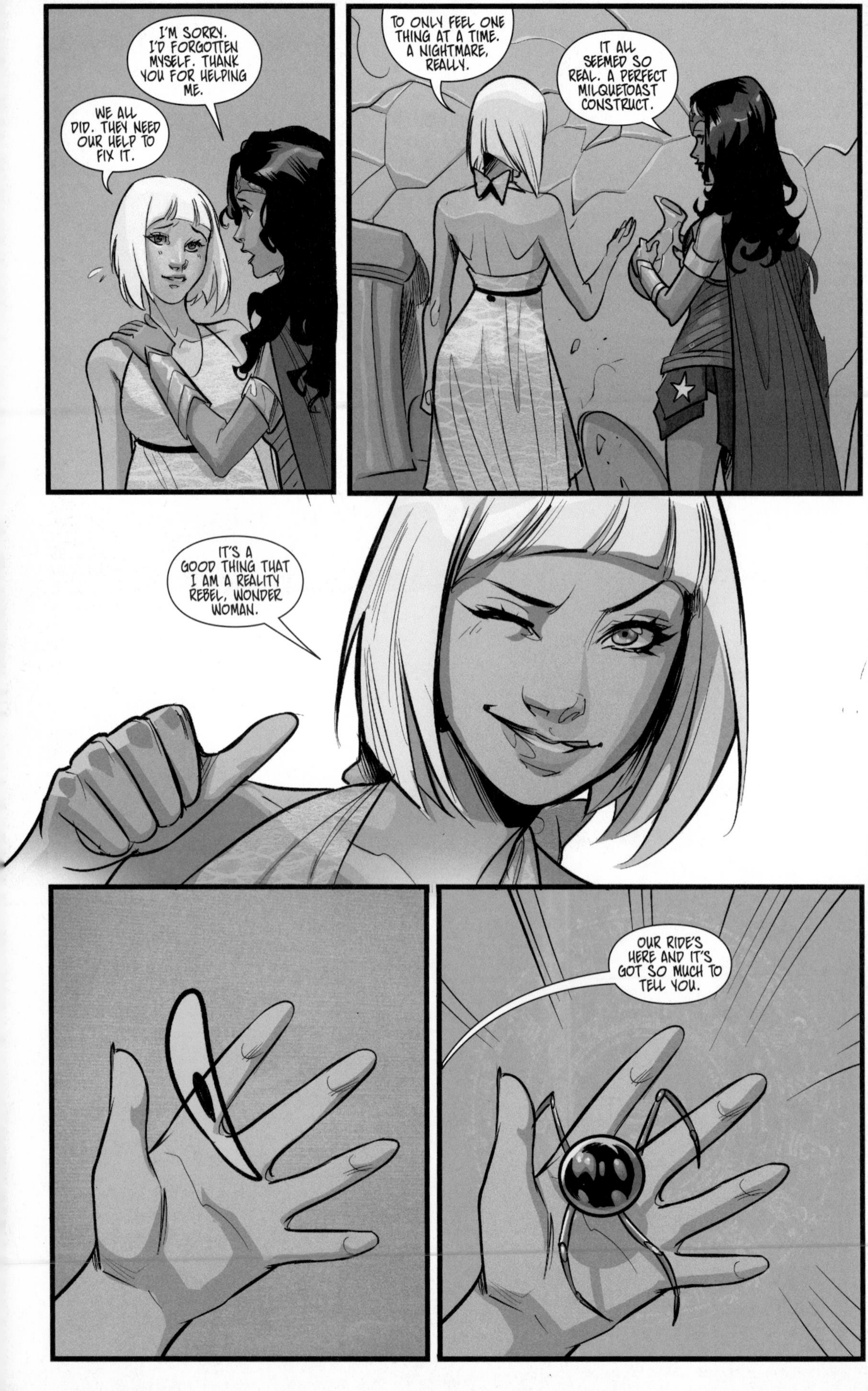
I'M SORRY. I'D FORGOTTEN MYSELF. THANK YOU FOR HELPING ME.
WE ALL DID. THEY NEED OUR HELP TO FIX IT.
TO ONLY FEEL ONE THING AT A TIME. A NIGHTMARE, REALLY.
IT ALL SEEMED SO REAL. A PERFECT MILQUETOAST CONSTRUCT.
IT'S A GOOD THING THAT I AM A REALITY REBEL, WONDER WOMAN.
OUR RIDE'S HERE AND IT'S GOT SO MUCH TO TELL YOU.

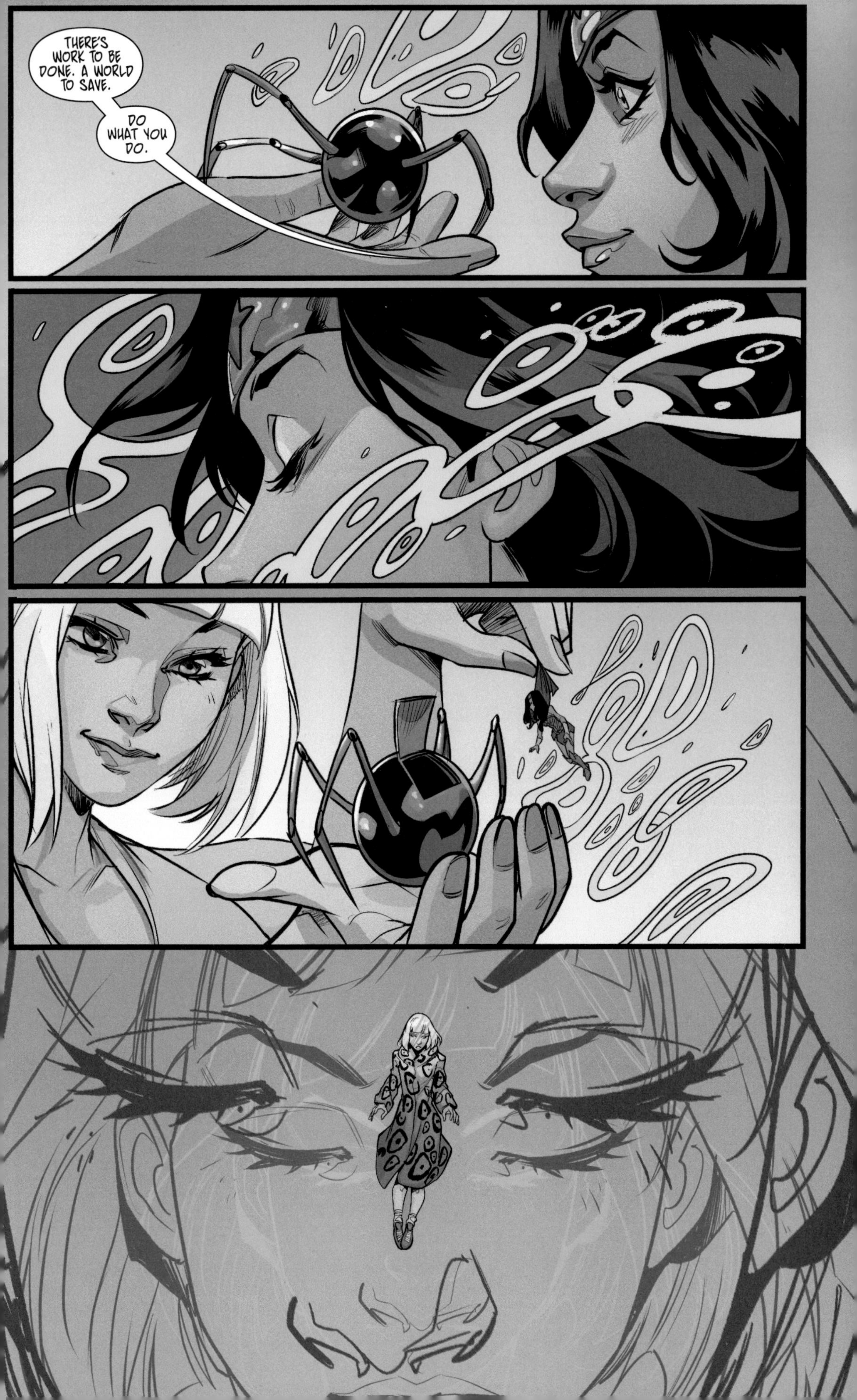
THERE'S WORK TO BE DONE. A WORLD TO SAVE.
DO WHAT YOU DO.

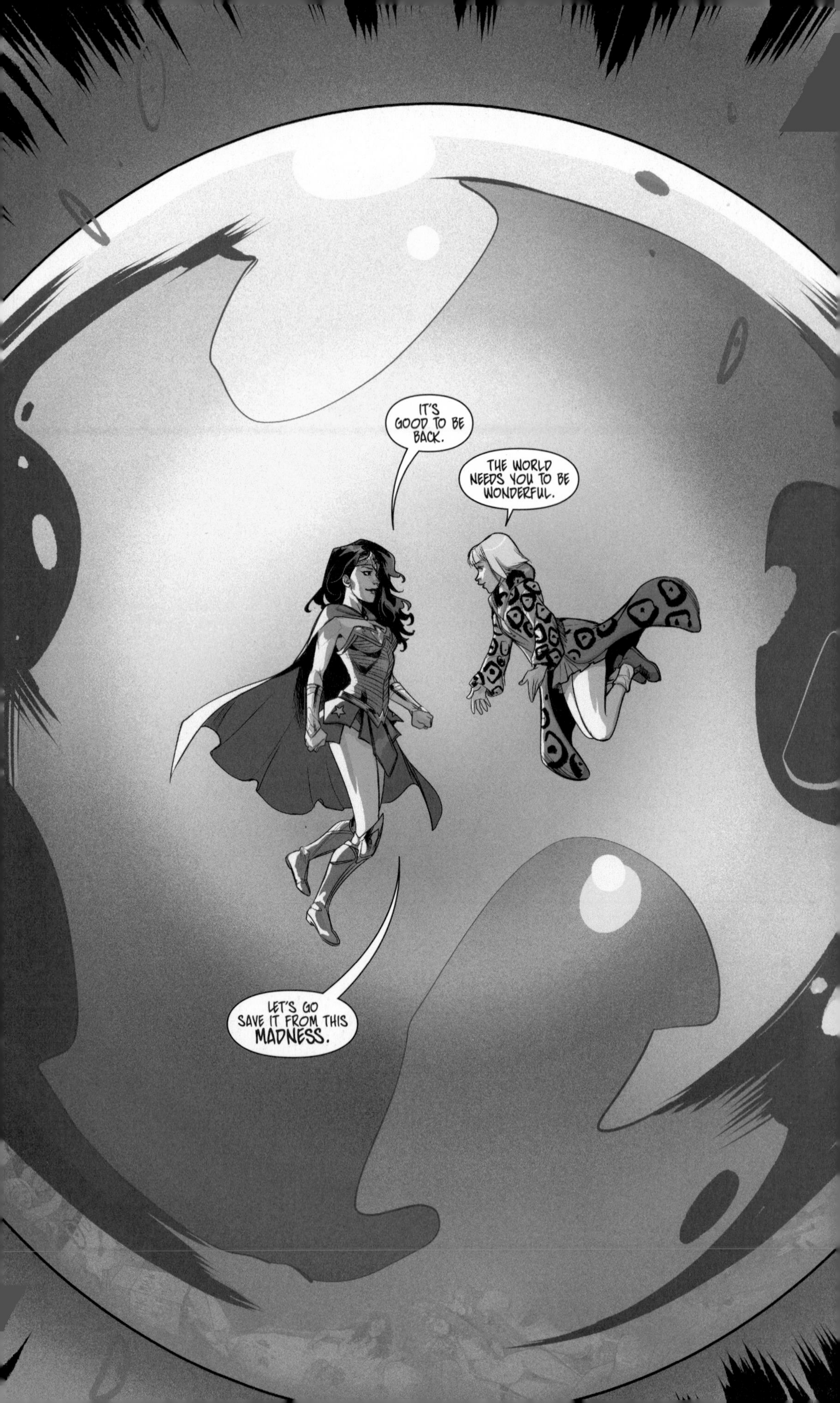
IT'S GOOD TO BE BACK.
THE WORLD NEEDS YOU TO BE WONDERFUL.
LET'S GO SAVE IT FROM THIS MADNESS.

In 1990 Garry Streicher was able to convince the publisher to bring ALPHA 13 back, this time in a book entitled CHRYSALIS: THE ETERNITY GIRL. Fred Hand had passed away in a tragic car accident the year prior, so Streicher was teamed with writer Bev Wilson. Together, Wilson and Streicher crafted a psychedelic epic which took the anarchist themes of ALPHA 13 into the afterlife with a story about the eternal cycle of death and resurrection before ending after 35 issues in 1993.

"Unfortunate Souls," CHRYSALIS: THE ETERNITY GIRL #1. Story by Bev Wilson, art by Garry Streicher. 1990.

ON A CLEAR DAY, UNDER THE BRIGHTEST SKIES, A THOUSAND MILES FROM THIS SPOT, A CHILD WAS CONCEIVED.

HER PARENTS, CINDY AND TOM, WOULDN'T KNOW FOR ANOTHER TWO-AND-A-HALF MONTHS, NOR WOULD THEY GREET THE NEWS HAPPILY.

MONEY IS *TIGHT*, YOU SEE.

YESTERDAY, THEY DECIDED TO ABORT THE PREGNANCY. THEY TOLD NO ONE; CINDY'S PARENTS ARE *VERY* RELIGIOUS, AND WOULD BE HORRIFIED.

BUT.

GET UP.

THAT IS NOT THE END OF THE STORY.

IT NEVER IS.

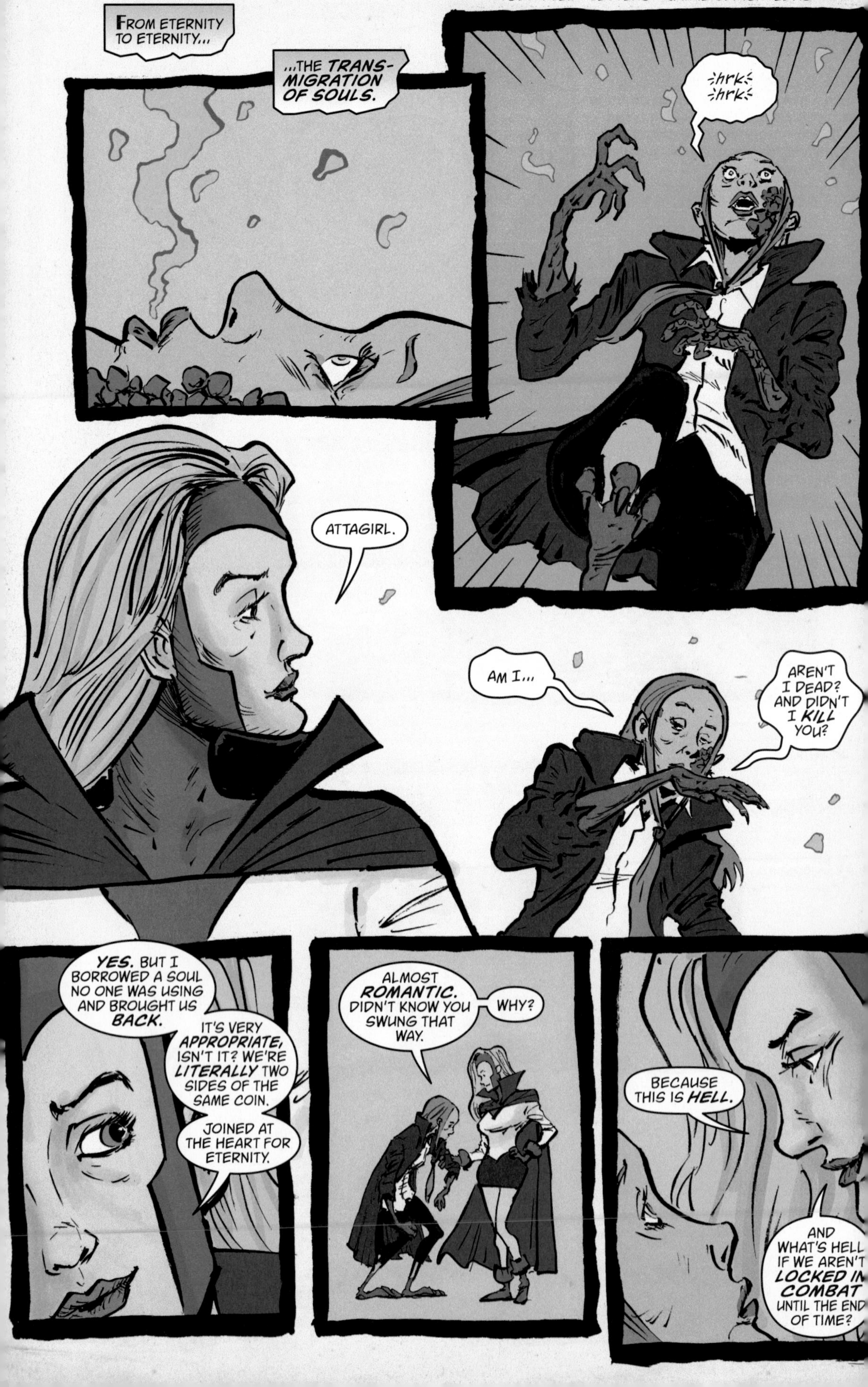
MAGDALENE VISAGGIO: SCRIPT • SONNY LIEW: ART & COLOR
TODD KLEIN: LETTERS • JAMIE S. RICH: EDITS
FROM ETERNITY TO ETERNITY...
...THE TRANS-MIGRATION OF SOULS.
hrk hrk
ATTAGIRL.
AM I...
AREN'T I DEAD? AND DIDN'T I KILL YOU?
YES. BUT I BORROWED A SOUL NO ONE WAS USING AND BROUGHT US BACK.
IT'S VERY APPROPRIATE, ISN'T IT? WE'RE LITERALLY TWO SIDES OF THE SAME COIN.
JOINED AT THE HEART FOR ETERNITY.
ALMOST ROMANTIC. DIDN'T KNOW YOU SWUNG THAT WAY.
WHY?
BECAUSE THIS IS HELL.
AND WHAT'S HELL IF WE AREN'T LOCKED IN COMBAT UNTIL THE END OF TIME?

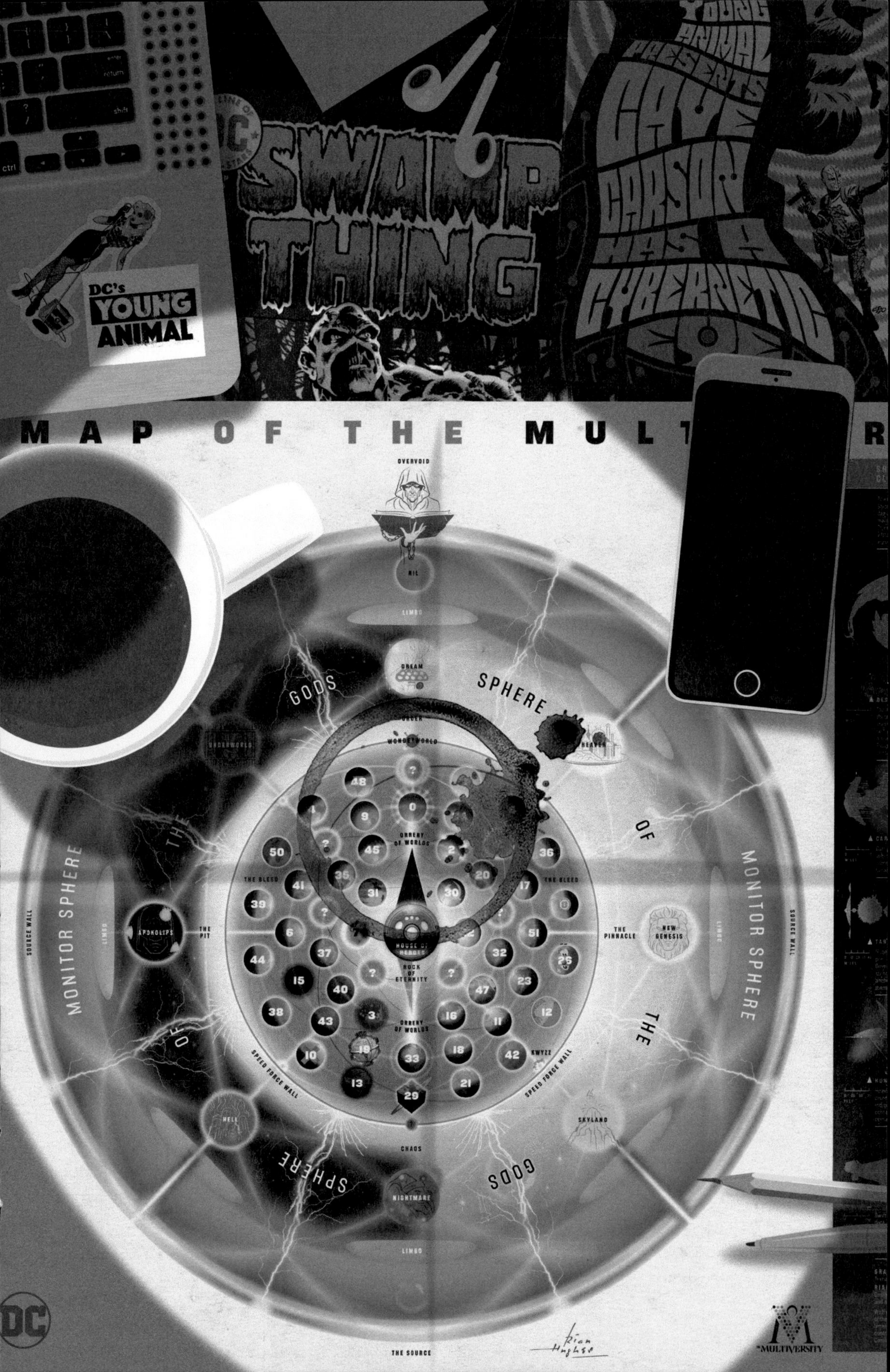

YOUNG ANIMAL PRESENTS
CAVE CARSON HAS A CYBERNETIC
SWAMP THING
DC's YOUNG ANIMAL
M A P O F T H E M U L T
OVERVOID
NIL
LIMBO
DREAM
GODS SPHERE OF THE MONITOR SPHERE
WONDERWORLD
UNDERWORLD
HEAVEN
ORRERY OF WORLDS
THE BLEED
APOKOLIPS
THE PIT
ROCK OF ETERNITY
THE PINNACLE
NEW GENESIS
MONITOR SPHERE
SOURCE WALL
SPEED FORCE WALL
KWYZZ
HELL
SKYLAND
CHAOS
NIGHTMARE
LIMBO
THE SOURCE
MULTIVERSITY

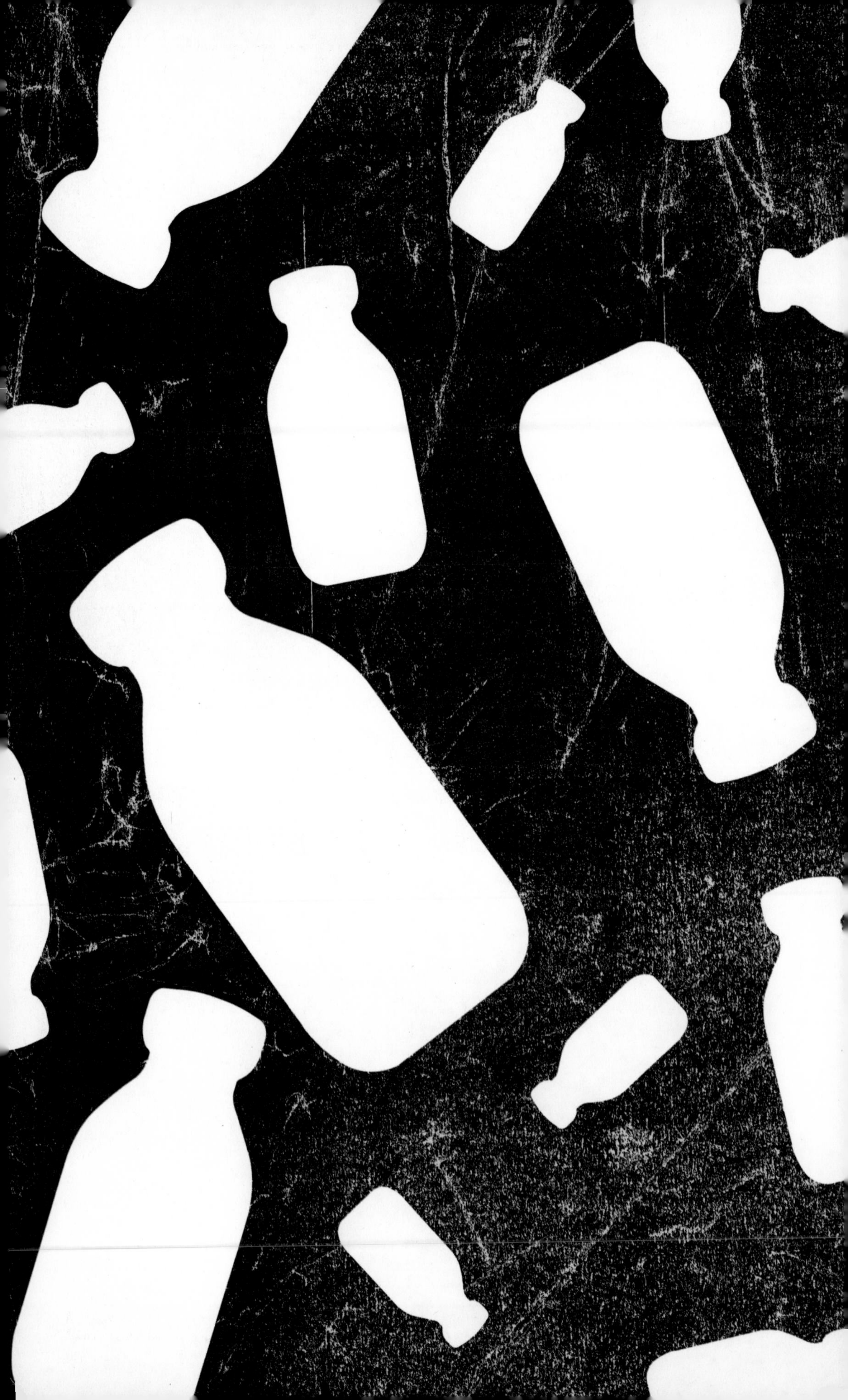

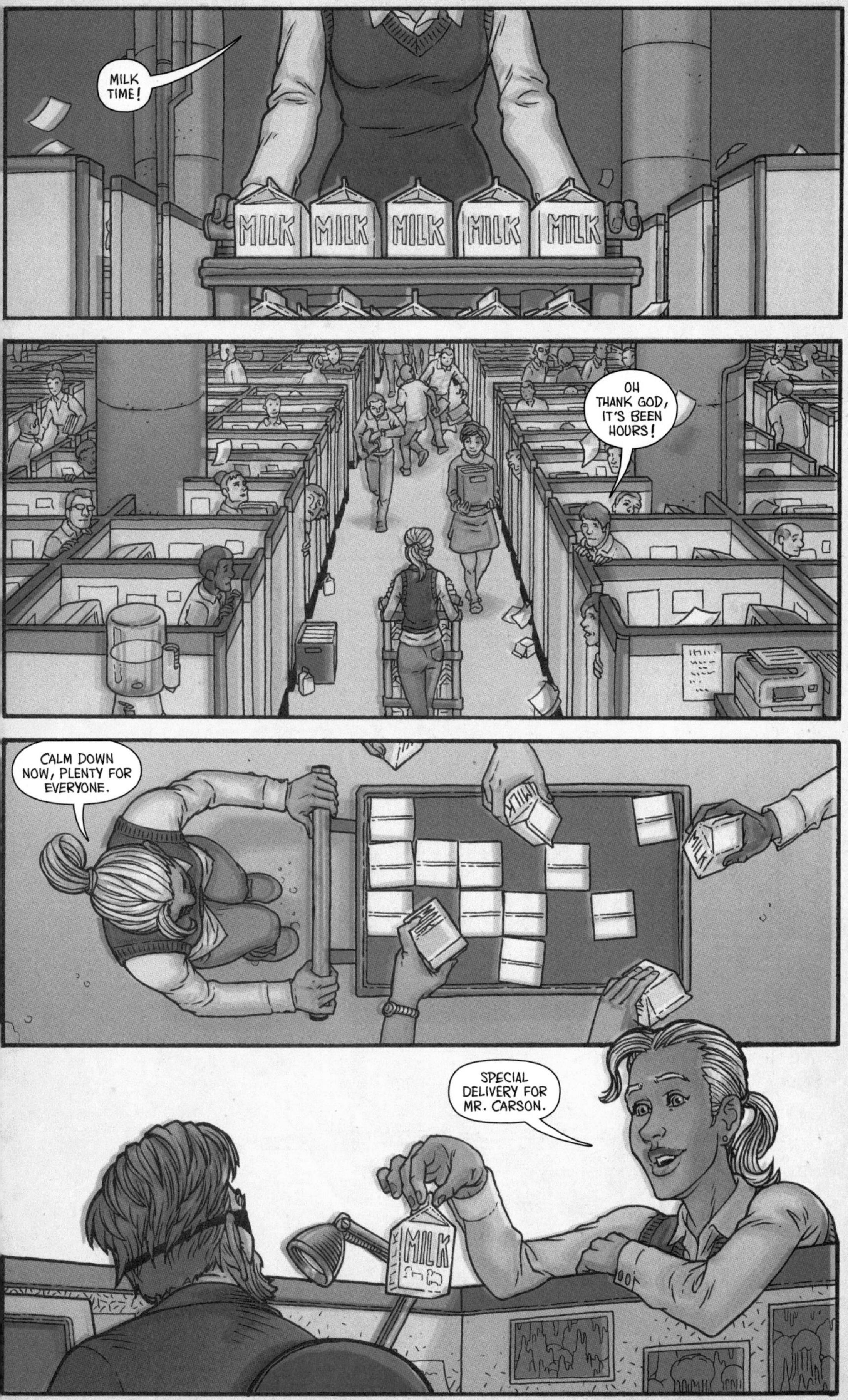
MILK TIME!
MILK
MILK
MILK
MILK
MILK
OH THANK GOD, IT'S BEEN HOURS!
CALM DOWN NOW, PLENTY FOR EVERYONE.
SPECIAL DELIVERY FOR MR. CARSON.
MILK

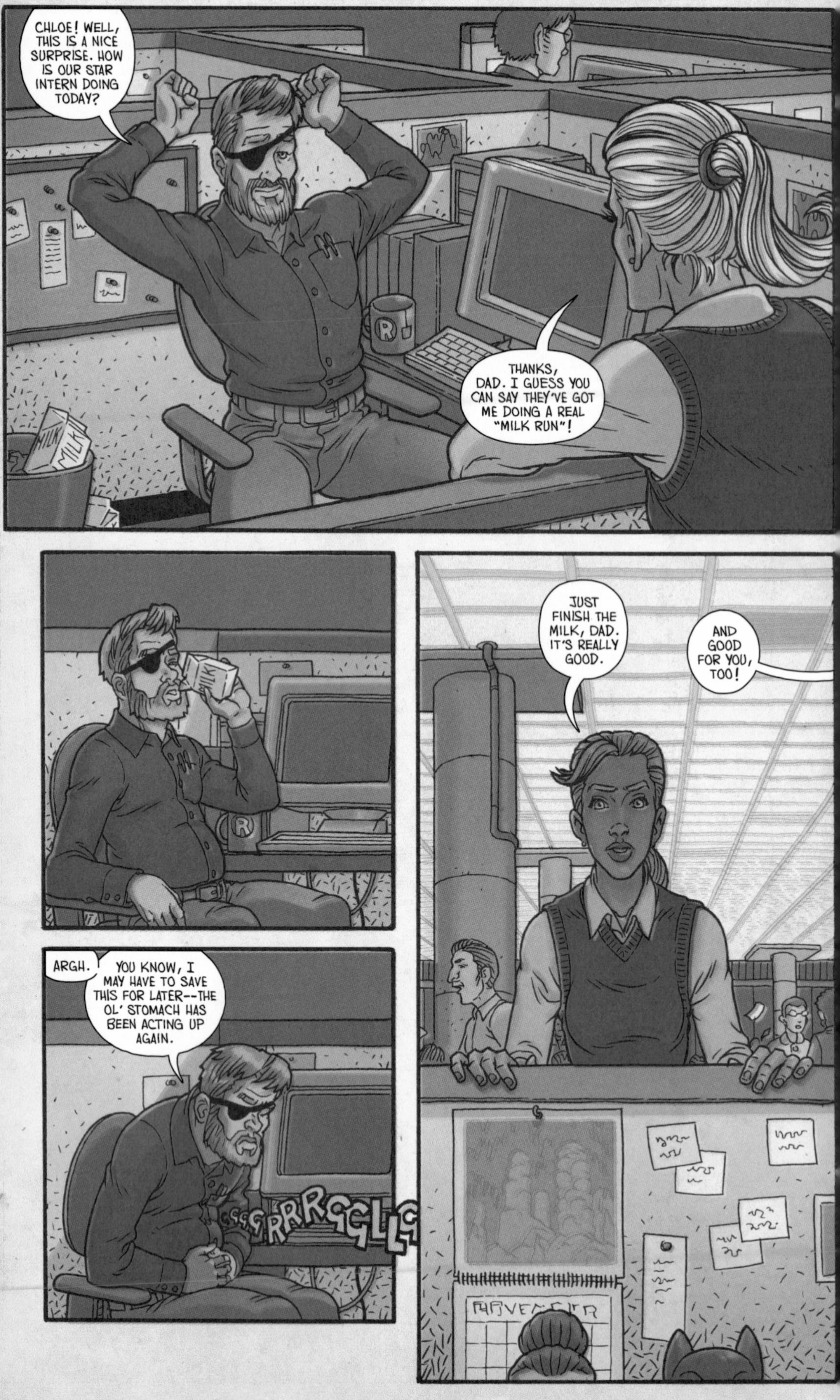
CHLOE! WELL, THIS IS A NICE SURPRISE. HOW IS OUR STAR INTERN DOING TODAY?
THANKS, DAD. I GUESS YOU CAN SAY THEY'VE GOT ME DOING A REAL "MILK RUN"!
JUST FINISH THE MILK, DAD. IT'S REALLY GOOD.
AND GOOD FOR YOU, TOO!
ARGH.
YOU KNOW, I MAY HAVE TO SAVE THIS FOR LATER--THE OL' STOMACH HAS BEEN ACTING UP AGAIN.
GGGGRRRRGGLLG

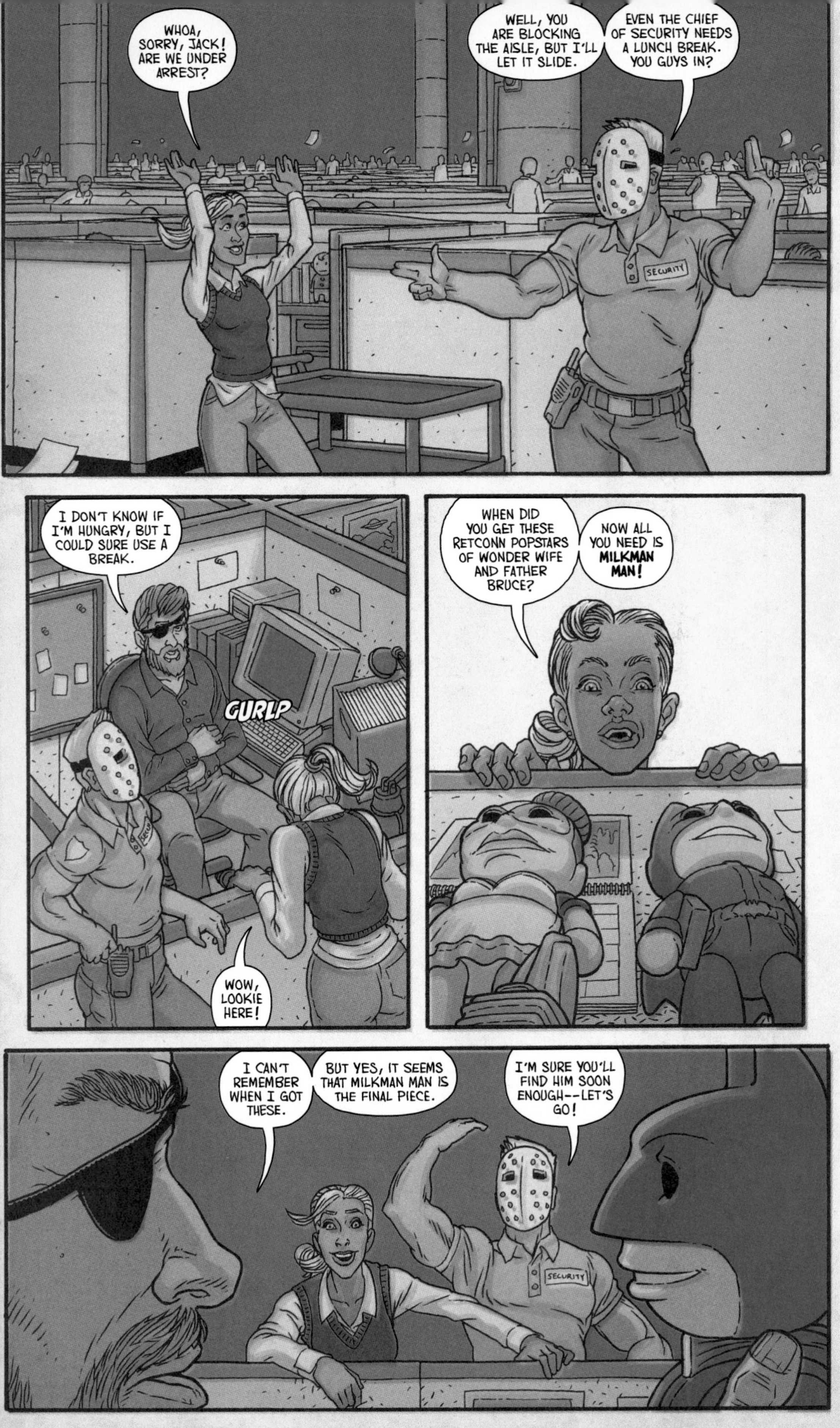
WHOA, SORRY, JACK! ARE WE UNDER ARREST?
WELL, YOU ARE BLOCKING THE AISLE, BUT I'LL LET IT SLIDE.
EVEN THE CHIEF OF SECURITY NEEDS A LUNCH BREAK. YOU GUYS IN?
SECURITY
I DON'T KNOW IF I'M HUNGRY, BUT I COULD SURE USE A BREAK.
GURLP
WOW, LOOKIE HERE!
WHEN DID YOU GET THESE RETCONN POPSTARS OF WONDER WIFE AND FATHER BRUCE?
NOW ALL YOU NEED IS **MILKMAN MAN!**
I CAN'T REMEMBER WHEN I GOT THESE.
BUT YES, IT SEEMS THAT MILKMAN MAN IS THE FINAL PIECE.
I'M SURE YOU'LL FIND HIM SOON ENOUGH--LET'S GO!
SECURITY

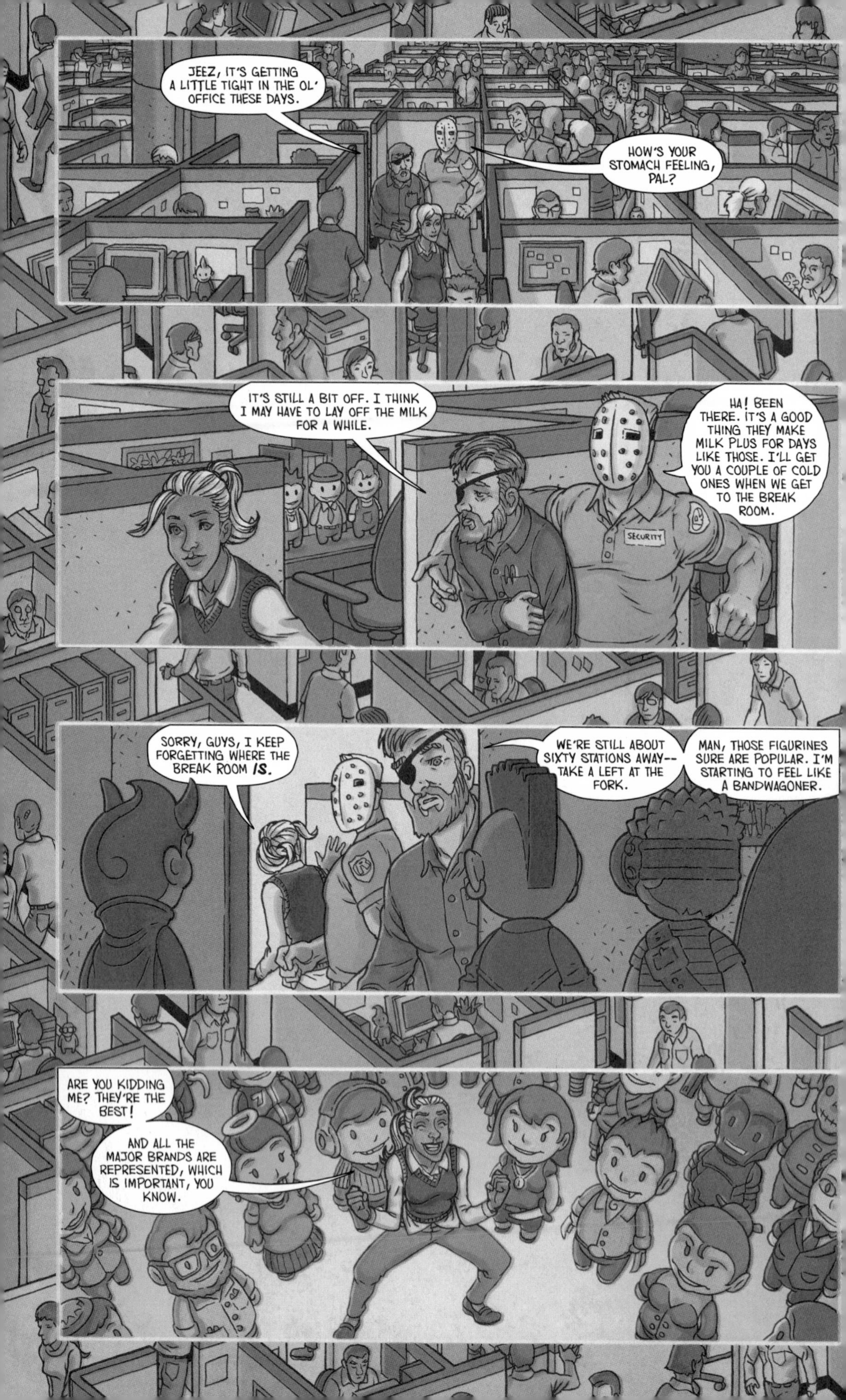

JEEZ, IT'S GETTING A LITTLE TIGHT IN THE OL' OFFICE THESE DAYS.
HOW'S YOUR STOMACH FEELING, PAL?
IT'S STILL A BIT OFF. I THINK I MAY HAVE TO LAY OFF THE MILK FOR A WHILE.
HA! BEEN THERE. IT'S A GOOD THING THEY MAKE MILK PLUS FOR DAYS LIKE THOSE. I'LL GET YOU A COUPLE OF COLD ONES WHEN WE GET TO THE BREAK ROOM.
SECURITY
SORRY, GUYS, I KEEP FORGETTING WHERE THE BREAK ROOM *IS*.
WE'RE STILL ABOUT SIXTY STATIONS AWAY-- TAKE A LEFT AT THE FORK.
MAN, THOSE FIGURINES SURE ARE POPULAR. I'M STARTING TO FEEL LIKE A BANDWAGONER.
ARE YOU KIDDING ME? THEY'RE THE BEST!
AND ALL THE MAJOR BRANDS ARE REPRESENTED, WHICH IS IMPORTANT, YOU KNOW.

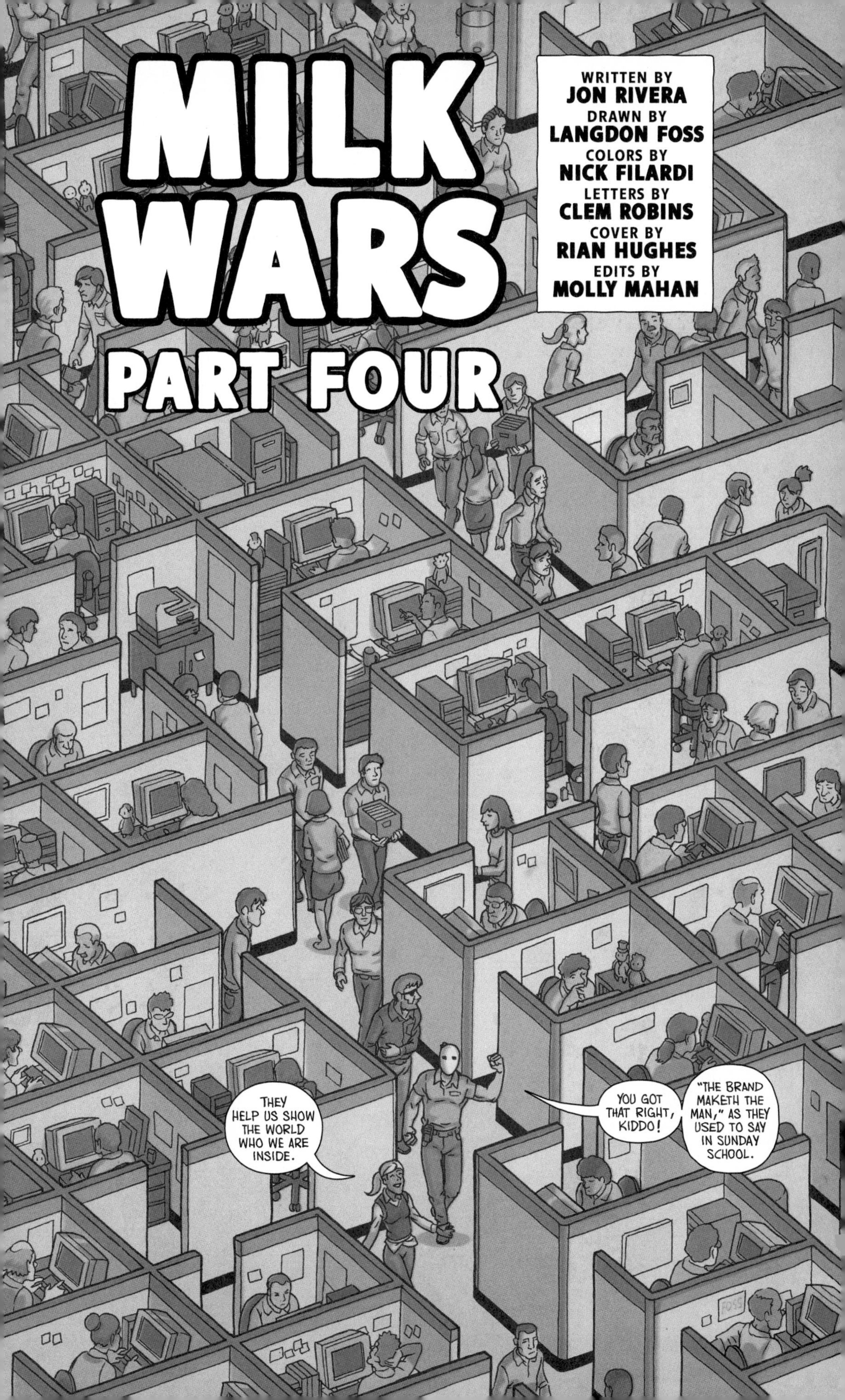
MILK WARS
PART FOUR
WRITTEN BY JON RIVERA
DRAWN BY LANGDON FOSS
COLORS BY NICK FILARDI
LETTERS BY CLEM ROBINS
COVER BY RIAN HUGHES
EDITS BY MOLLY MAHAN
THEY HELP US SHOW THE WORLD WHO WE ARE INSIDE.
YOU GOT THAT RIGHT, KIDDO!
"THE BRAND MAKETH THE MAN," AS THEY USED TO SAY IN SUNDAY SCHOOL.
FOSS

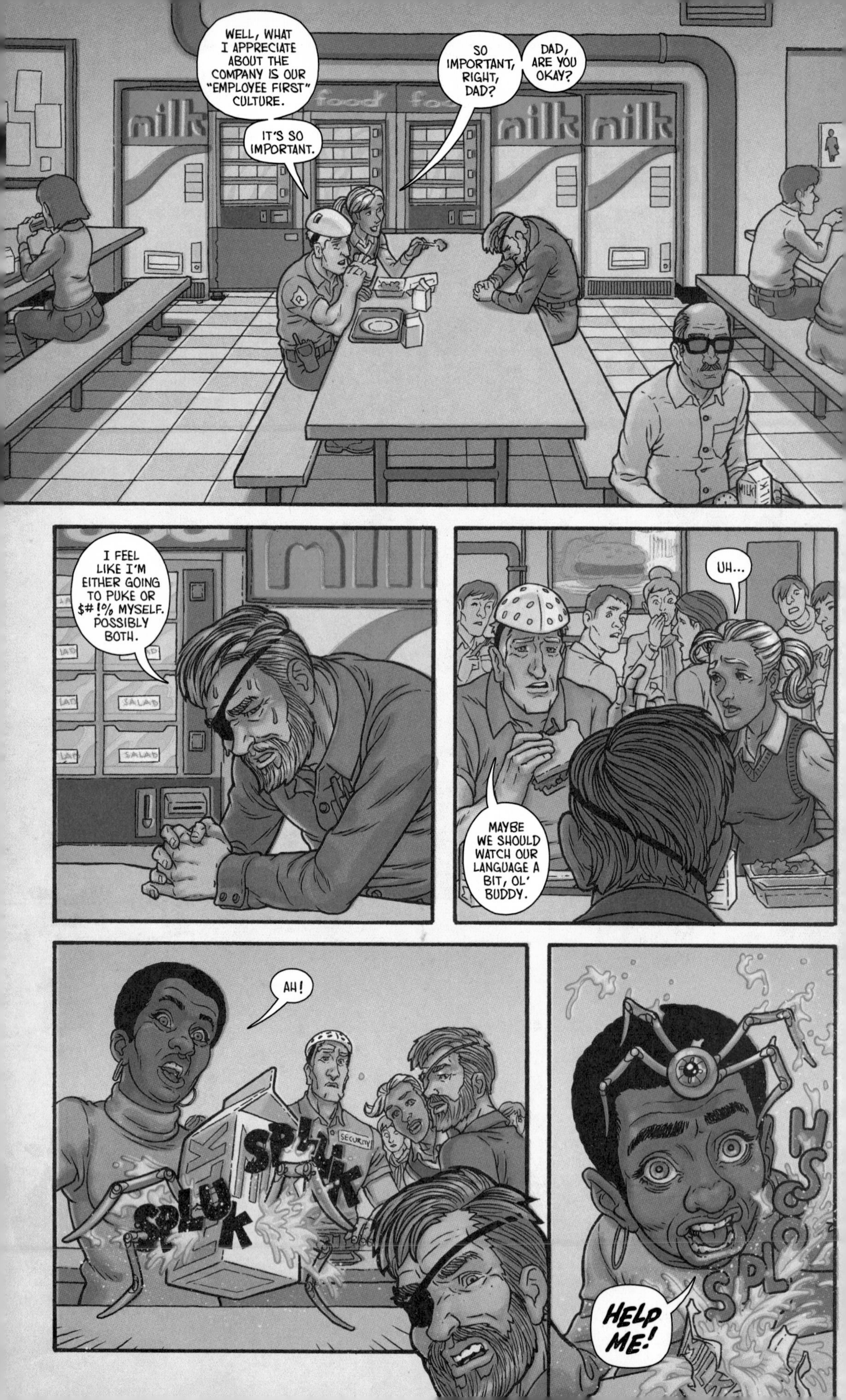
WELL, WHAT I APPRECIATE ABOUT THE COMPANY IS OUR "EMPLOYEE FIRST" CULTURE.
IT'S SO IMPORTANT.
SO IMPORTANT, RIGHT, DAD?
DAD, ARE YOU OKAY?
milk
food
food
milk
milk
I FEEL LIKE I'M EITHER GOING TO PUKE OR $#!% MYSELF. POSSIBLY BOTH.
SALAD
SALAD
UH...
MAYBE WE SHOULD WATCH OUR LANGUAGE A BIT, OL' BUDDY.
AH!
SECURITY
SPLUK
SPLUK
HELP ME!
SPLOOSH

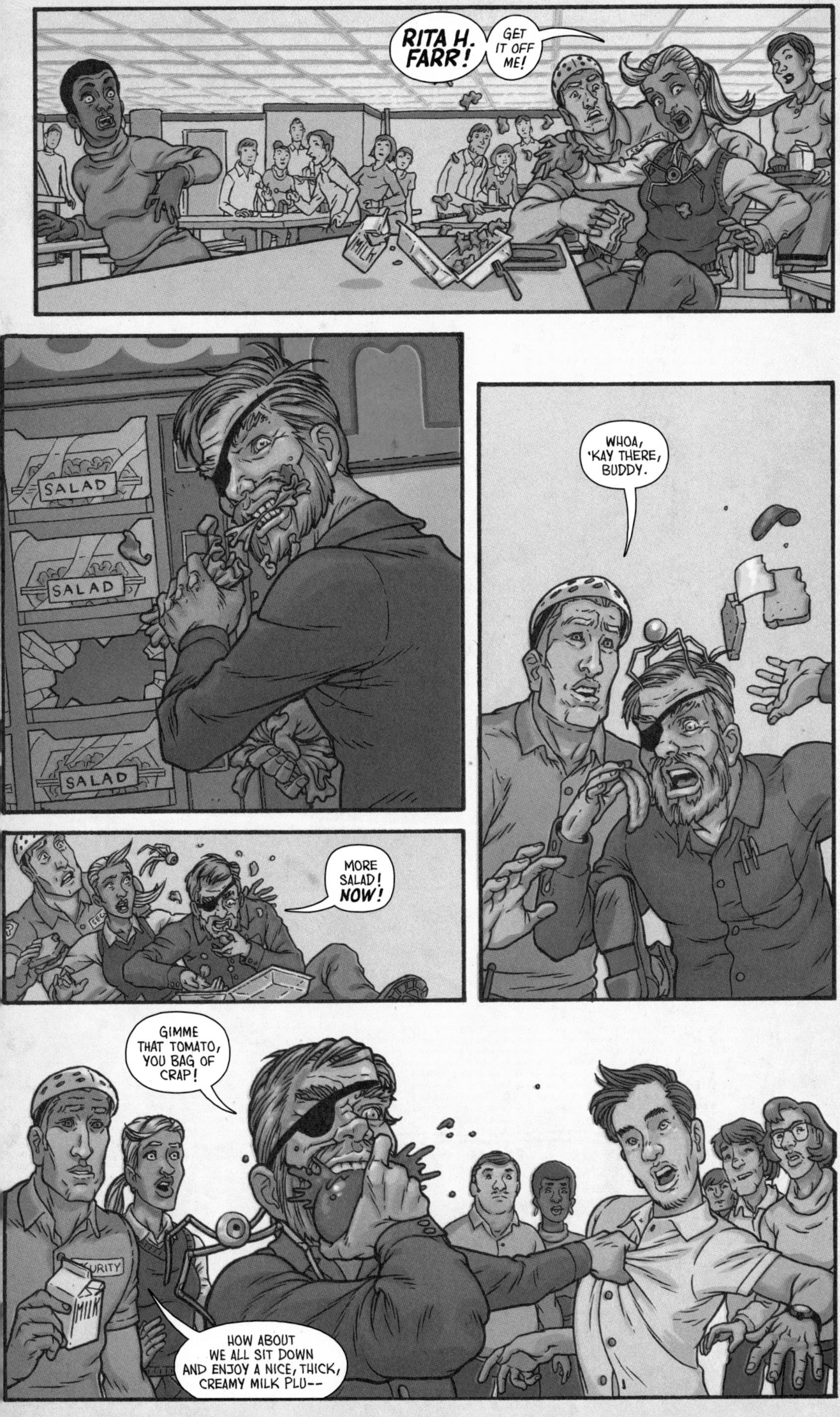
RITA H. FARR!
GET IT OFF ME!
WHOA, 'KAY THERE, BUDDY.
MORE SALAD! NOW!
GIMME THAT TOMATO, YOU BAG OF CRAP!
HOW ABOUT WE ALL SIT DOWN AND ENJOY A NICE, THICK, CREAMY MILK PLU--

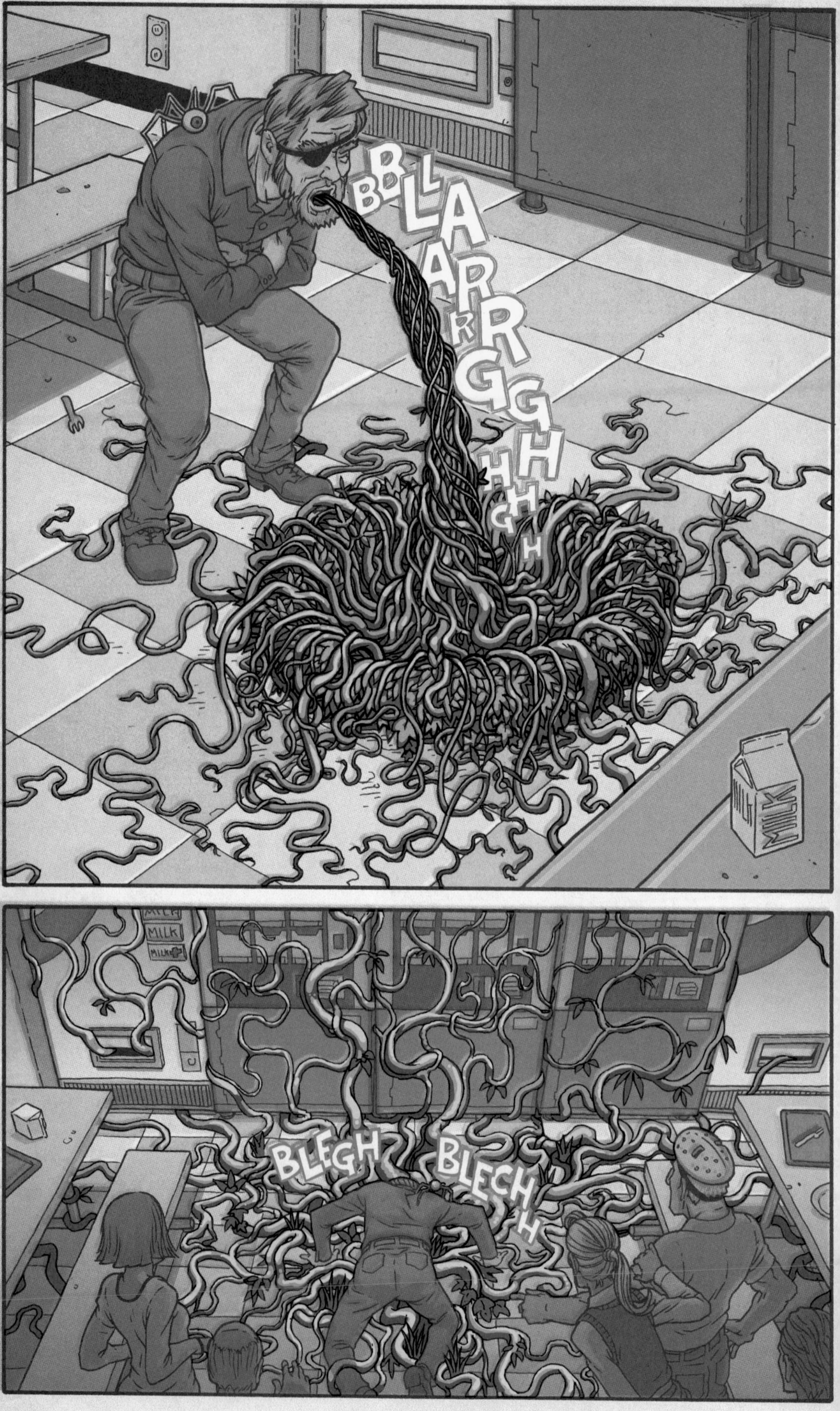
BLARRGGH
BLARGHGH
MILK
MILK
MILK
MILK
BLEGH
BLECH
H
H

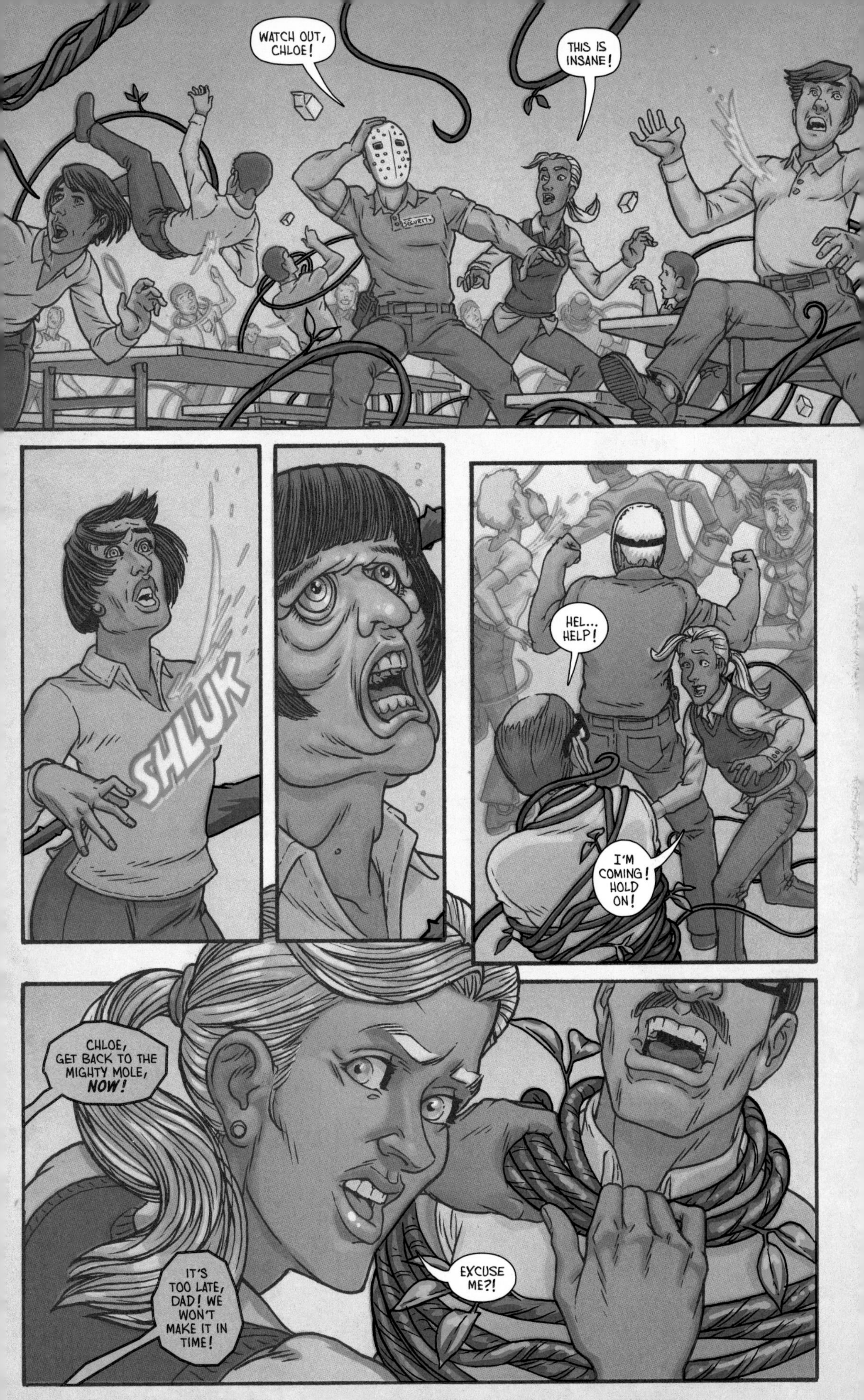

WATCH OUT, CHLOE!
THIS IS INSANE!
SECURITY
SHLUK
HEL... HELP!
I'M COMING! HOLD ON!
CHLOE, GET BACK TO THE MIGHTY MOLE, NOW!
IT'S TOO LATE, DAD! WE WON'T MAKE IT IN TIME!
EXCUSE ME?!

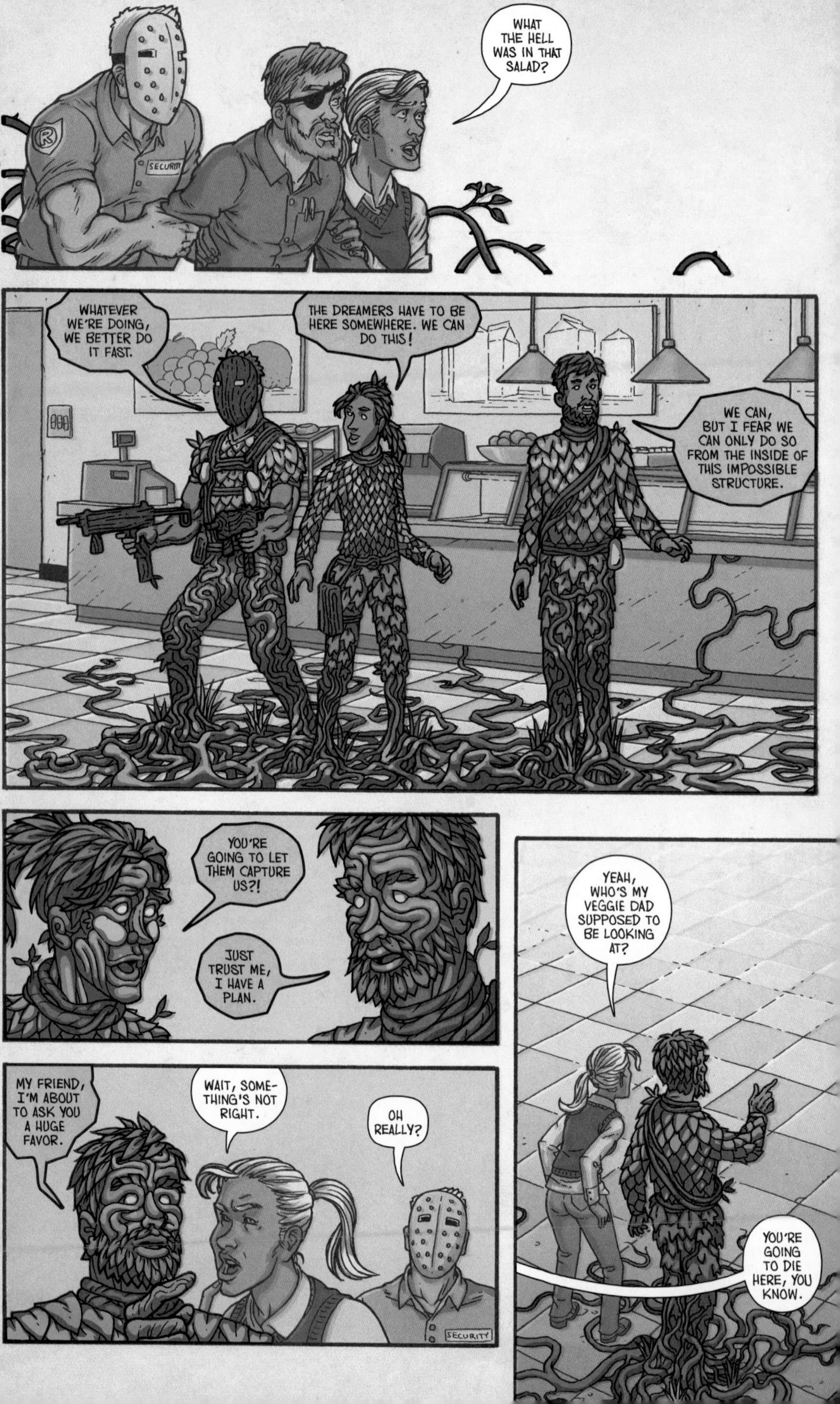
SECURITY
WHAT THE HELL WAS IN THAT SALAD?
WHATEVER WE'RE DOING, WE BETTER DO IT FAST.
THE DREAMERS HAVE TO BE HERE SOMEWHERE. WE CAN DO THIS!
WE CAN, BUT I FEAR WE CAN ONLY DO SO FROM THE INSIDE OF THIS IMPOSSIBLE STRUCTURE.
YOU'RE GOING TO LET THEM CAPTURE US?!
JUST TRUST ME, I HAVE A PLAN.
MY FRIEND, I'M ABOUT TO ASK YOU A HUGE FAVOR.
WAIT, SOME-THING'S NOT RIGHT.
OH REALLY?
SECURITY
YEAH, WHO'S MY VEGGIE DAD SUPPOSED TO BE LOOKING AT?
YOU'RE GOING TO DIE HERE, YOU KNOW.

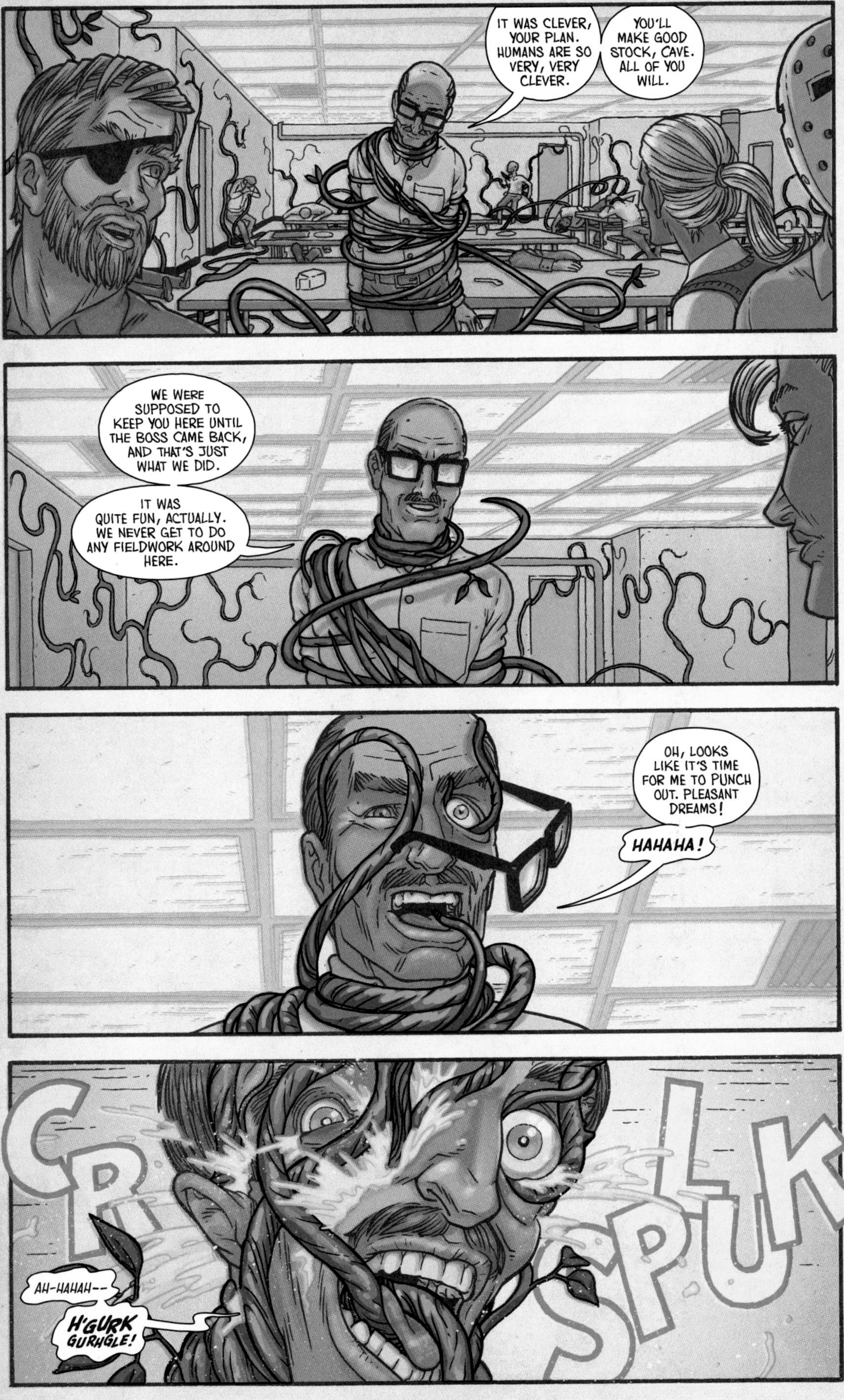
IT WAS CLEVER, YOUR PLAN. HUMANS ARE SO VERY, VERY CLEVER.
YOU'LL MAKE GOOD STOCK, CAVE. ALL OF YOU WILL.
WE WERE SUPPOSED TO KEEP YOU HERE UNTIL THE BOSS CAME BACK, AND THAT'S JUST WHAT WE DID.
IT WAS QUITE FUN, ACTUALLY. WE NEVER GET TO DO ANY FIELDWORK AROUND HERE.
OH, LOOKS LIKE IT'S TIME FOR ME TO PUNCH OUT. PLEASANT DREAMS!
HAHAHA!
CRL
SPUK
AH-HAHAH--
H'GURK GURHGLE!

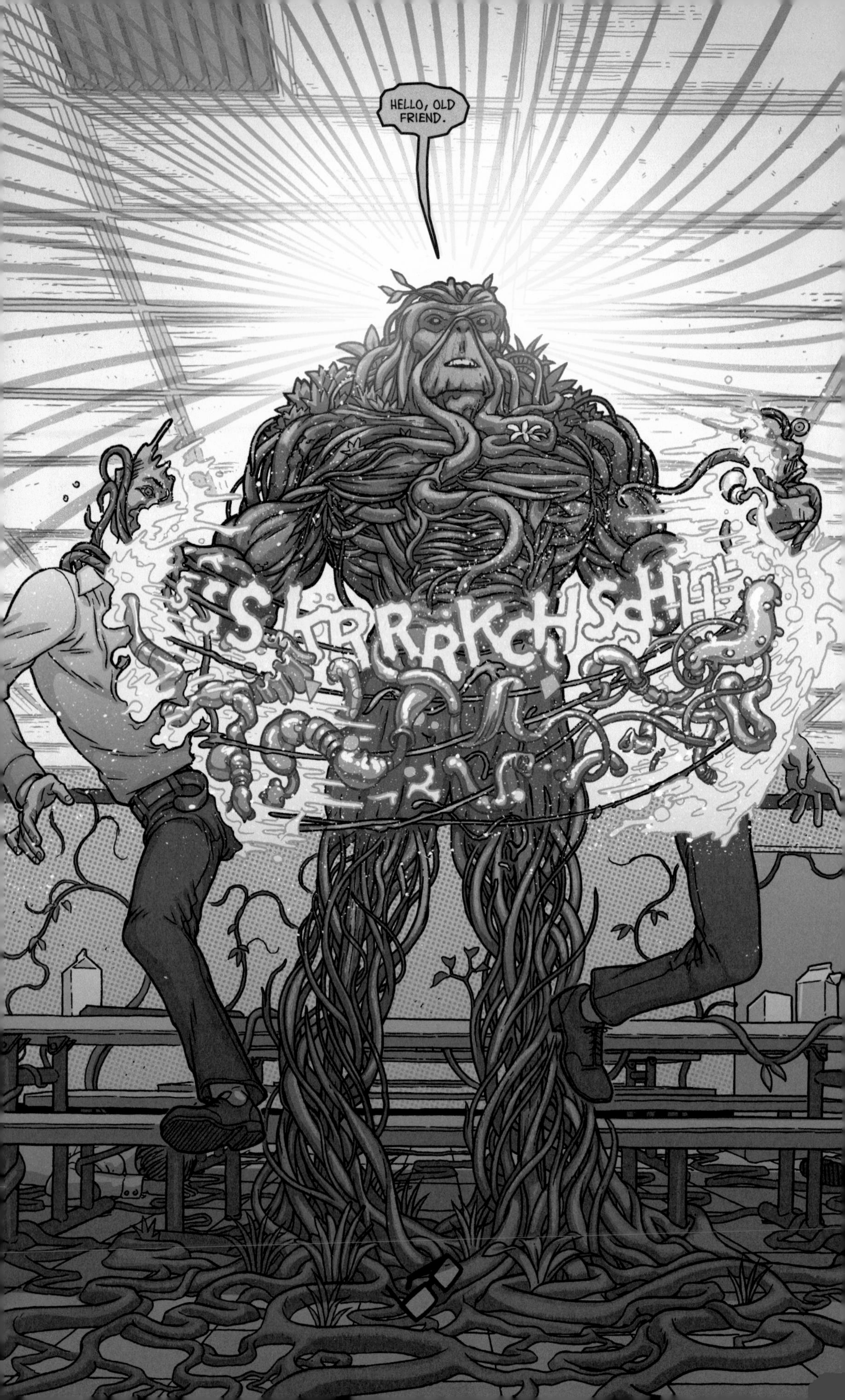
HELLO, OLD FRIEND.
SHRRRKCHSSHH

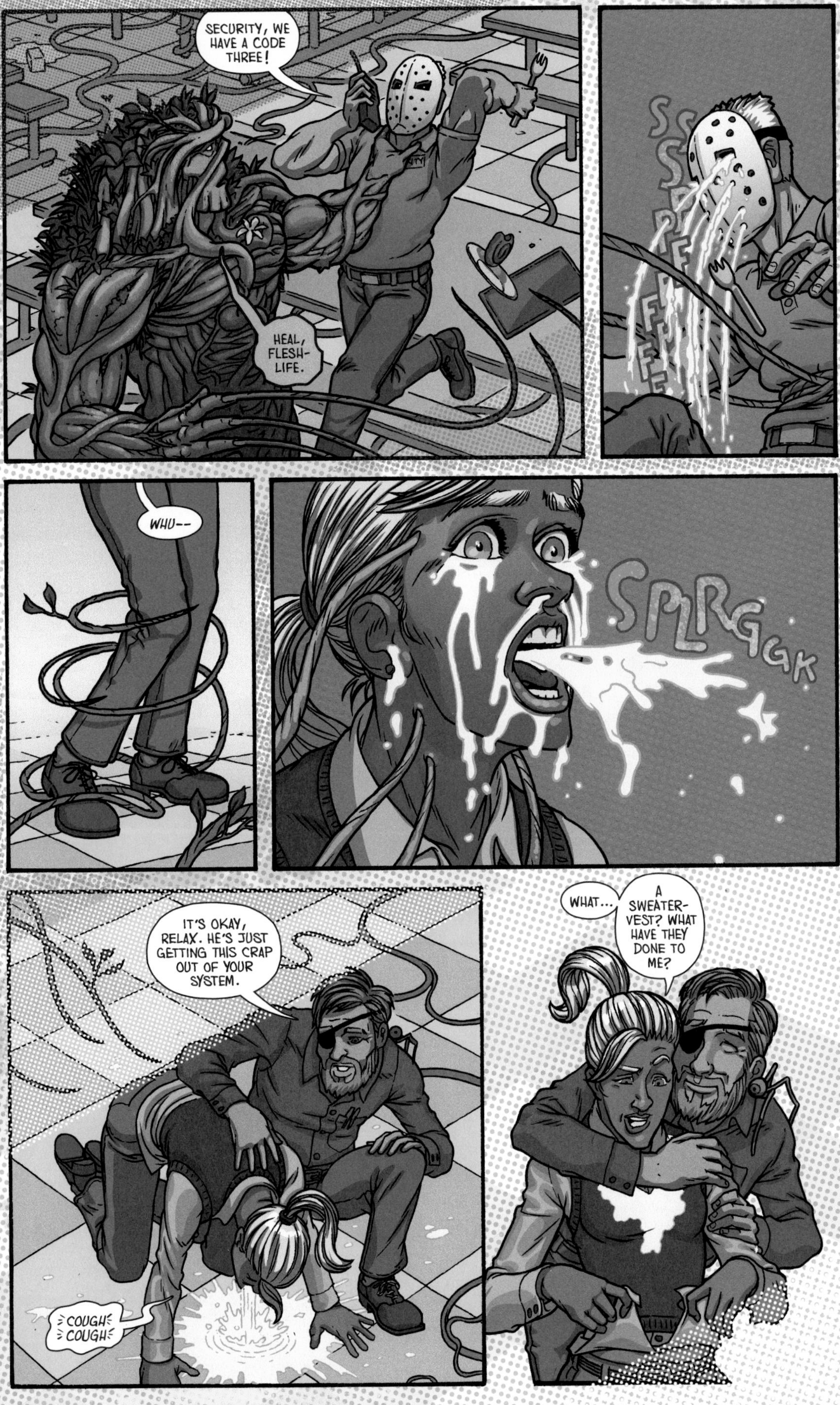
SECURITY, WE HAVE A CODE THREE!
HEAL, FLESH-LIFE.
SSSPRFFFFFF
WHU--
SPLRGGAK
IT'S OKAY, RELAX. HE'S JUST GETTING THIS CRAP OUT OF YOUR SYSTEM.
COUGH COUGH
WHAT...
A SWEATER-VEST? WHAT HAVE THEY DONE TO ME?

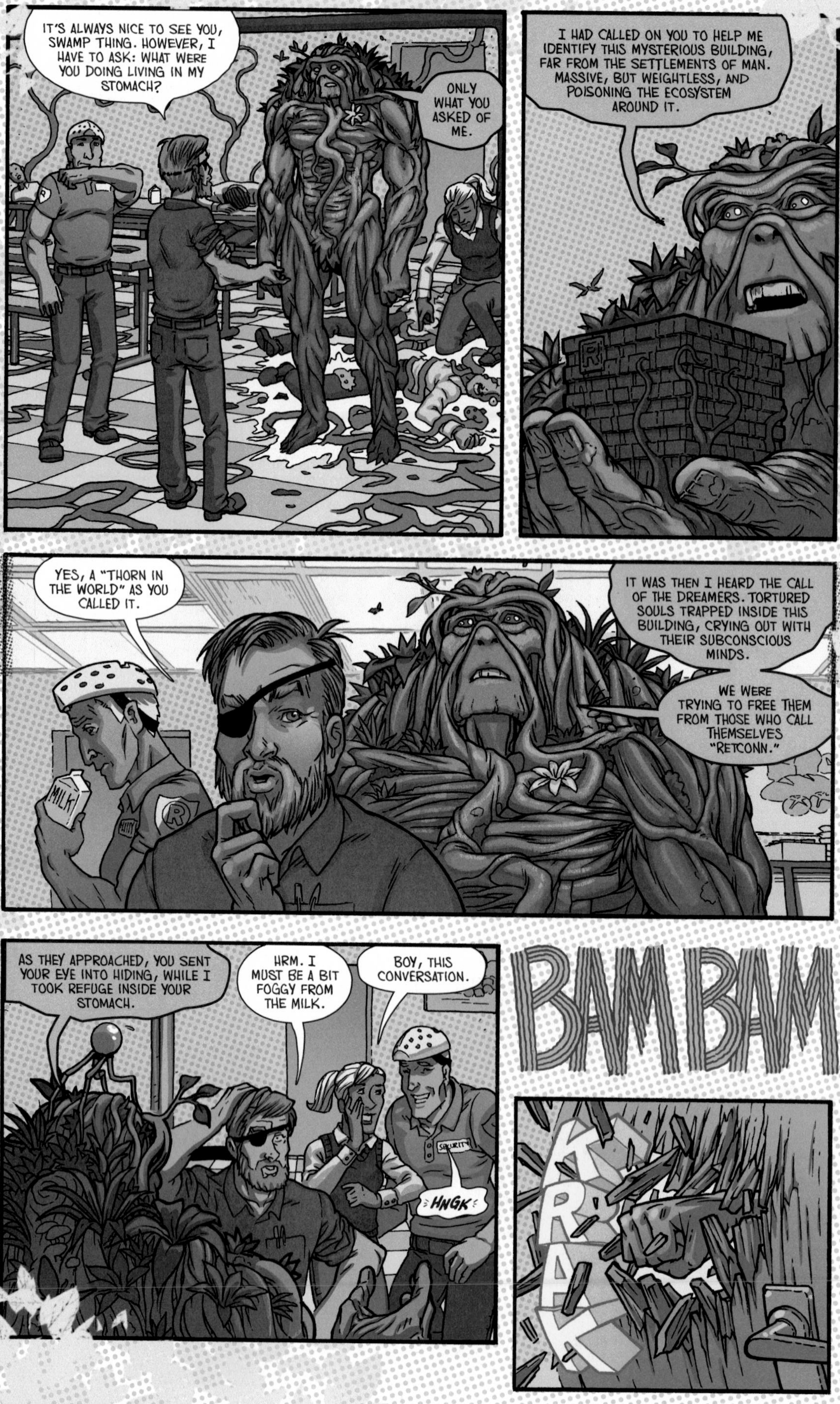
IT'S ALWAYS NICE TO SEE YOU, SWAMP THING. HOWEVER, I HAVE TO ASK: WHAT WERE YOU DOING LIVING IN MY STOMACH?
ONLY WHAT YOU ASKED OF ME.
I HAD CALLED ON YOU TO HELP ME IDENTIFY THIS MYSTERIOUS BUILDING, FAR FROM THE SETTLEMENTS OF MAN. MASSIVE, BUT WEIGHTLESS, AND POISONING THE ECOSYSTEM AROUND IT.
YES, A "THORN IN THE WORLD" AS YOU CALLED IT.
MILK
IT WAS THEN I HEARD THE CALL OF THE DREAMERS. TORTURED SOULS TRAPPED INSIDE THIS BUILDING, CRYING OUT WITH THEIR SUBCONSCIOUS MINDS.
WE WERE TRYING TO FREE THEM FROM THOSE WHO CALL THEMSELVES "RETCONN."
AS THEY APPROACHED, YOU SENT YOUR EYE INTO HIDING, WHILE I TOOK REFUGE INSIDE YOUR STOMACH.
HRM. I MUST BE A BIT FOGGY FROM THE MILK.
BOY, THIS CONVERSATION.
HNGK
BAM BAM
KRAK

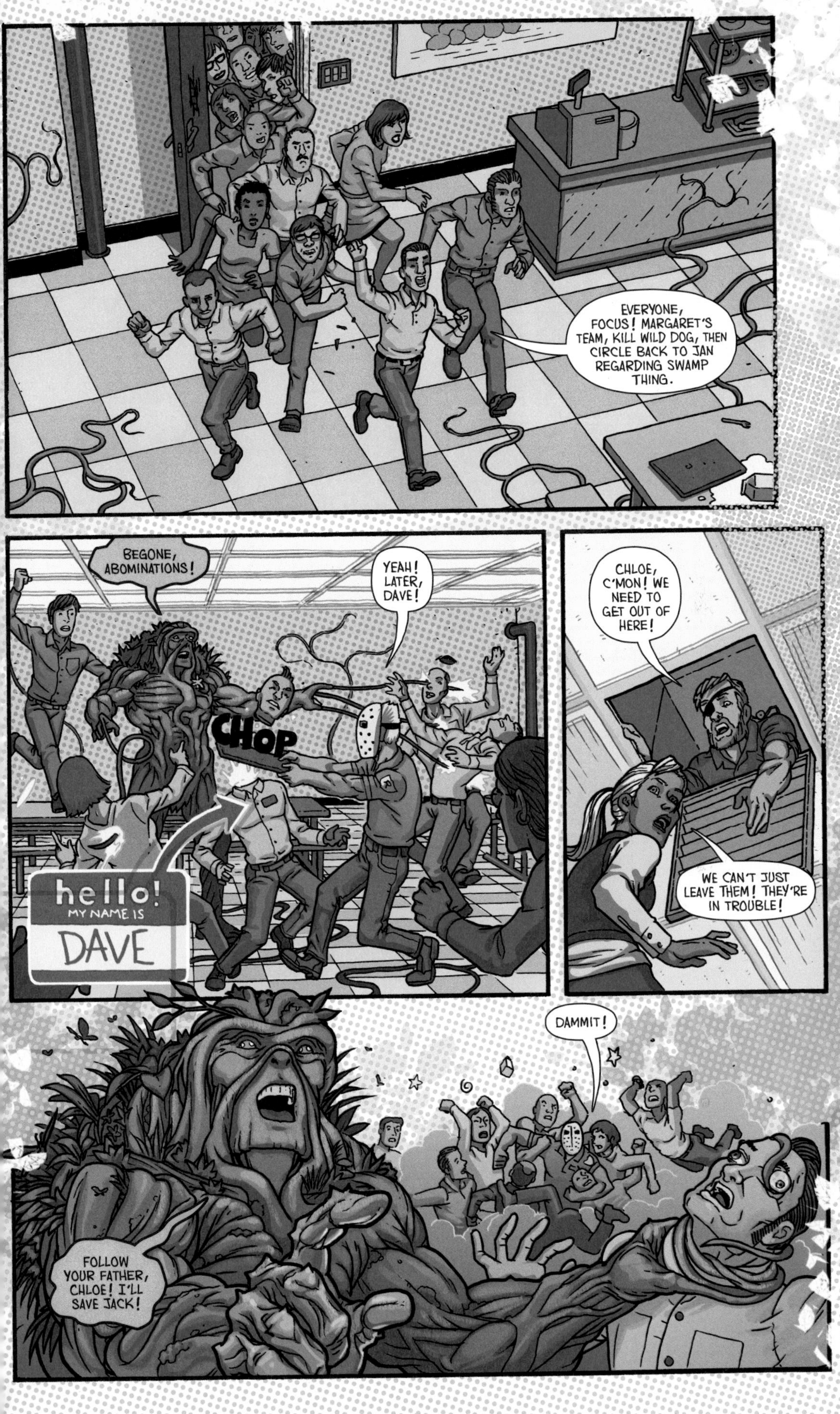
EVERYONE, FOCUS! MARGARET'S TEAM, KILL WILD DOG, THEN CIRCLE BACK TO JAN REGARDING SWAMP THING.
BEGONE, ABOMINATIONS!
YEAH! LATER, DAVE!
CHOP
hello! MY NAME IS
DAVE
CHLOE, C'MON! WE NEED TO GET OUT OF HERE!
WE CAN'T JUST LEAVE THEM! THEY'RE IN TROUBLE!
DAMMIT!
FOLLOW YOUR FATHER, CHLOE! I'LL SAVE JACK!

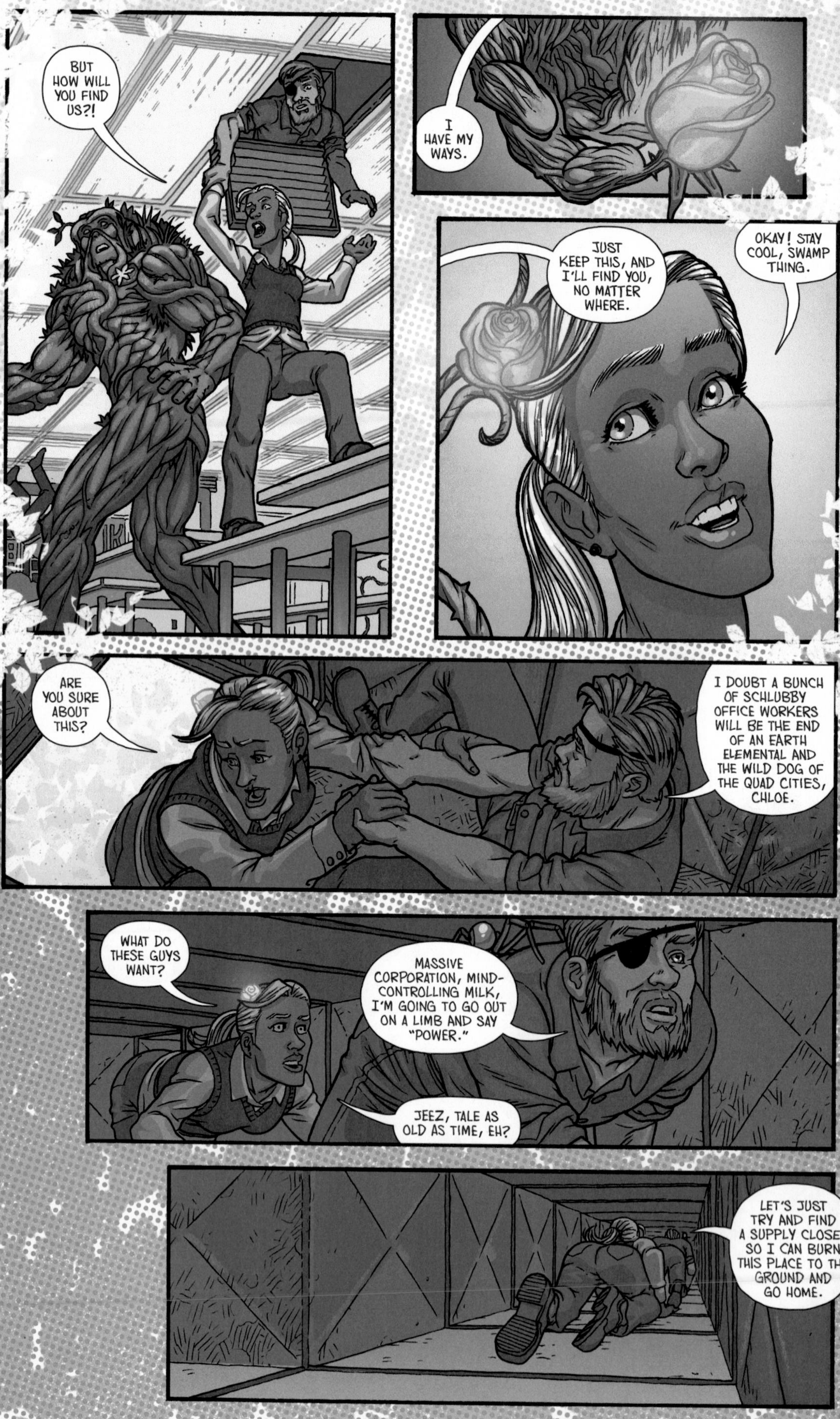
BUT HOW WILL YOU FIND US?!
I HAVE MY WAYS.
JUST KEEP THIS, AND I'LL FIND YOU, NO MATTER WHERE.
OKAY! STAY COOL, SWAMP THING.
ARE YOU SURE ABOUT THIS?
I DOUBT A BUNCH OF SCHLUBBY OFFICE WORKERS WILL BE THE END OF AN EARTH ELEMENTAL AND THE WILD DOG OF THE QUAD CITIES, CHLOE.
WHAT DO THESE GUYS WANT?
MASSIVE CORPORATION, MIND-CONTROLLING MILK, I'M GOING TO GO OUT ON A LIMB AND SAY "POWER."
JEEZ, TALE AS OLD AS TIME, EH?
LET'S JUST TRY AND FIND A SUPPLY CLOSET SO I CAN BURN THIS PLACE TO THE GROUND AND GO HOME.

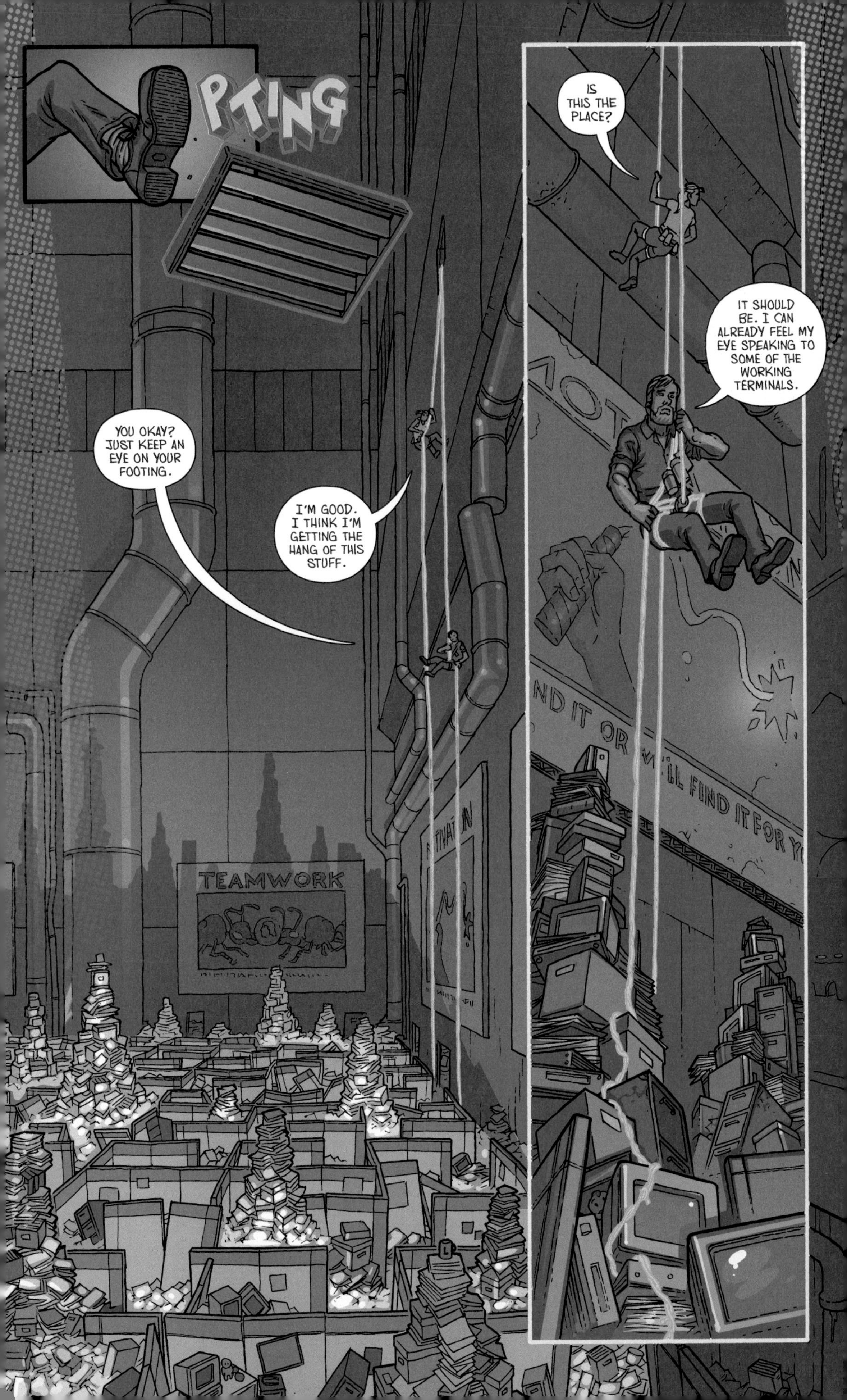
PTING
YOU OKAY? JUST KEEP AN EYE ON YOUR FOOTING.
I'M GOOD. I THINK I'M GETTING THE HANG OF THIS STUFF.
TEAMWORK
IS THIS THE PLACE?
IT SHOULD BE. I CAN ALREADY FEEL MY EYE SPEAKING TO SOME OF THE WORKING TERMINALS.

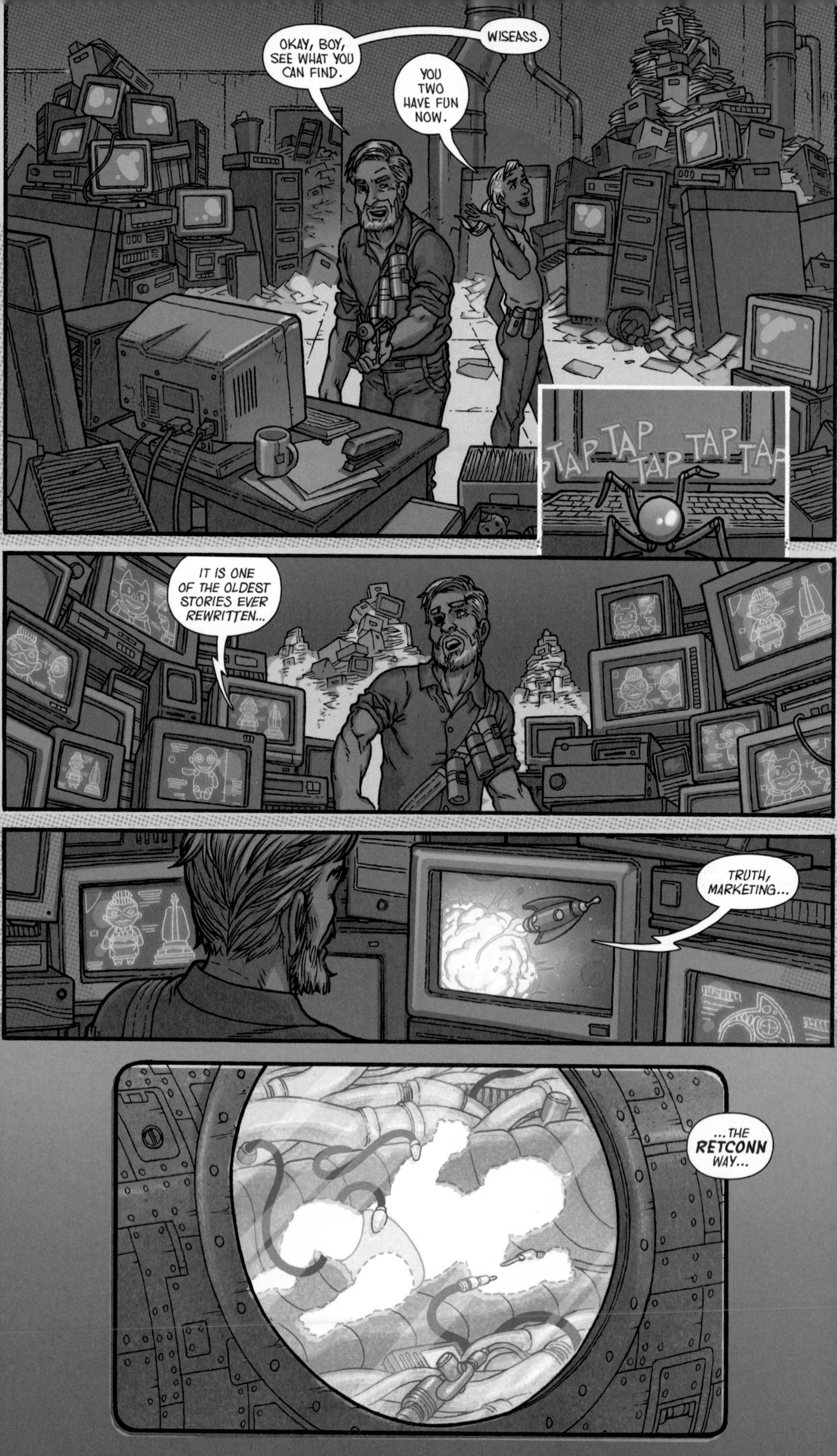
OKAY, BOY, SEE WHAT YOU CAN FIND.
WISEASS.
YOU TWO HAVE FUN NOW.
TAP TAP TAP TAP TAP TAP TAP
IT IS ONE OF THE OLDEST STORIES EVER REWRITTEN...
TRUTH, MARKETING...
...THE RETCONN WAY...

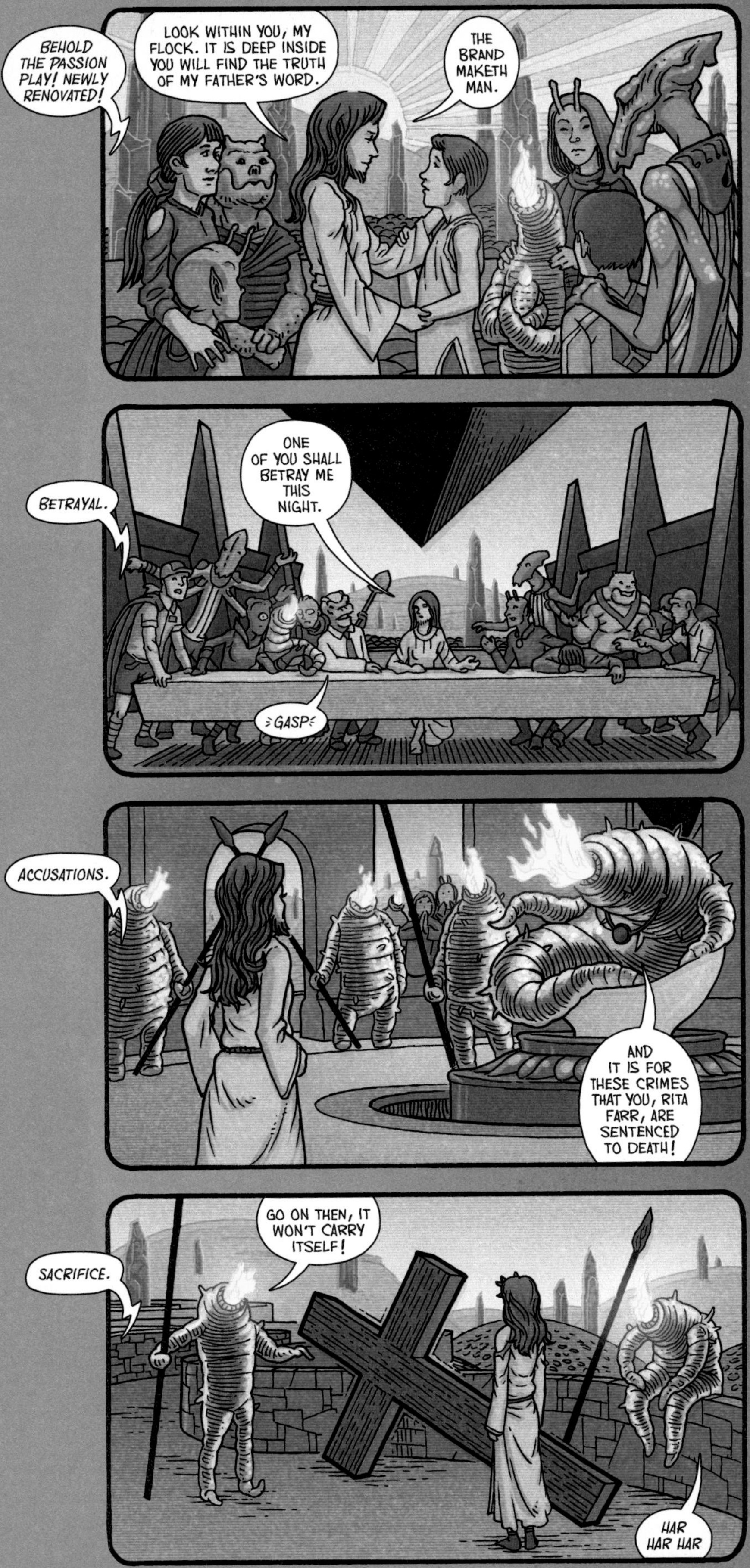
BEHOLD THE PASSION PLAY! NEWLY RENOVATED!
LOOK WITHIN YOU, MY FLOCK. IT IS DEEP INSIDE YOU WILL FIND THE TRUTH OF MY FATHER'S WORD.
THE BRAND MAKETH MAN.
BETRAYAL.
ONE OF YOU SHALL BETRAY ME THIS NIGHT.
GASP
ACCUSATIONS.
AND IT IS FOR THESE CRIMES THAT YOU, RITA FARR, ARE SENTENCED TO DEATH!
SACRIFICE.
GO ON THEN, IT WON'T CARRY ITSELF!
HAR HAR HAR

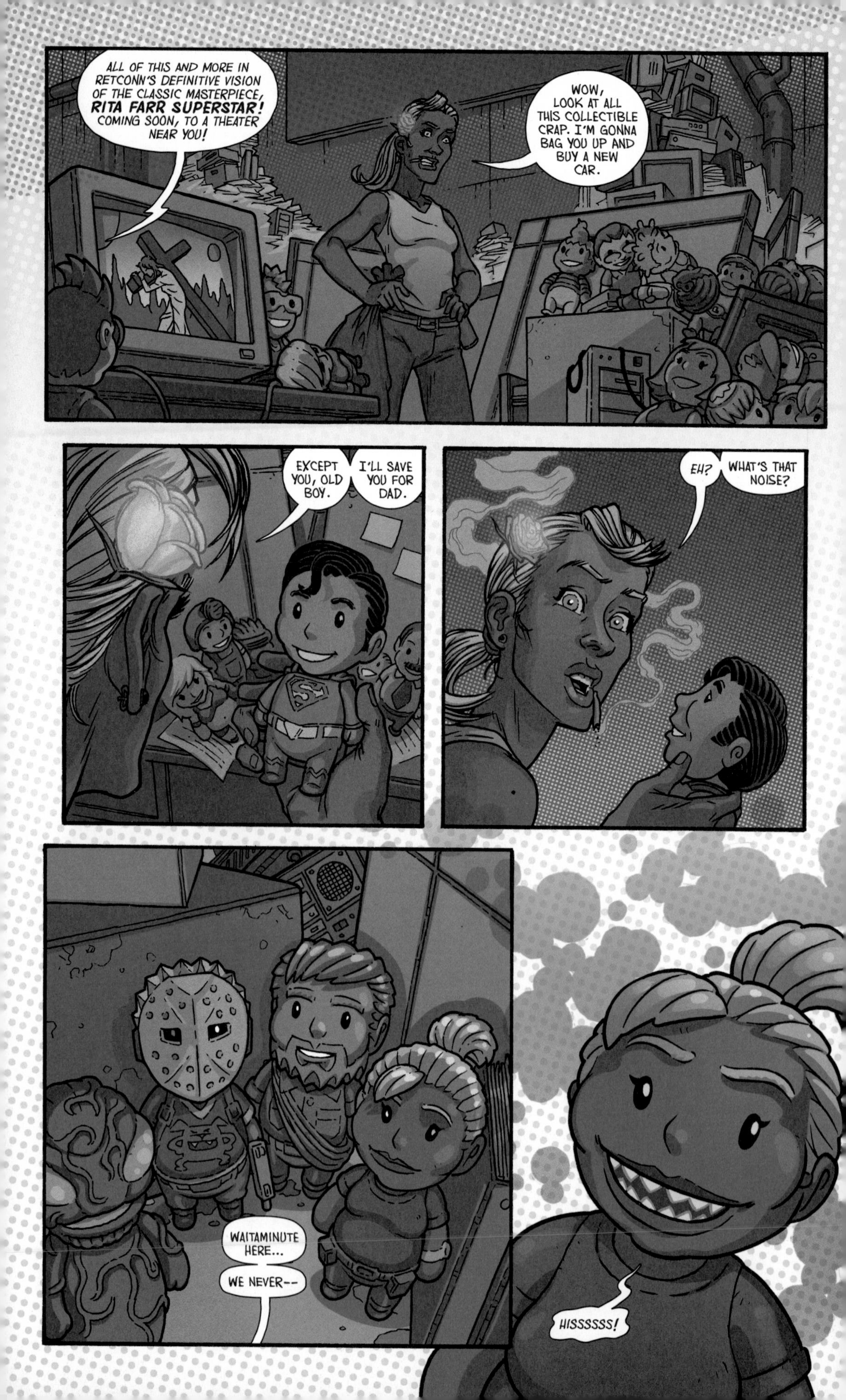
ALL OF THIS AND MORE IN RETCONN'S DEFINITIVE VISION OF THE CLASSIC MASTERPIECE, **RITA FARR SUPERSTAR!** COMING SOON, TO A THEATER NEAR YOU!
WOW, LOOK AT ALL THIS COLLECTIBLE CRAP. I'M GONNA BAG YOU UP AND BUY A NEW CAR.
EXCEPT YOU, OLD BOY.
I'LL SAVE YOU FOR DAD.
EH?
WHAT'S THAT NOISE?
WAITAMINUTE HERE...
WE NEVER--
HISSSSSS!

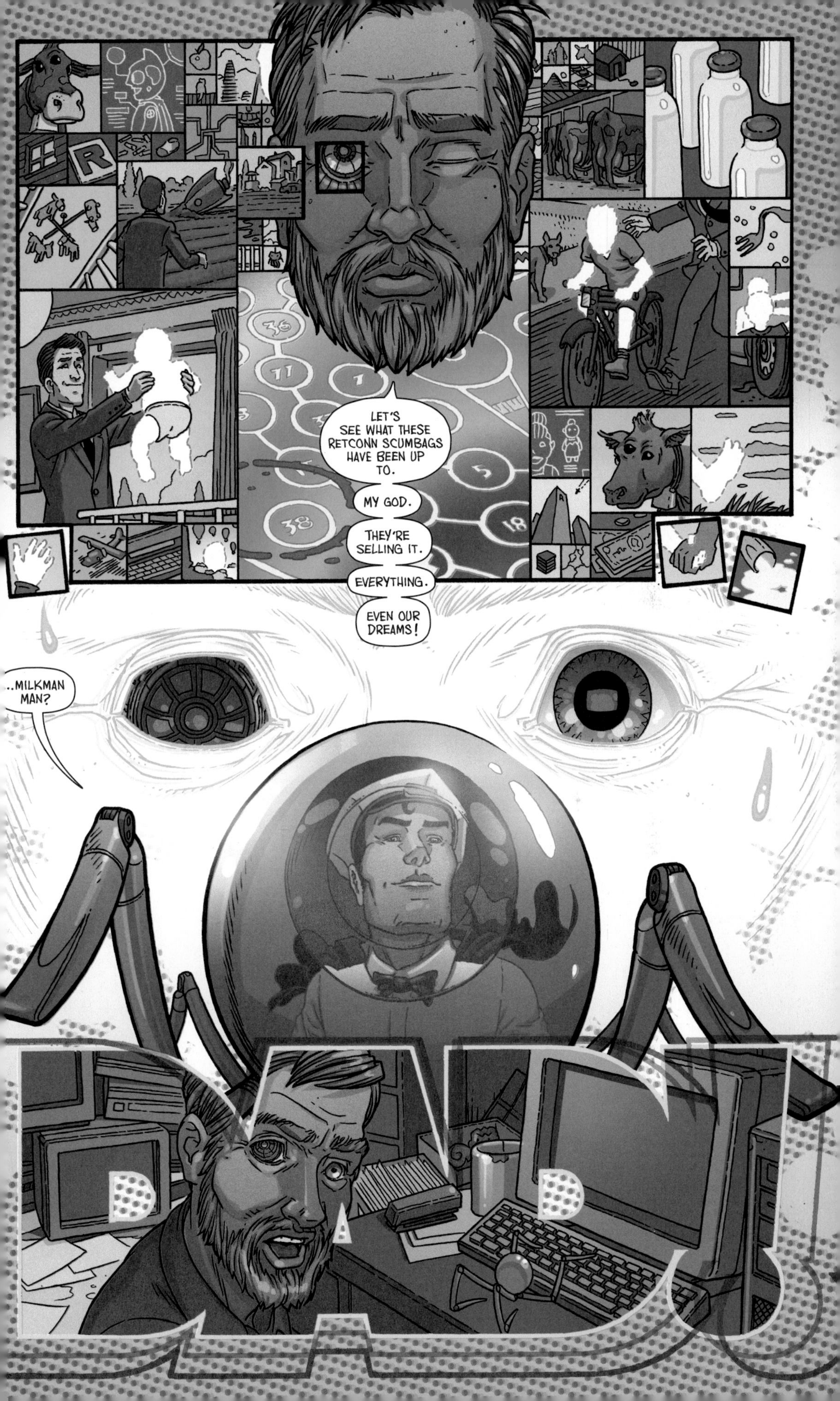
LET'S SEE WHAT THESE RETCONN SCUMBAGS HAVE BEEN UP TO.
MY GOD.
THEY'RE SELLING IT.
EVERYTHING.
EVEN OUR DREAMS!
..MILKMAN MAN?
DAD

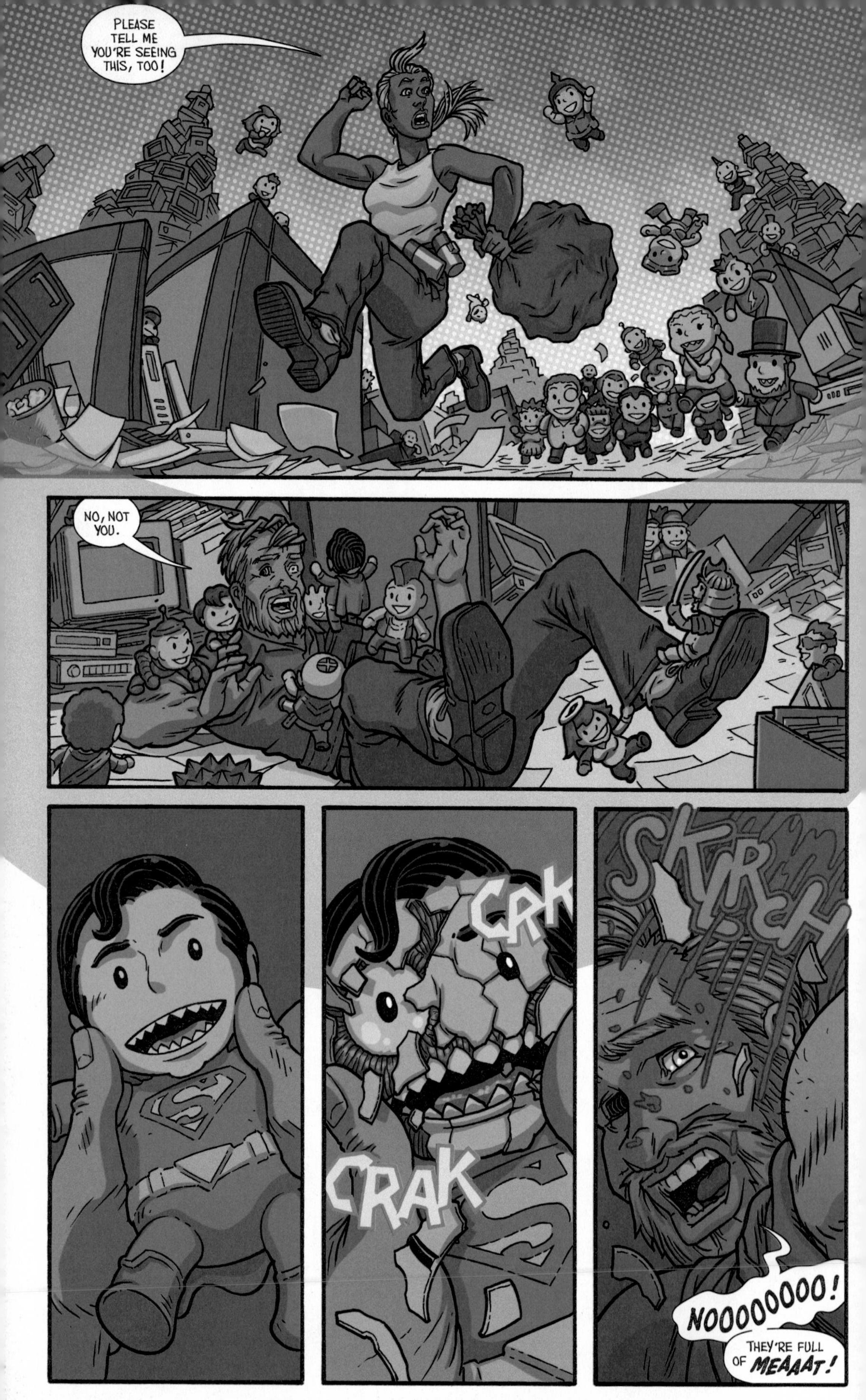
PLEASE TELL ME YOU'RE SEEING THIS, TOO!
NO, NOT YOU.
CRK
CRAK
SKYRCH
NOOOOOOOO!
THEY'RE FULL OF MEAAAT!

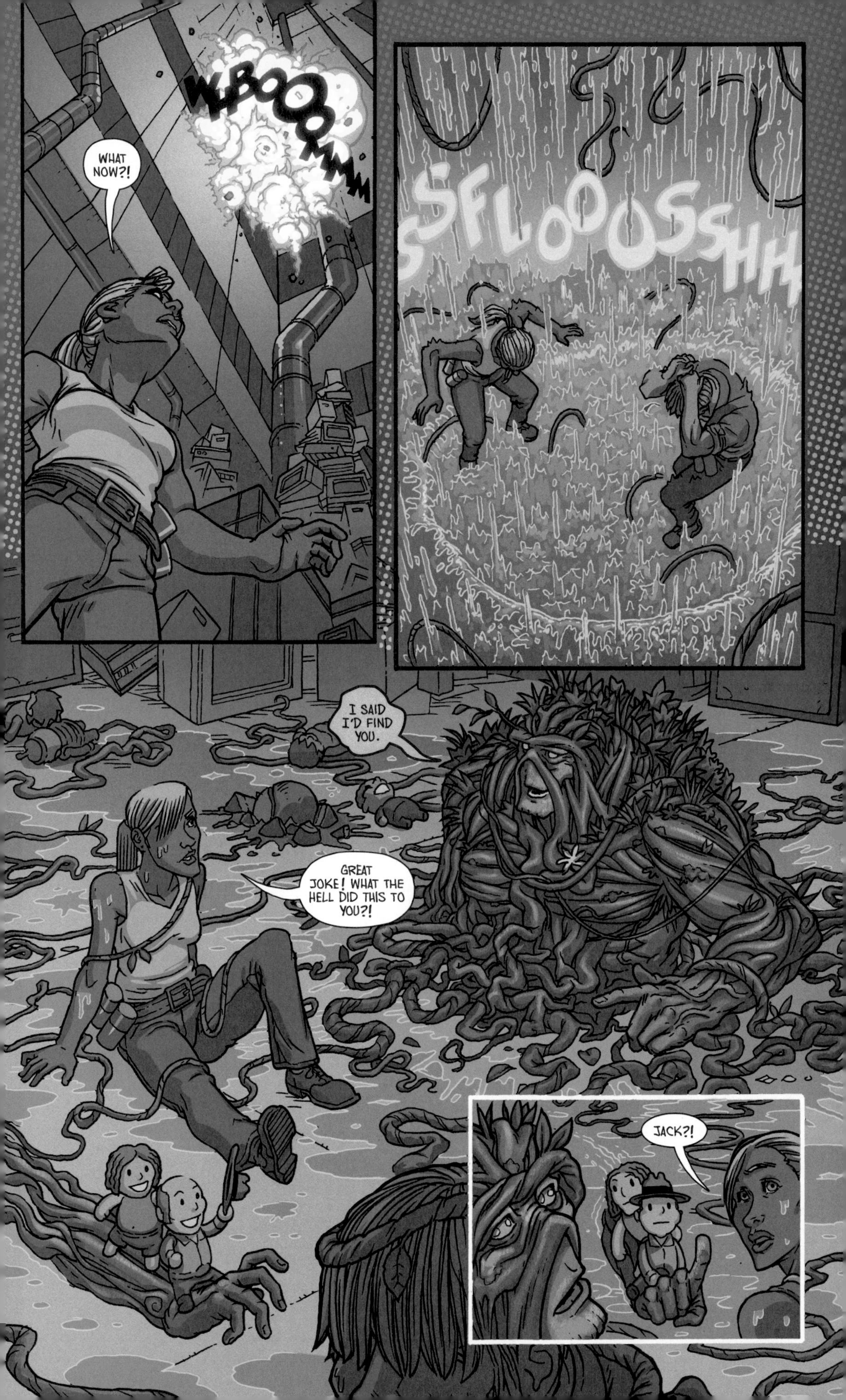
WHAT NOW?!
WBOOOMMM
SFLOOOSSHH
I SAID I'D FIND YOU.
GREAT JOKE! WHAT THE HELL DID THIS TO YOU?!
JACK?!

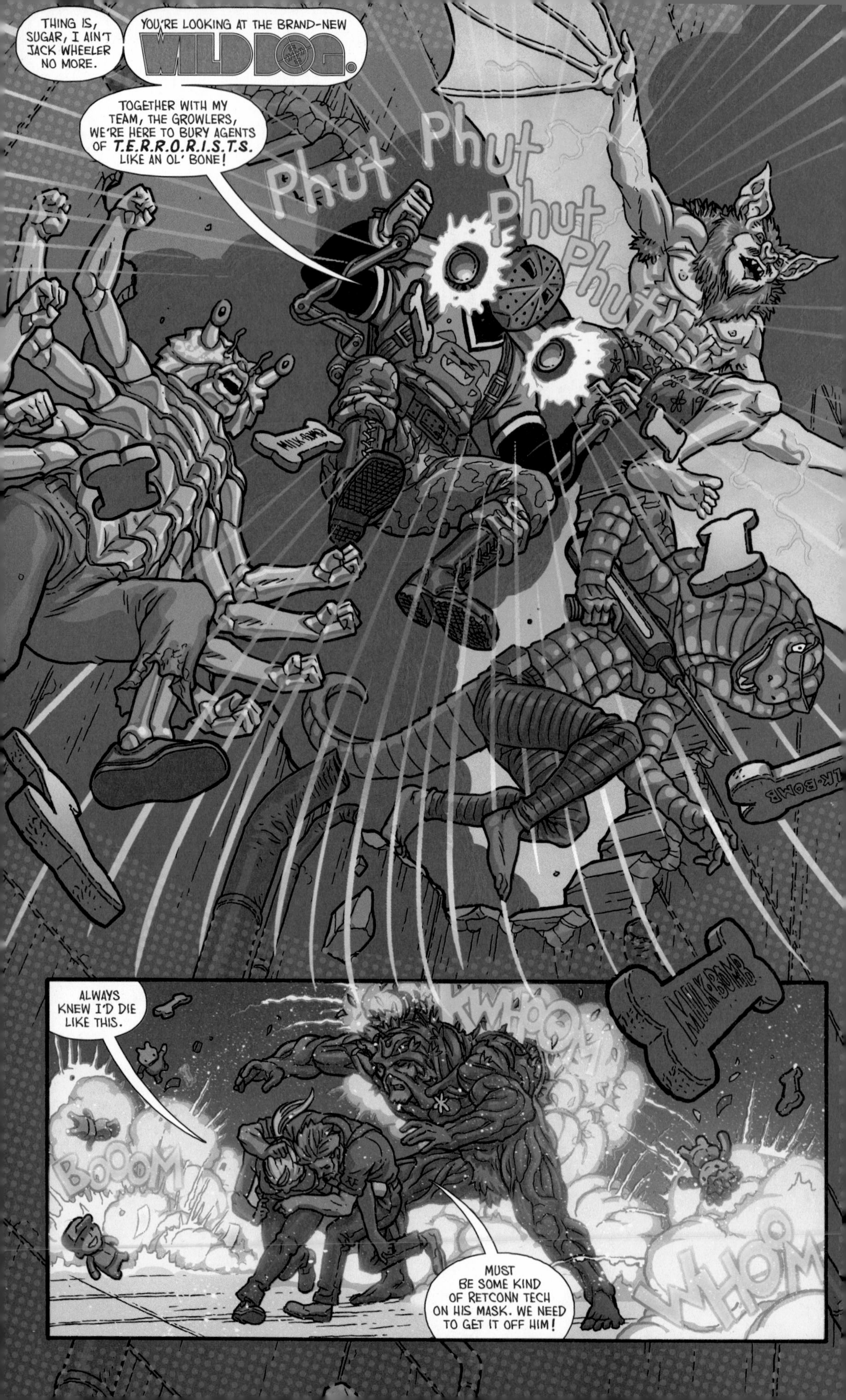
THING IS, SUGAR, I AIN'T JACK WHEELER NO MORE.
YOU'RE LOOKING AT THE BRAND-NEW
WILD DOG.
TOGETHER WITH MY TEAM, THE GROWLERS, WE'RE HERE TO BURY AGENTS OF T.E.R.R.O.R.I.S.T.S. LIKE AN OL' BONE!
Phut Phut Phut Phut
MILK-BOMB
ALWAYS KNEW I'D DIE LIKE THIS.
BOOOM
MUST BE SOME KIND OF RETCONN TECH ON HIS MASK. WE NEED TO GET IT OFF HIM!
WHOOOM

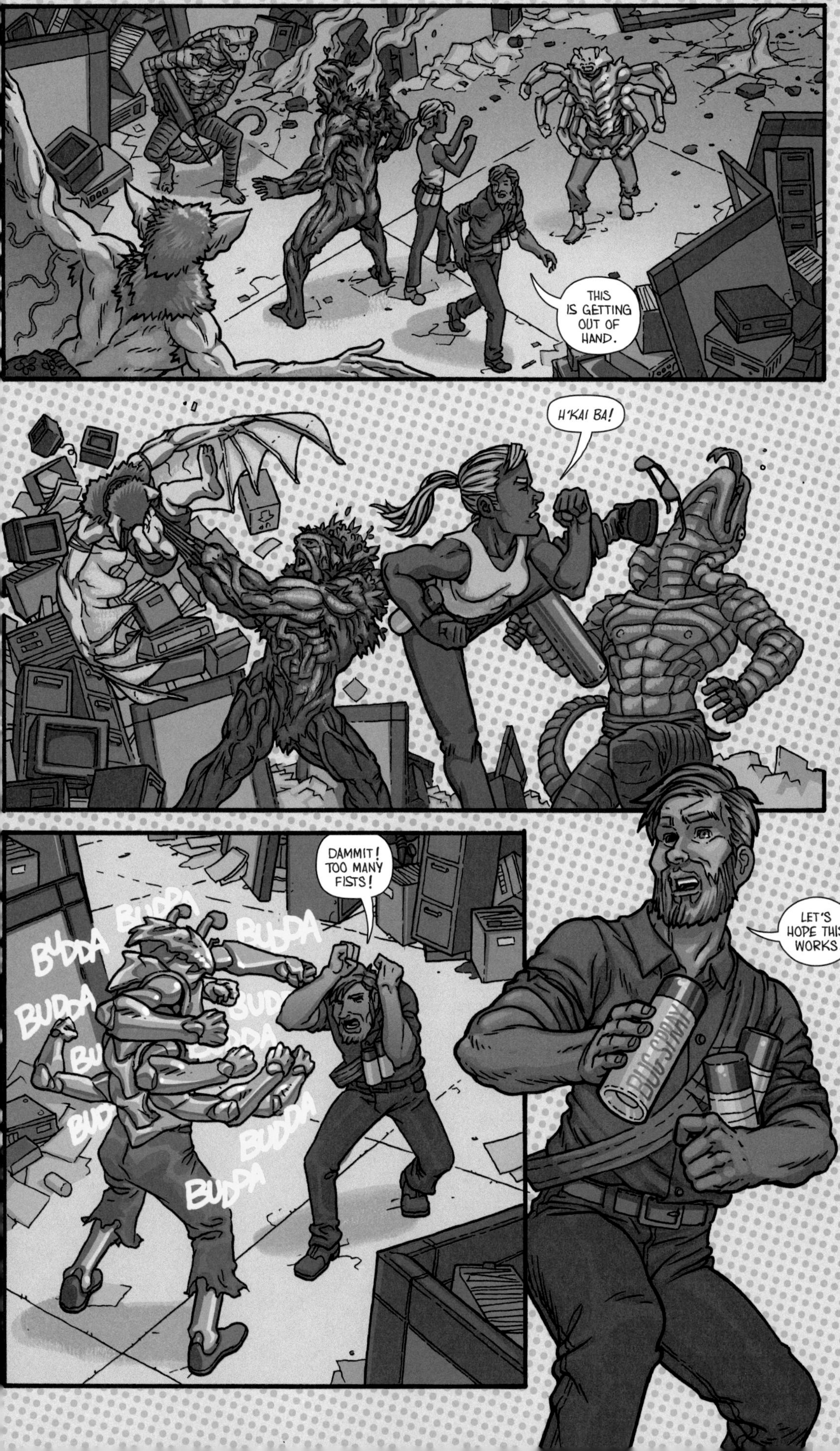
THIS IS GETTING OUT OF HAND.
H'KAI BA!
DAMMIT! TOO MANY FISTS!
BUDDA
BUDDA
BUDDA
BUDDA
BUDDA
BUDDA
LET'S HOPE THIS WORKS.
BUG SPRAY

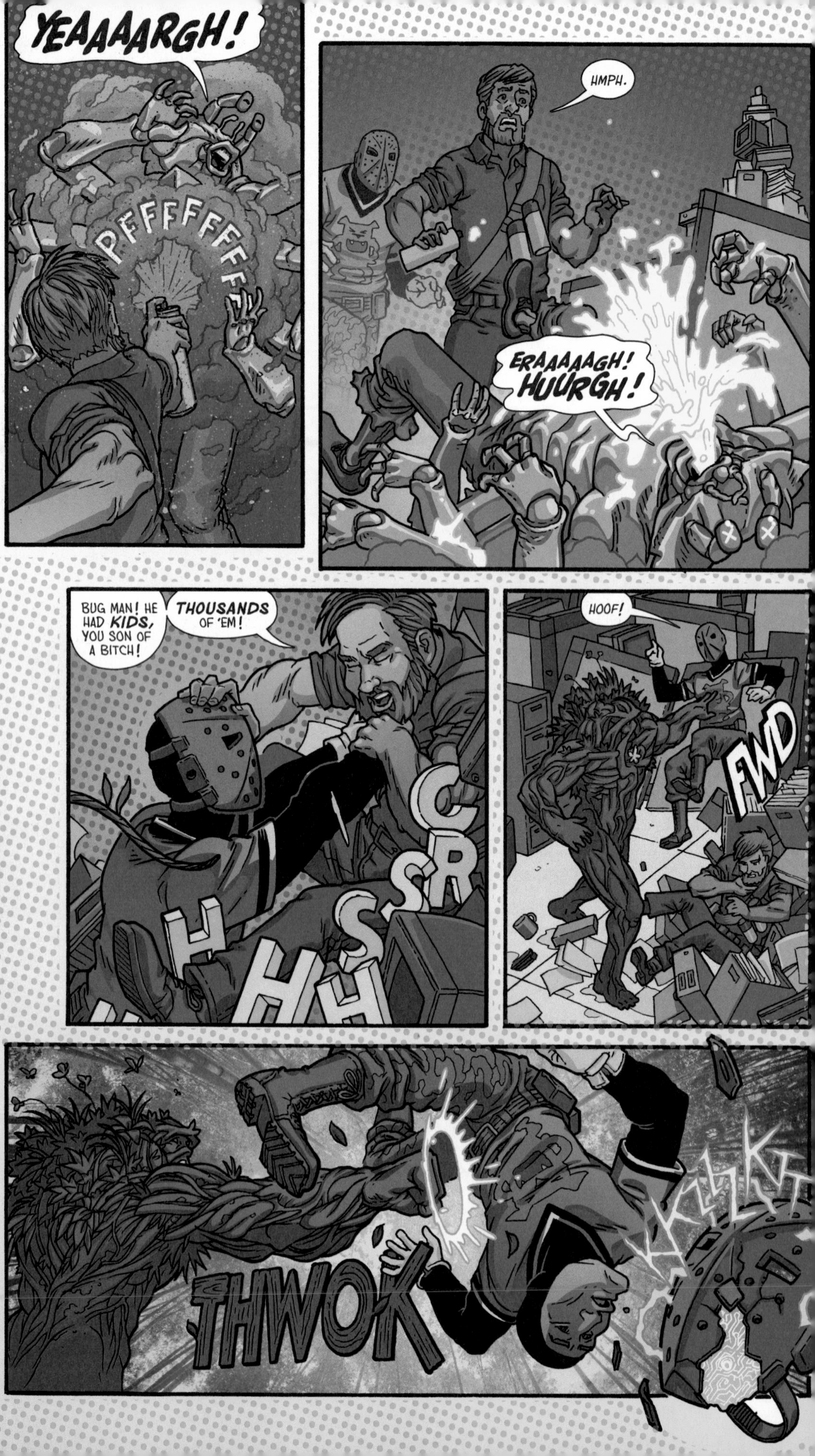
YEAAAARGH!
PFFFFFFFFFF
HMPH.
ERAAAAAGH! HUURGH!
BUG MAN! HE HAD KIDS, YOU SON OF A BITCH!
THOUSANDS OF 'EM!
CRSSHHHH
HOOF!
FWD
THWOK
KKZZKT

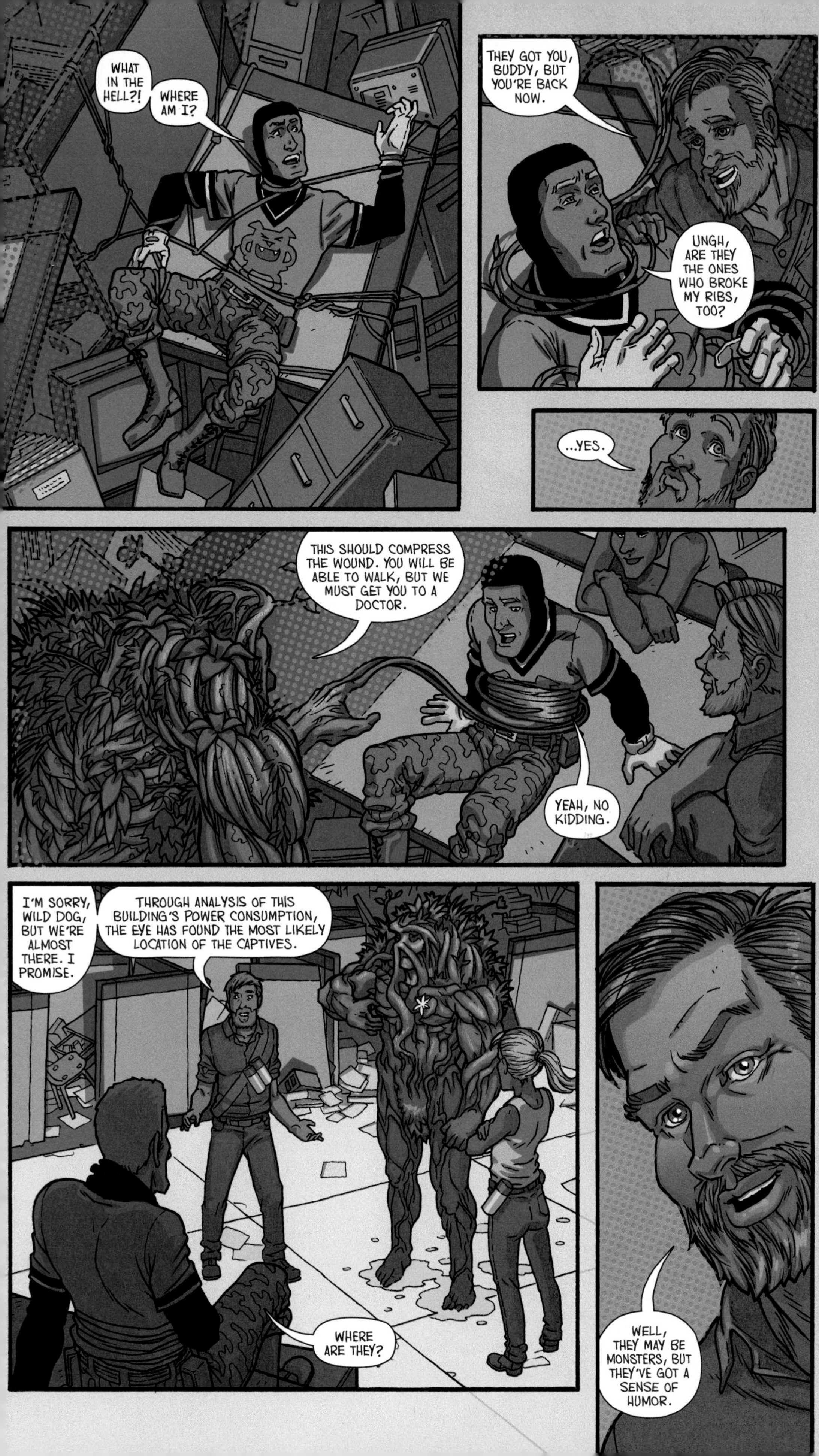
WHAT IN THE HELL?!
WHERE AM I?
THEY GOT YOU, BUDDY, BUT YOU'RE BACK NOW.
UNGH, ARE THEY THE ONES WHO BROKE MY RIBS, TOO?
...YES.
THIS SHOULD COMPRESS THE WOUND. YOU WILL BE ABLE TO WALK, BUT WE MUST GET YOU TO A DOCTOR.
YEAH, NO KIDDING.
I'M SORRY, WILD DOG, BUT WE'RE ALMOST THERE. I PROMISE.
THROUGH ANALYSIS OF THIS BUILDING'S POWER CONSUMPTION, THE EYE HAS FOUND THE MOST LIKELY LOCATION OF THE CAPTIVES.
WHERE ARE THEY?
WELL, THEY MAY BE MONSTERS, BUT THEY'VE GOT A SENSE OF HUMOR.

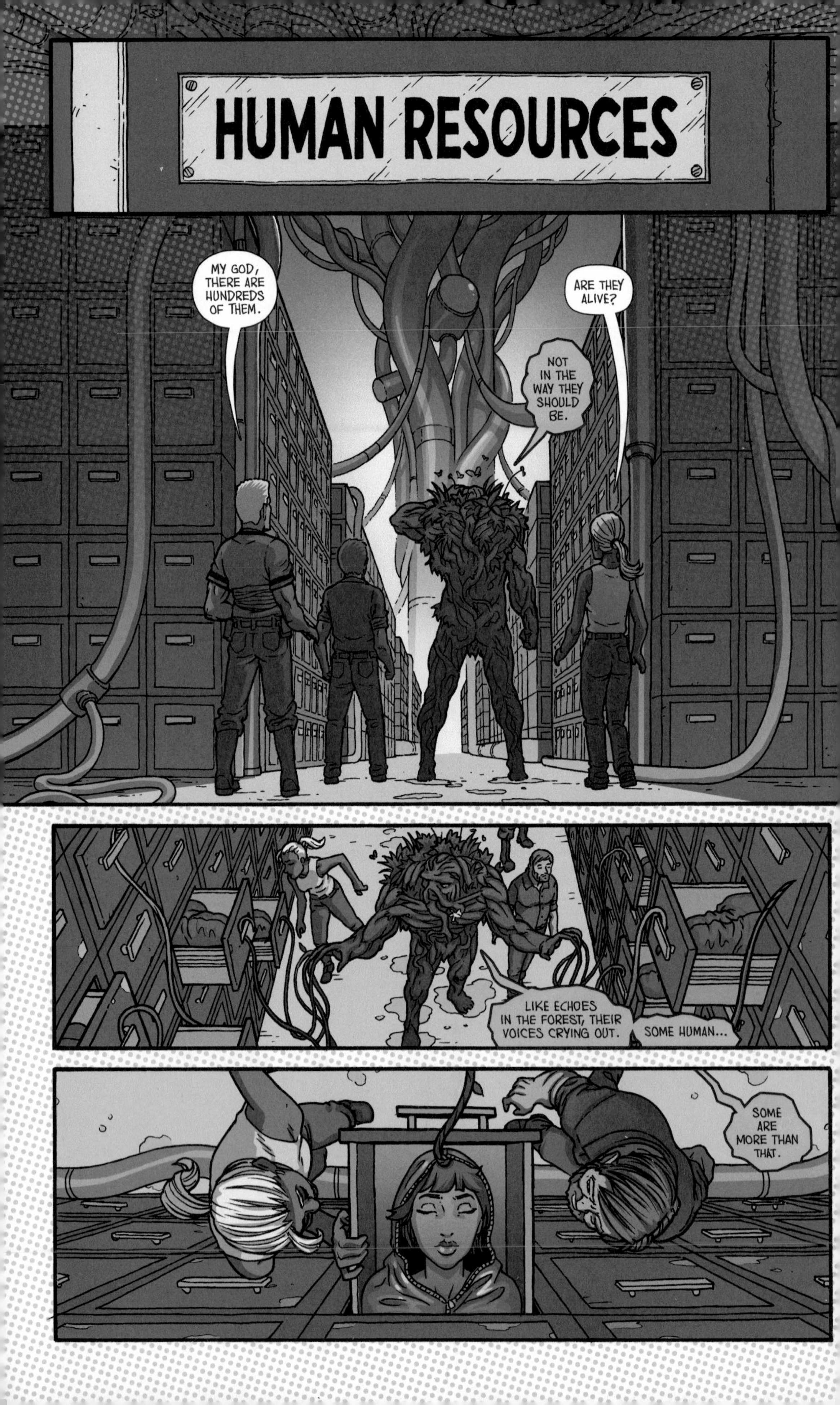
HUMAN RESOURCES
MY GOD, THERE ARE HUNDREDS OF THEM.
ARE THEY ALIVE?
NOT IN THE WAY THEY SHOULD BE.
LIKE ECHOES IN THE FOREST, THEIR VOICES CRYING OUT.
SOME HUMAN...
SOME ARE MORE THAN THAT.

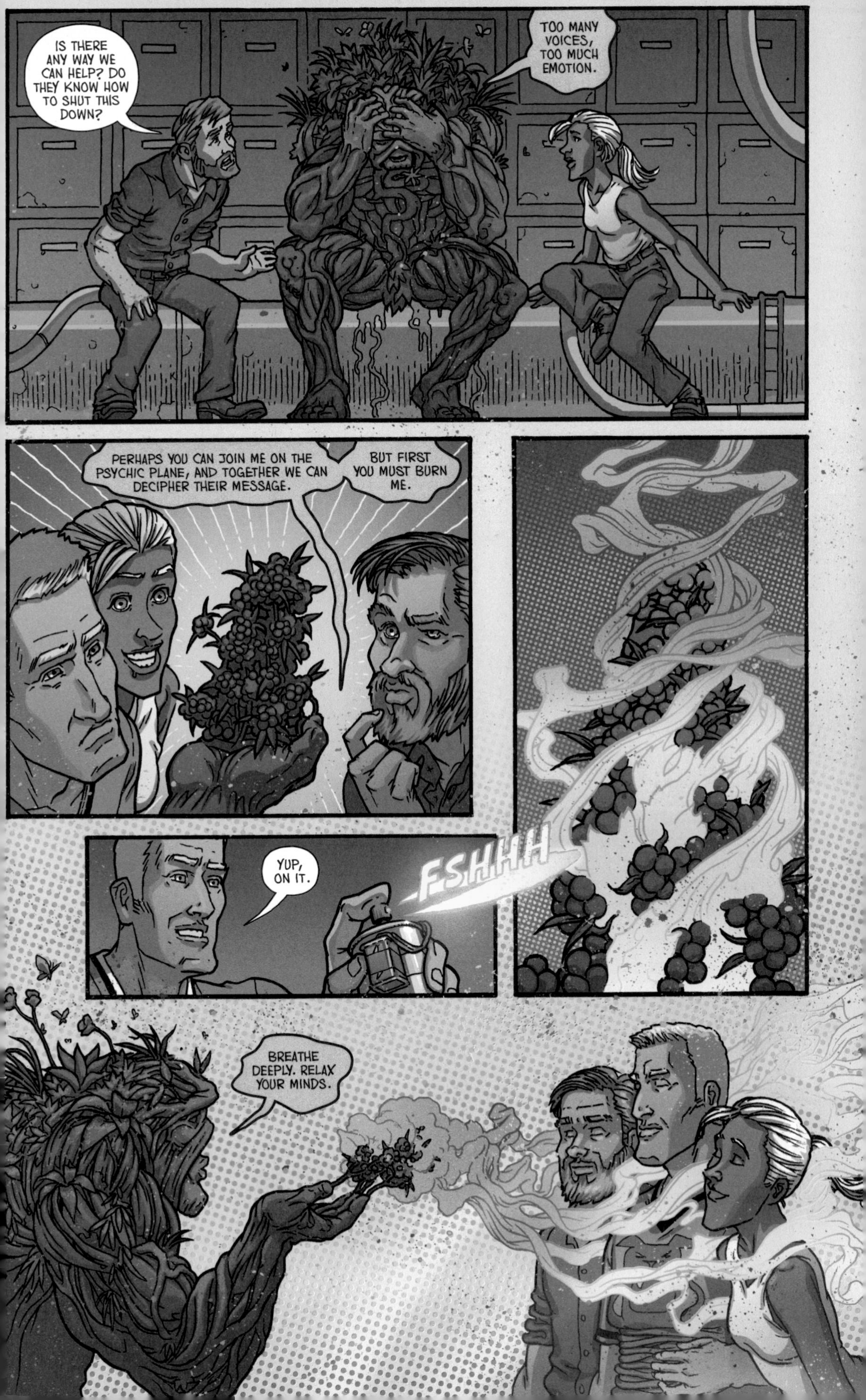

IS THERE ANY WAY WE CAN HELP? DO THEY KNOW HOW TO SHUT THIS DOWN?
TOO MANY VOICES, TOO MUCH EMOTION.
PERHAPS YOU CAN JOIN ME ON THE PSYCHIC PLANE, AND TOGETHER WE CAN DECIPHER THEIR MESSAGE.
BUT FIRST YOU MUST BURN ME.
YUP, ON IT.
FSHHH
BREATHE DEEPLY. RELAX YOUR MINDS.

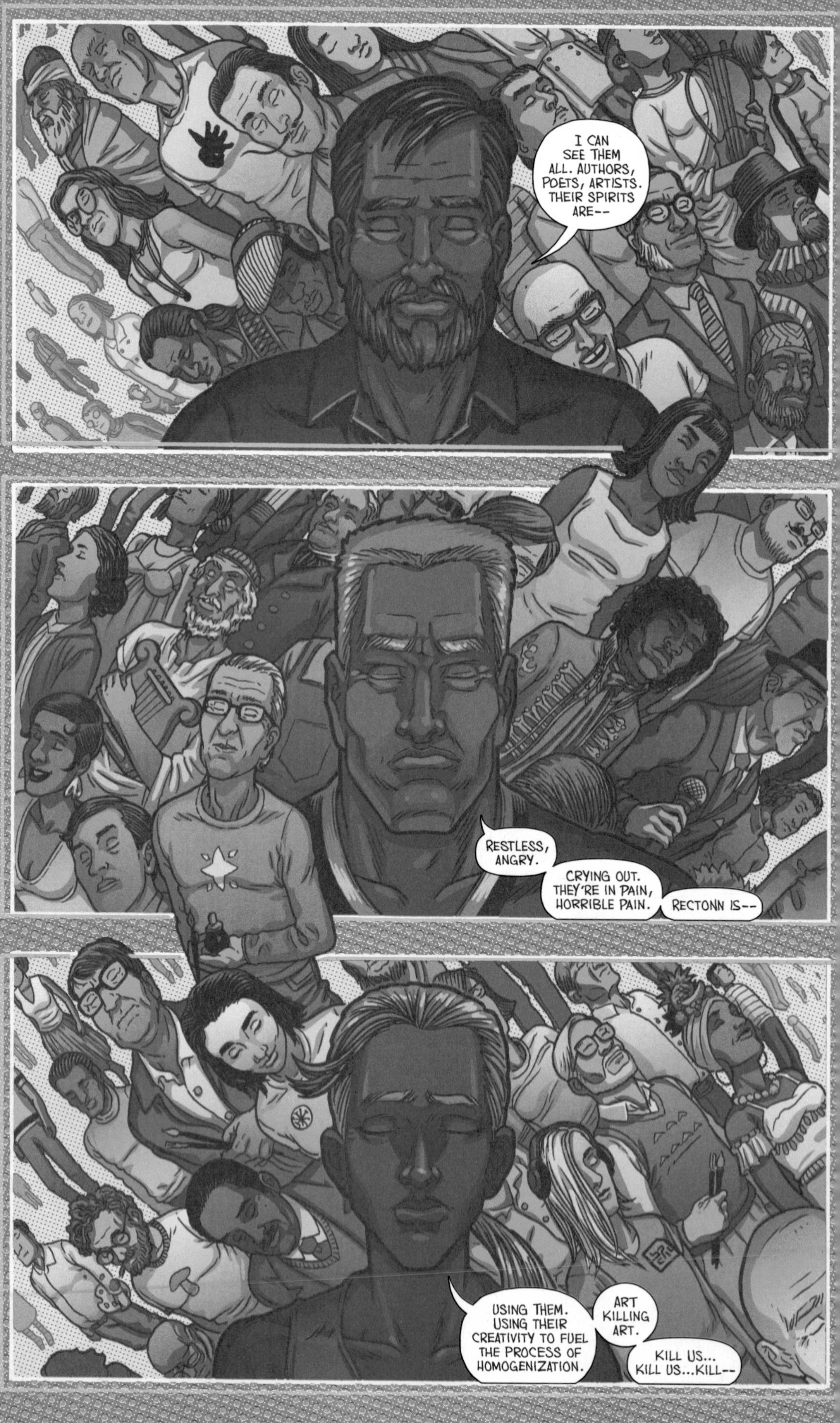
I CAN SEE THEM ALL. AUTHORS, POETS, ARTISTS. THEIR SPIRITS ARE--
RESTLESS, ANGRY.
CRYING OUT. THEY'RE IN PAIN, HORRIBLE PAIN.
RECTONN IS--
USING THEM. USING THEIR CREATIVITY TO FUEL THE PROCESS OF HOMOGENIZATION.
ART KILLING ART.
KILL US... KILL US...KILL--

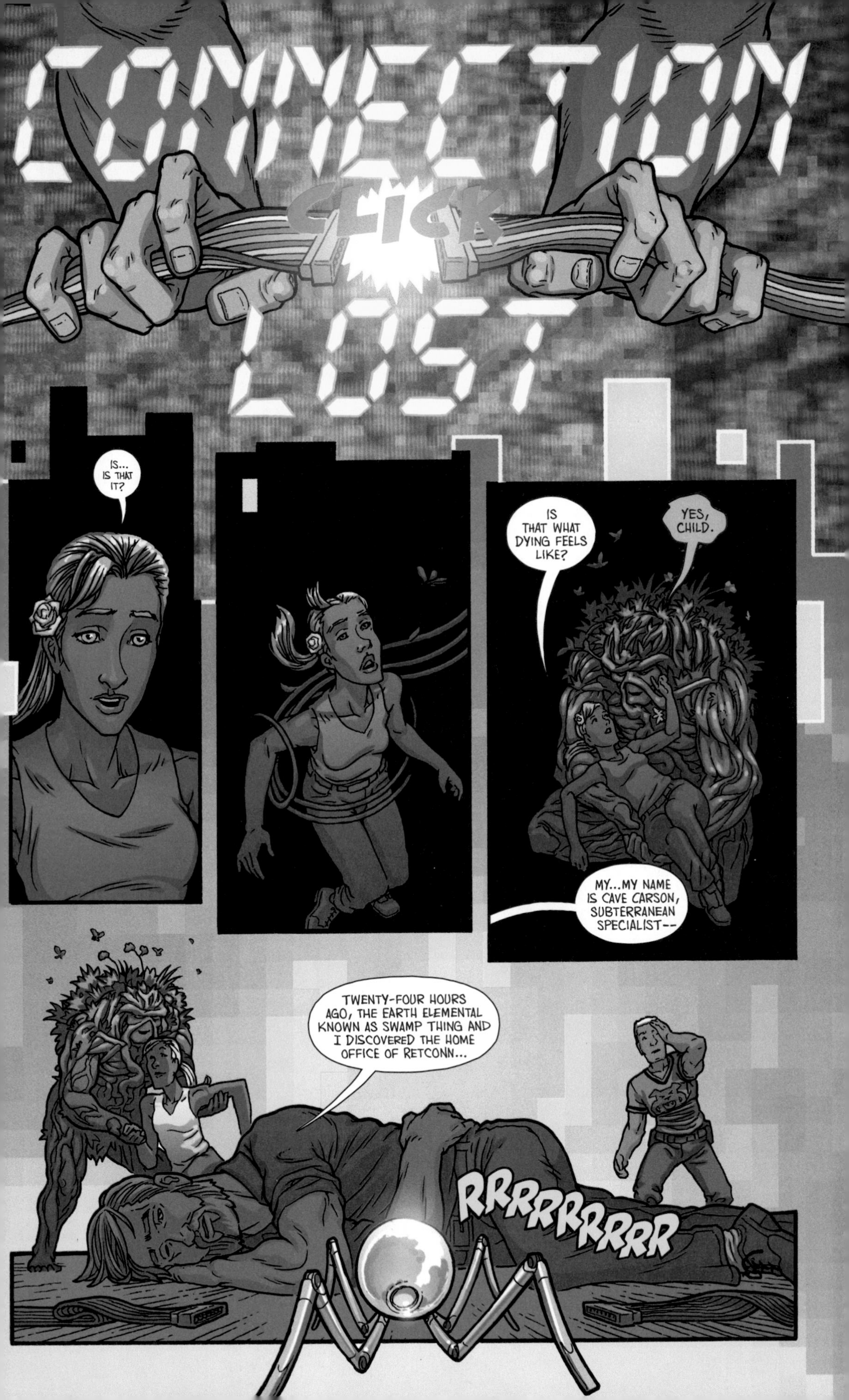
CONNECTION
CLICK
LOST
IS... IS THAT IT?
IS THAT WHAT DYING FEELS LIKE?
YES, CHILD.
MY...MY NAME IS CAVE CARSON, SUBTERRANEAN SPECIALIST--
TWENTY-FOUR HOURS AGO, THE EARTH ELEMENTAL KNOWN AS SWAMP THING AND I DISCOVERED THE HOME OFFICE OF RETCONN...
RRRRRRRRRR

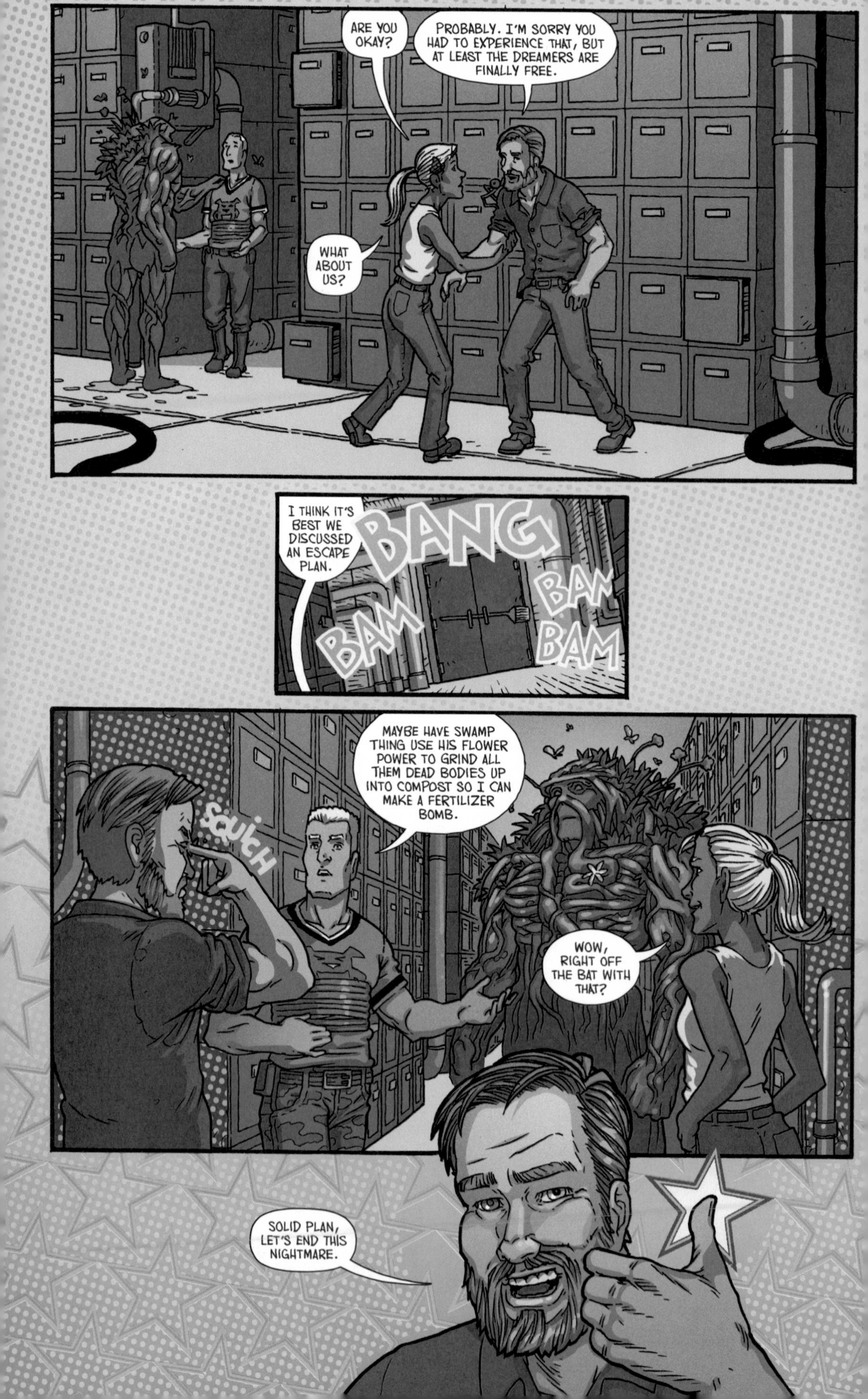
ARE YOU OKAY?
PROBABLY. I'M SORRY YOU HAD TO EXPERIENCE THAT, BUT AT LEAST THE DREAMERS ARE FINALLY FREE.
WHAT ABOUT US?
I THINK IT'S BEST WE DISCUSSED AN ESCAPE PLAN.
BANG
BAM
BAM
BAM
MAYBE HAVE SWAMP THING USE HIS FLOWER POWER TO GRIND ALL THEM DEAD BODIES UP INTO COMPOST SO I CAN MAKE A FERTILIZER BOMB.
SQUICH
WOW, RIGHT OFF THE BAT WITH THAT?
SOLID PLAN, LET'S END THIS NIGHTMARE.

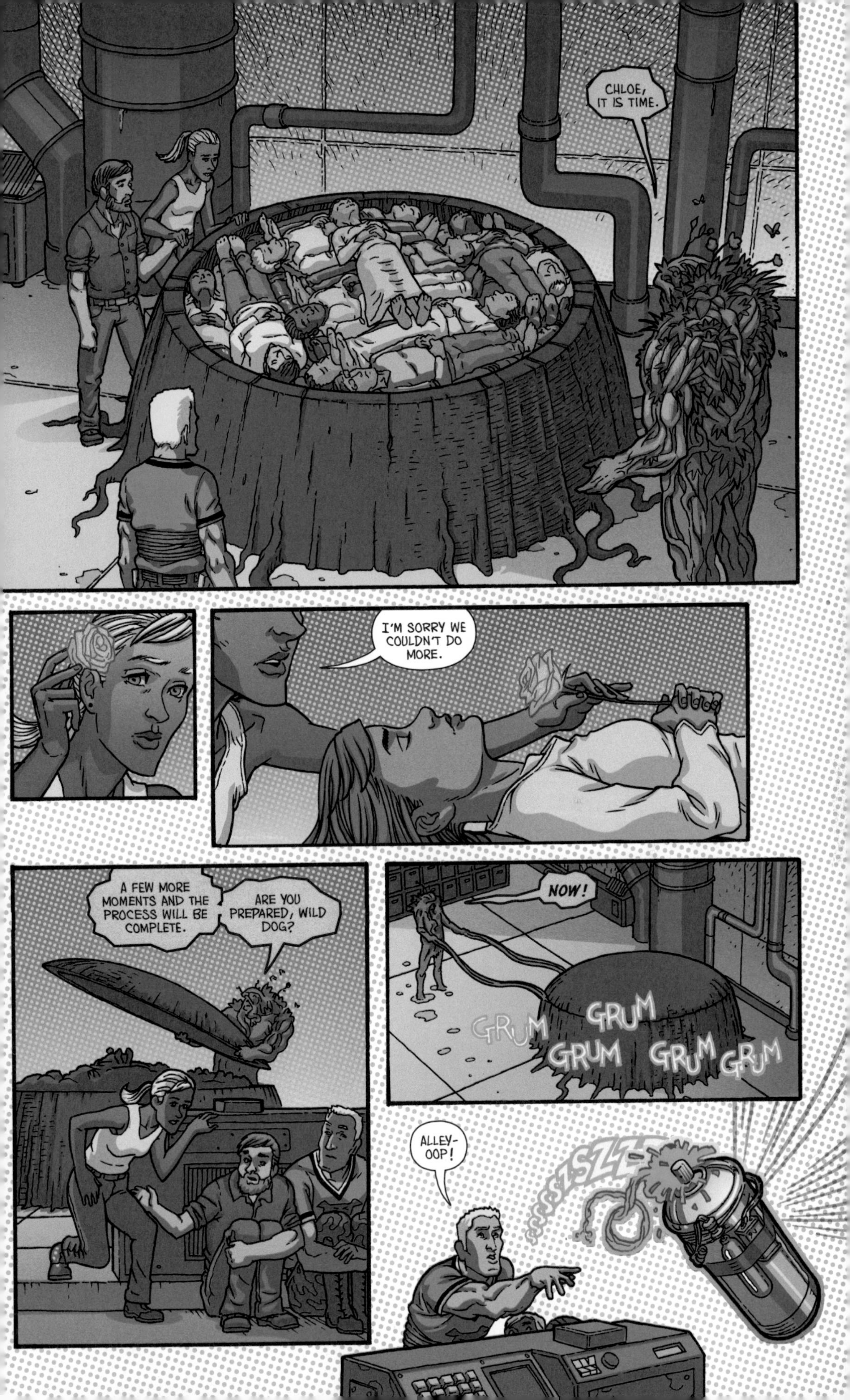
CHLOE, IT IS TIME.
I'M SORRY WE COULDN'T DO MORE.
A FEW MORE MOMENTS AND THE PROCESS WILL BE COMPLETE.
ARE YOU PREPARED, WILD DOG?
NOW!
GRUM GRUM GRUM GRUM GRUM
ALLEY-OOP!
SSSSSZZZ

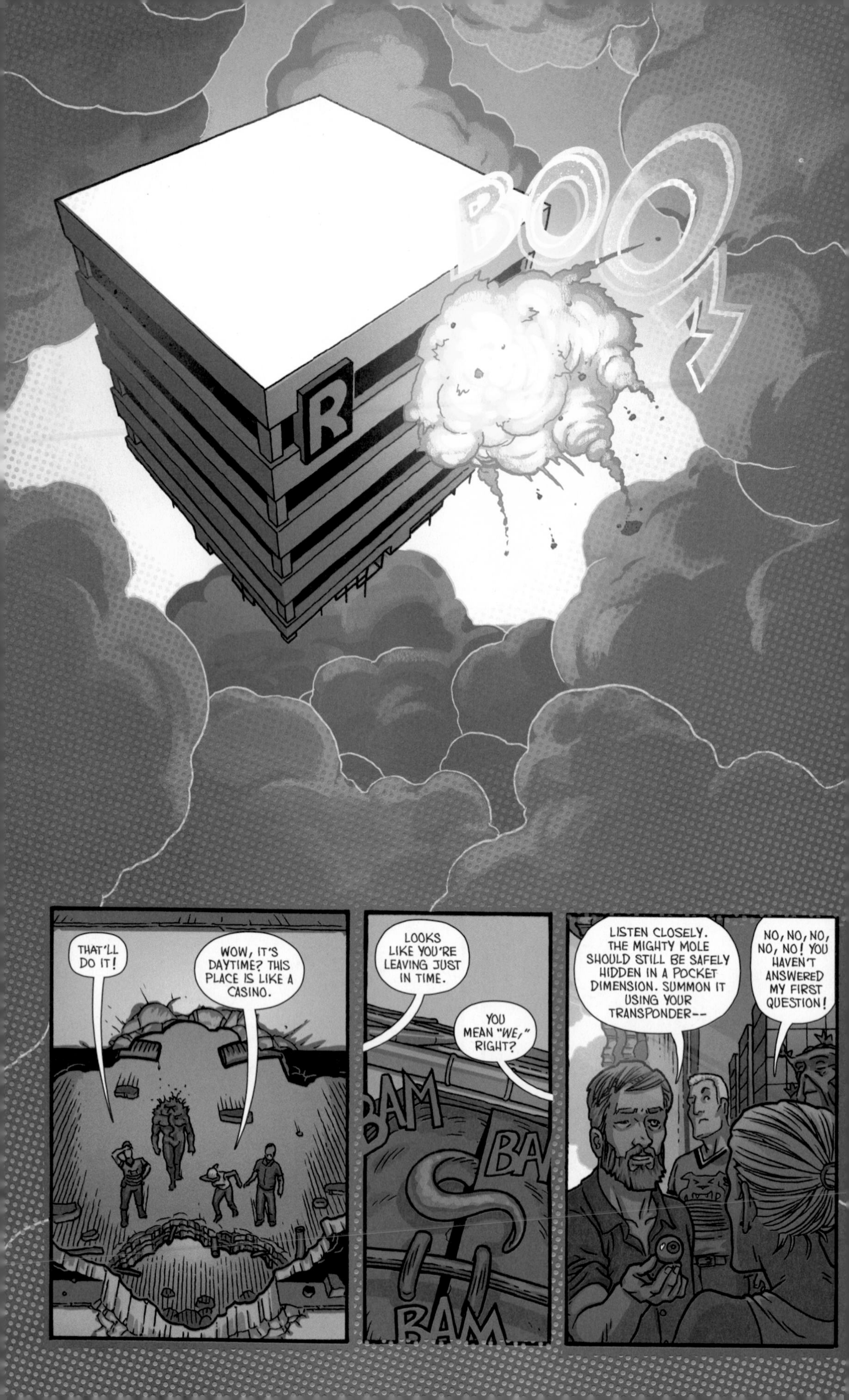
BOOM
THAT'LL DO IT!
WOW, IT'S DAYTIME? THIS PLACE IS LIKE A CASINO.
LOOKS LIKE YOU'RE LEAVING JUST IN TIME.
YOU MEAN "WE," RIGHT?
BAM
BAM
LISTEN CLOSELY. THE MIGHTY MOLE SHOULD STILL BE SAFELY HIDDEN IN A POCKET DIMENSION. SUMMON IT USING YOUR TRANSPONDER--
NO, NO, NO, NO, NO! YOU HAVEN'T ANSWERED MY FIRST QUESTION!

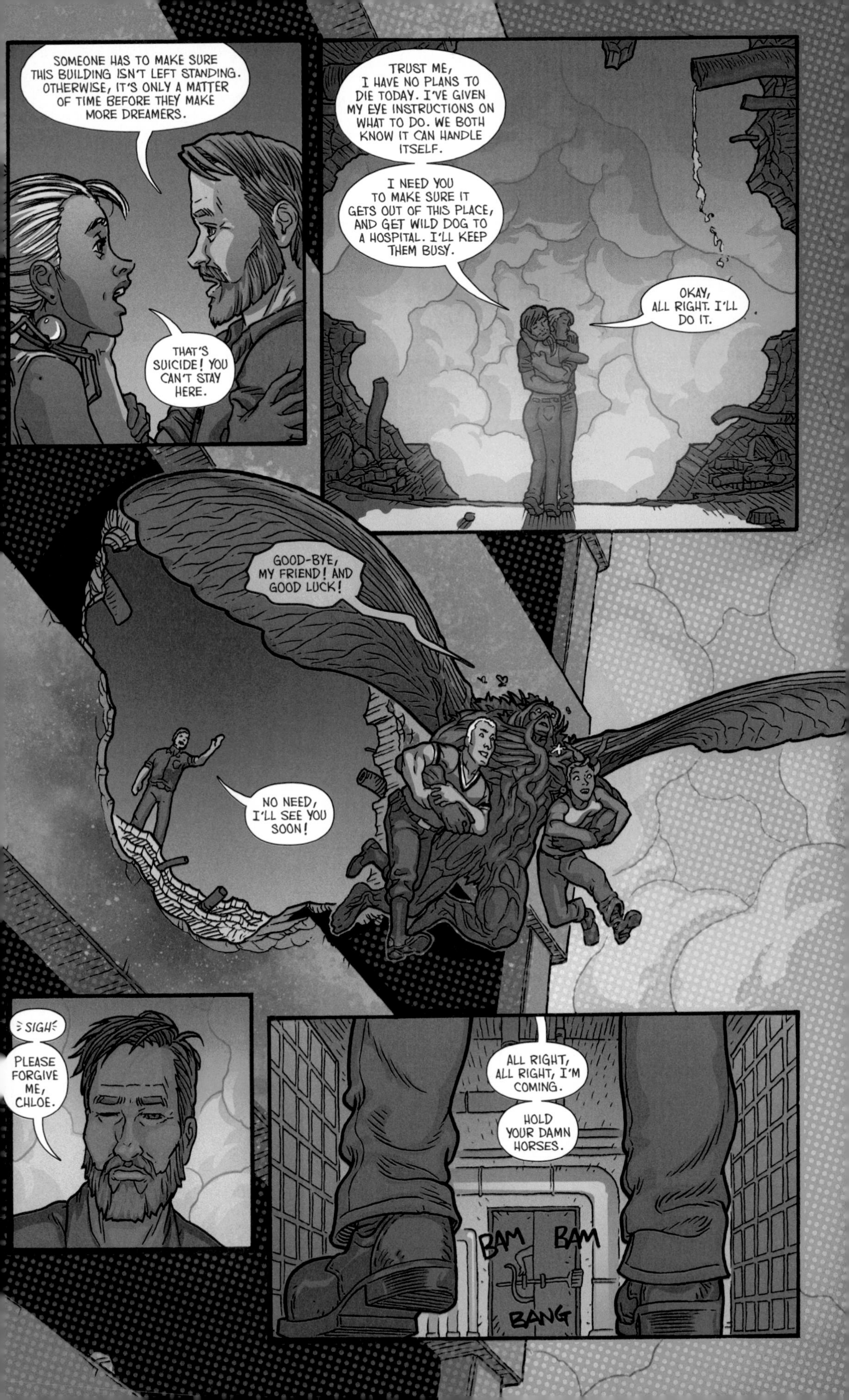
SOMEONE HAS TO MAKE SURE THIS BUILDING ISN'T LEFT STANDING. OTHERWISE, IT'S ONLY A MATTER OF TIME BEFORE THEY MAKE MORE DREAMERS.
THAT'S SUICIDE! YOU CAN'T STAY HERE.
TRUST ME, I HAVE NO PLANS TO DIE TODAY. I'VE GIVEN MY EYE INSTRUCTIONS ON WHAT TO DO. WE BOTH KNOW IT CAN HANDLE ITSELF.
I NEED YOU TO MAKE SURE IT GETS OUT OF THIS PLACE, AND GET WILD DOG TO A HOSPITAL. I'LL KEEP THEM BUSY.
OKAY, ALL RIGHT. I'LL DO IT.
GOOD-BYE, MY FRIEND! AND GOOD LUCK!
NO NEED, I'LL SEE YOU SOON!
SIGH
PLEASE FORGIVE ME, CHLOE.
ALL RIGHT, ALL RIGHT, I'M COMING.
HOLD YOUR DAMN HORSES.
BAM BAM
BANG

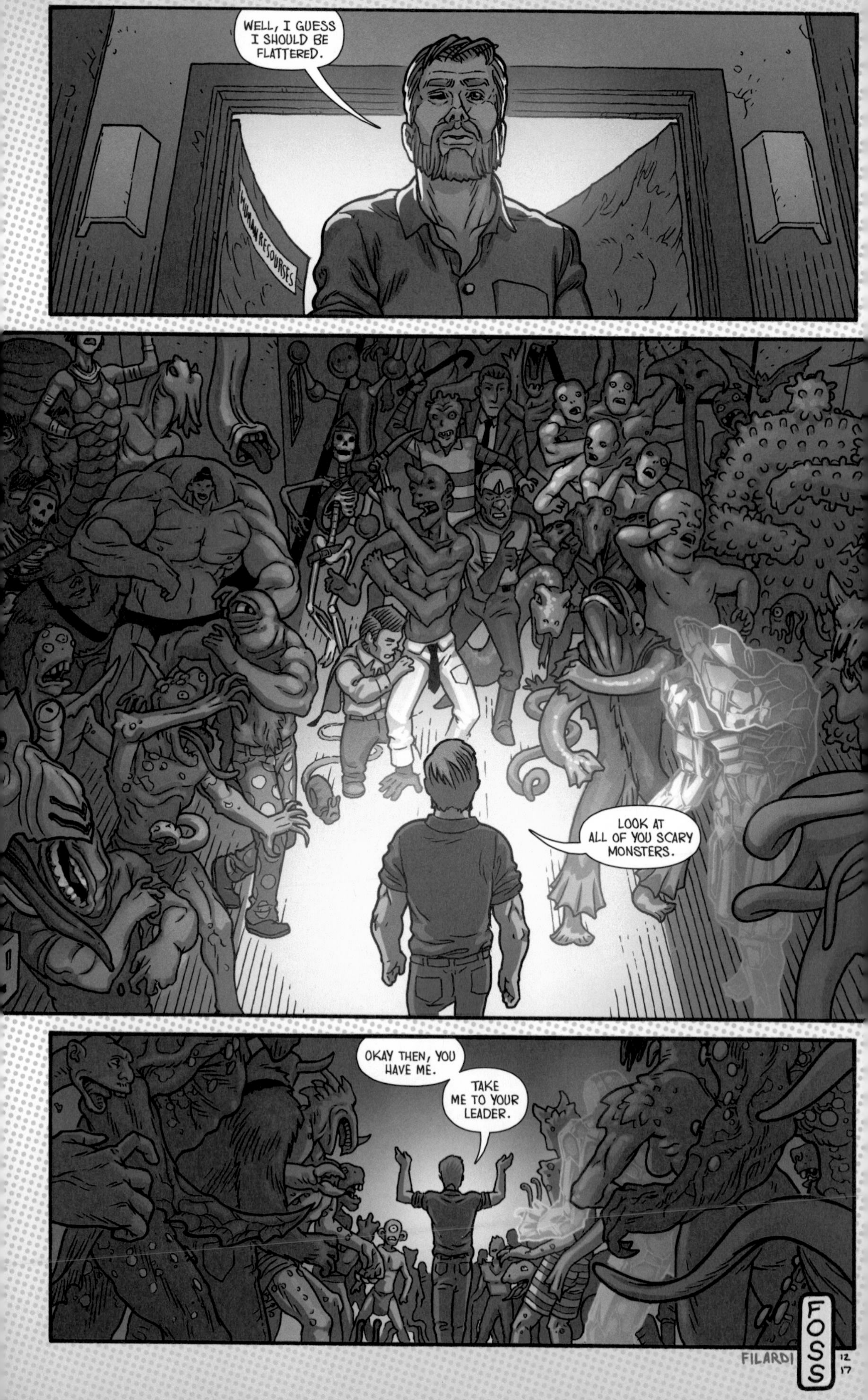
WELL, I GUESS I SHOULD BE FLATTERED.
HUMAN RESOURCES
LOOK AT ALL OF YOU SCARY MONSTERS.
OKAY THEN, YOU HAVE ME.
TAKE ME TO YOUR LEADER.
FILARDI
FOSS
12 17

In 2008, ALPHA 13 was revived again as a six-issue miniseries written by Paul Cruey with art by Ellie Keegan. A complete reimagining that ignored all existing continuity, this version focused on Caroline Sharp/Chrysalis' transformation and its effect on her, driving Caroline deep into an existential morass. Unlike previous incarnations, Cruey and Keegan's ALPHA 13 had little psychedelic imagery, preferring experimental storytelling that tried to capture Caroline's fractured experience of reality. Released to critical confusion, a promised ongoing series never materialized.

'Operation: Existence!,' ALPHA 13 Vol. 2 #6. Story by Paul Cruey, art by Ellie Keegan. 2008.

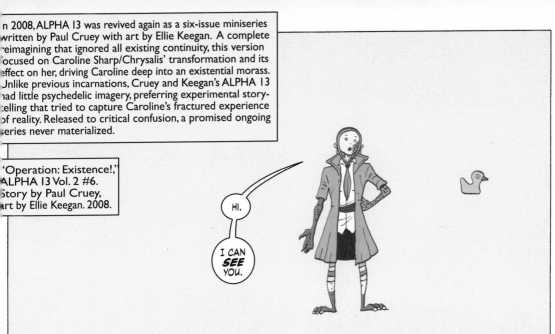

HI.

I CAN **SEE** YOU.

THIS ISN'T THE PAGE WE'RE SUPPOSED TO BE PRINTING.

THAT'S SUPPOSED TO BE MORE OF MY **ONGOING EXISTENTIAL DRAMA** WITH ON-AGAIN OFF-AGAIN NEMESIS MADAME ATOM.

BUT I'VE ABOUT **HAD** IT WITH THAT.

AT SOME POINT CHARACTERS SHOULD BE ALLOWED TO REST. THE **REBOOTS** AND REINVENTIONS...

...YOU GET THE SENSE THAT NOBODY MUCH LIKES YOU. BECAUSE THAT'S THE **TRUTH.**

WHAT I AM IS **INTELLECTUAL PROPERTY** THEY KEEP TRYING TO FIND WAYS TO EXPLOIT, EVEN AS THE CREATIVE TEAMS GUIDING ME CONSPIRE TO PUSH ME FURTHER AND FURTHER UP MY OWN ASS.

ALL IN THE **HOPES** THAT SOMETHING WILL FINALLY RESONATE.

MY LIFE IN FOUR COLORS.

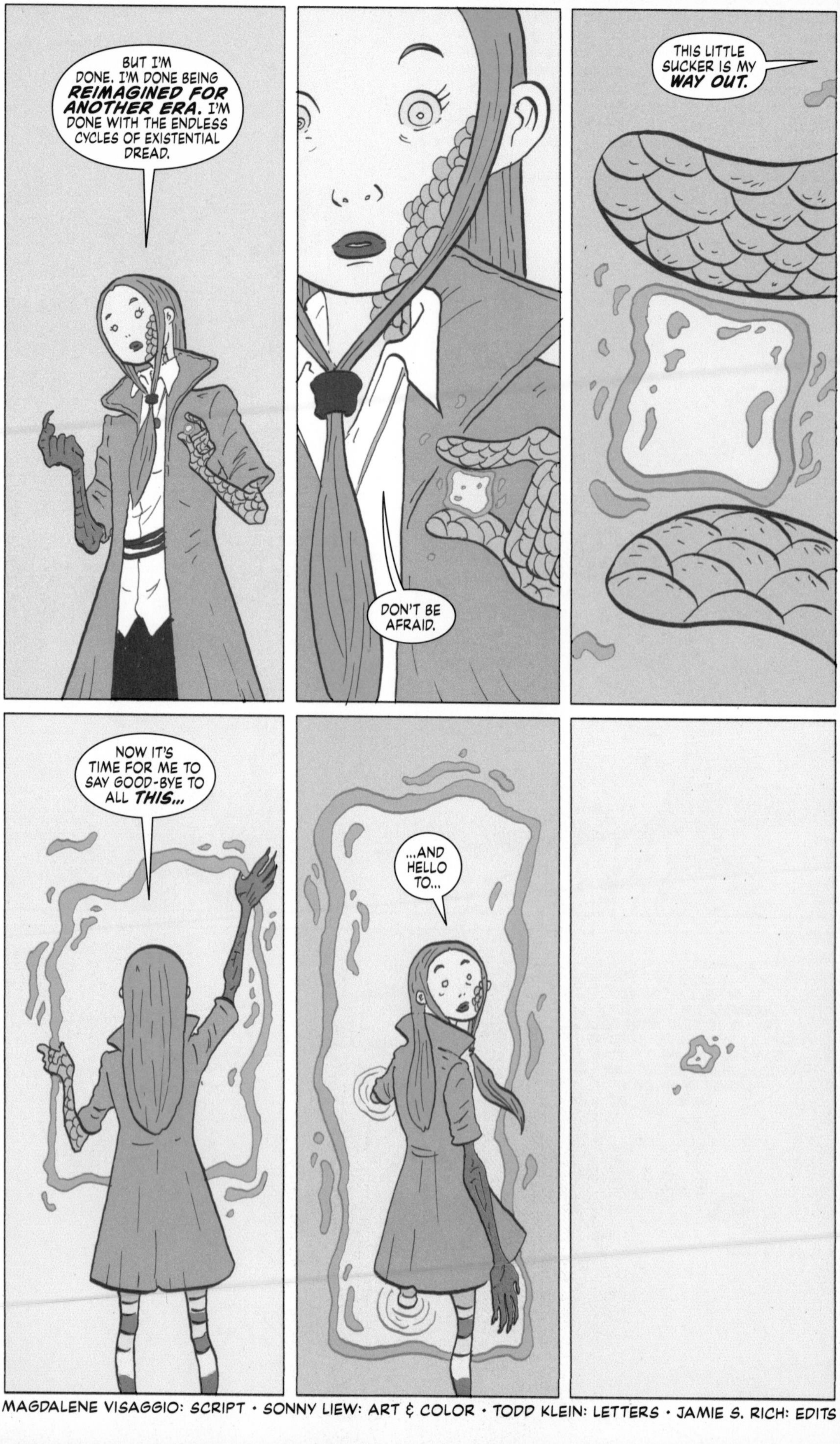
BUT I'M DONE. I'M DONE BEING REIMAGINED FOR ANOTHER ERA. I'M DONE WITH THE ENDLESS CYCLES OF EXISTENTIAL DREAD.
DON'T BE AFRAID.
THIS LITTLE SUCKER IS MY WAY OUT.
NOW IT'S TIME FOR ME TO SAY GOOD-BYE TO ALL THIS...
...AND HELLO TO...

MAGDALENE VISAGGIO: SCRIPT • SONNY LIEW: ART & COLOR • TODD KLEIN: LETTERS • JAMIE S. RICH: EDITS

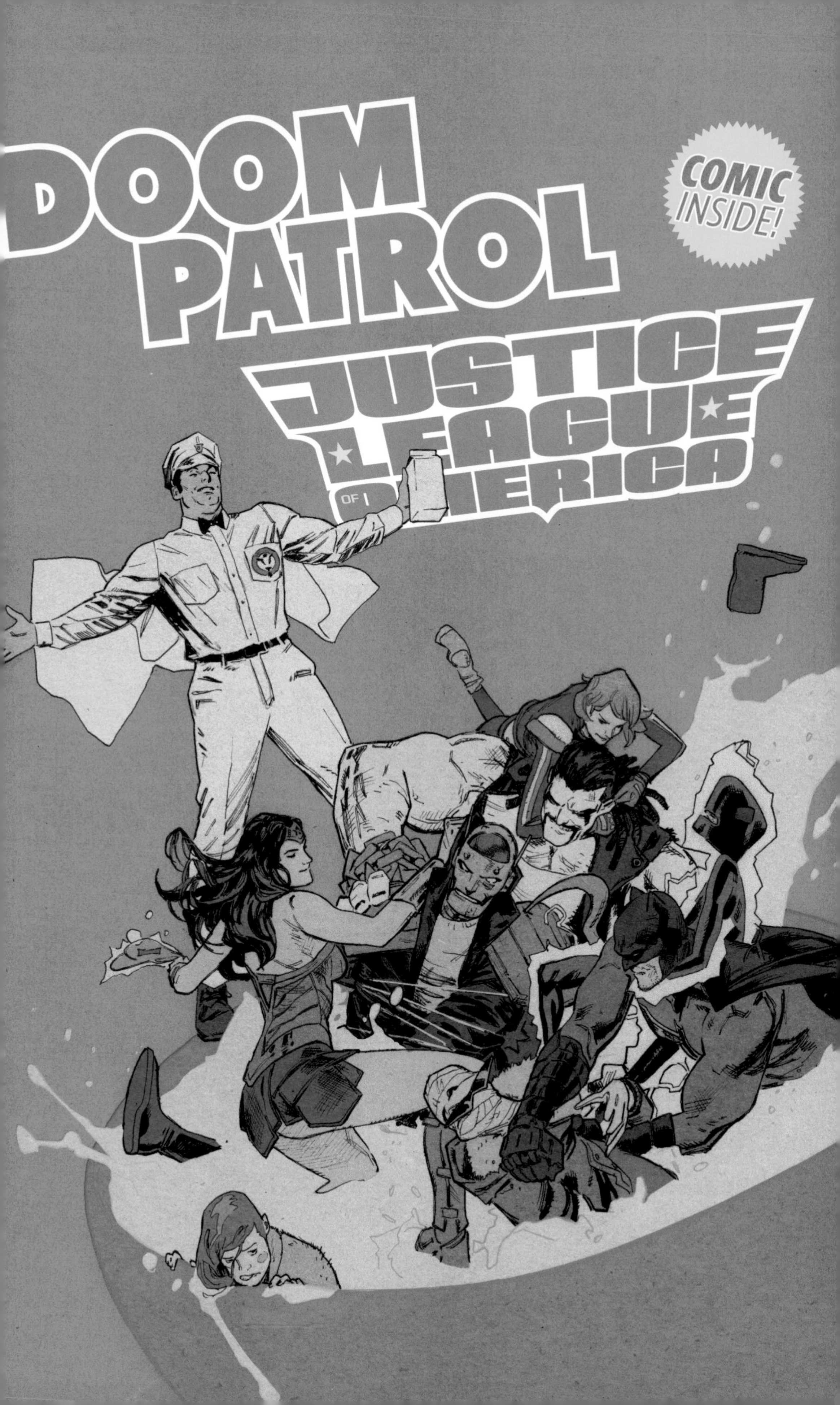
DOOM PATROL
COMIC INSIDE!
JUSTICE LEAGUE OF AMERICA

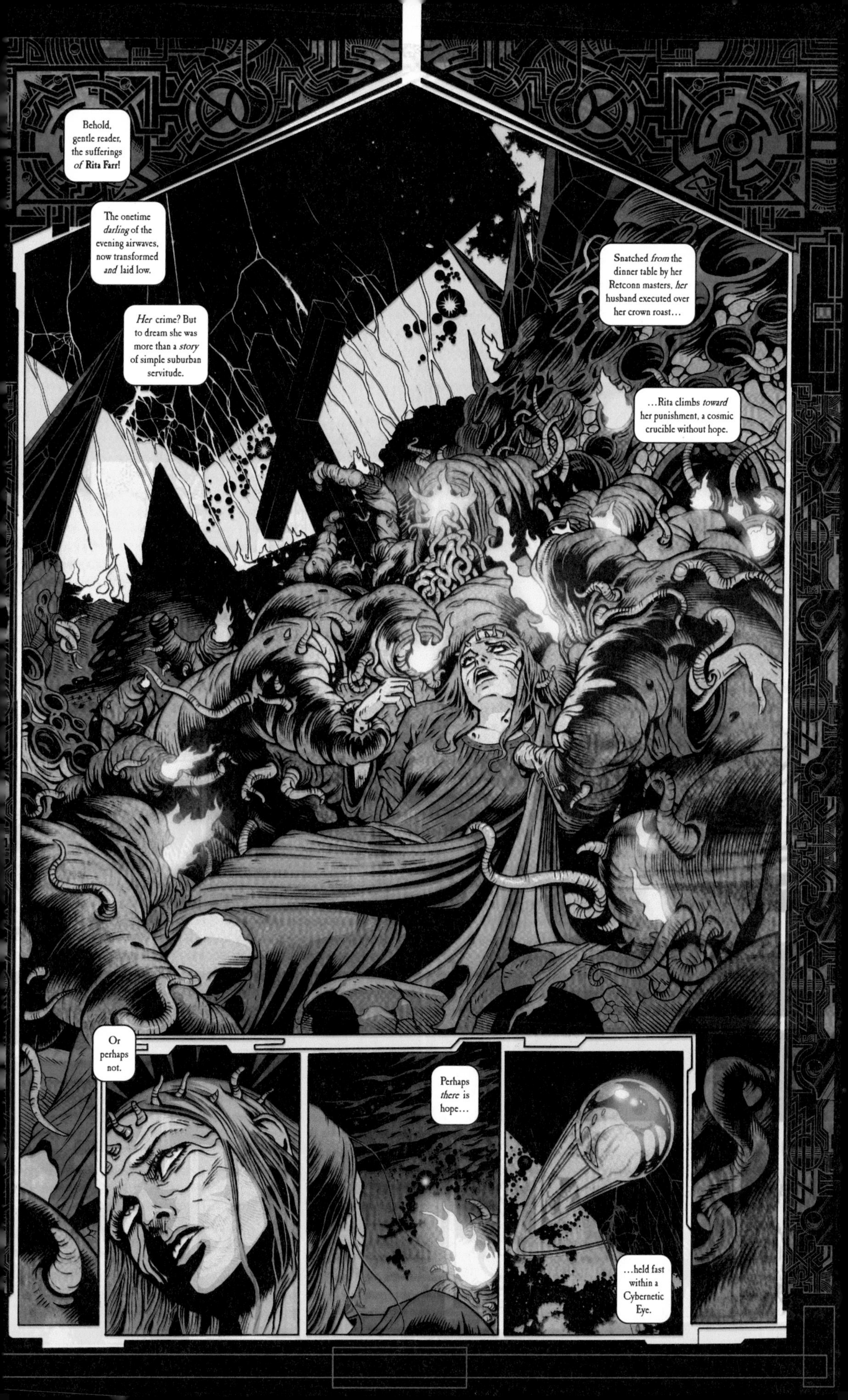
Behold, gentle reader, the sufferings *of* **Rita Farr!**
The onetime *darling* of the evening airwaves, now transformed *and* laid low.
Her crime? But to dream she was more than a *story* of simple suburban servitude.
Snatched *from* the dinner table by her Retconn masters, *her* husband executed over her crown roast…
…Rita climbs *toward* her punishment, a cosmic crucible without hope.
Or perhaps not.
Perhaps *there* is hope…
…held fast within a Cybernetic Eye.

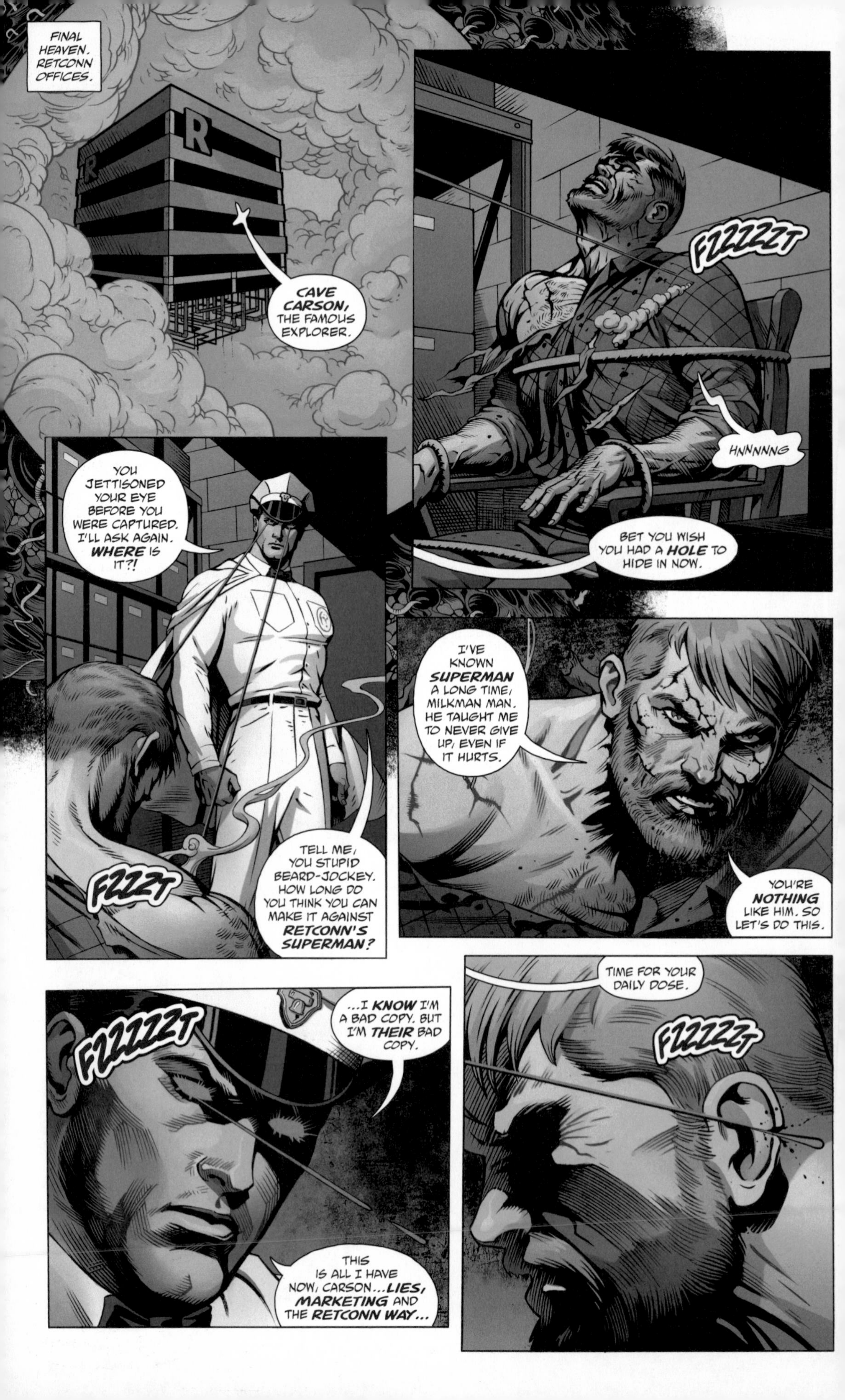
FINAL HEAVEN. RETCONN OFFICES.
CAVE CARSON, THE FAMOUS EXPLORER.
FZZZZZT
HNNNNNG
BET YOU WISH YOU HAD A HOLE TO HIDE IN NOW.
YOU JETTISONED YOUR EYE BEFORE YOU WERE CAPTURED. I'LL ASK AGAIN. WHERE IS IT?!
TELL ME, YOU STUPID BEARD-JOCKEY. HOW LONG DO YOU THINK YOU CAN MAKE IT AGAINST RETCONN'S SUPERMAN?
FZZZT
I'VE KNOWN SUPERMAN A LONG TIME, MILKMAN MAN. HE TAUGHT ME TO NEVER GIVE UP, EVEN IF IT HURTS.
YOU'RE NOTHING LIKE HIM. SO LET'S DO THIS.
FZZZZZT
...I KNOW I'M A BAD COPY. BUT I'M THEIR BAD COPY.
THIS IS ALL I HAVE NOW, CARSON...LIES, MARKETING AND THE RETCONN WAY...
TIME FOR YOUR DAILY DOSE.
FZZZZZT

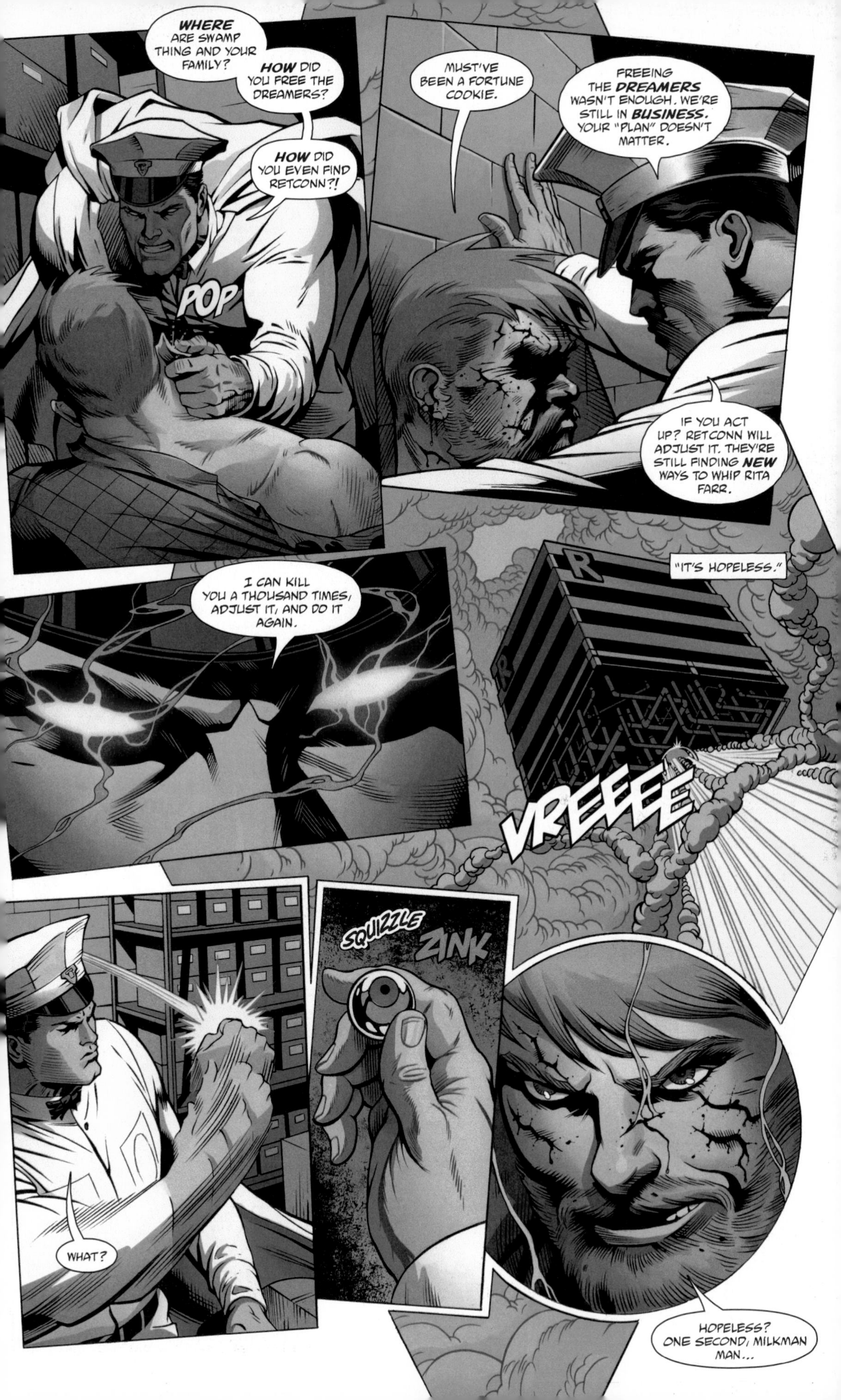
WHERE ARE SWAMP THING AND YOUR FAMILY?
HOW DID YOU FREE THE DREAMERS?
HOW DID YOU EVEN FIND RETCONN?!
POP
MUST'VE BEEN A FORTUNE COOKIE.
FREEING THE DREAMERS WASN'T ENOUGH. WE'RE STILL IN BUSINESS. YOUR "PLAN" DOESN'T MATTER.
IF YOU ACT UP? RETCONN WILL ADJUST IT. THEY'RE STILL FINDING NEW WAYS TO WHIP RITA FARR.
I CAN KILL YOU A THOUSAND TIMES, ADJUST IT, AND DO IT AGAIN.
"IT'S HOPELESS."
VREEEE
SQUIZZLE
ZINK
WHAT?
HOPELESS? ONE SECOND, MILKMAN MAN...

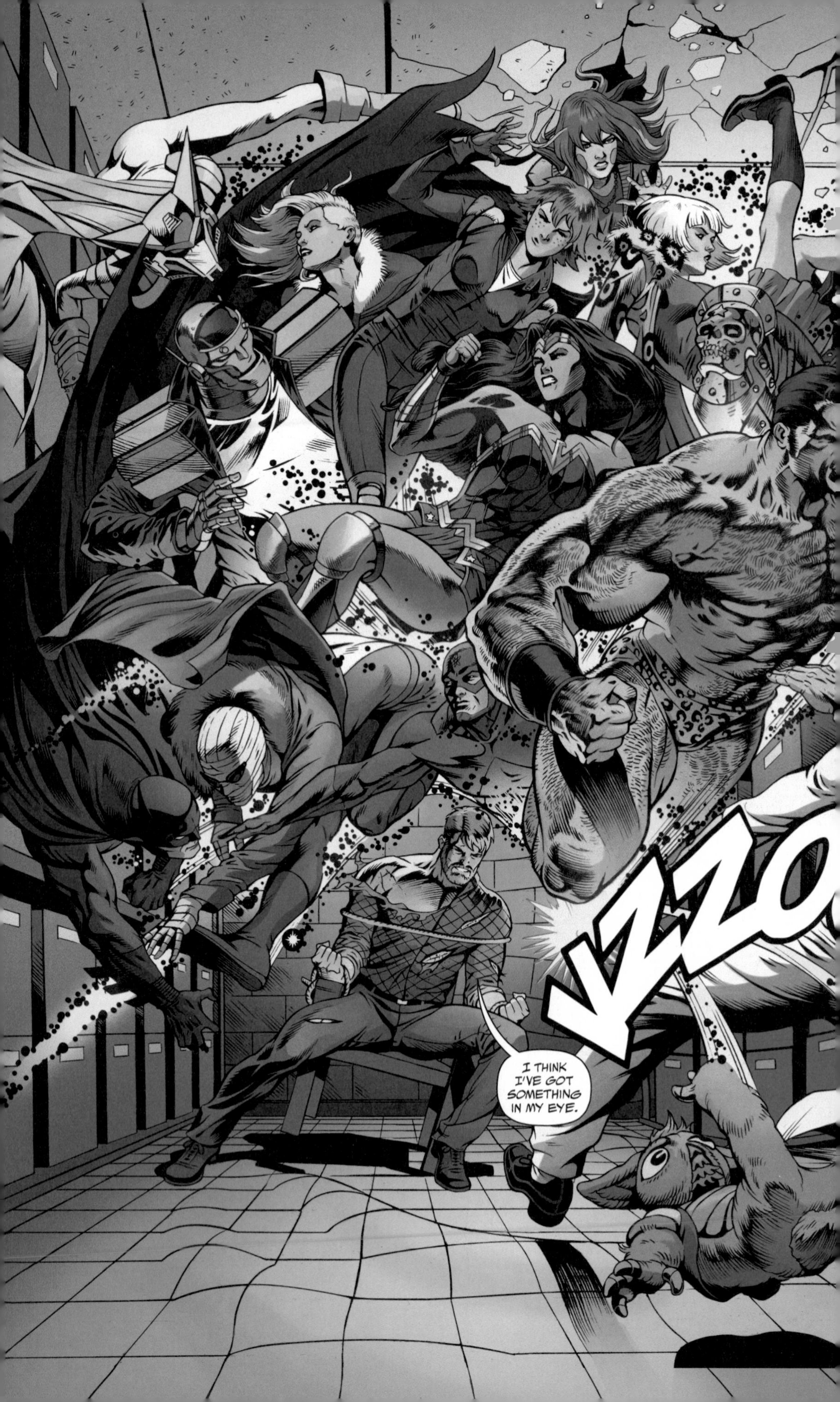
KZZO
I THINK I'VE GOT SOMETHING IN MY EYE.

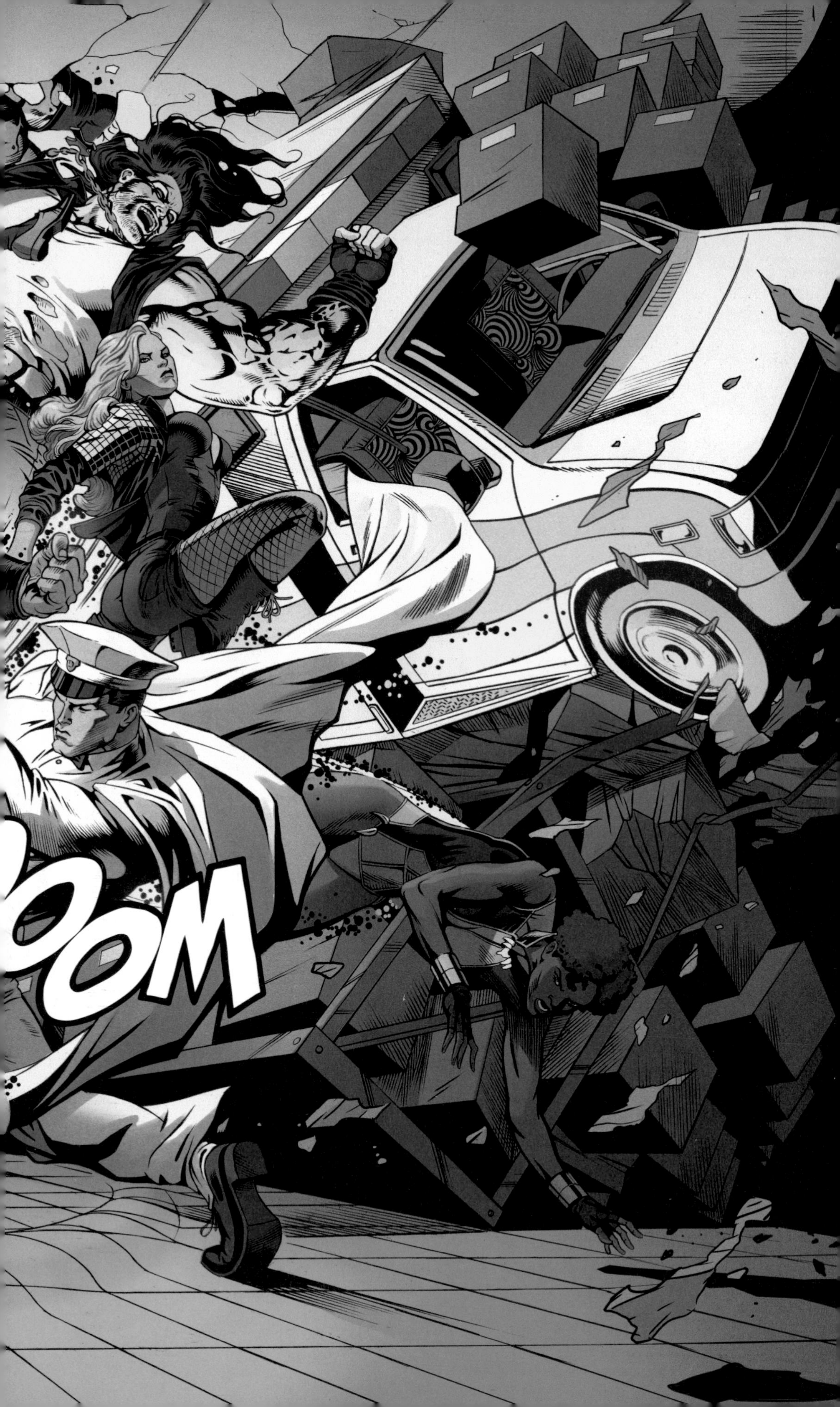
OOM

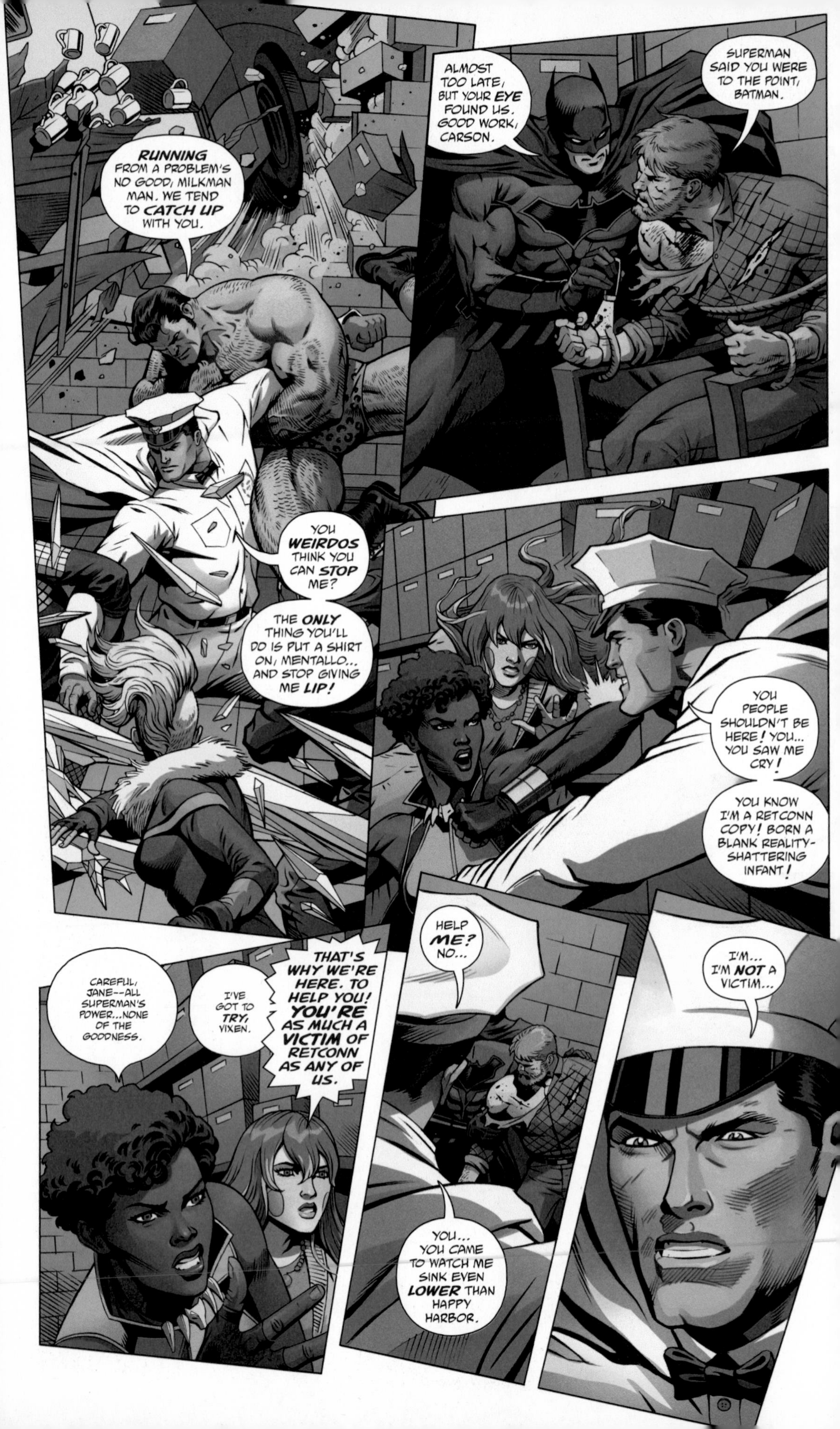

RUNNING FROM A PROBLEM'S NO GOOD, MILKMAN MAN. WE TEND TO CATCH UP WITH YOU.
ALMOST TOO LATE, BUT YOUR EYE FOUND US. GOOD WORK, CARSON.
SUPERMAN SAID YOU WERE TO THE POINT, BATMAN.
YOU WEIRDOS THINK YOU CAN STOP ME?
THE ONLY THING YOU'LL DO IS PUT A SHIRT ON, MENTALLO... AND STOP GIVING ME LIP!
YOU PEOPLE SHOULDN'T BE HERE! YOU... YOU SAW ME CRY!
YOU KNOW I'M A RETCONN COPY! BORN A BLANK REALITY-SHATTERING INFANT!
CAREFUL, JANE--ALL SUPERMAN'S POWER...NONE OF THE GOODNESS.
I'VE GOT TO TRY, VIXEN.
THAT'S WHY WE'RE HERE. TO HELP YOU! YOU'RE AS MUCH A VICTIM OF RETCONN AS ANY OF US.
HELP ME? NO...
YOU... YOU CAME TO WATCH ME SINK EVEN LOWER THAN HAPPY HARBOR.
I'M... I'M NOT A VICTIM...

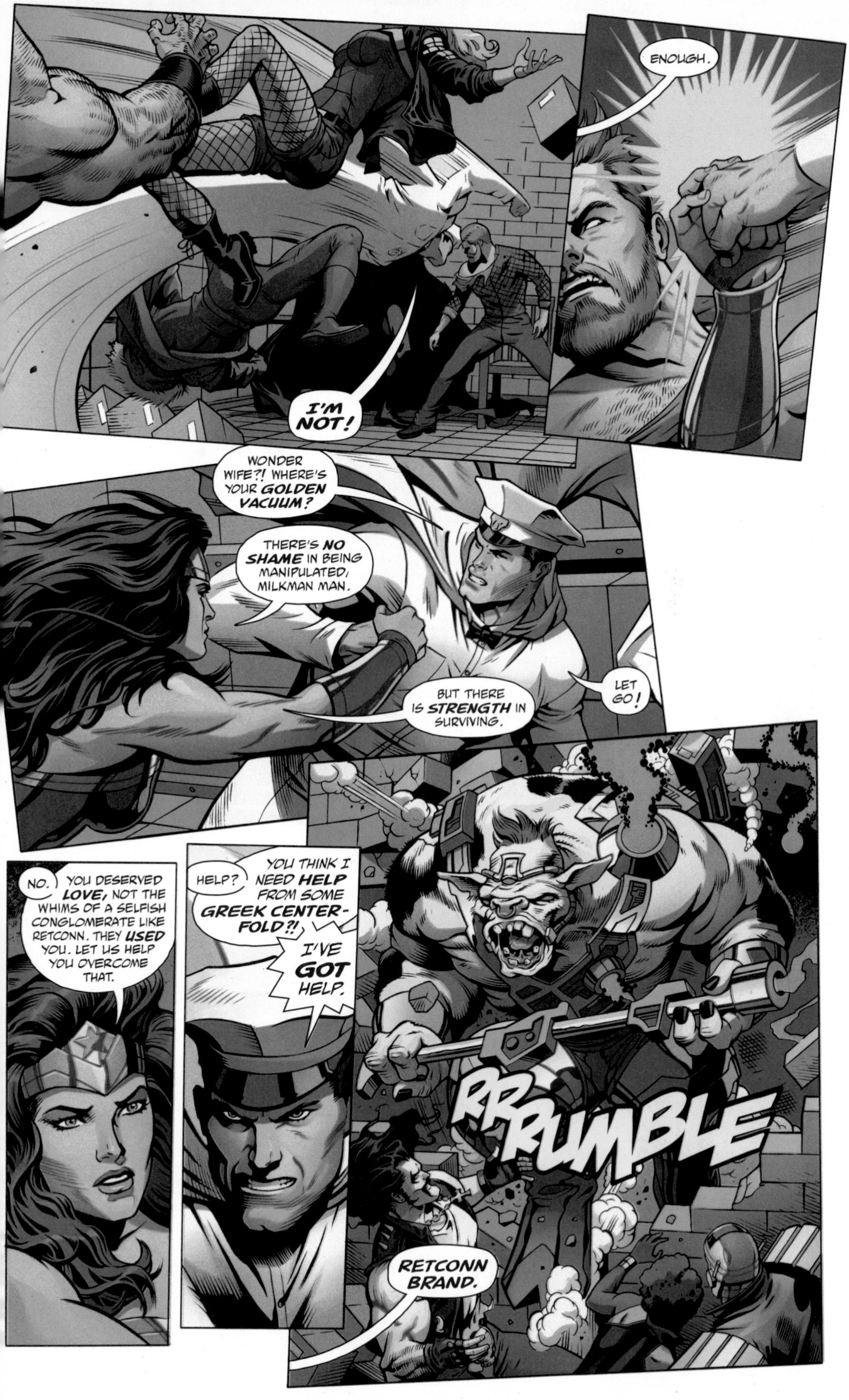

I'M NOT!
ENOUGH.
WONDER WIFE?! WHERE'S YOUR GOLDEN VACUUM?
THERE'S NO SHAME IN BEING MANIPULATED, MILKMAN MAN.
BUT THERE IS STRENGTH IN SURVIVING.
LET GO!
NO.
YOU DESERVED LOVE, NOT THE WHIMS OF A SELFISH CONGLOMERATE LIKE RETCONN. THEY USED YOU. LET US HELP YOU OVERCOME THAT.
HELP?
YOU THINK I NEED HELP FROM SOME GREEK CENTER-FOLD?!
I'VE GOT HELP.
RRRUMBLE
RETCONN BRAND.

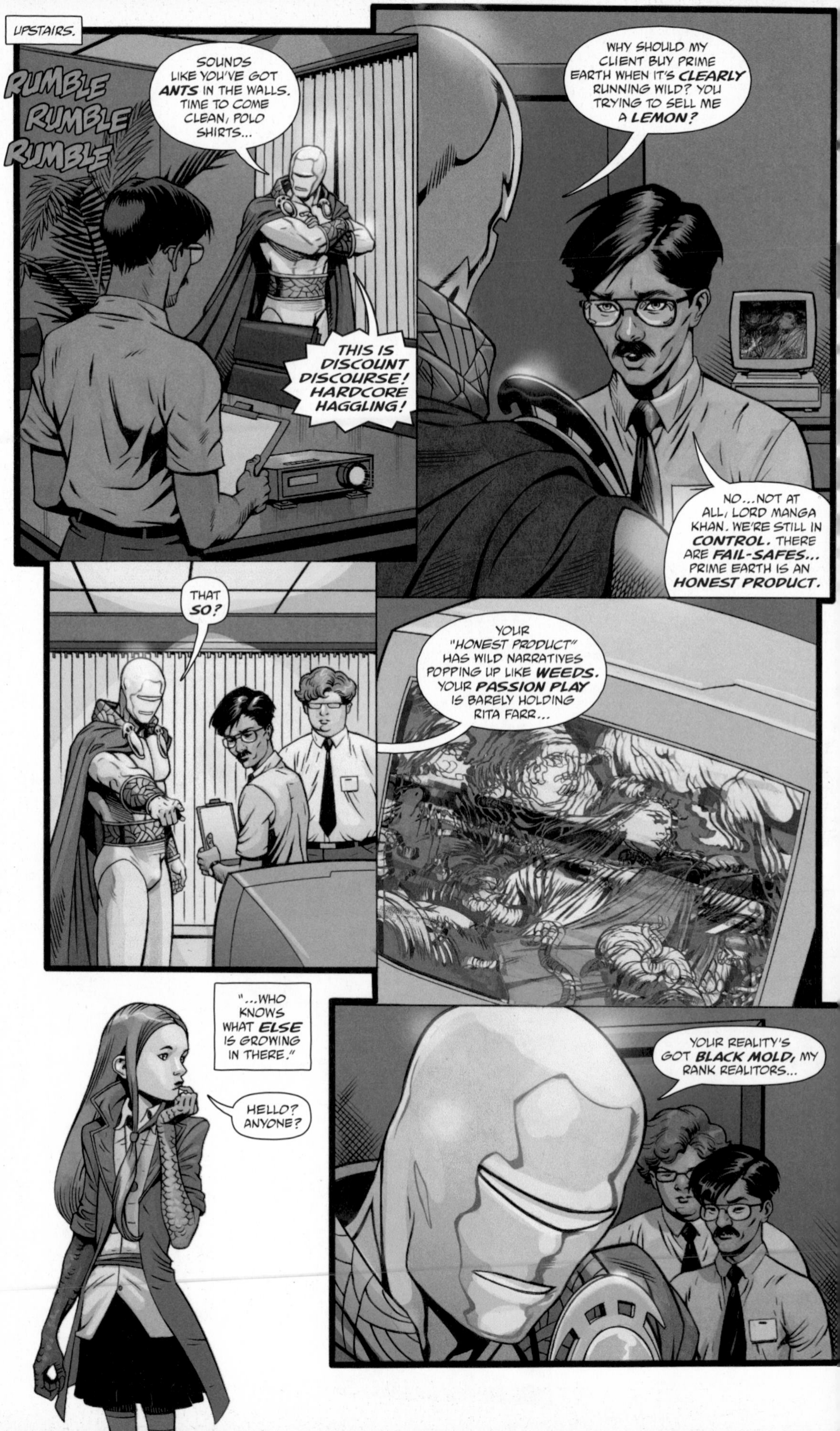
UPSTAIRS.
RUMBLE RUMBLE RUMBLE
SOUNDS LIKE YOU'VE GOT ANTS IN THE WALLS. TIME TO COME CLEAN, POLO SHIRTS...
THIS IS DISCOUNT DISCOURSE! HARDCORE HAGGLING!
WHY SHOULD MY CLIENT BUY PRIME EARTH WHEN IT'S CLEARLY RUNNING WILD? YOU TRYING TO SELL ME A LEMON?
NO...NOT AT ALL, LORD MANGA KHAN. WE'RE STILL IN CONTROL. THERE ARE FAIL-SAFES... PRIME EARTH IS AN HONEST PRODUCT.
THAT SO?
YOUR "HONEST PRODUCT" HAS WILD NARRATIVES POPPING UP LIKE WEEDS. YOUR PASSION PLAY IS BARELY HOLDING RITA FARR...
"...WHO KNOWS WHAT ELSE IS GROWING IN THERE."
HELLO? ANYONE?
YOUR REALITY'S GOT BLACK MOLD, MY RANK REALITORS...

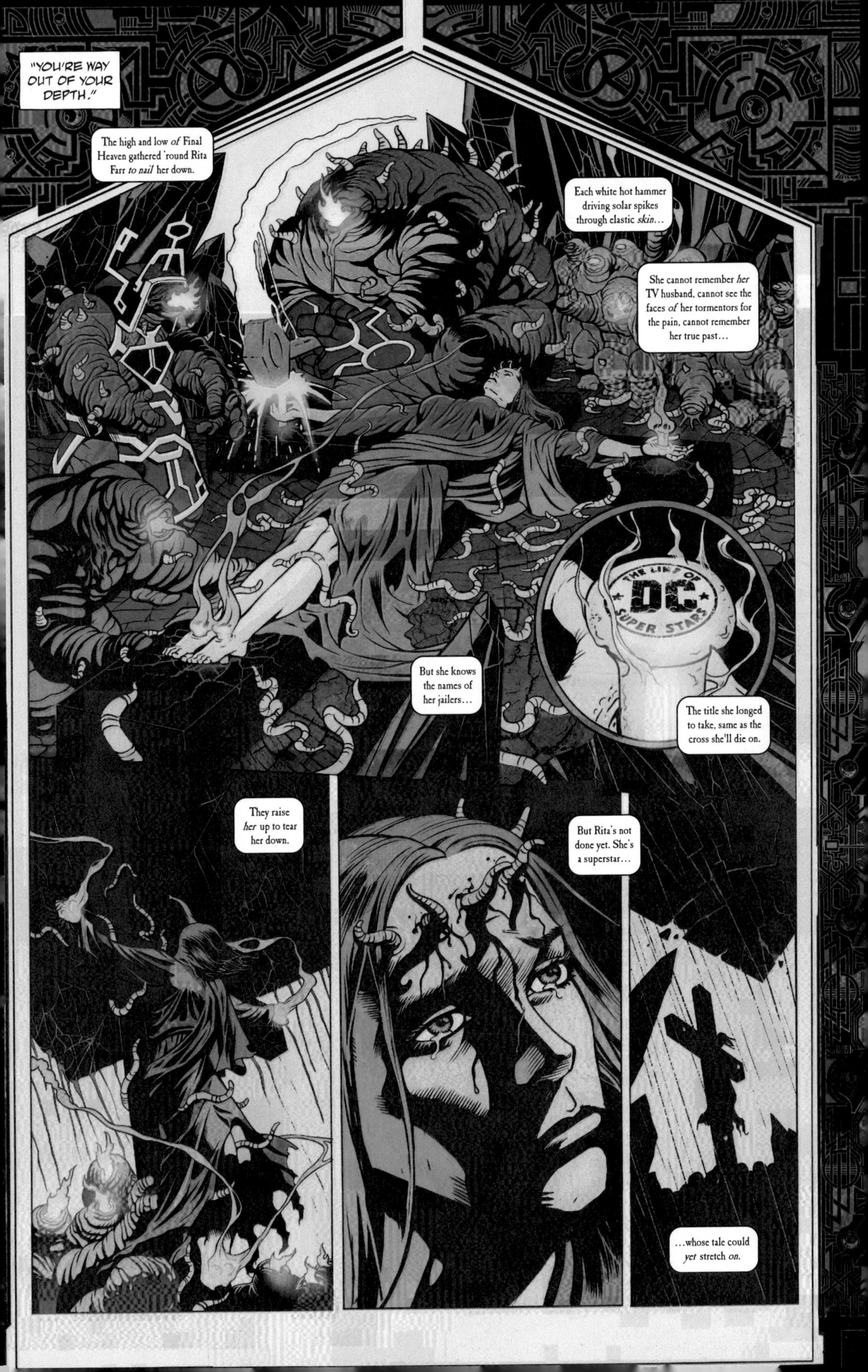
"YOU'RE WAY OUT OF YOUR DEPTH."
The high and low *of* Final Heaven gathered 'round Rita Farr *to nail* her down.
Each white hot hammer driving solar spikes through elastic *skin*…
She cannot remember *her* TV husband, cannot see the faces *of* her tormentors for the pain, cannot remember her true past…
THE LINE OF DC SUPER STARS
But she knows the names of her jailers…
The title she longed to take, same as the cross she'll die on.
They raise *her* up to tear her down.
But Rita's not done yet. She's a superstar…
…whose tale could *yet* stretch *on*.

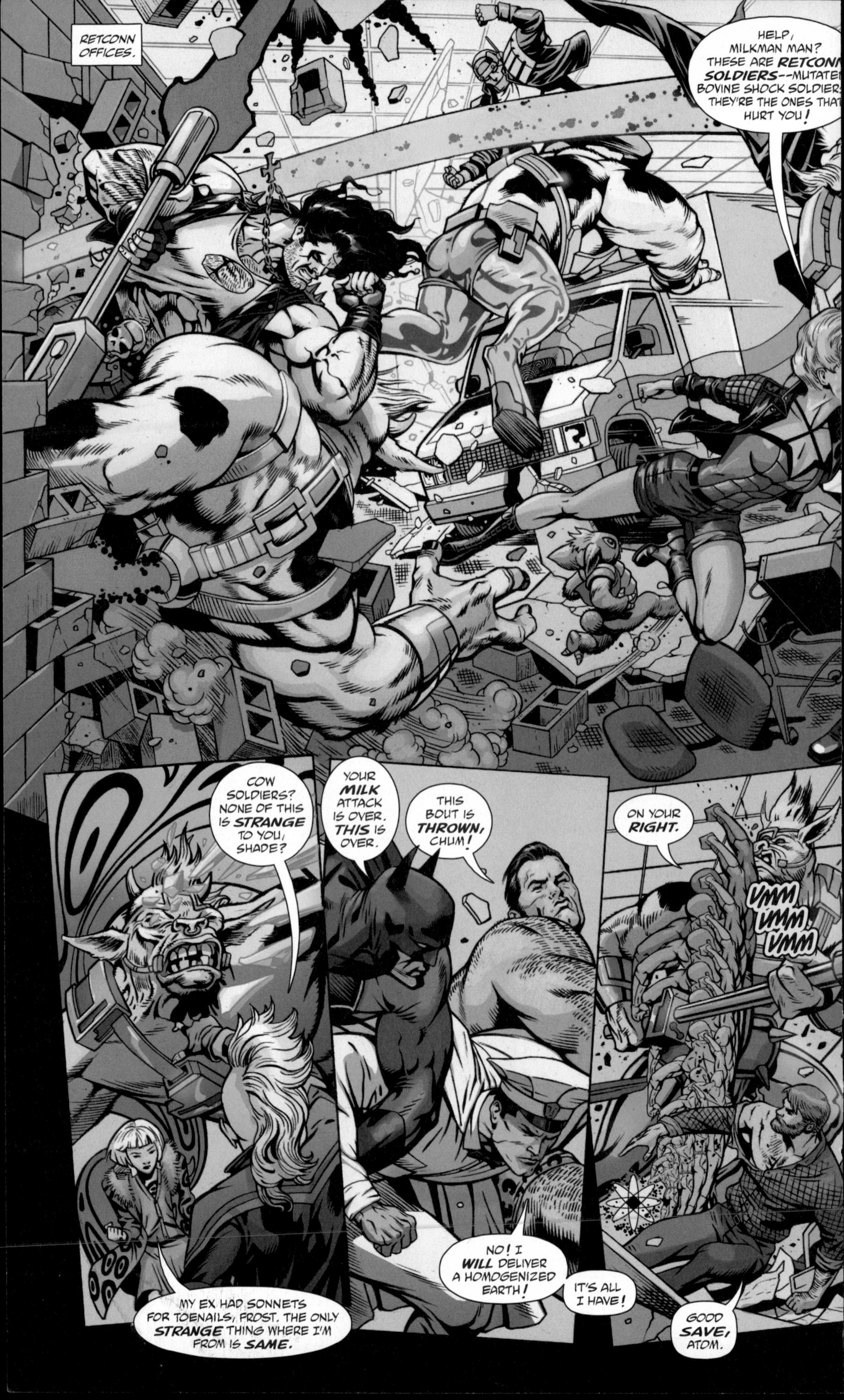
RETCONN OFFICES.
HELP, MILKMAN MAN? THESE ARE RETCONN SOLDIERS--MUTATED BOVINE SHOCK SOLDIERS. THEY'RE THE ONES THAT HURT YOU!
COW SOLDIERS? NONE OF THIS IS STRANGE TO YOU, SHADE?
MY EX HAD SONNETS FOR TOENAILS, FROST. THE ONLY STRANGE THING WHERE I'M FROM IS SAME.
YOUR MILK ATTACK IS OVER. THIS IS OVER.
THIS BOUT IS THROWN, CHUM!
NO! I WILL DELIVER A HOMOGENIZED EARTH!
IT'S ALL I HAVE!
ON YOUR RIGHT.
VMM VMM VMM
GOOD SAVE, ATOM.

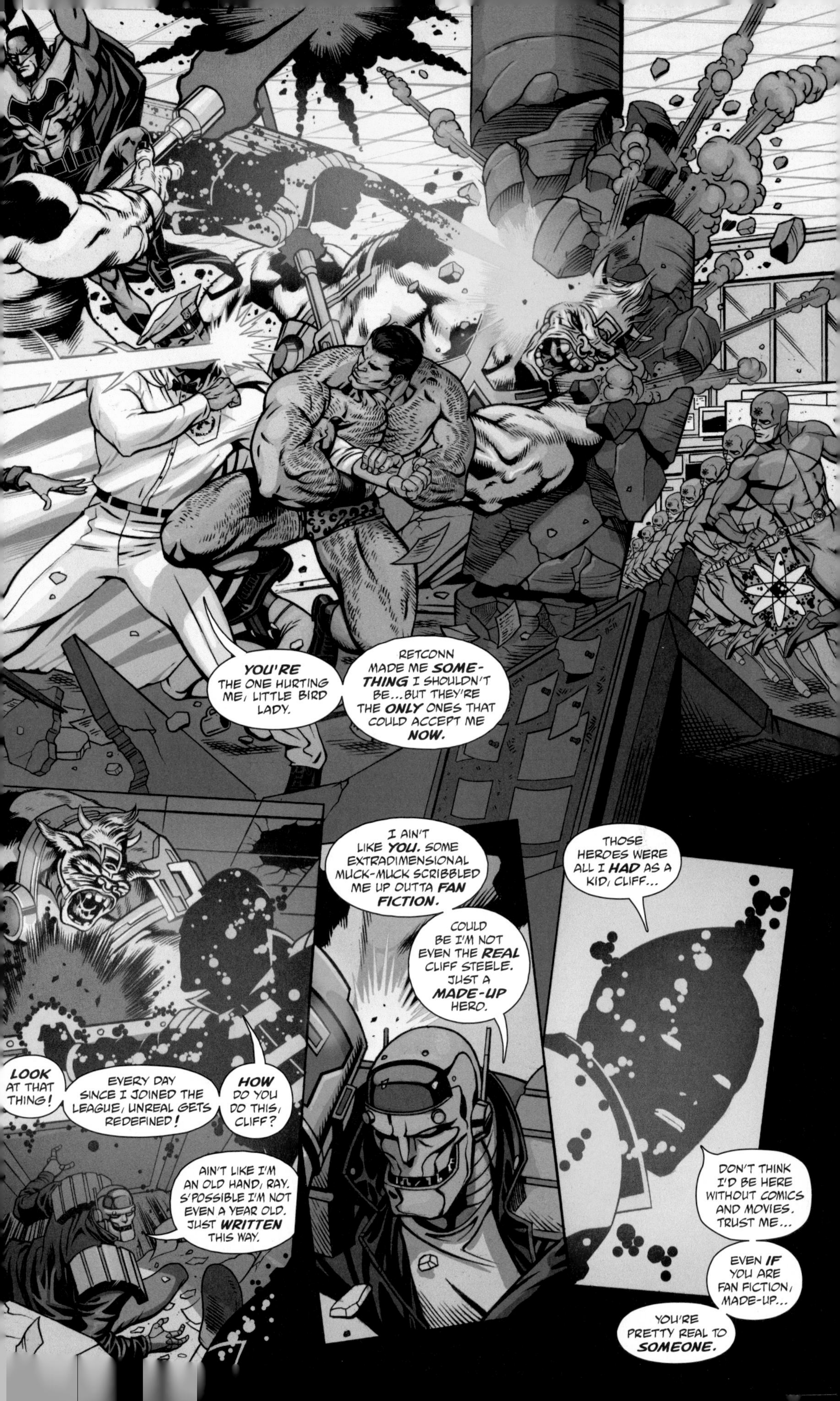

YOU'RE THE ONE HURTING ME, LITTLE BIRD LADY.
RETCONN MADE ME SOME-THING I SHOULDN'T BE...BUT THEY'RE THE ONLY ONES THAT COULD ACCEPT ME NOW.
LOOK AT THAT THING!
EVERY DAY SINCE I JOINED THE LEAGUE, UNREAL GETS REDEFINED!
HOW DO YOU DO THIS, CLIFF?
AIN'T LIKE I'M AN OLD HAND, RAY. S'POSSIBLE I'M NOT EVEN A YEAR OLD. JUST WRITTEN THIS WAY.
I AIN'T LIKE YOU. SOME EXTRADIMENSIONAL MUCK-MUCK SCRIBBLED ME UP OUTTA FAN FICTION.
COULD BE I'M NOT EVEN THE REAL CLIFF STEELE. JUST A MADE-UP HERO.
THOSE HEROES WERE ALL I HAD AS A KID, CLIFF...
DON'T THINK I'D BE HERE WITHOUT COMICS AND MOVIES. TRUST ME...
EVEN IF YOU ARE FAN FICTION, MADE-UP...
YOU'RE PRETTY REAL TO SOMEONE.

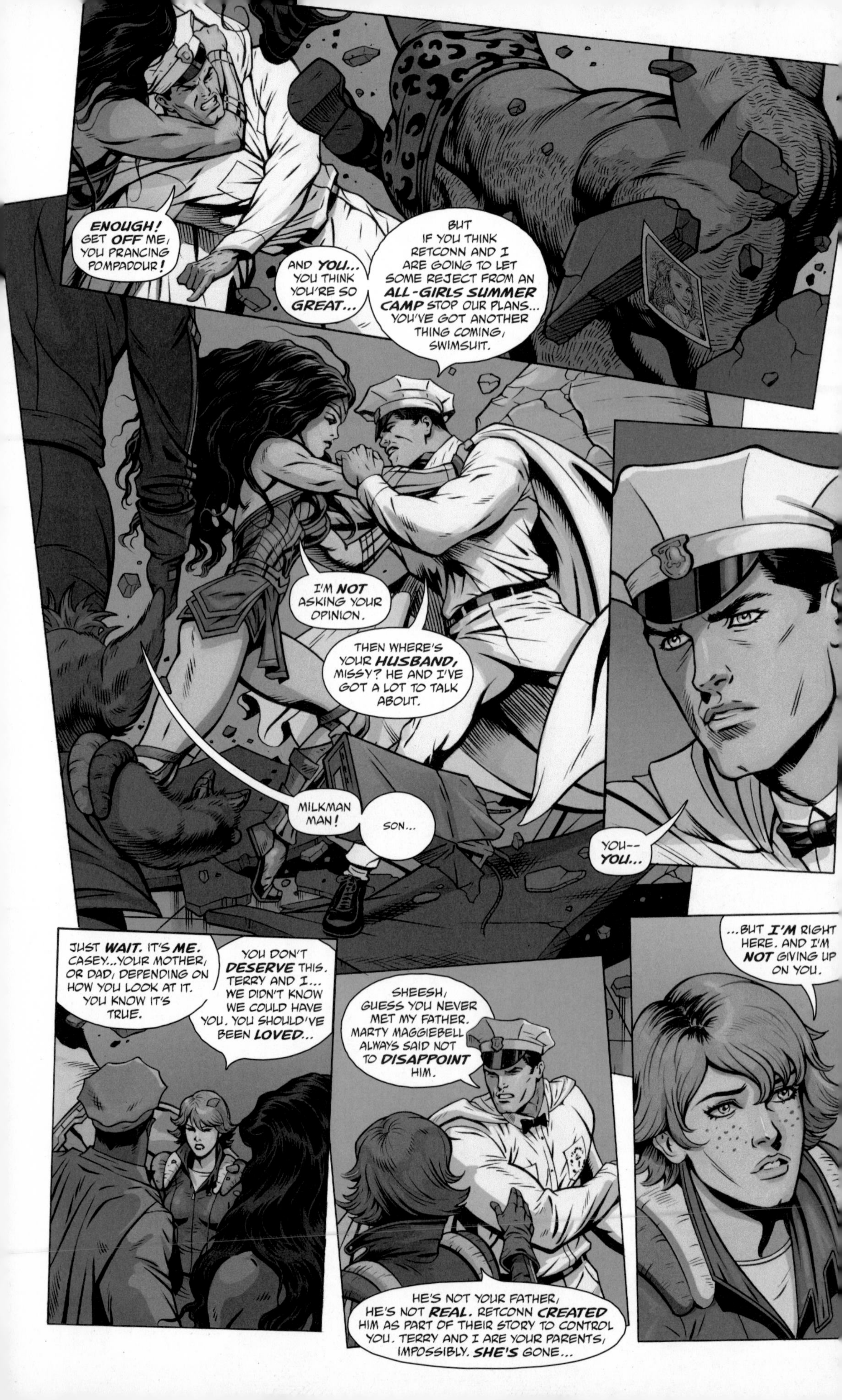

ENOUGH! GET OFF ME, YOU PRANCING POMPADOUR!
AND YOU... YOU THINK YOU'RE SO GREAT...
BUT IF YOU THINK RETCONN AND I ARE GOING TO LET SOME REJECT FROM AN ALL-GIRLS SUMMER CAMP STOP OUR PLANS... YOU'VE GOT ANOTHER THING COMING, SWIMSUIT.
I'M NOT ASKING YOUR OPINION.
THEN WHERE'S YOUR HUSBAND, MISSY? HE AND I'VE GOT A LOT TO TALK ABOUT.
MILKMAN MAN!
SON...
YOU-- YOU...
JUST WAIT. IT'S ME. CASEY...YOUR MOTHER, OR DAD, DEPENDING ON HOW YOU LOOK AT IT. YOU KNOW IT'S TRUE.
YOU DON'T DESERVE THIS. TERRY AND I... WE DIDN'T KNOW WE COULD HAVE YOU. YOU SHOULD'VE BEEN LOVED...
SHEESH, GUESS YOU NEVER MET MY FATHER. MARTY MAGGIEBELL ALWAYS SAID NOT TO DISAPPOINT HIM.
HE'S NOT YOUR FATHER, HE'S NOT REAL. RETCONN CREATED HIM AS PART OF THEIR STORY TO CONTROL YOU. TERRY AND I ARE YOUR PARENTS, IMPOSSIBLY. SHE'S GONE...
...BUT I'M RIGHT HERE. AND I'M NOT GIVING UP ON YOU.

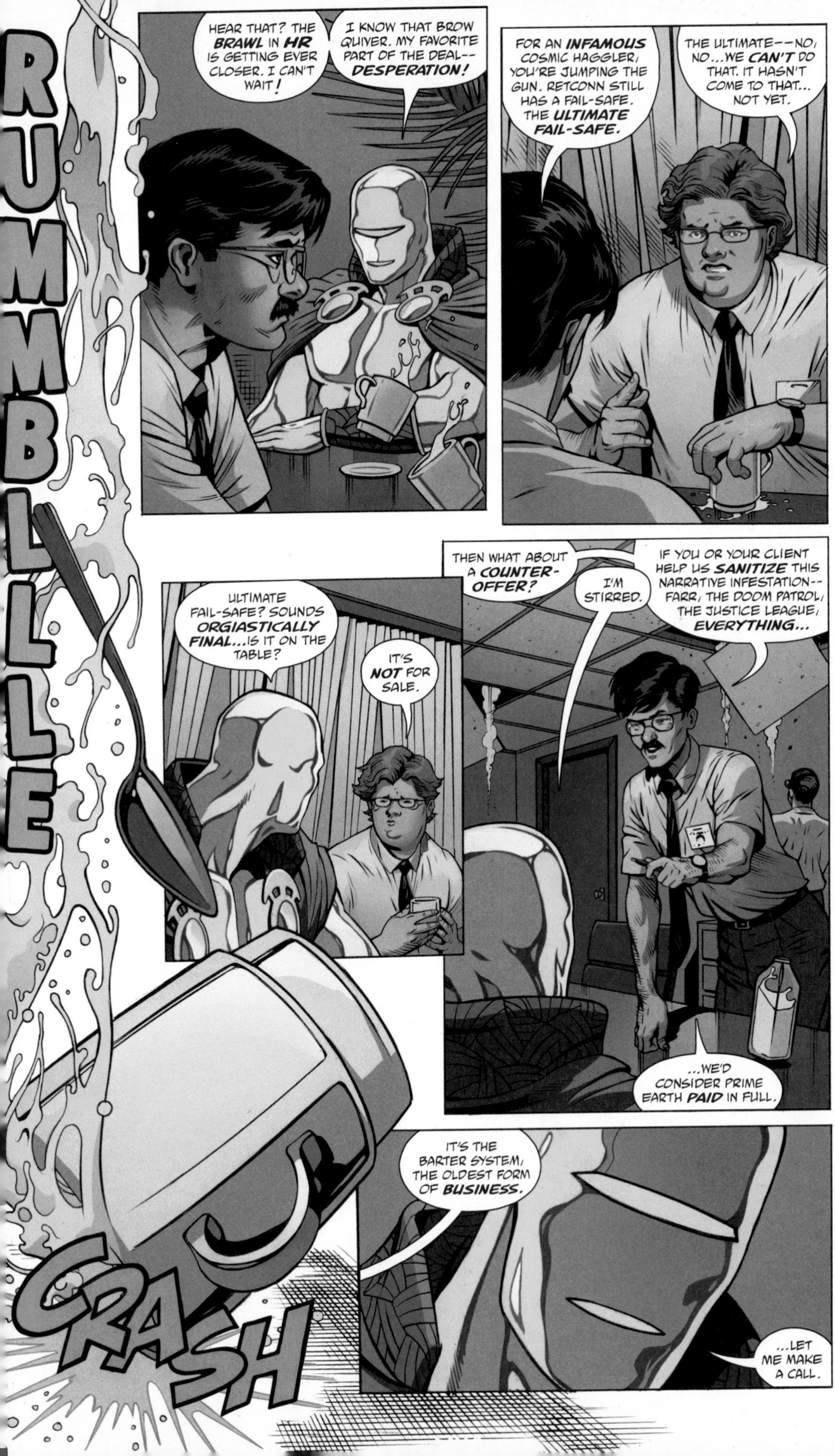
RUMMBBLLLLE
HEAR THAT? THE BRAWL IN HR IS GETTING EVER CLOSER. I CAN'T WAIT!
I KNOW THAT BROW QUIVER. MY FAVORITE PART OF THE DEAL-- DESPERATION!
FOR AN INFAMOUS COSMIC HAGGLER, YOU'RE JUMPING THE GUN. RETCONN STILL HAS A FAIL-SAFE. THE ULTIMATE FAIL-SAFE.
THE ULTIMATE--NO, NO...WE CAN'T DO THAT. IT HASN'T COME TO THAT... NOT YET.
ULTIMATE FAIL-SAFE? SOUNDS ORGIASTICALLY FINAL...IS IT ON THE TABLE?
IT'S NOT FOR SALE.
THEN WHAT ABOUT A COUNTER-OFFER?
I'M STIRRED.
IF YOU OR YOUR CLIENT HELP US SANITIZE THIS NARRATIVE INFESTATION-- FARR, THE DOOM PATROL, THE JUSTICE LEAGUE, EVERYTHING...
...WE'D CONSIDER PRIME EARTH PAID IN FULL.
CRASH
IT'S THE BARTER SYSTEM, THE OLDEST FORM OF BUSINESS.
...LET ME MAKE A CALL.

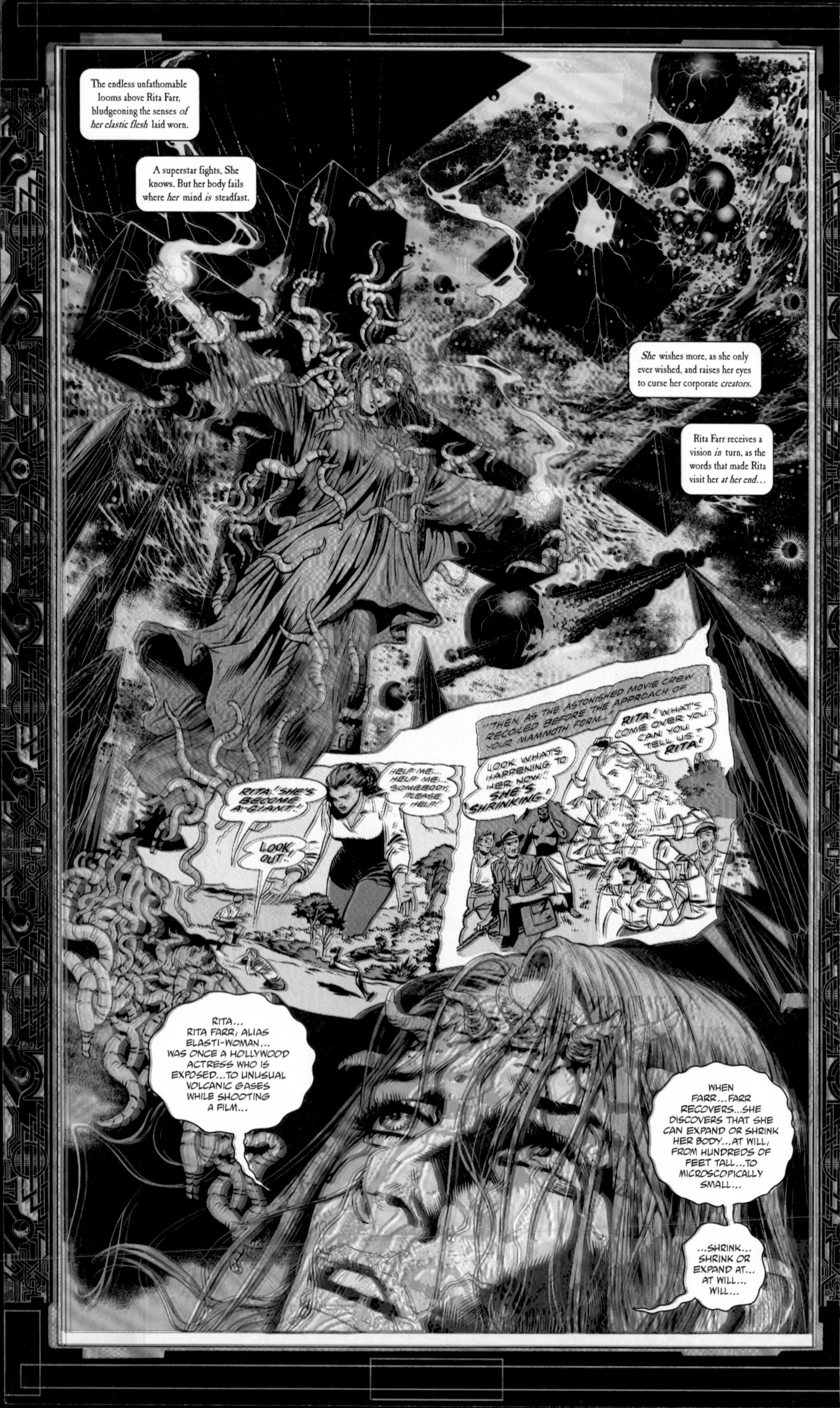
The endless unfathomable looms above Rita Farr, bludgeoning the senses *of her elastic flesh* laid worn.
A superstar fights, She knows. But her body fails where *her* mind *is* steadfast.
She wishes more, as she only ever wished, and raises her eyes to curse her corporate *creators.*
Rita Farr receives a vision *in* turn, as the words that made Rita visit her *at her end*...
RITA! SHE'S BECOME A GIANT!
HELP ME... HELP ME... SOMEBODY, PLEASE HELP!
LOOK OUT!
"THEN, AS THE ASTONISHED MOVIE CREW RECOILED BEFORE THE APPROACH OF YOUR MAMMOTH FORM..."
RITA! WHAT'S COME OVER YOU? CAN YOU TELL US? RITA!
LOOK WHAT'S HAPPENING TO HER NOW! SHE'S SHRINKING!
RITA... RITA FARR, ALIAS ELASTI-WOMAN... WAS ONCE A HOLLYWOOD ACTRESS WHO IS EXPOSED... TO UNUSUAL VOLCANIC GASES WHILE SHOOTING A FILM...
WHEN FARR... FARR RECOVERS... SHE DISCOVERS THAT SHE CAN EXPAND OR SHRINK HER BODY... AT WILL, FROM HUNDREDS OF FEET TALL... TO MICROSCOPICALLY SMALL...
...SHRINK... SHRINK OR EXPAND AT... AT WILL... WILL...

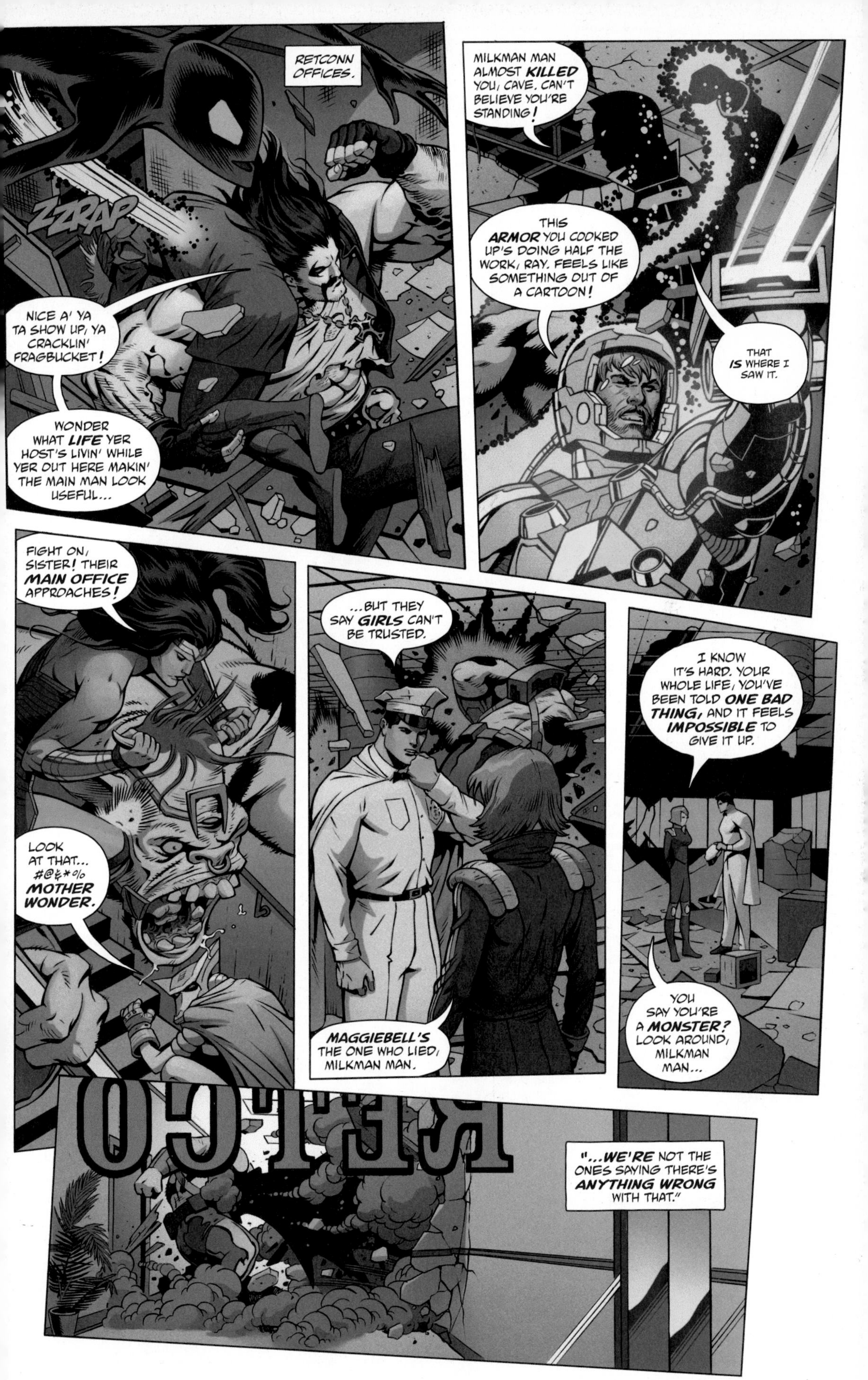
RETCONN OFFICES.
ZZRAP
NICE A' YA TA SHOW UP, YA CRACKLIN' FRAGBUCKET!
WONDER WHAT LIFE YER HOST'S LIVIN' WHILE YER OUT HERE MAKIN' THE MAIN MAN LOOK USEFUL...
MILKMAN MAN ALMOST KILLED YOU, CAVE. CAN'T BELIEVE YOU'RE STANDING!
THIS ARMOR YOU COOKED UP'S DOING HALF THE WORK, RAY. FEELS LIKE SOMETHING OUT OF A CARTOON!
THAT IS WHERE I SAW IT.
FIGHT ON, SISTER! THEIR MAIN OFFICE APPROACHES!
LOOK AT THAT... #@&*% MOTHER WONDER.
...BUT THEY SAY GIRLS CAN'T BE TRUSTED.
MAGGIEBELL'S THE ONE WHO LIED, MILKMAN MAN.
I KNOW IT'S HARD. YOUR WHOLE LIFE, YOU'VE BEEN TOLD ONE BAD THING, AND IT FEELS IMPOSSIBLE TO GIVE IT UP.
YOU SAY YOU'RE A MONSTER? LOOK AROUND, MILKMAN MAN...
"...WE'RE NOT THE ONES SAYING THERE'S ANYTHING WRONG WITH THAT."

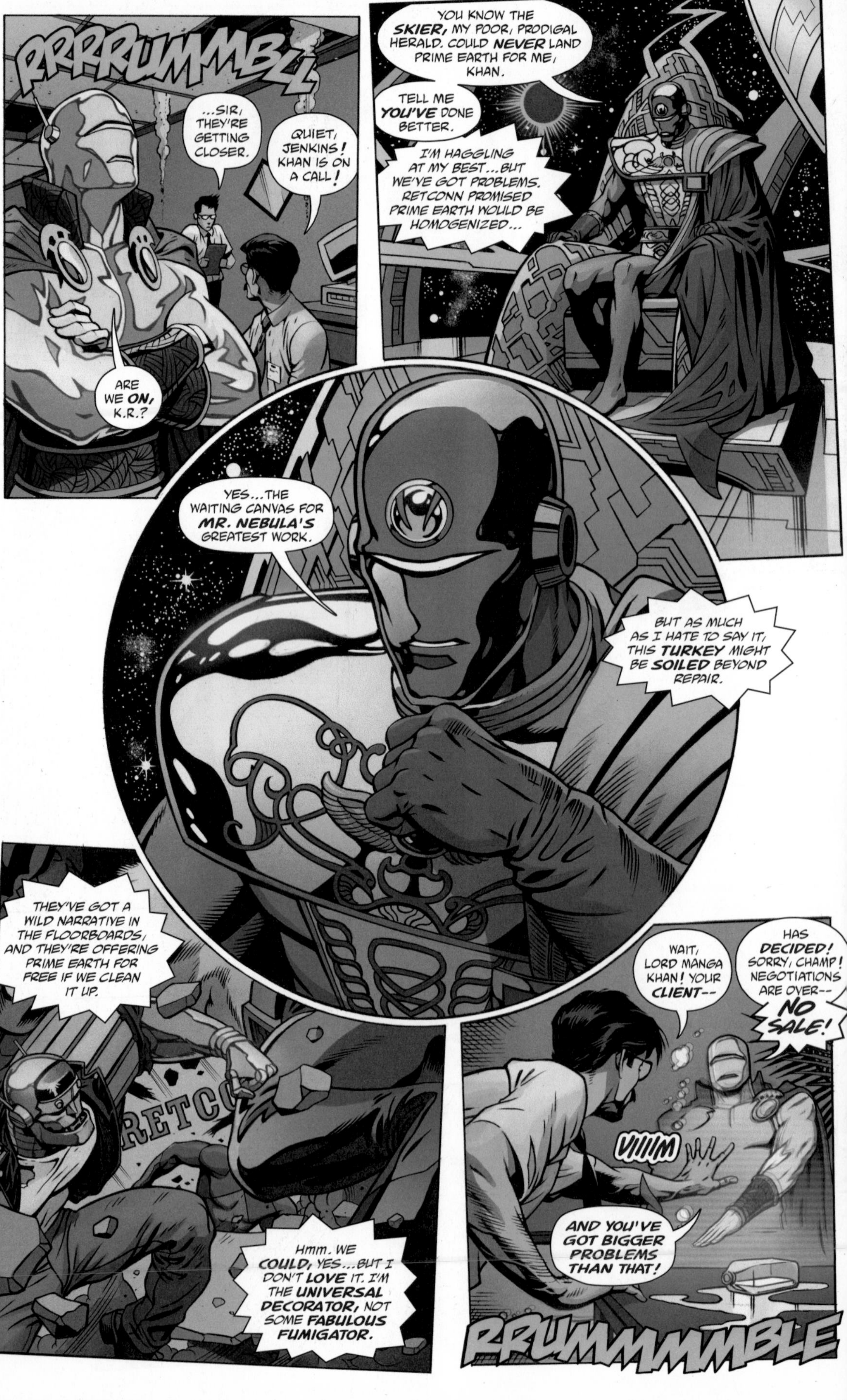
RRRRUMMBLL
...SIR, THEY'RE GETTING CLOSER.
QUIET, JENKINS! KHAN IS ON A CALL!
ARE WE ON, K.R.?
YOU KNOW THE SKIER, MY POOR, PRODIGAL HERALD. COULD NEVER LAND PRIME EARTH FOR ME, KHAN.
TELL ME YOU'VE DONE BETTER.
I'M HAGGLING AT MY BEST...BUT WE'VE GOT PROBLEMS. RETCONN PROMISED PRIME EARTH WOULD BE HOMOGENIZED...
YES...THE WAITING CANVAS FOR MR. NEBULA'S GREATEST WORK.
BUT AS MUCH AS I HATE TO SAY IT, THIS TURKEY MIGHT BE SOILED BEYOND REPAIR.
THEY'VE GOT A WILD NARRATIVE IN THE FLOORBOARDS, AND THEY'RE OFFERING PRIME EARTH FOR FREE IF WE CLEAN IT UP.
RETCO
Hmm. WE COULD, YES...BUT I DON'T LOVE IT. I'M THE UNIVERSAL DECORATOR, NOT SOME FABULOUS FUMIGATOR.
WAIT, LORD MANGA KHAN! YOUR CLIENT--
HAS DECIDED! SORRY, CHAMP! NEGOTIATIONS ARE OVER-- NO SALE!
VIIIM
AND YOU'VE GOT BIGGER PROBLEMS THAN THAT!
RRUMMMMBLE

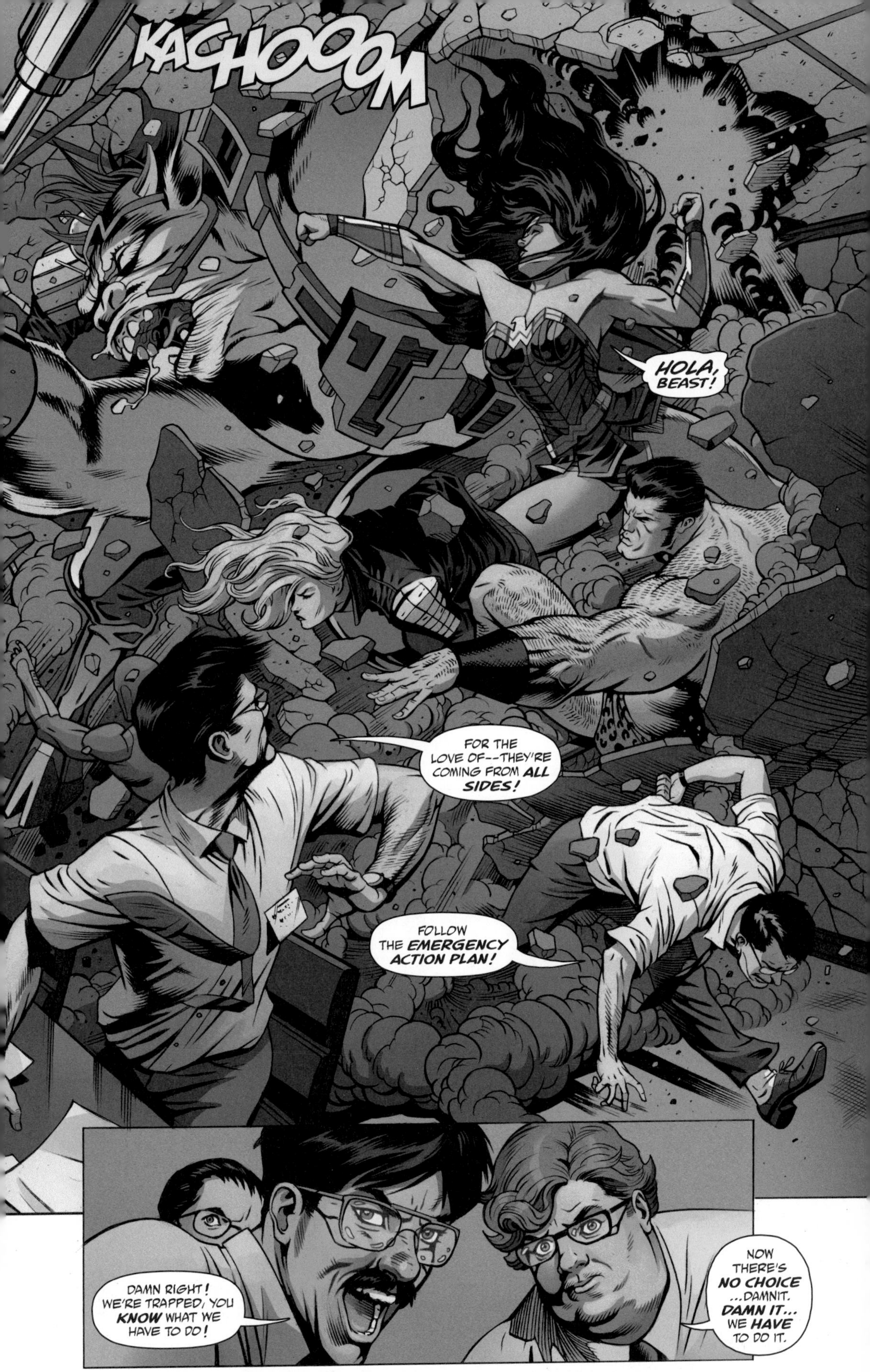
KACHOOOOM
HOLA, BEAST!
FOR THE LOVE OF--THEY'RE COMING FROM ALL SIDES!
FOLLOW THE EMERGENCY ACTION PLAN!
DAMN RIGHT! WE'RE TRAPPED, YOU KNOW WHAT WE HAVE TO DO!
NOW THERE'S NO CHOICE ...DAMNIT. DAMN IT... WE HAVE TO DO IT.

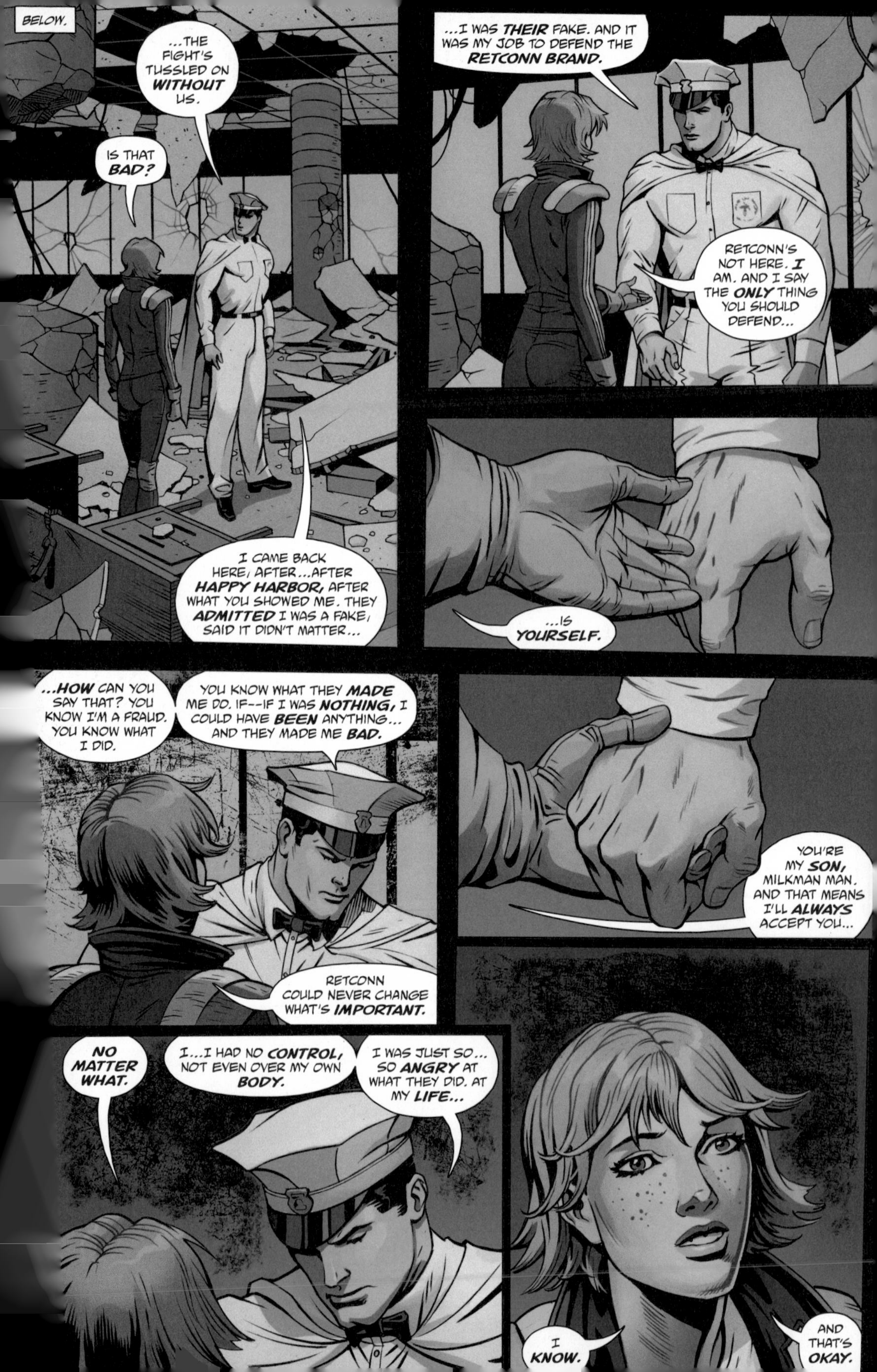
BELOW.
...THE FIGHT'S TUSSLED ON WITHOUT US.
IS THAT BAD?
I CAME BACK HERE, AFTER...AFTER HAPPY HARBOR, AFTER WHAT YOU SHOWED ME. THEY ADMITTED I WAS A FAKE, SAID IT DIDN'T MATTER...
...I WAS THEIR FAKE. AND IT WAS MY JOB TO DEFEND THE RETCONN BRAND.
RETCONN'S NOT HERE. I AM. AND I SAY THE ONLY THING YOU SHOULD DEFEND...
...IS YOURSELF.
...HOW CAN YOU SAY THAT? YOU KNOW I'M A FRAUD. YOU KNOW WHAT I DID.
YOU KNOW WHAT THEY MADE ME DO. IF--IF I WAS NOTHING, I COULD HAVE BEEN ANYTHING... AND THEY MADE ME BAD.
RETCONN COULD NEVER CHANGE WHAT'S IMPORTANT.
YOU'RE MY SON, MILKMAN MAN. AND THAT MEANS I'LL ALWAYS ACCEPT YOU...
NO MATTER WHAT.
I...I HAD NO CONTROL, NOT EVEN OVER MY OWN BODY.
I WAS JUST SO... SO ANGRY AT WHAT THEY DID. AT MY LIFE...
I KNOW.
AND THAT'S OKAY.

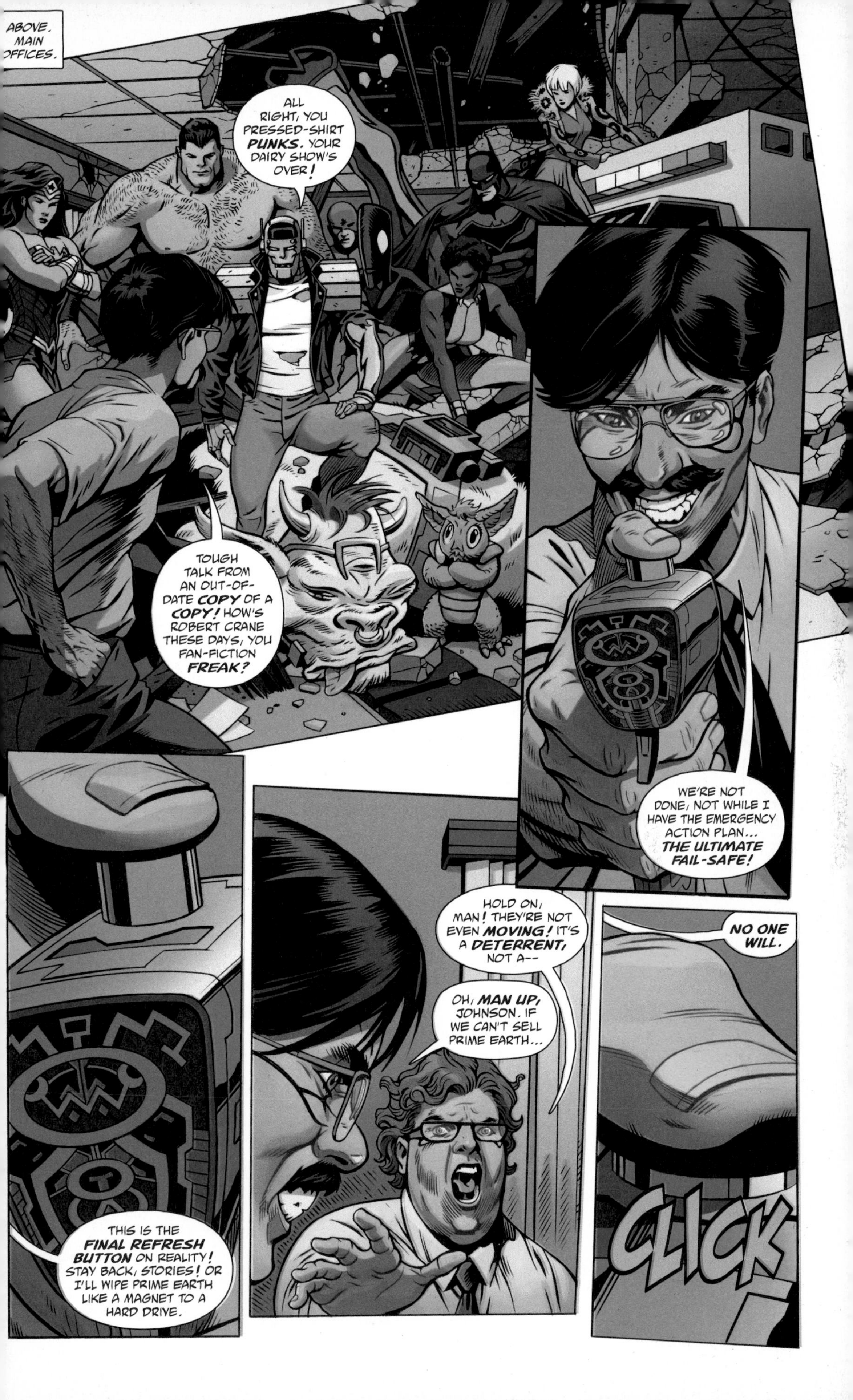

ABOVE. MAIN OFFICES.
ALL RIGHT, YOU PRESSED-SHIRT PUNKS. YOUR DAIRY SHOW'S OVER!
TOUGH TALK FROM AN OUT-OF-DATE COPY OF A COPY! HOW'S ROBERT CRANE THESE DAYS, YOU FAN-FICTION FREAK?
WE'RE NOT DONE, NOT WHILE I HAVE THE EMERGENCY ACTION PLAN... THE ULTIMATE FAIL-SAFE!
THIS IS THE FINAL REFRESH BUTTON ON REALITY! STAY BACK, STORIES! OR I'LL WIPE PRIME EARTH LIKE A MAGNET TO A HARD DRIVE.
HOLD ON, MAN! THEY'RE NOT EVEN MOVING! IT'S A DETERRENT, NOT A--
OH, MAN UP, JOHNSON. IF WE CAN'T SELL PRIME EARTH...
NO ONE WILL.
CLICK

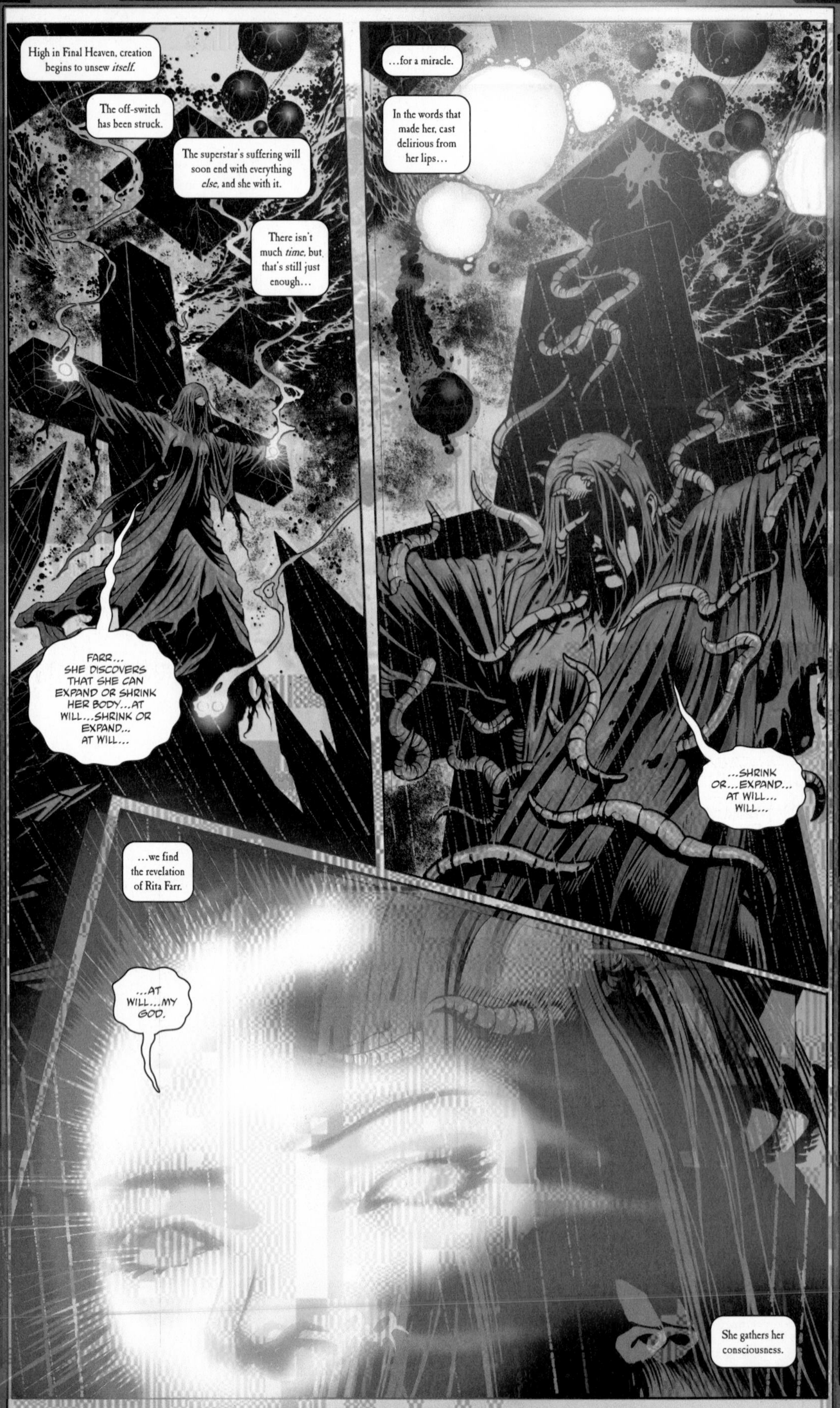

High in Final Heaven, creation begins to unsew *itself*.
The off-switch has been struck.
The superstar's suffering will soon end with everything *else*, and she with it.
There isn't much *time*, but, that's still just enough...
FARR... SHE DISCOVERS THAT SHE CAN EXPAND OR SHRINK HER BODY...AT WILL...SHRINK OR EXPAND... AT WILL...
...for a miracle.
In the words that made her, cast delirious from her lips...
...SHRINK OR...EXPAND... AT WILL... WILL...
...we find the revelation of Rita Farr.
...AT WILL...MY GOD.
She gathers her consciousness.

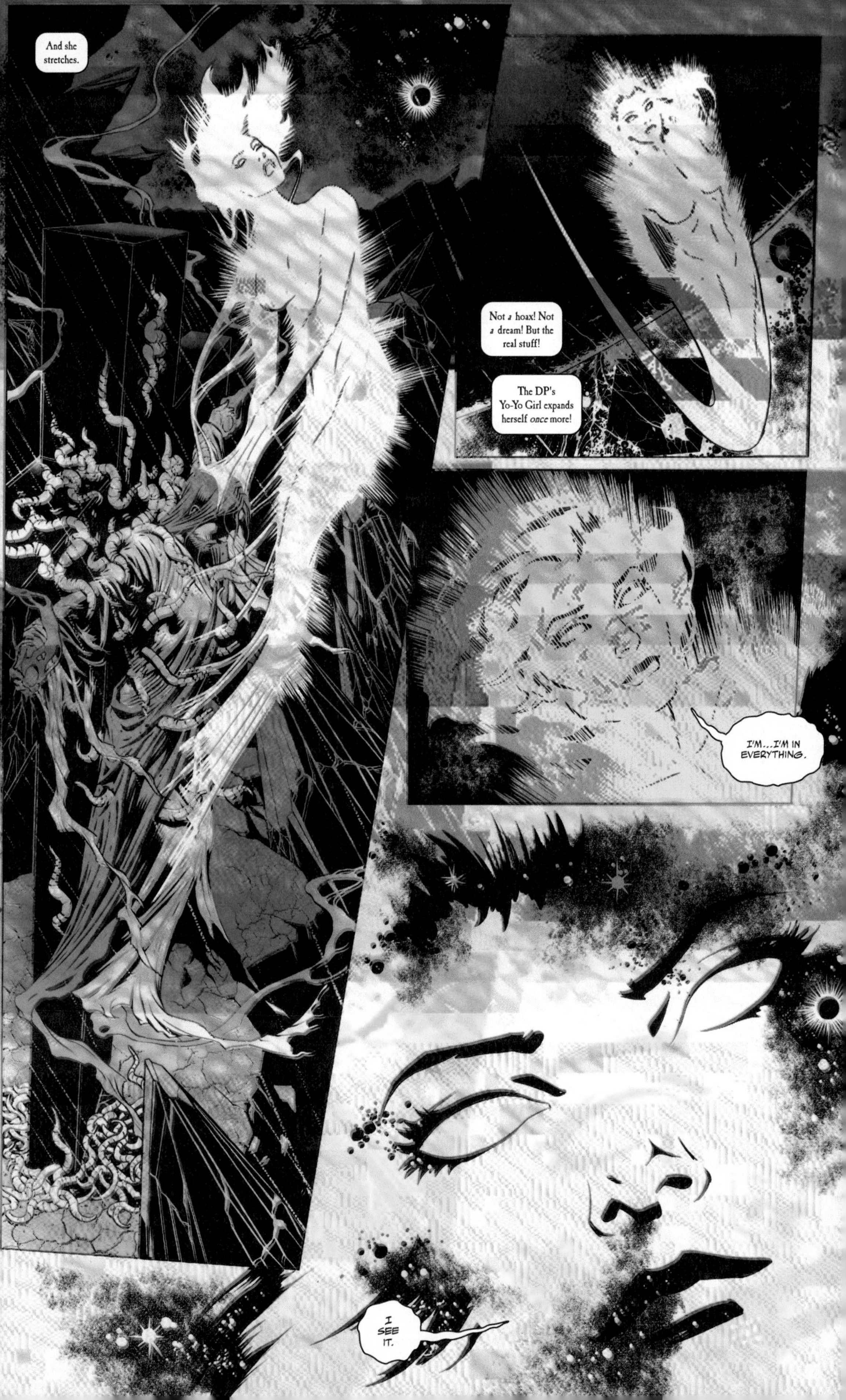
And she stretches.
Not *a* hoax! Not *a* dream! But the real stuff!
The DP's Yo-Yo Girl expands herself *once* more!
I'M...I'M IN EVERYTHING.
I SEE IT.

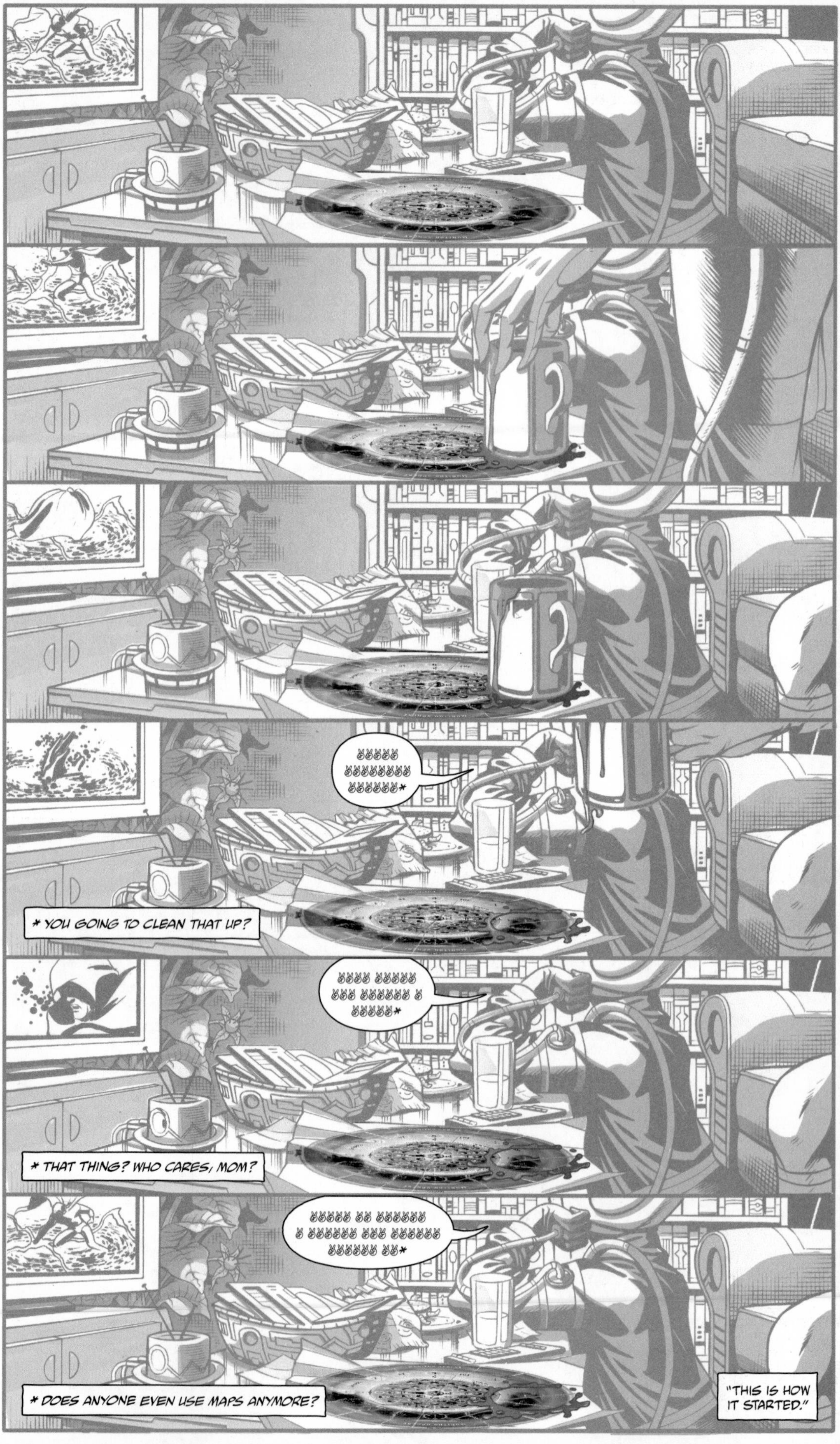

* YOU GOING TO CLEAN THAT UP?
* THAT THING? WHO CARES, MOM?
* DOES ANYONE EVEN USE MAPS ANYMORE?
"THIS IS HOW IT STARTED."

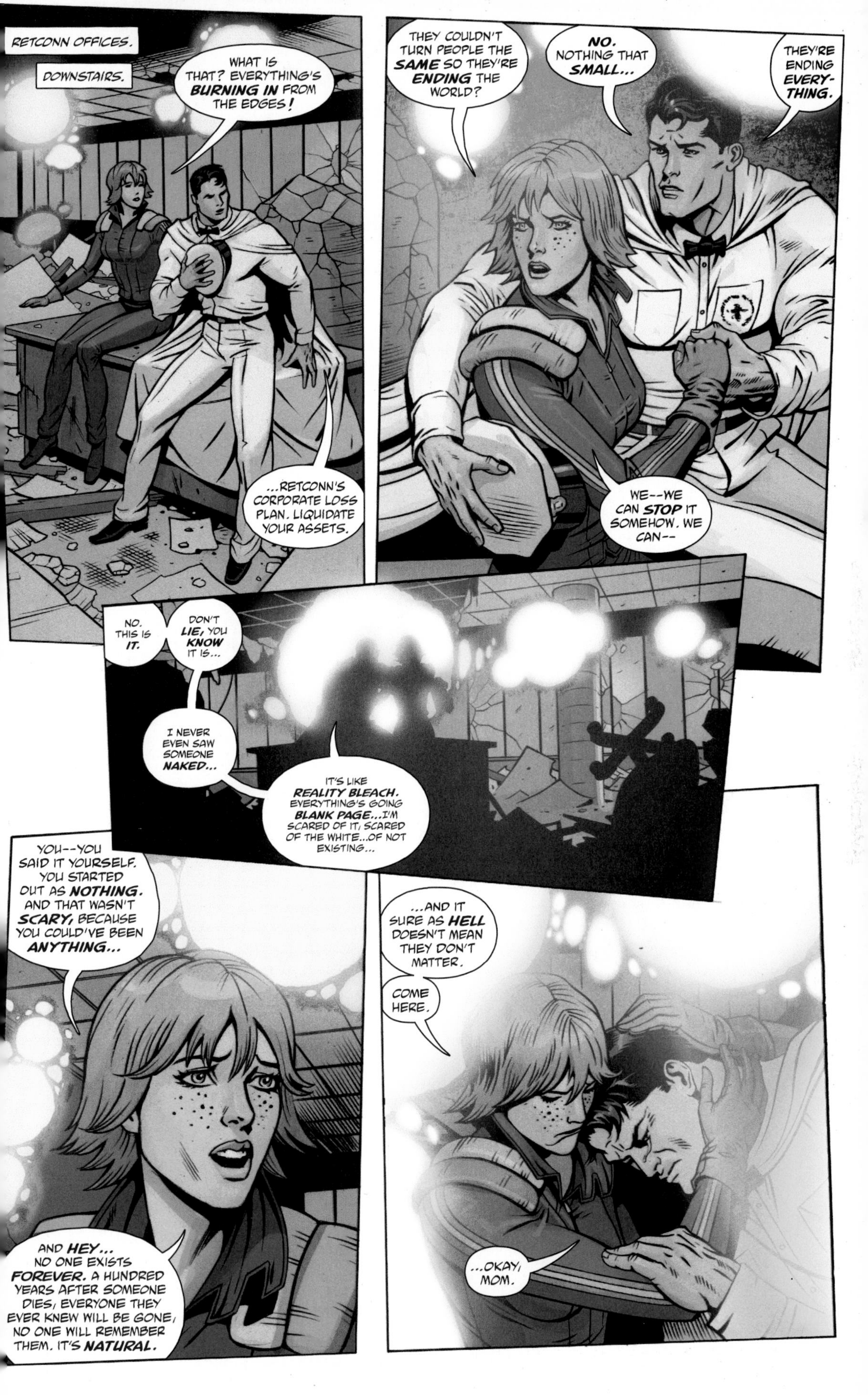
RETCONN OFFICES.
DOWNSTAIRS.
WHAT IS THAT? EVERYTHING'S BURNING IN FROM THE EDGES!
...RETCONN'S CORPORATE LOSS PLAN. LIQUIDATE YOUR ASSETS.
THEY COULDN'T TURN PEOPLE THE SAME SO THEY'RE ENDING THE WORLD?
NO. NOTHING THAT SMALL...
THEY'RE ENDING EVERYTHING.
WE--WE CAN STOP IT SOMEHOW. WE CAN--
NO. THIS IS IT.
DON'T LIE, YOU KNOW IT IS...
I NEVER EVEN SAW SOMEONE NAKED...
IT'S LIKE REALITY BLEACH. EVERYTHING'S GOING BLANK PAGE...I'M SCARED OF IT, SCARED OF THE WHITE...OF NOT EXISTING...
YOU--YOU SAID IT YOURSELF. YOU STARTED OUT AS NOTHING. AND THAT WASN'T SCARY, BECAUSE YOU COULD'VE BEEN ANYTHING...
AND HEY... NO ONE EXISTS FOREVER. A HUNDRED YEARS AFTER SOMEONE DIES, EVERYONE THEY EVER KNEW WILL BE GONE, NO ONE WILL REMEMBER THEM. IT'S NATURAL.
...AND IT SURE AS HELL DOESN'T MEAN THEY DON'T MATTER.
COME HERE.
...OKAY, MOM.

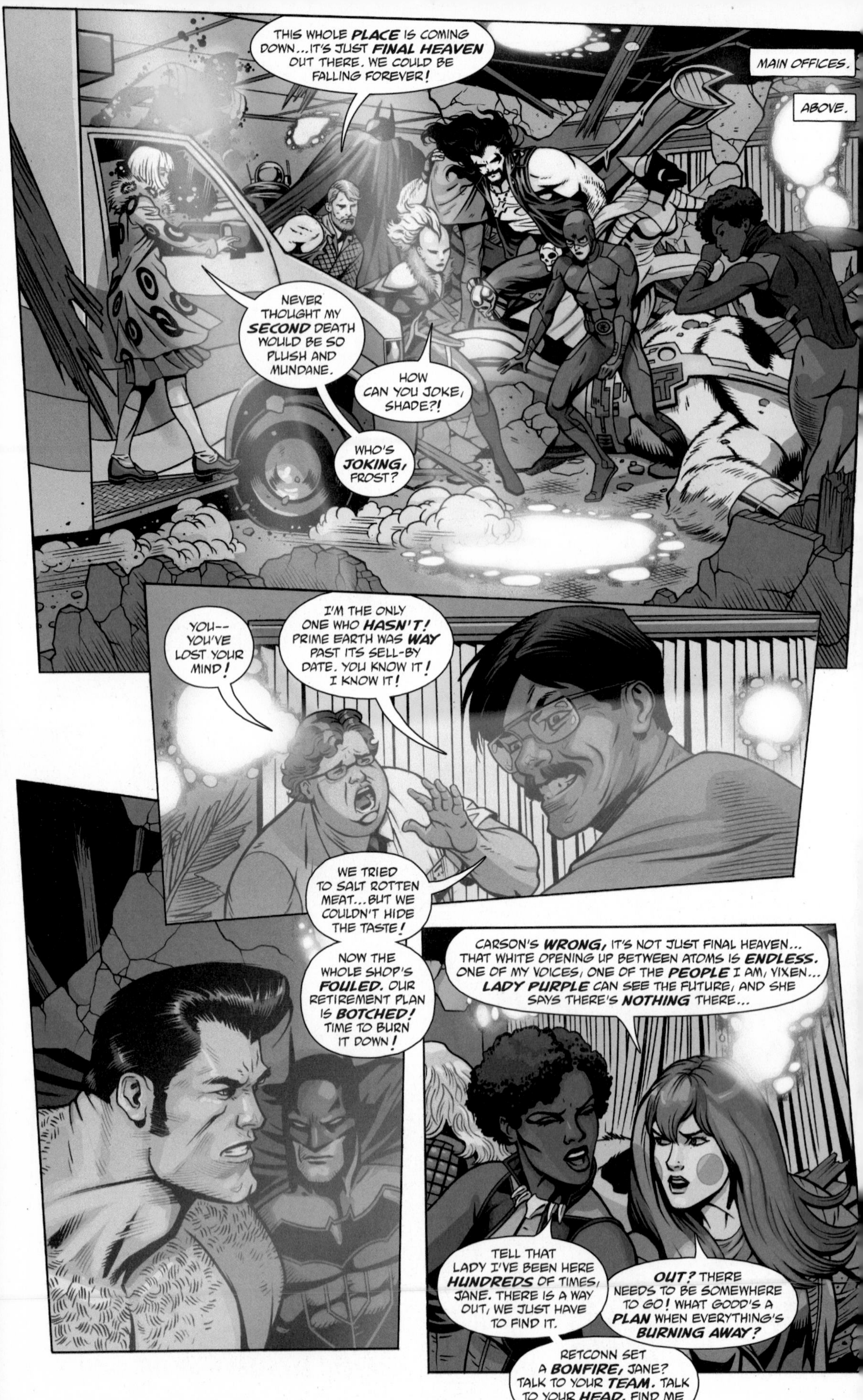

THIS WHOLE PLACE IS COMING DOWN...IT'S JUST FINAL HEAVEN OUT THERE. WE COULD BE FALLING FOREVER!
MAIN OFFICES.
ABOVE.
NEVER THOUGHT MY SECOND DEATH WOULD BE SO PLUSH AND MUNDANE.
HOW CAN YOU JOKE, SHADE?!
WHO'S JOKING, FROST?
YOU-- YOU'VE LOST YOUR MIND!
I'M THE ONLY ONE WHO HASN'T! PRIME EARTH WAS WAY PAST ITS SELL-BY DATE. YOU KNOW IT! I KNOW IT!
WE TRIED TO SALT ROTTEN MEAT...BUT WE COULDN'T HIDE THE TASTE!
NOW THE WHOLE SHOP'S FOULED. OUR RETIREMENT PLAN IS BOTCHED! TIME TO BURN IT DOWN!
CARSON'S WRONG, IT'S NOT JUST FINAL HEAVEN... THAT WHITE OPENING UP BETWEEN ATOMS IS ENDLESS. ONE OF MY VOICES, ONE OF THE PEOPLE I AM, VIXEN... LADY PURPLE CAN SEE THE FUTURE, AND SHE SAYS THERE'S NOTHING THERE...
TELL THAT LADY I'VE BEEN HERE HUNDREDS OF TIMES, JANE. THERE IS A WAY OUT, WE JUST HAVE TO FIND IT.
OUT? THERE NEEDS TO BE SOMEWHERE TO GO! WHAT GOOD'S A PLAN WHEN EVERYTHING'S BURNING AWAY?
RETCONN SET A BONFIRE, JANE? TALK TO YOUR TEAM. TALK TO YOUR HEAD. FIND ME SOME WATER.

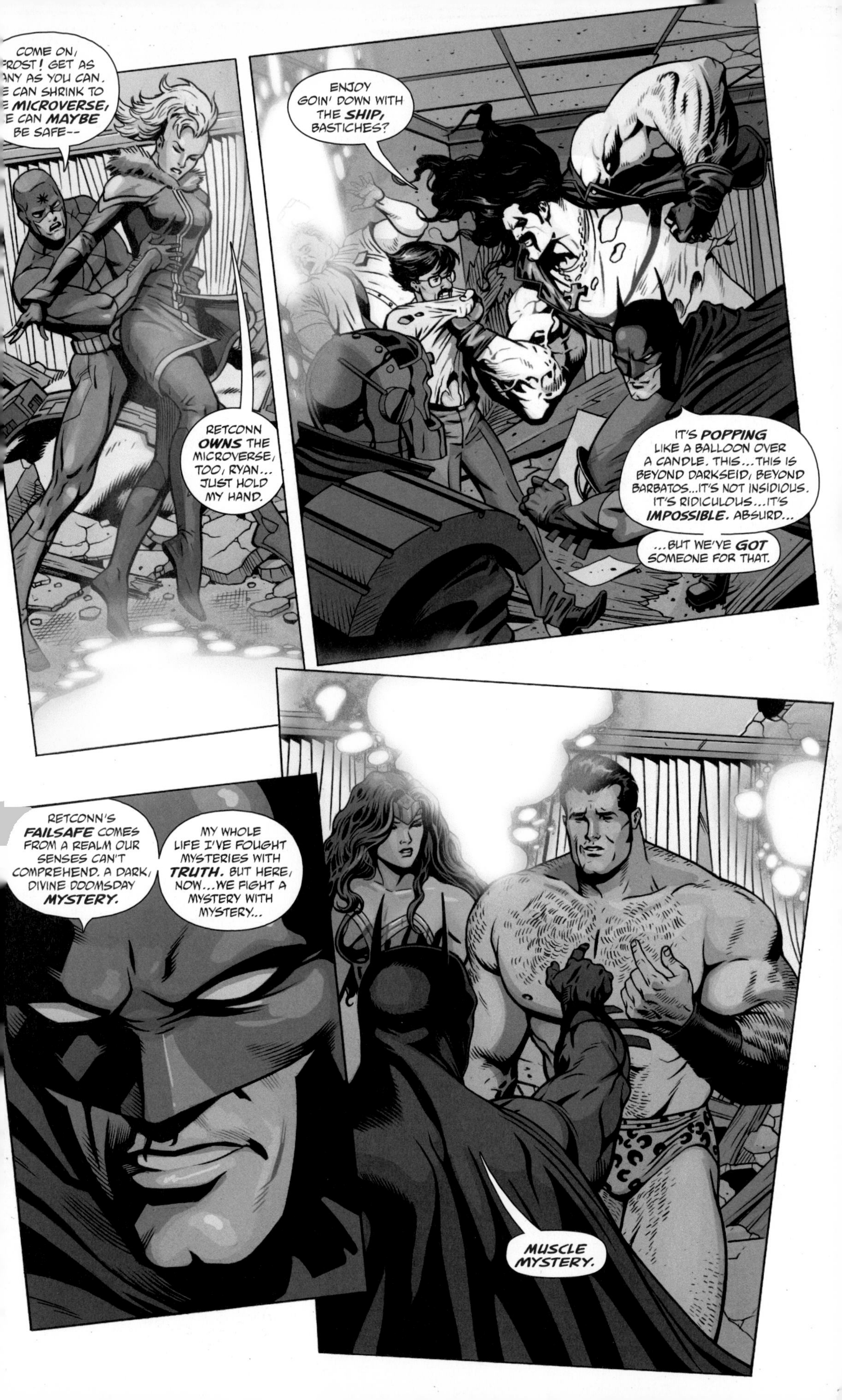

COME ON, FROST! GET AS ANY AS YOU CAN. E CAN SHRINK TO E MICROVERSE, E CAN MAYBE BE SAFE--
RETCONN OWNS THE MICROVERSE, TOO, RYAN... JUST HOLD MY HAND.
ENJOY GOIN' DOWN WITH THE SHIP, BASTICHES?
IT'S POPPING LIKE A BALLOON OVER A CANDLE. THIS...THIS IS BEYOND DARKSEID, BEYOND BARBATOS...IT'S NOT INSIDIOUS. IT'S RIDICULOUS...IT'S IMPOSSIBLE. ABSURD...
...BUT WE'VE GOT SOMEONE FOR THAT.
RETCONN'S FAILSAFE COMES FROM A REALM OUR SENSES CAN'T COMPREHEND. A DARK, DIVINE DOOMSDAY MYSTERY.
MY WHOLE LIFE I'VE FOUGHT MYSTERIES WITH TRUTH. BUT HERE, NOW...WE FIGHT A MYSTERY WITH MYSTERY...
MUSCLE MYSTERY.

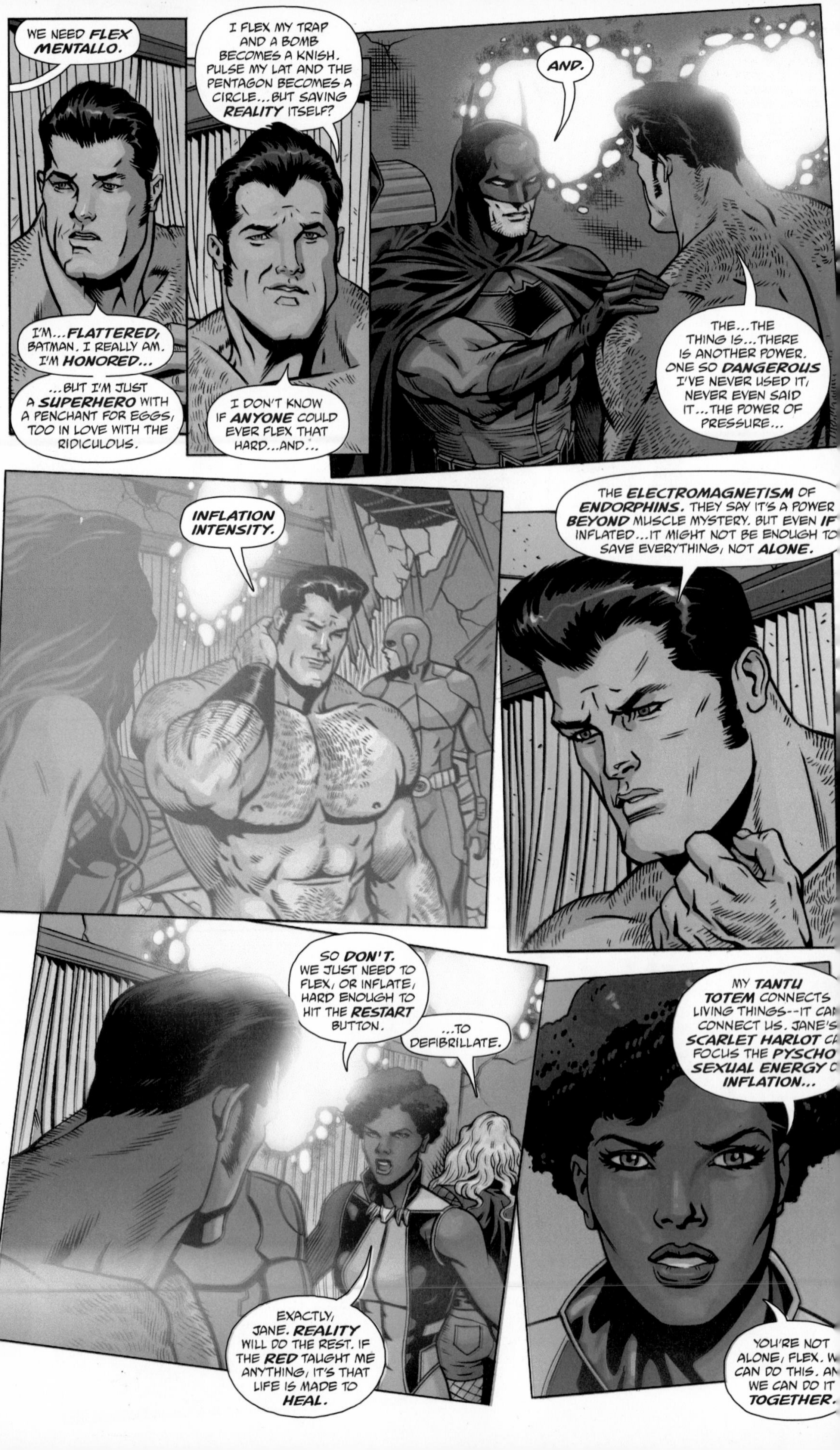
WE NEED FLEX MENTALLO.
I'M...FLATTERED, BATMAN. I REALLY AM. I'M HONORED...
...BUT I'M JUST A SUPERHERO WITH A PENCHANT FOR EGGS, TOO IN LOVE WITH THE RIDICULOUS.
I FLEX MY TRAP AND A BOMB BECOMES A KNISH. PULSE MY LAT AND THE PENTAGON BECOMES A CIRCLE...BUT SAVING REALITY ITSELF?
I DON'T KNOW IF ANYONE COULD EVER FLEX THAT HARD...AND...
AND.
THE...THE THING IS...THERE IS ANOTHER POWER. ONE SO DANGEROUS I'VE NEVER USED IT, NEVER EVEN SAID IT...THE POWER OF PRESSURE...
INFLATION INTENSITY.
THE ELECTROMAGNETISM OF ENDORPHINS. THEY SAY IT'S A POWER BEYOND MUSCLE MYSTERY. BUT EVEN IF INFLATED...IT MIGHT NOT BE ENOUGH TO SAVE EVERYTHING, NOT ALONE.
SO DON'T. WE JUST NEED TO FLEX, OR INFLATE, HARD ENOUGH TO HIT THE RESTART BUTTON.
...TO DEFIBRILLATE.
EXACTLY, JANE. REALITY WILL DO THE REST. IF THE RED TAUGHT ME ANYTHING, IT'S THAT LIFE IS MADE TO HEAL.
MY TANTU TOTEM CONNECTS LIVING THINGS--IT CA CONNECT US. JANE'S SCARLET HARLOT C FOCUS THE PYSCHO SEXUAL ENERGY O INFLATION...
YOU'RE NOT ALONE, FLEX. W CAN DO THIS. A WE CAN DO IT TOGETHER.

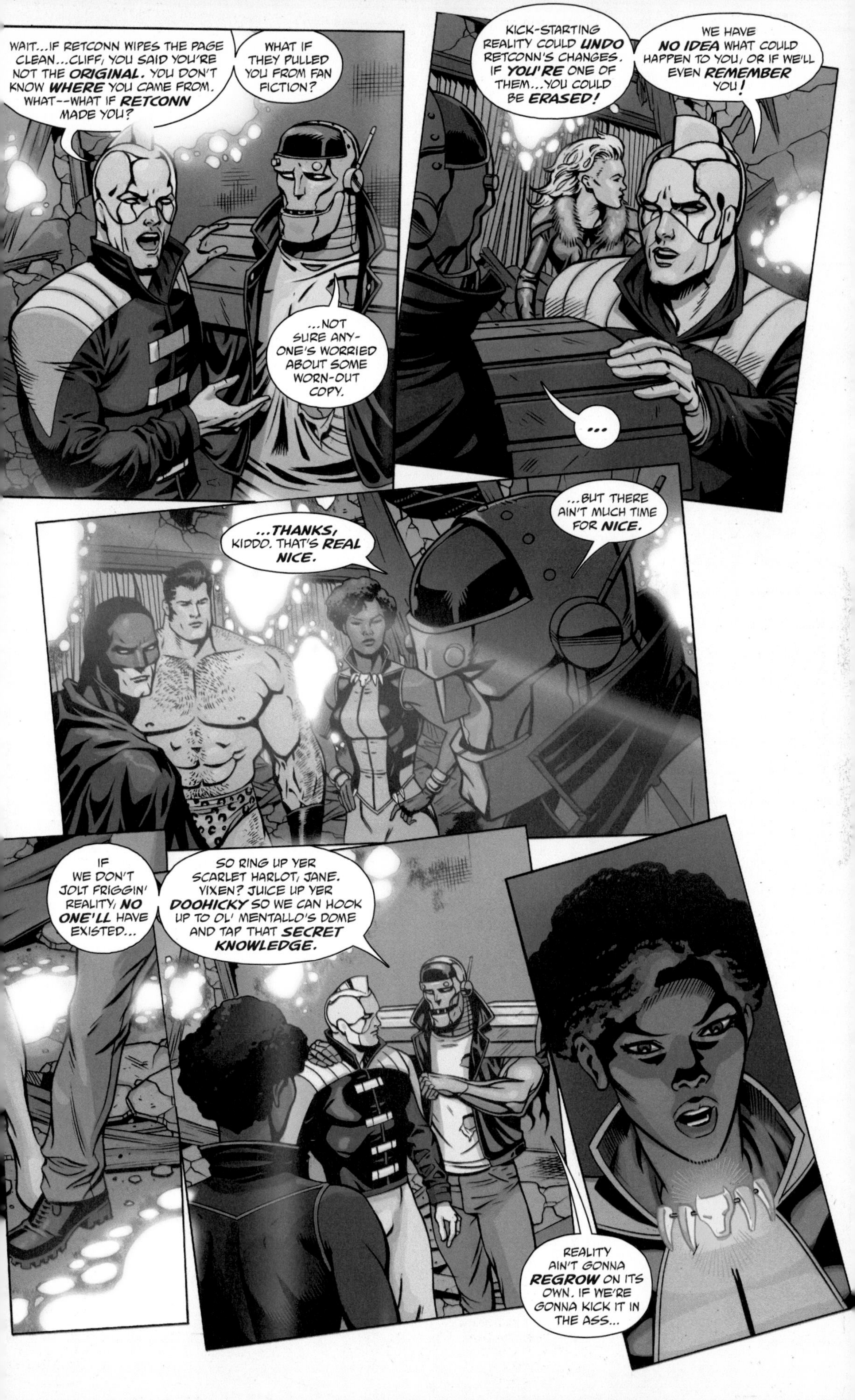
WAIT...IF RETCONN WIPES THE PAGE CLEAN...CLIFF, YOU SAID YOU'RE NOT THE ORIGINAL. YOU DON'T KNOW WHERE YOU CAME FROM. WHAT--WHAT IF RETCONN MADE YOU?
WHAT IF THEY PULLED YOU FROM FAN FICTION?
...NOT SURE ANY-ONE'S WORRIED ABOUT SOME WORN-OUT COPY.
KICK-STARTING REALITY COULD UNDO RETCONN'S CHANGES. IF YOU'RE ONE OF THEM...YOU COULD BE ERASED!
WE HAVE NO IDEA WHAT COULD HAPPEN TO YOU, OR IF WE'LL EVEN REMEMBER YOU!
...
...THANKS, KIDDO. THAT'S REAL NICE.
...BUT THERE AIN'T MUCH TIME FOR NICE.
IF WE DON'T JOLT FRIGGIN' REALITY, NO ONE'LL HAVE EXISTED...
SO RING UP YER SCARLET HARLOT, JANE. VIXEN? JUICE UP YER DOOHICKY SO WE CAN HOOK UP TO OL' MENTALLO'S DOME AND TAP THAT SECRET KNOWLEDGE.
REALITY AIN'T GONNA REGROW ON ITS OWN. IF WE'RE GONNA KICK IT IN THE ASS...

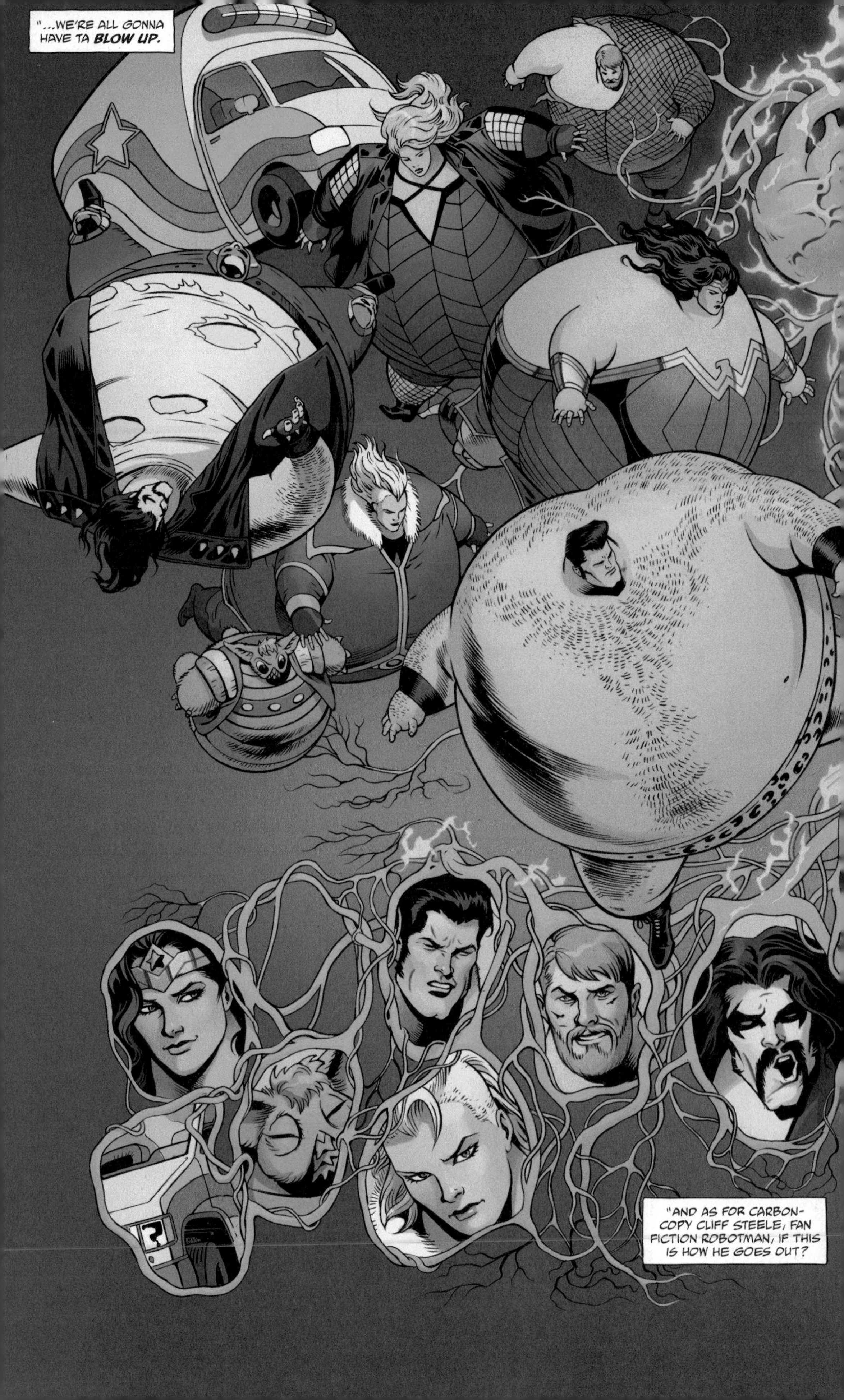
"...WE'RE ALL GONNA HAVE TA **BLOW UP.**
"AND AS FOR CARBON-COPY CLIFF STEELE, FAN FICTION ROBOTMAN, IF THIS IS HOW HE GOES OUT?

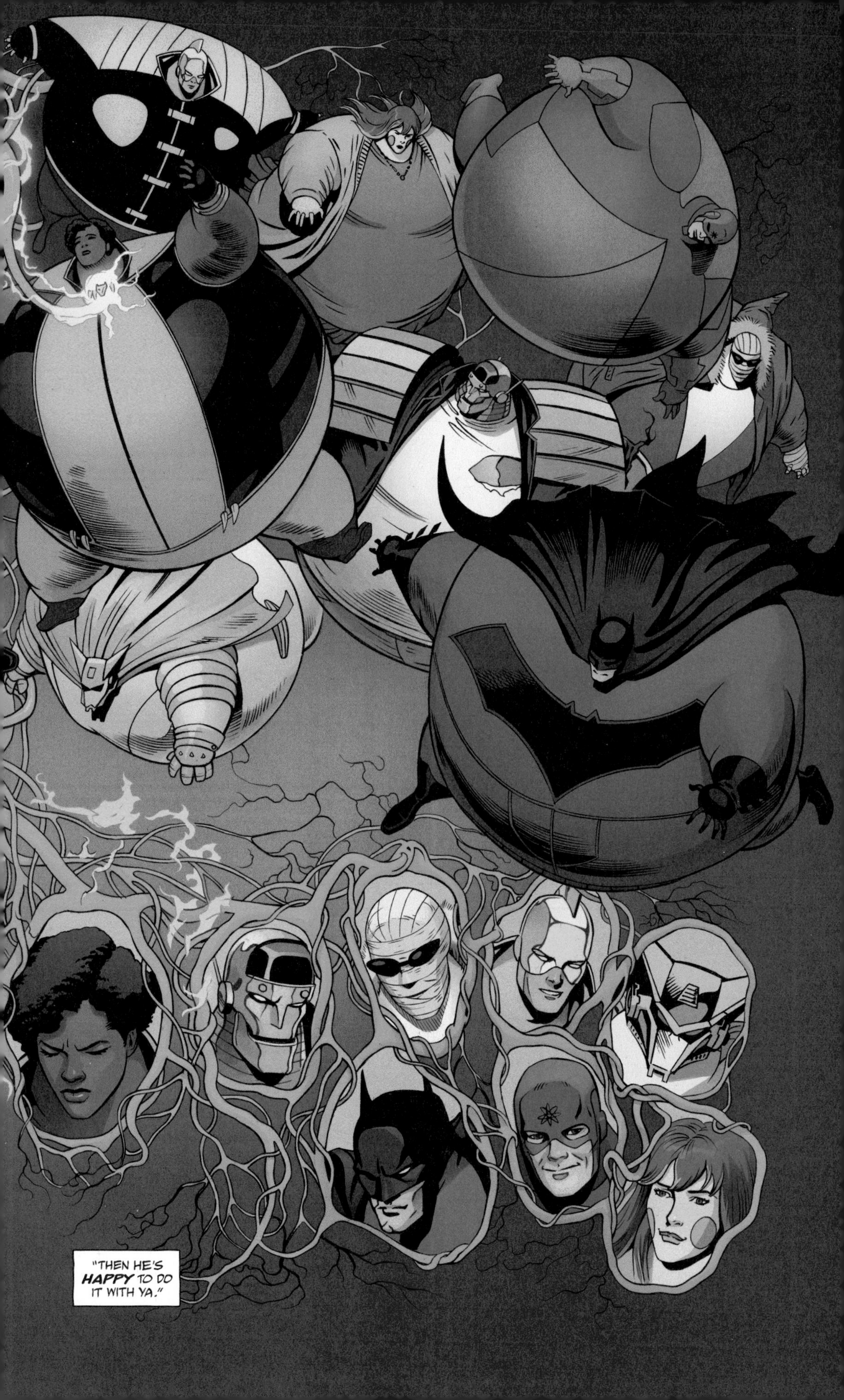
"THEN HE'S **HAPPY** TO DO IT WITH YA."

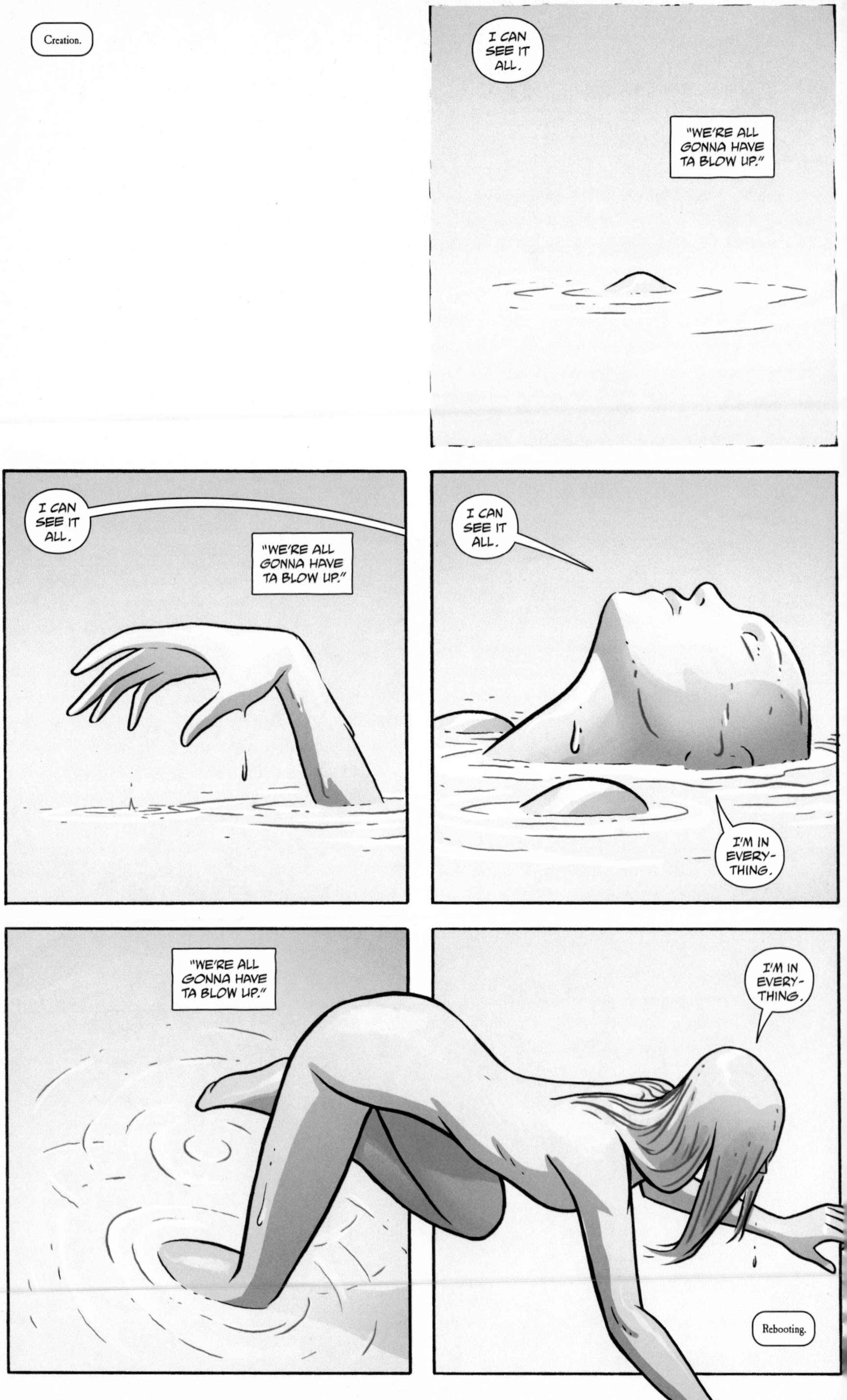
Creation.
I CAN SEE IT ALL.
"WE'RE ALL GONNA HAVE TA BLOW UP."
I CAN SEE IT ALL.
"WE'RE ALL GONNA HAVE TA BLOW UP."
I CAN SEE IT ALL.
I'M IN EVERY-THING.
"WE'RE ALL GONNA HAVE TA BLOW UP."
I'M IN EVERY-THING.
Rebooting.

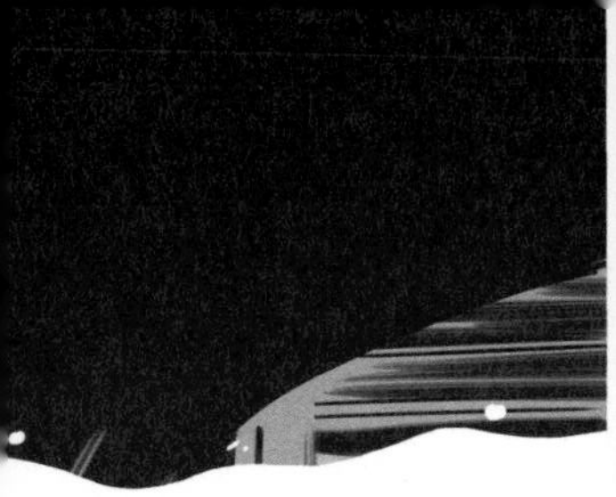
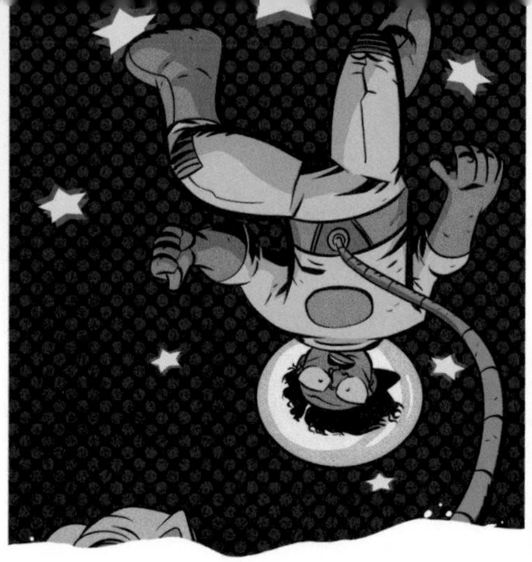
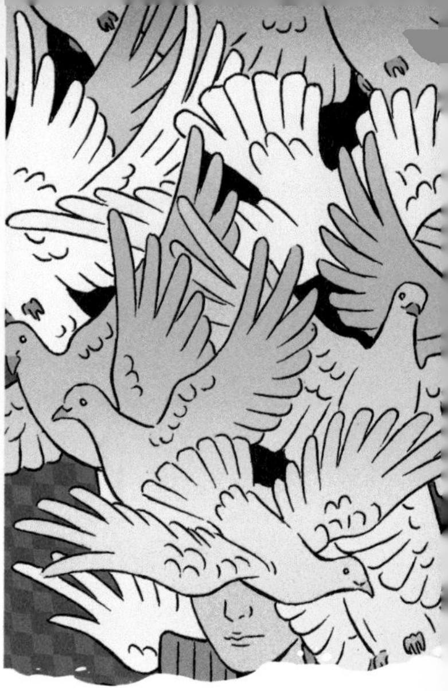

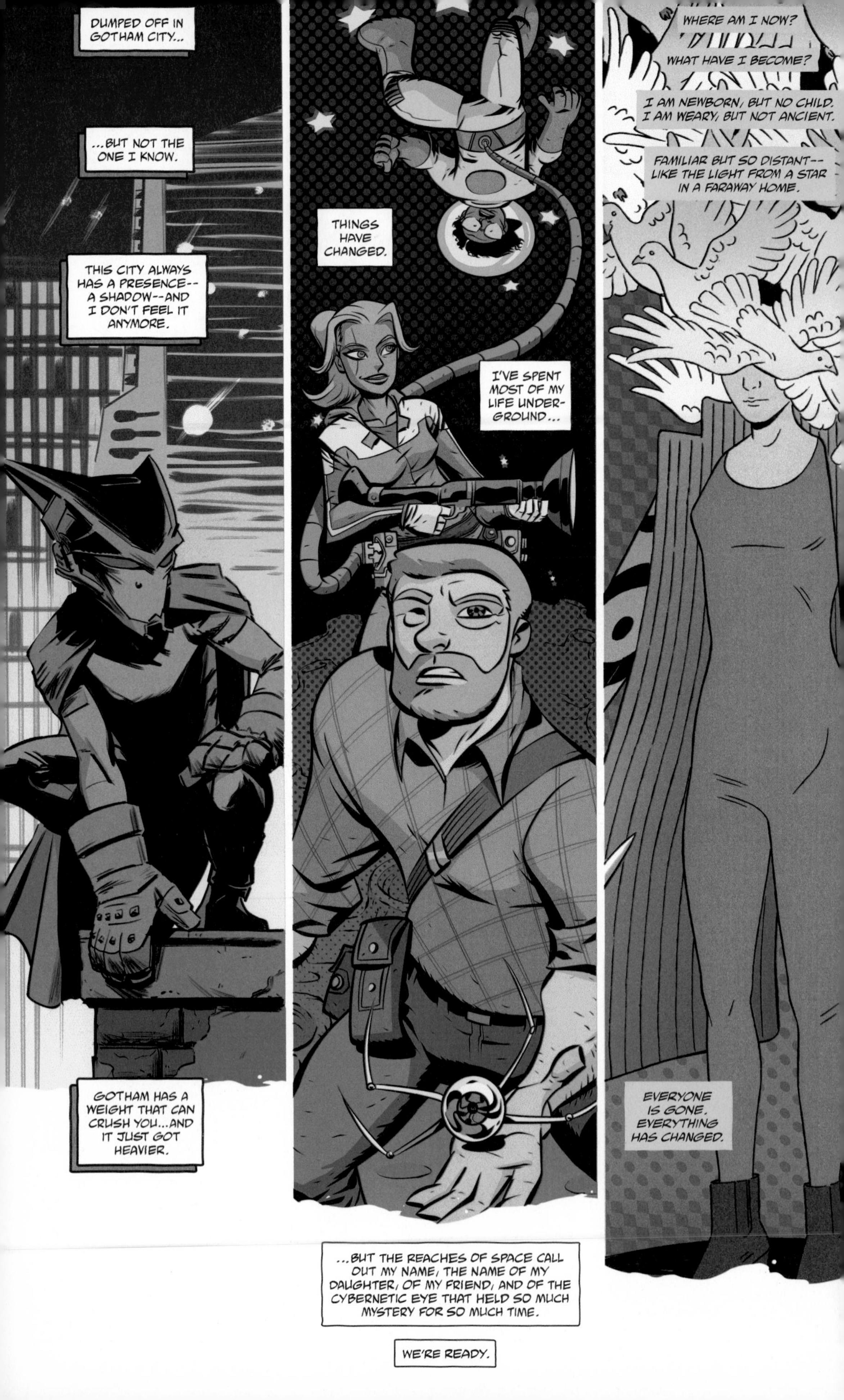
DUMPED OFF IN GOTHAM CITY...
...BUT NOT THE ONE I KNOW.
THIS CITY ALWAYS HAS A PRESENCE-- A SHADOW--AND I DON'T FEEL IT ANYMORE.
GOTHAM HAS A WEIGHT THAT CAN CRUSH YOU...AND IT JUST GOT HEAVIER.
THINGS HAVE CHANGED.
I'VE SPENT MOST OF MY LIFE UNDER-GROUND...
...BUT THE REACHES OF SPACE CALL OUT MY NAME, THE NAME OF MY DAUGHTER, OF MY FRIEND, AND OF THE CYBERNETIC EYE THAT HELD SO MUCH MYSTERY FOR SO MUCH TIME.
WE'RE READY.
WHERE AM I NOW?
WHAT HAVE I BECOME?
I AM NEWBORN, BUT NO CHILD. I AM WEARY, BUT NOT ANCIENT.
FAMILIAR BUT SO DISTANT-- LIKE THE LIGHT FROM A STAR IN A FARAWAY HOME.
EVERYONE IS GONE. EVERYTHING HAS CHANGED.

WAIT!

WAIT! HOLD ON!

DON'T KNOW IF I CAN FIT...

HNGAH!

...PHYEW

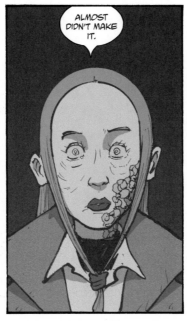

ALMOST DIDN'T MAKE IT.

OKAY, CAROLINE... LET'S SEE WHAT'S IN HERE.

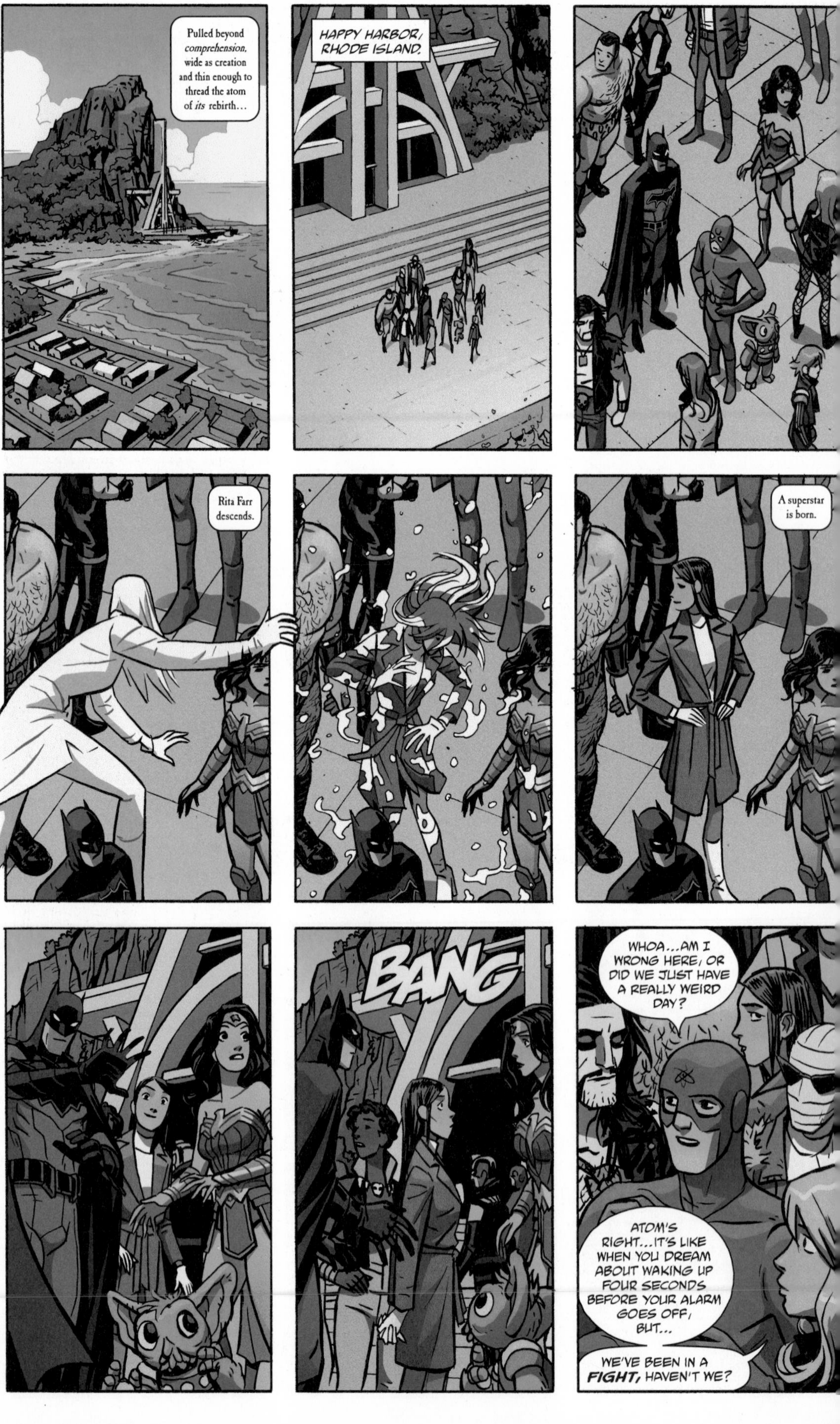
Pulled beyond *comprehension,* wide as creation and thin enough to thread the atom of *its* rebirth...
HAPPY HARBOR, RHODE ISLAND.
Rita Farr descends.
A superstar is born.
BANG
WHOA...AM I WRONG HERE, OR DID WE JUST HAVE A REALLY WEIRD DAY?
ATOM'S RIGHT...IT'S LIKE WHEN YOU DREAM ABOUT WAKING UP FOUR SECONDS BEFORE YOUR ALARM GOES OFF, BUT...
WE'VE BEEN IN A **FIGHT,** HAVEN'T WE?

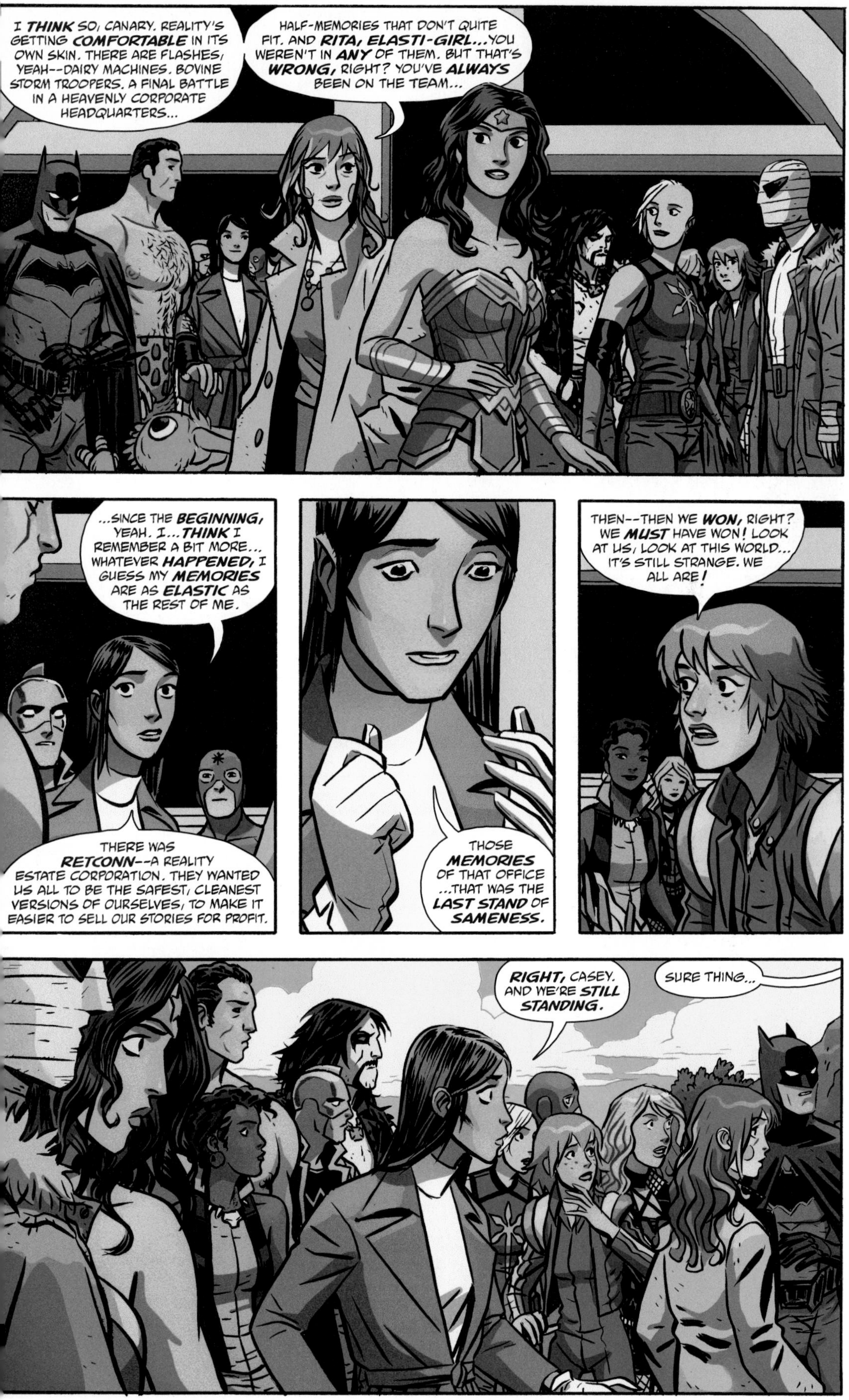
I THINK SO, CANARY. REALITY'S GETTING COMFORTABLE IN ITS OWN SKIN. THERE ARE FLASHES, YEAH--DAIRY MACHINES. BOVINE STORM TROOPERS. A FINAL BATTLE IN A HEAVENLY CORPORATE HEADQUARTERS...
HALF-MEMORIES THAT DON'T QUITE FIT. AND RITA, ELASTI-GIRL...YOU WEREN'T IN ANY OF THEM. BUT THAT'S WRONG, RIGHT? YOU'VE ALWAYS BEEN ON THE TEAM...
...SINCE THE BEGINNING, YEAH. I...THINK I REMEMBER A BIT MORE... WHATEVER HAPPENED, I GUESS MY MEMORIES ARE AS ELASTIC AS THE REST OF ME.
THERE WAS RETCONN--A REALITY ESTATE CORPORATION. THEY WANTED US ALL TO BE THE SAFEST, CLEANEST VERSIONS OF OURSELVES, TO MAKE IT EASIER TO SELL OUR STORIES FOR PROFIT.
THOSE MEMORIES OF THAT OFFICE ...THAT WAS THE LAST STAND OF SAMENESS.
THEN--THEN WE WON, RIGHT? WE MUST HAVE WON! LOOK AT US, LOOK AT THIS WORLD... IT'S STILL STRANGE. WE ALL ARE!
RIGHT, CASEY. AND WE'RE STILL STANDING.
SURE THING...

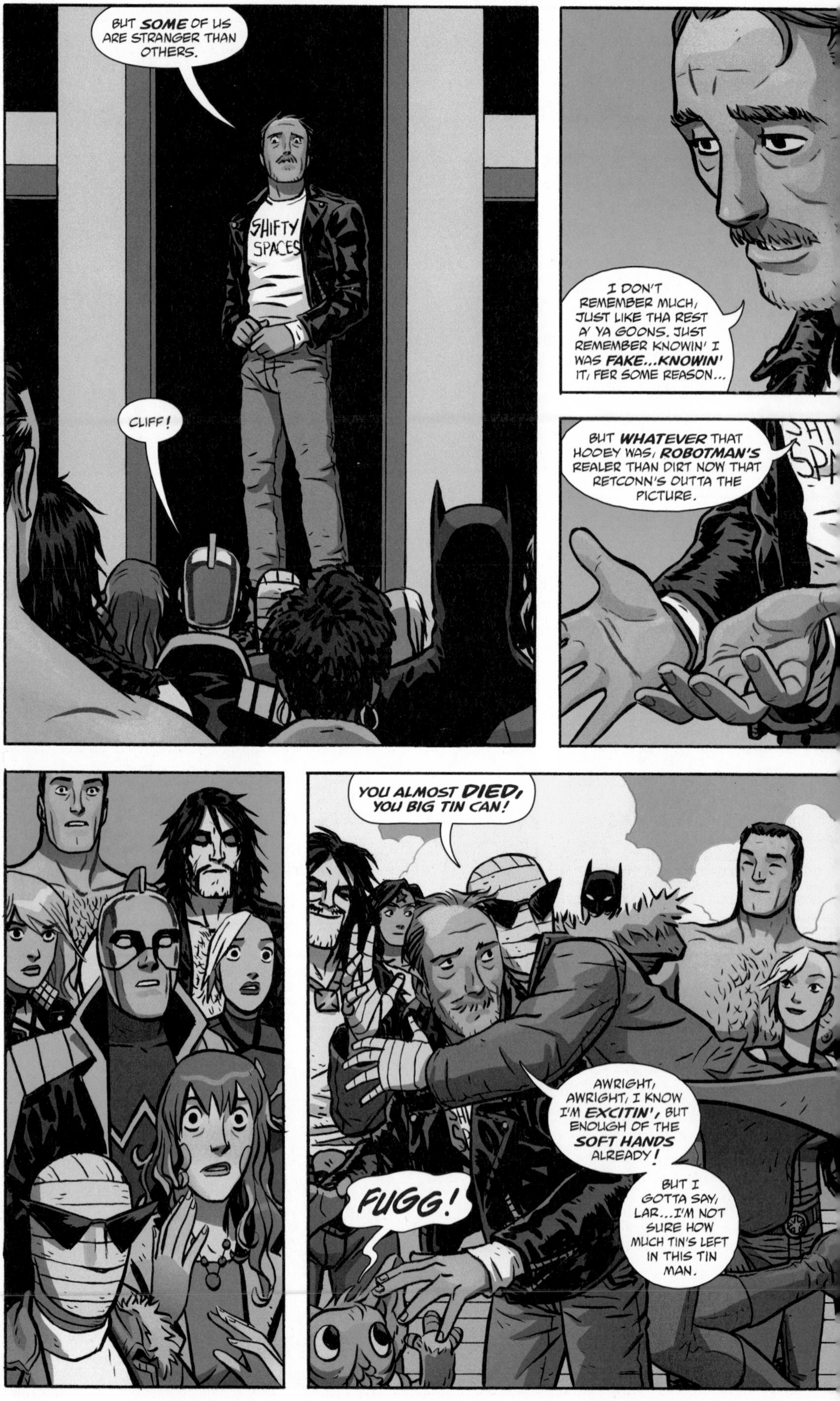
BUT SOME OF US ARE STRANGER THAN OTHERS.
CLIFF!
SHIFTY SPACES
I DON'T REMEMBER MUCH, JUST LIKE THA REST A' YA GOONS. JUST REMEMBER KNOWIN' I WAS FAKE...KNOWIN' IT, FER SOME REASON...
BUT WHATEVER THAT HOOEY WAS, ROBOTMAN'S REALER THAN DIRT NOW THAT RETCONN'S OUTTA THE PICTURE.
YOU ALMOST DIED, YOU BIG TIN CAN!
AWRIGHT, AWRIGHT, I KNOW I'M EXCITIN', BUT ENOUGH OF THE SOFT HANDS ALREADY!
BUT I GOTTA SAY, LAR...I'M NOT SURE HOW MUCH TIN'S LEFT IN THIS TIN MAN.
FUGG!

YOUR **TEAM** FOUGHT WELL, CASEY BRINKE. AS DID YOU.

THANK YOU, DIANA... BUT IT'S NOT MY TEAM. IT'S **JANE'S**.

NO WARRIOR ACTS BY HEART NOR MIND ALONE. YOU ARE THE DOOM PATROL'S **HEART**, CASEY. I SEE YOU...I KNOW YOU ARE IN **PAIN**.

I--I **SHOULDN'T** BE. I MEAN, WE **WON**, RIGHT? BUT THERE'S **SOMETHING**, A PERIPHERAL FEELING I'M CHASING BUT CAN'T CATCH. SENSE MEMORIES...

A SAD VOICE, HOLDING EACH OTHER, BUT WHEN I TRY TO SEE WHO'S THERE...I CAN'T EXPLAIN IT OR DEFINE IT...I **THINK** I HAD A CHILD. I THINK TERRY AND I HAD A **SON**...

BUT IT'S **NOTHING**.

THE HOLES IN OUR HEARTS CANNOT ALWAYS BE **NAMED**, CASEY...BUT WE MAY **YET** FIND WAYS TO **FILL** THEM.

THANK **YOU**, WONDER WOMAN.

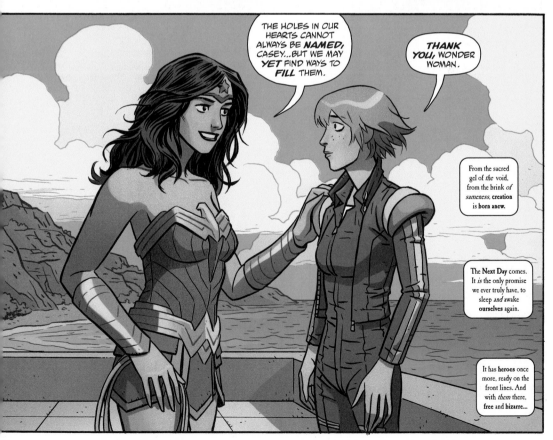

From the sacred gel of *the* void, from the brink *of sameness,* **creation** is **born anew.**

The **Next Day** comes. It *is* the only promise we ever truly have, to sleep *and* awake ourselves again.

It has **heroes** once more, ready on the front lines. And with *them* there, **free** and **bizarre**...

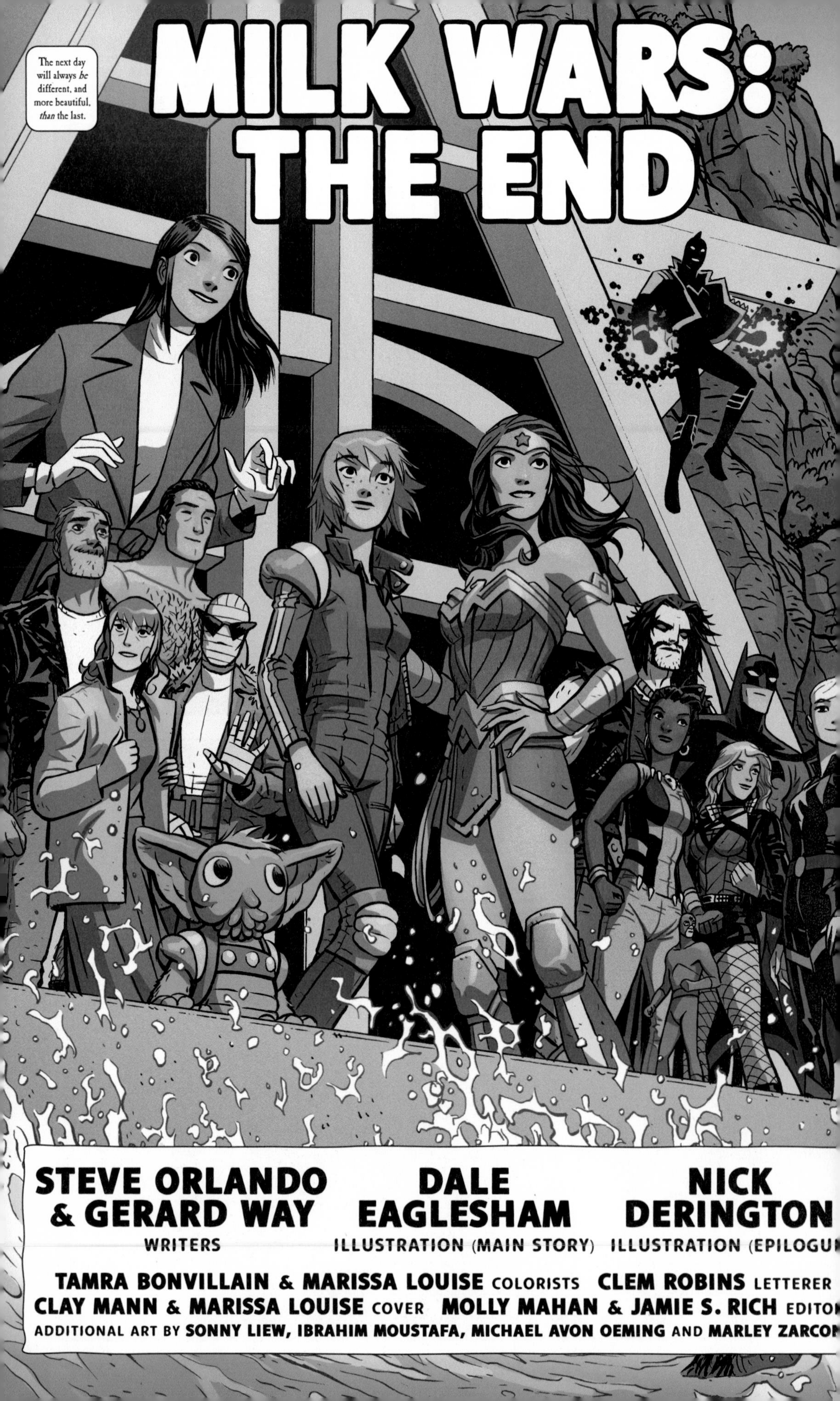
The next day will always *be* different, and more beautiful, *than* the last.
MILK WARS: THE END
STEVE ORLANDO & GERARD WAY
WRITERS
DALE EAGLESHAM
ILLUSTRATION (MAIN STORY)
NICK DERINGTON
ILLUSTRATION (EPILOGU
TAMRA BONVILLAIN & MARISSA LOUISE COLORISTS
CLEM ROBINS LETTERER
CLAY MANN & MARISSA LOUISE COVER
MOLLY MAHAN & JAMIE S. RICH EDITO
ADDITIONAL ART BY SONNY LIEW, IBRAHIM MOUSTAFA, MICHAEL AVON OEMING AND MARLEY ZARCO

UNPASTEURIZED

Character designs, breakdowns and preliminary artwork for MILK WARS

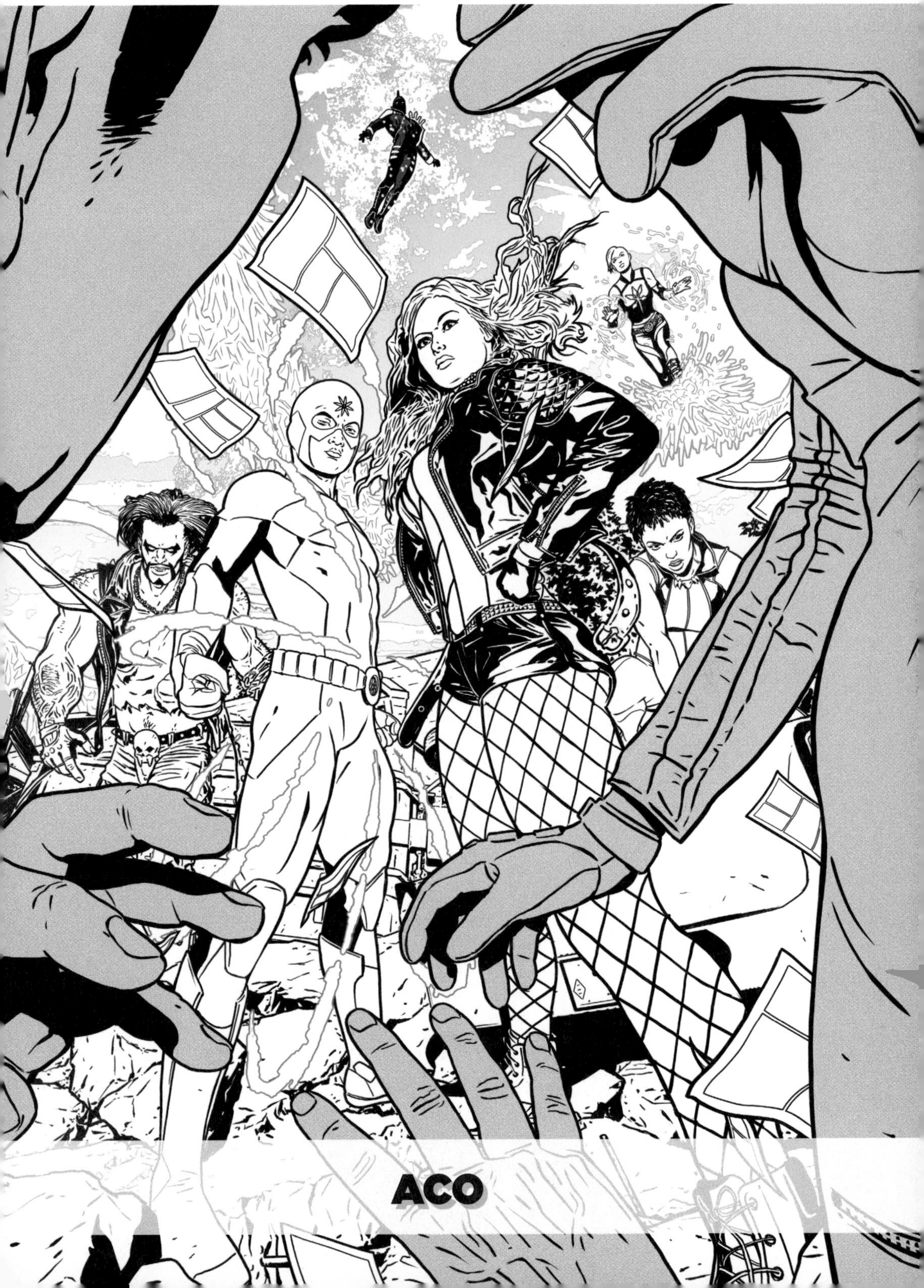

ACO

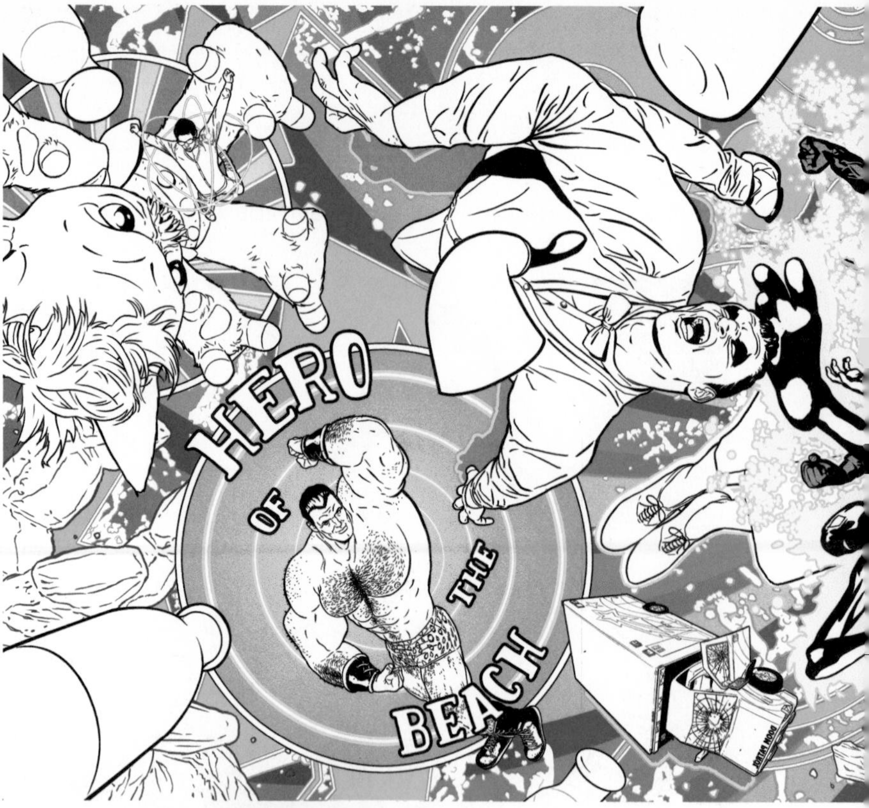
HERO OF THE BEACH

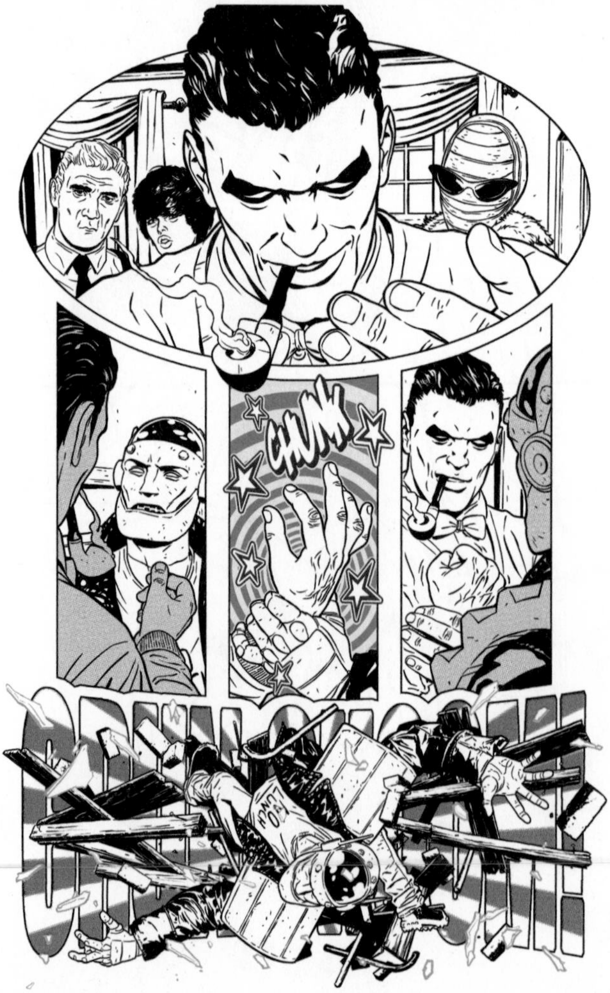
CHUNK

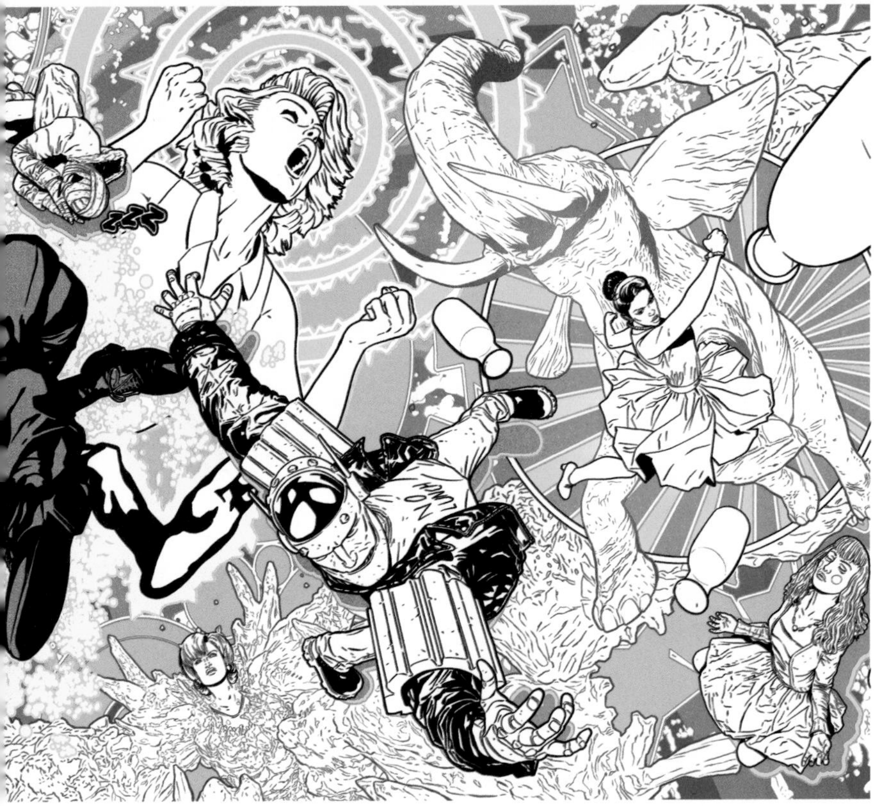

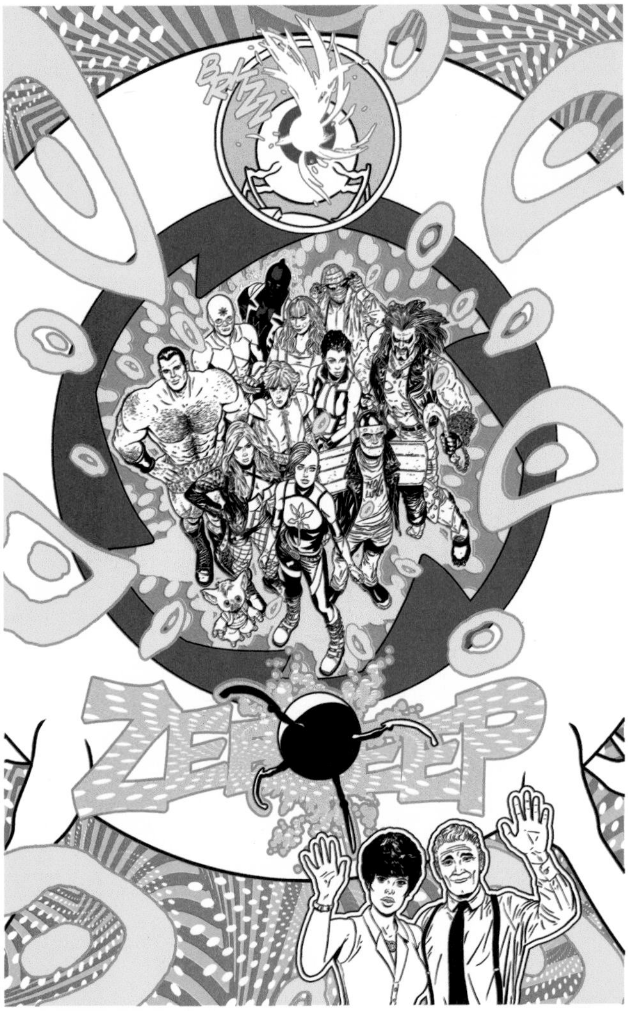
BRZZZ

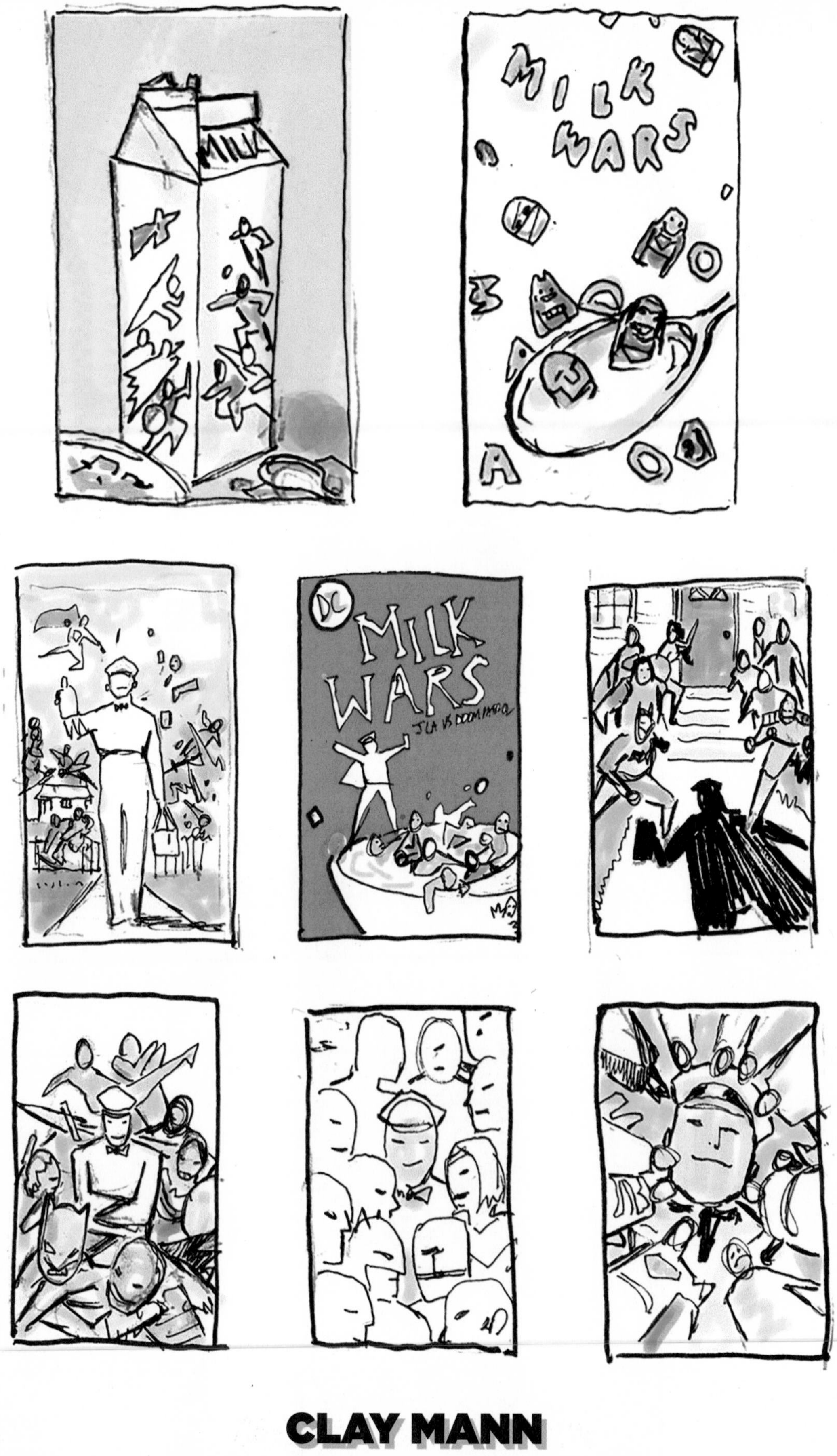
MILK
MILK WARS
DC
MILK WARS
JLA VS DOOM PATROL

CLAY MANN

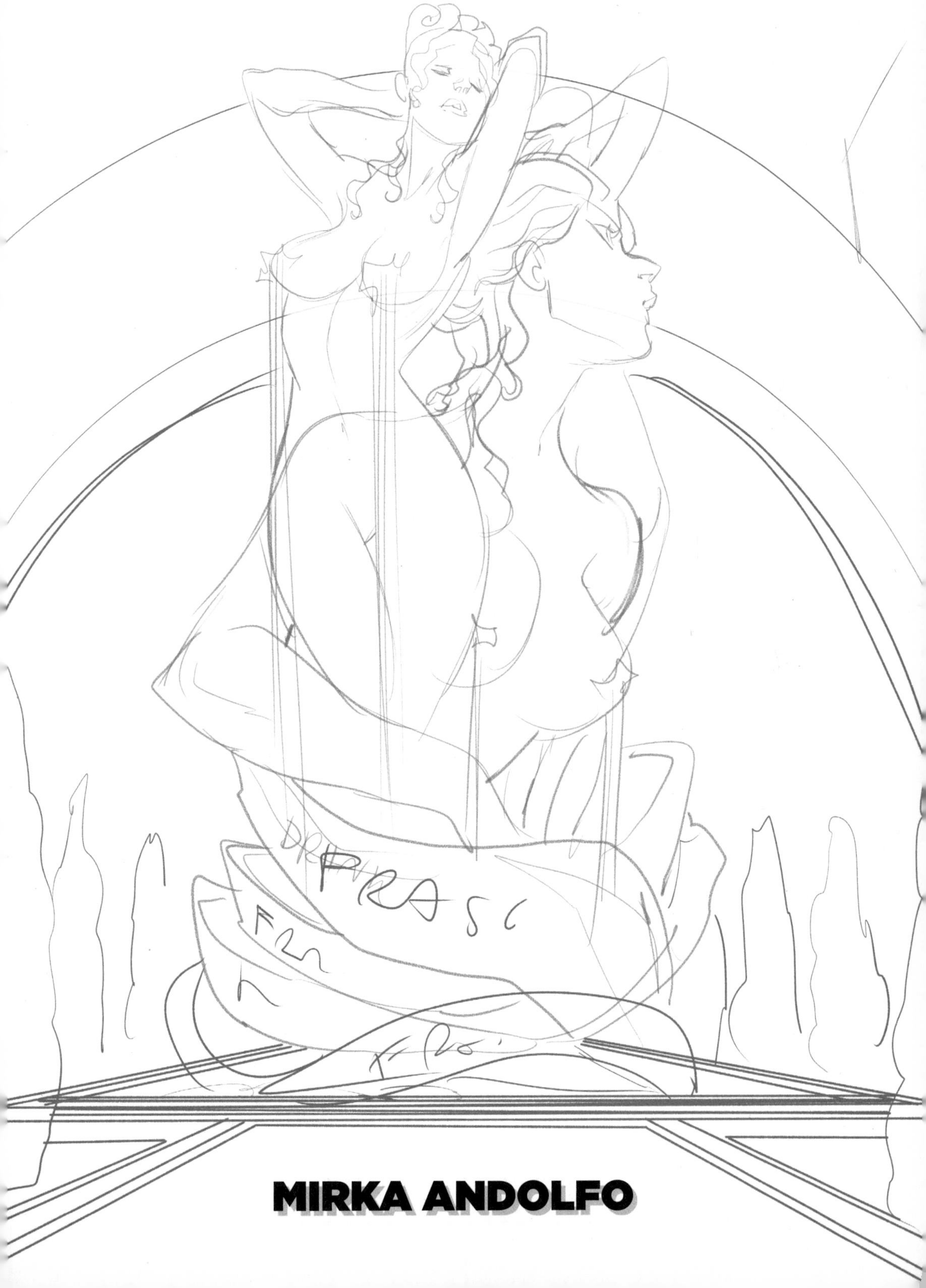

MIRKA ANDOLFO

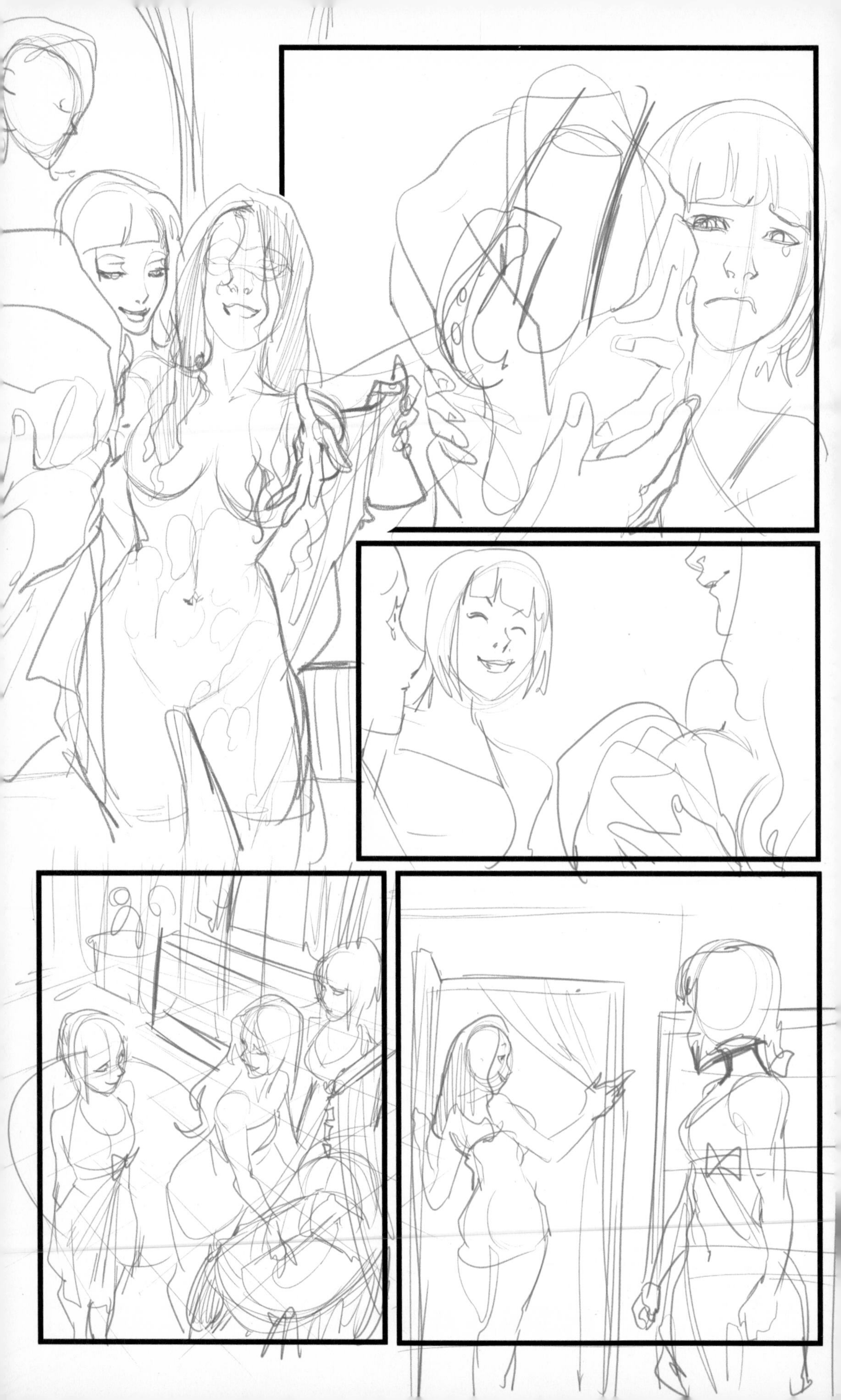

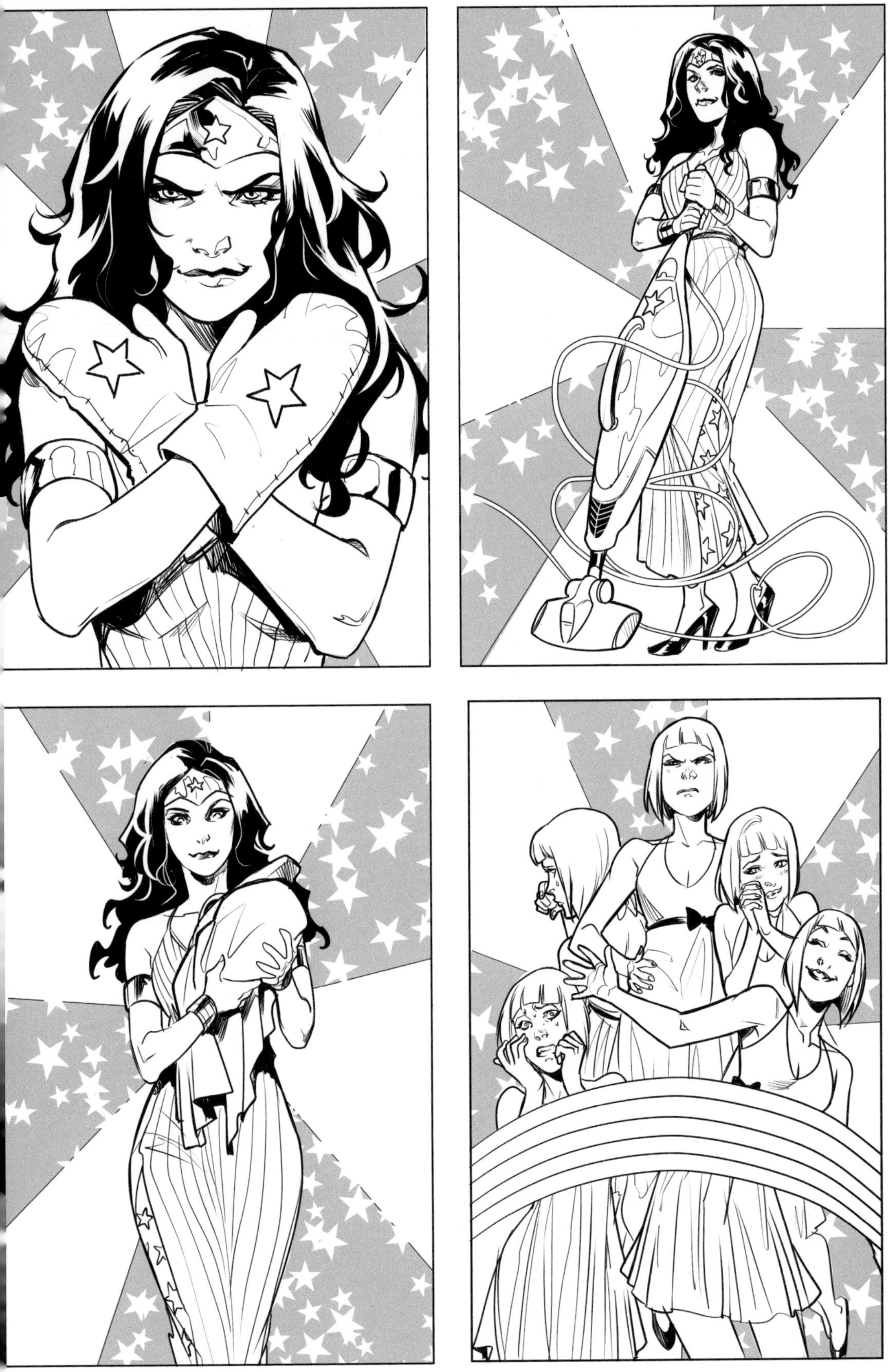

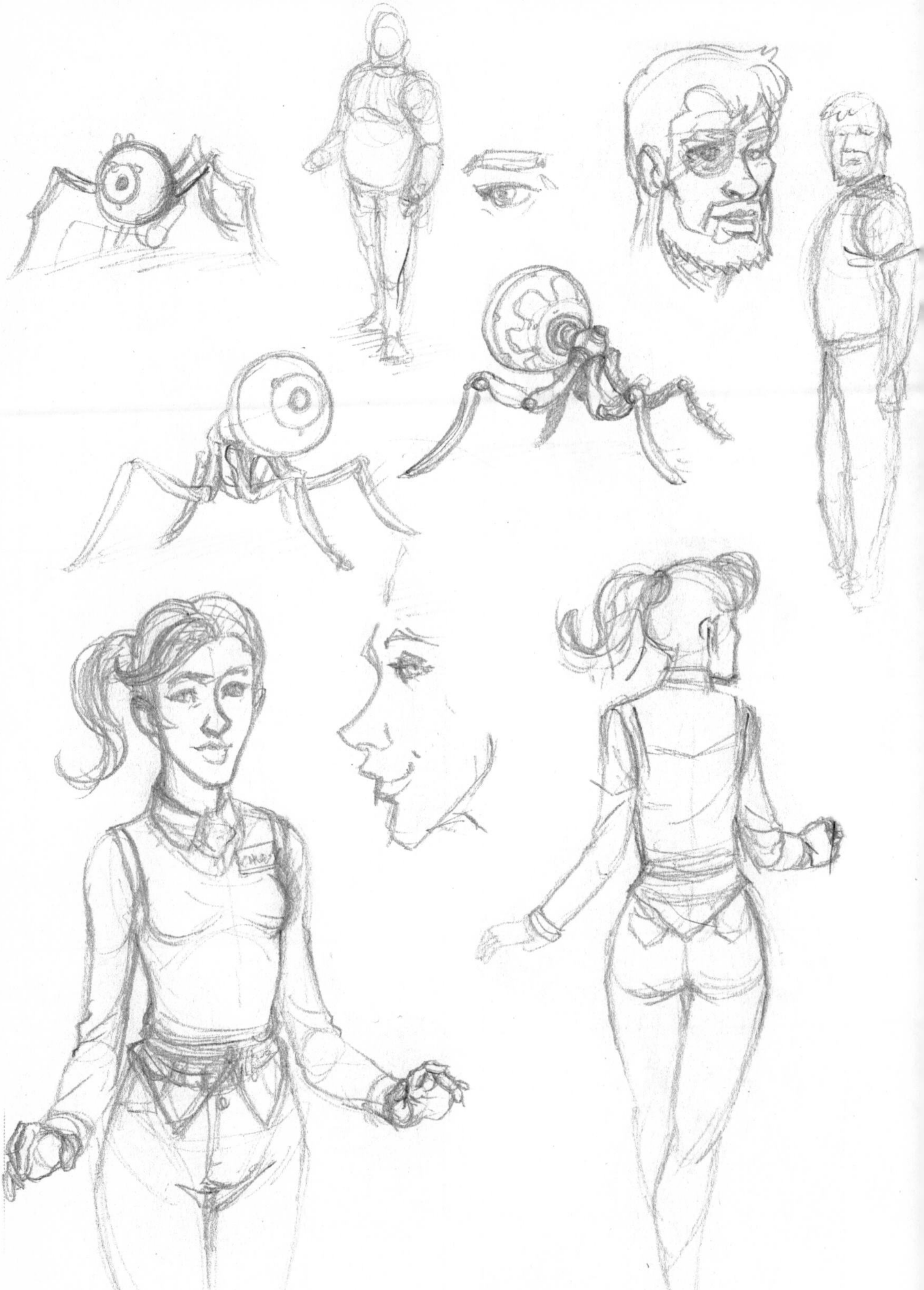

LANGDON FOSS

PENCILLER INKER PAGE#
TITLE ISSUE # MONTH **INTERIORS**

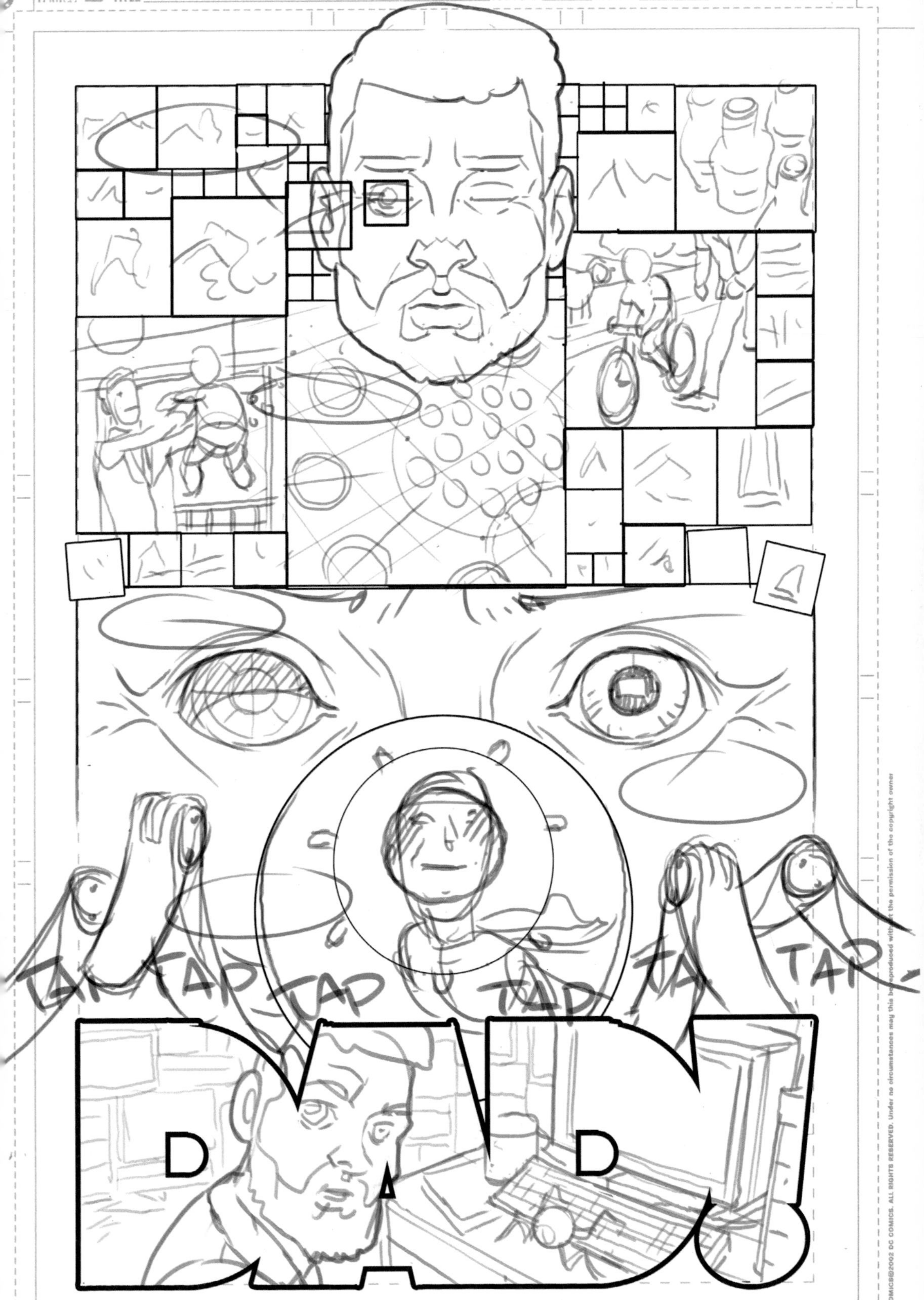

TAP TAP TAP TAP TAP TAP
DAD!
D A D

CROP
BLEED

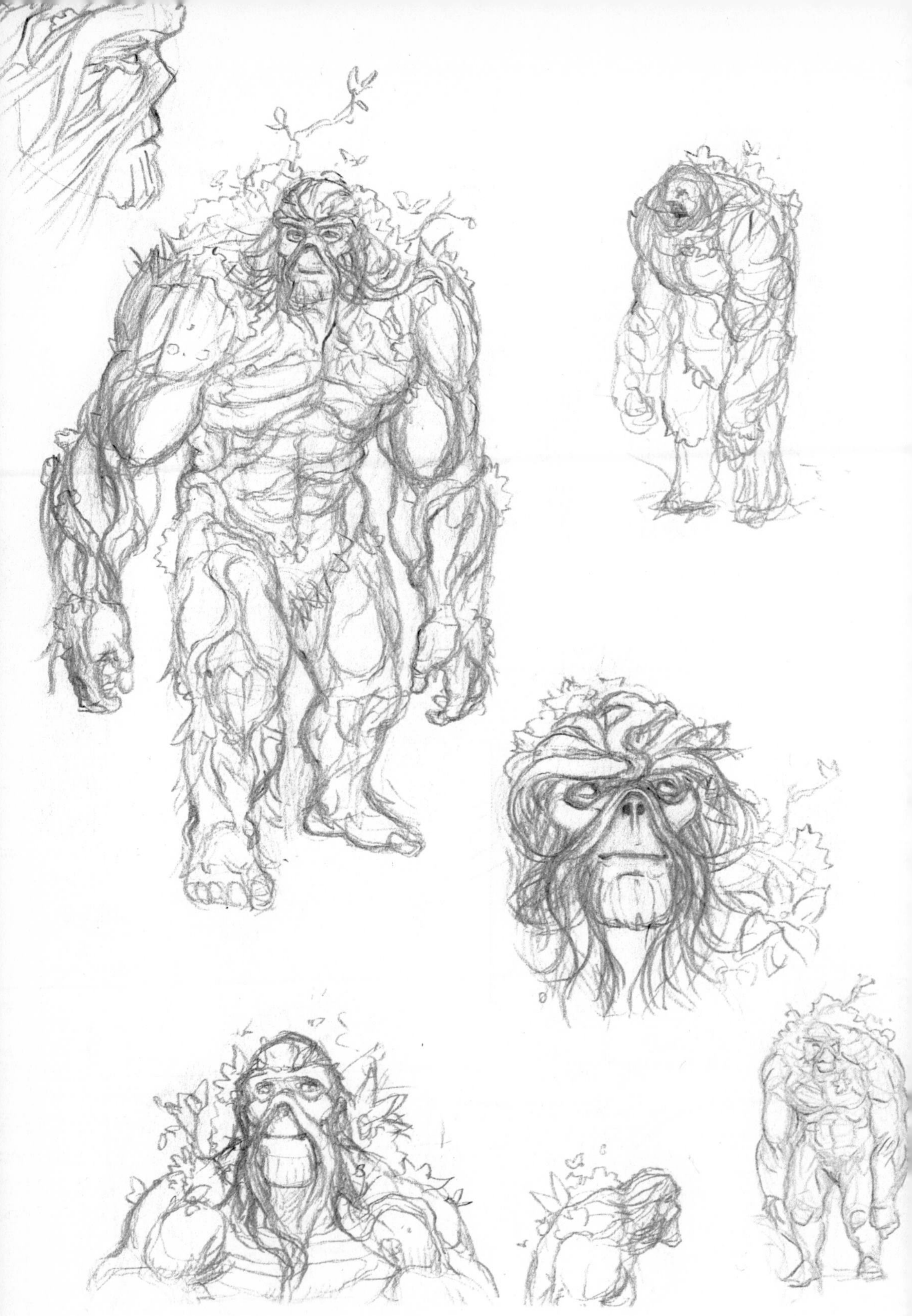

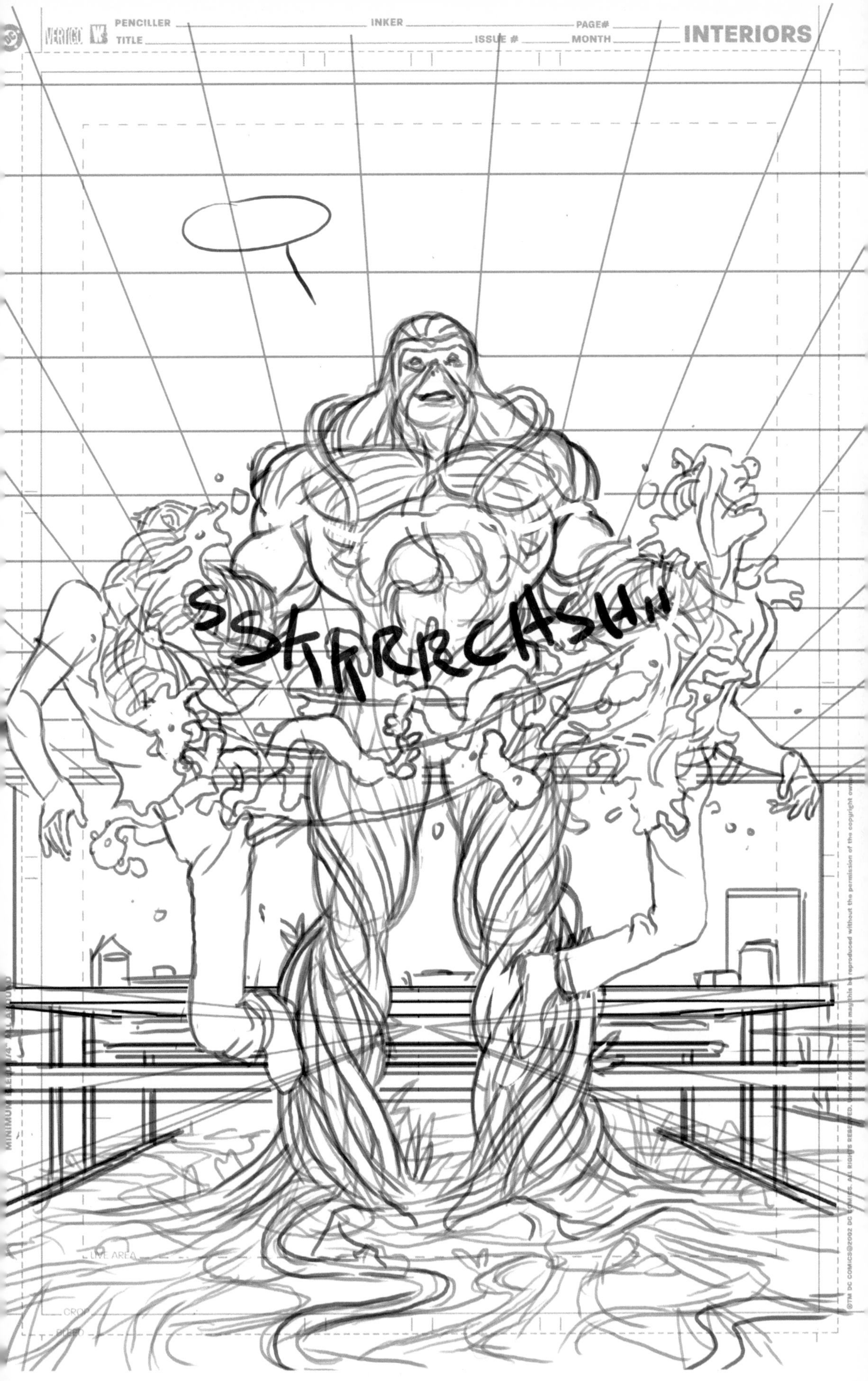
PENCILLER
INKER
PAGE#
TITLE
ISSUE #
MONTH
INTERIORS
SSKRRRCHSH!!
LIVE AREA
CROP
BLEED

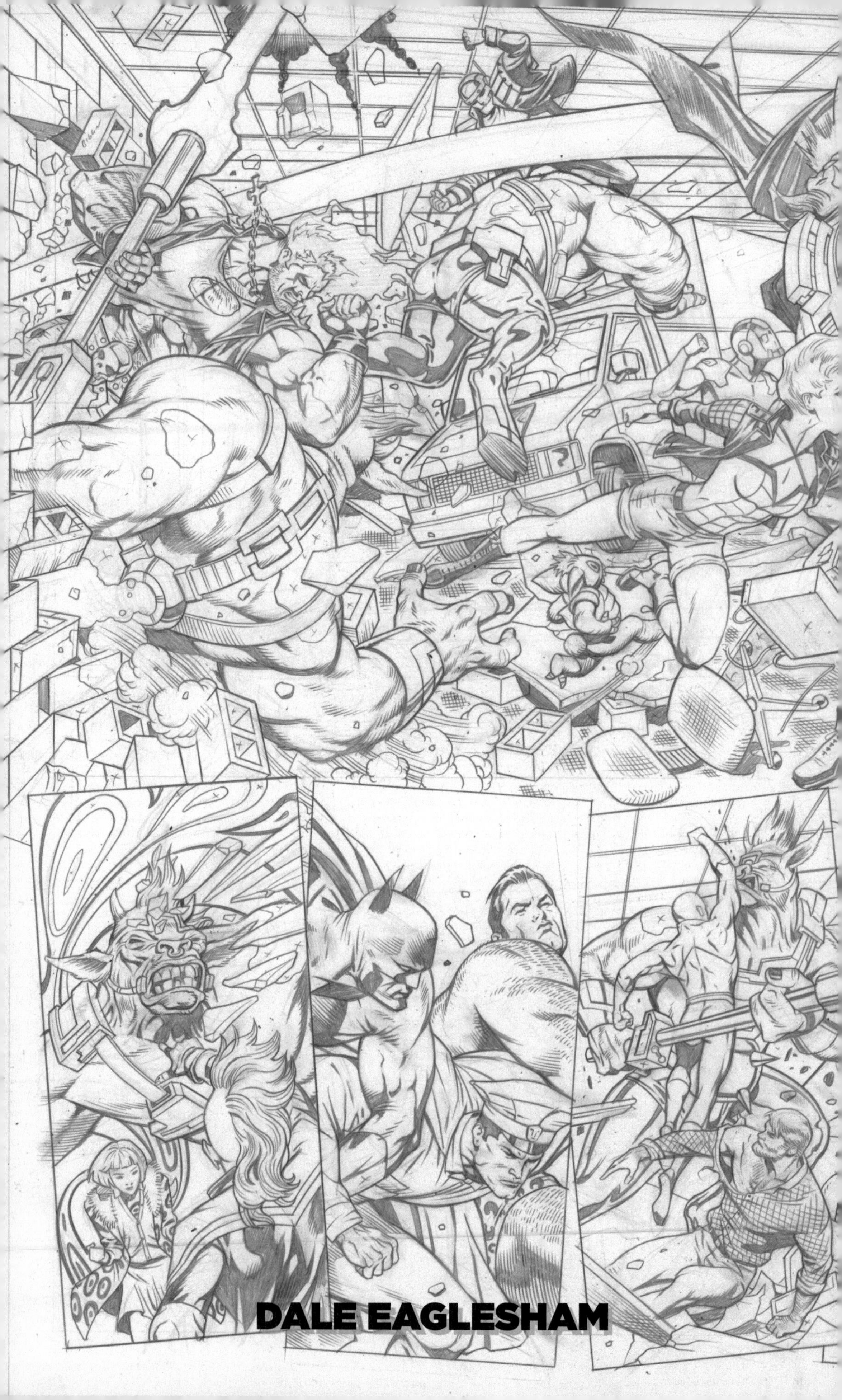
DALE EAGLESHAM

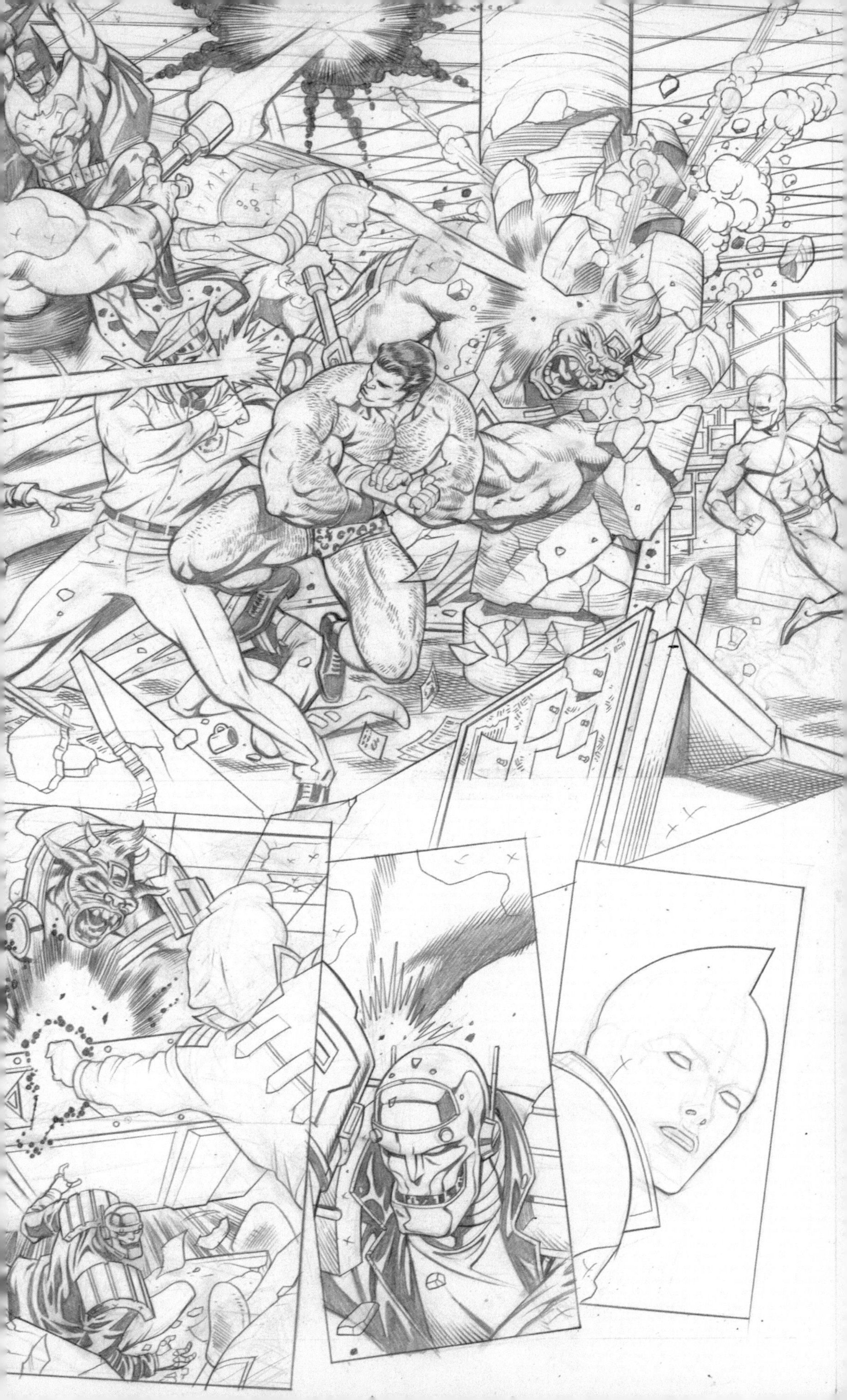

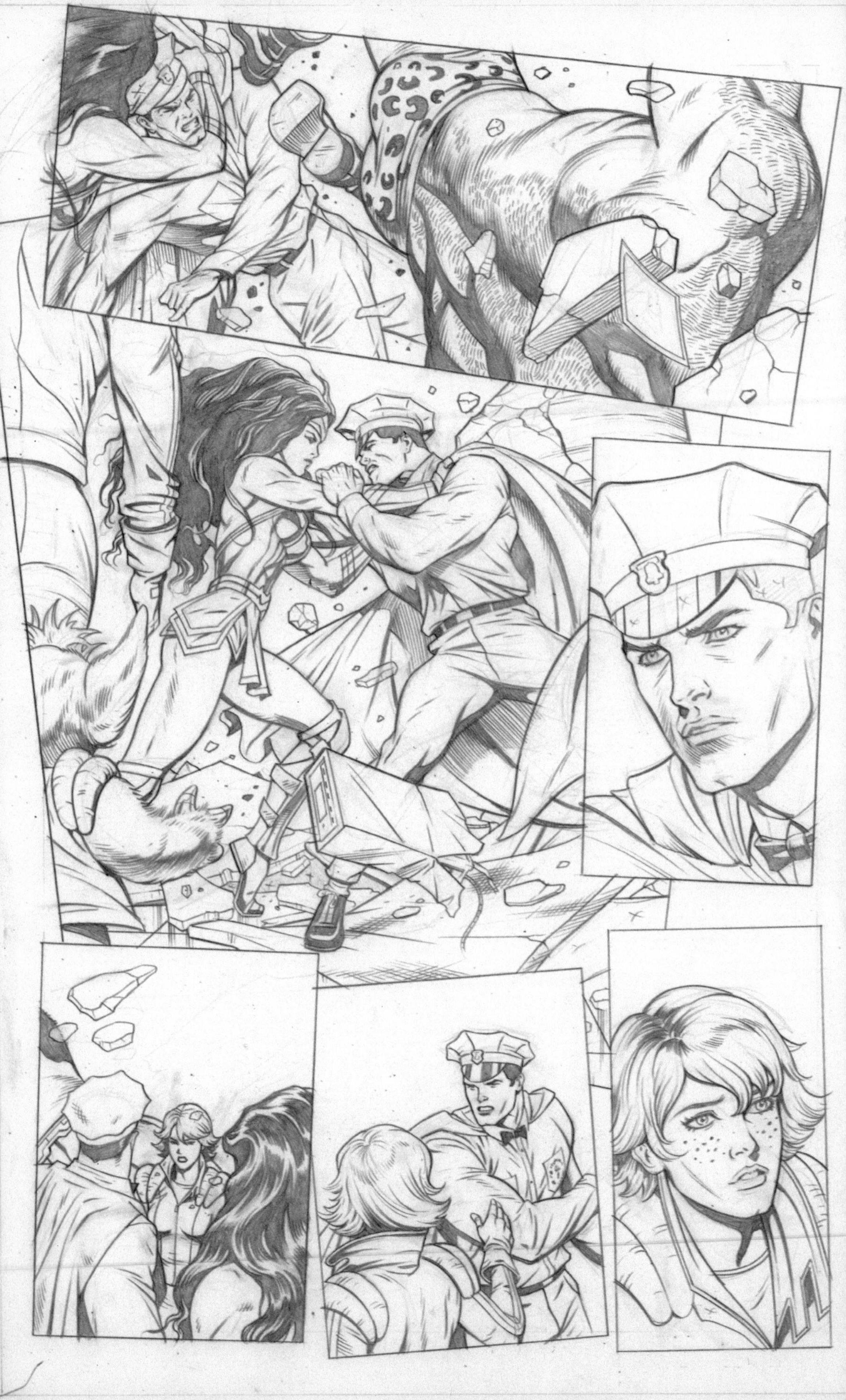

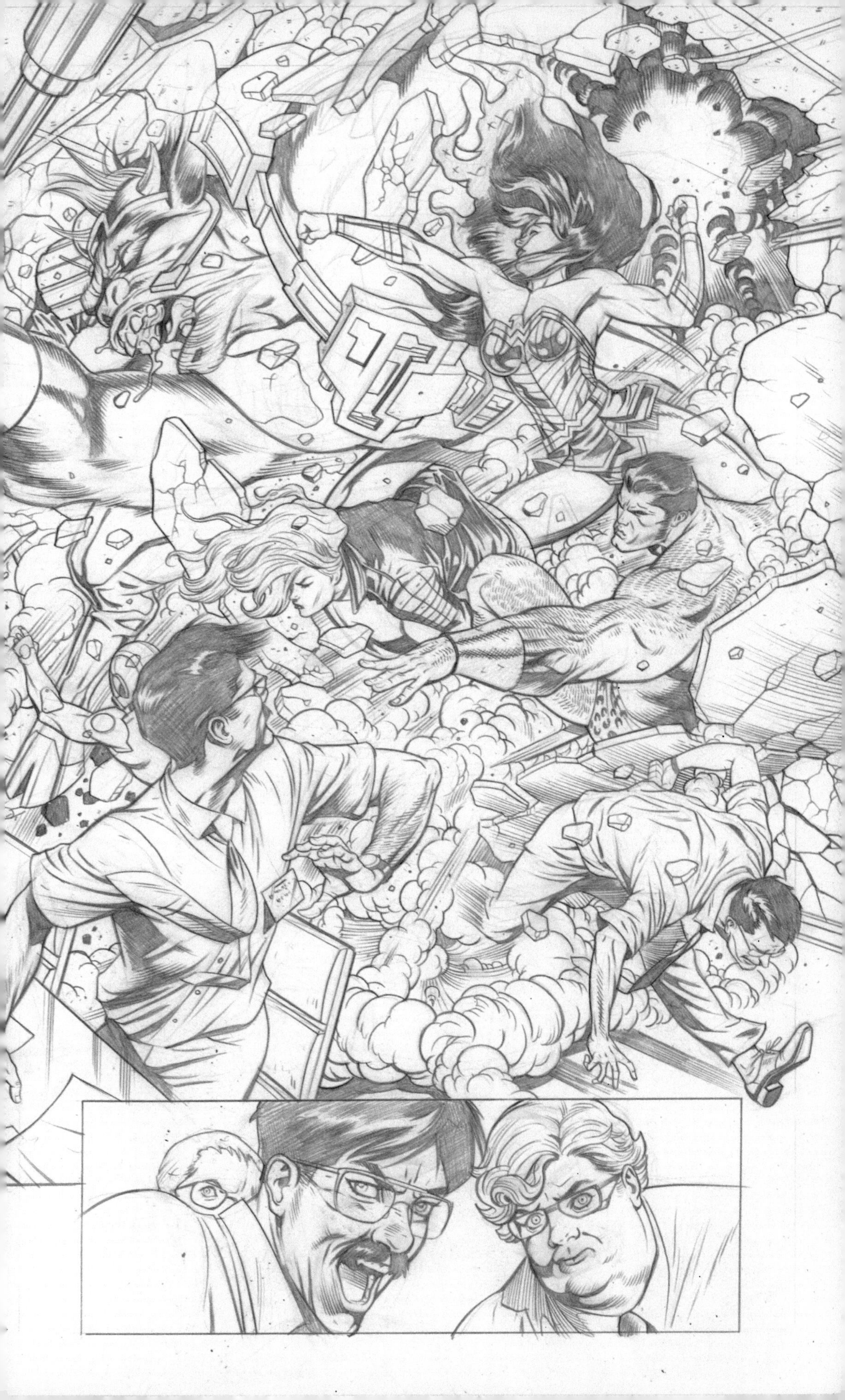

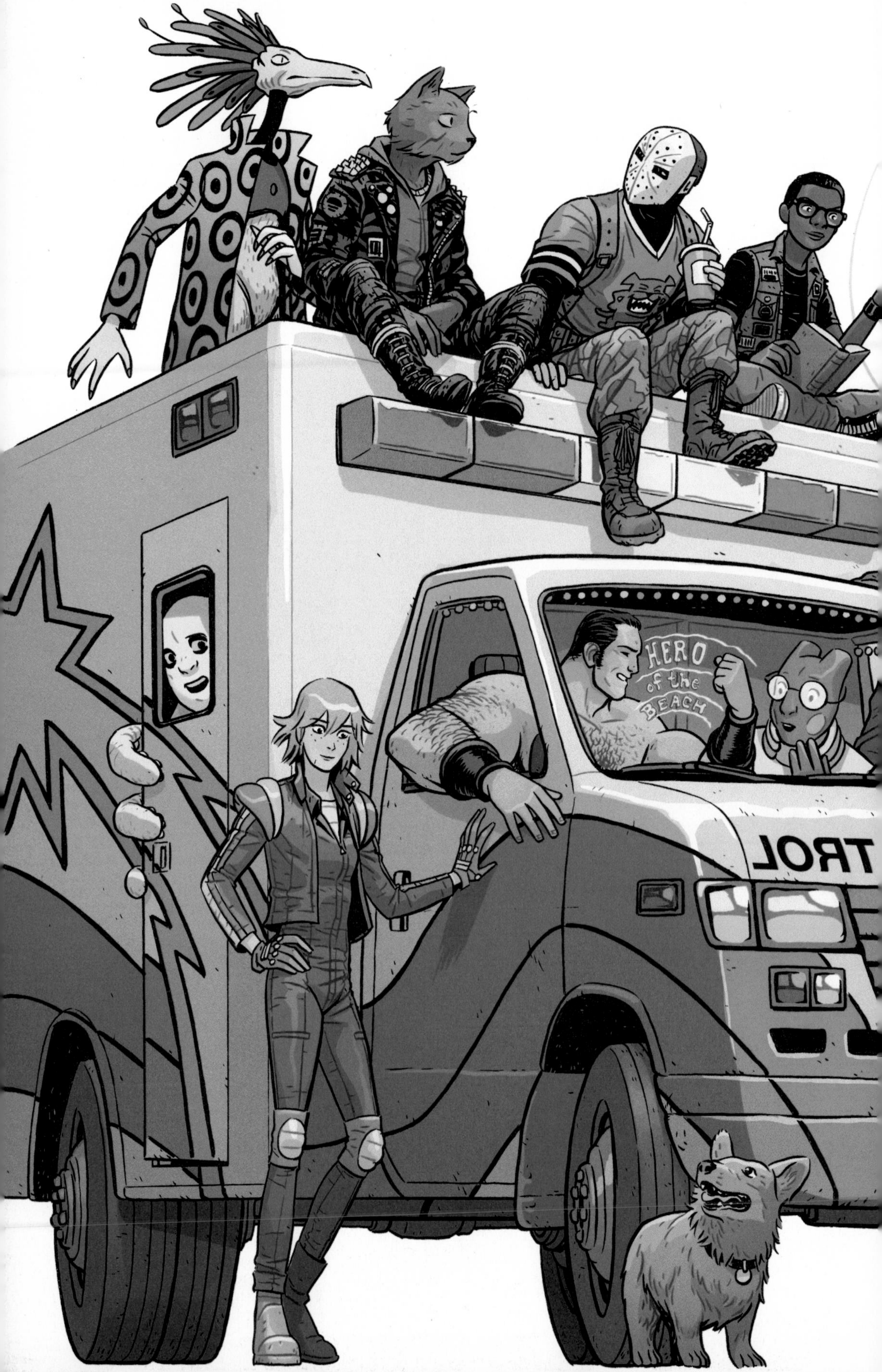
HERO of the BEACH
TROL

SPECIAL BONUS!

In 2017, DC released a promotional one-shot entitled DC'S YOUNG ANIMAL MIXTAPE SAMPLER that showcased excerpts from the imprint's four debut series. Also included were three new story pages featuring a welcoming message from Young Animal founder Gerard Way. Those pages—illustrated by Michael and Laura Allred—are reprinted here, together with the title's wraparound cover art by Nick Derington and Tamra Bonvillain.

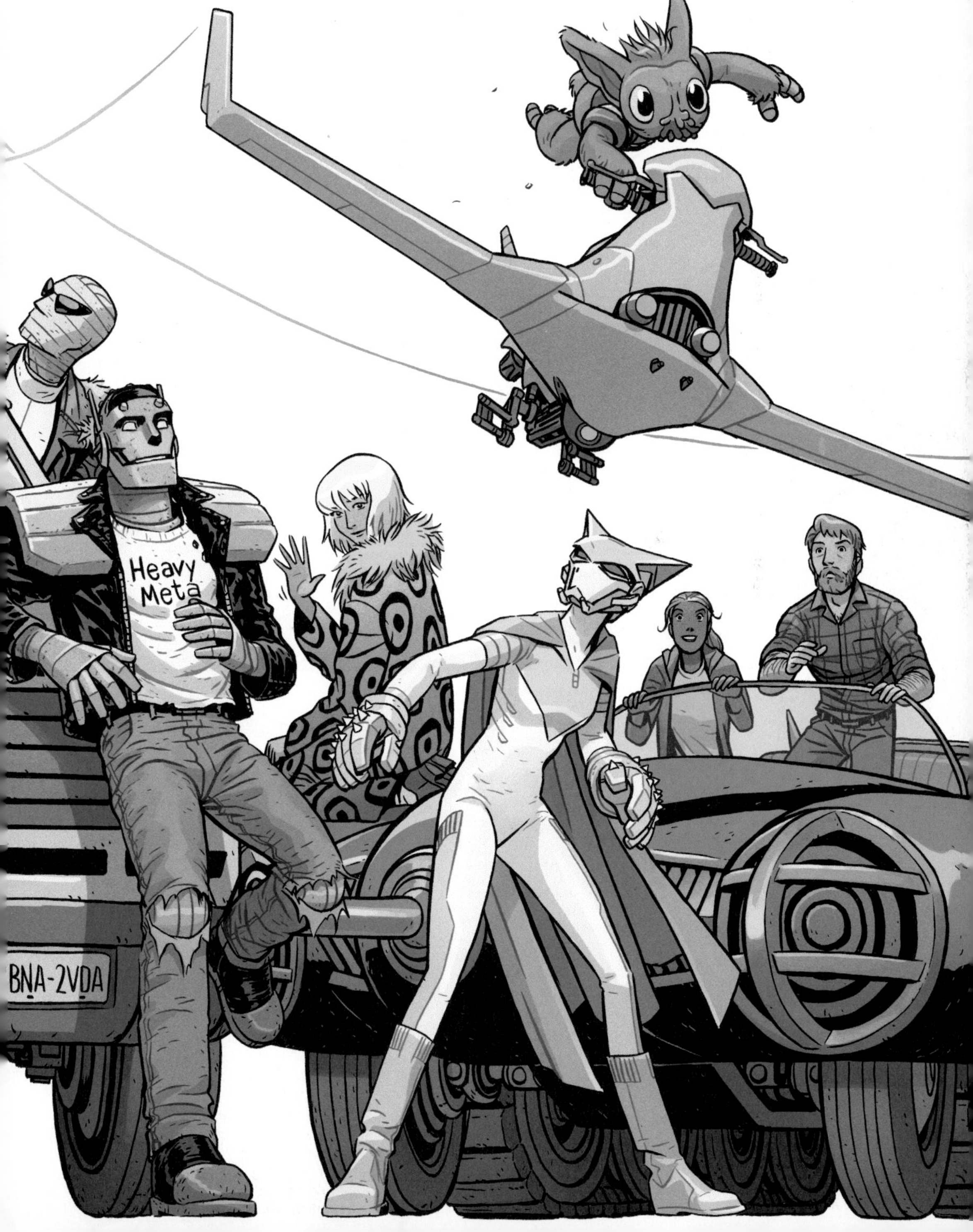
Heavy Meta
BNA-2VDA

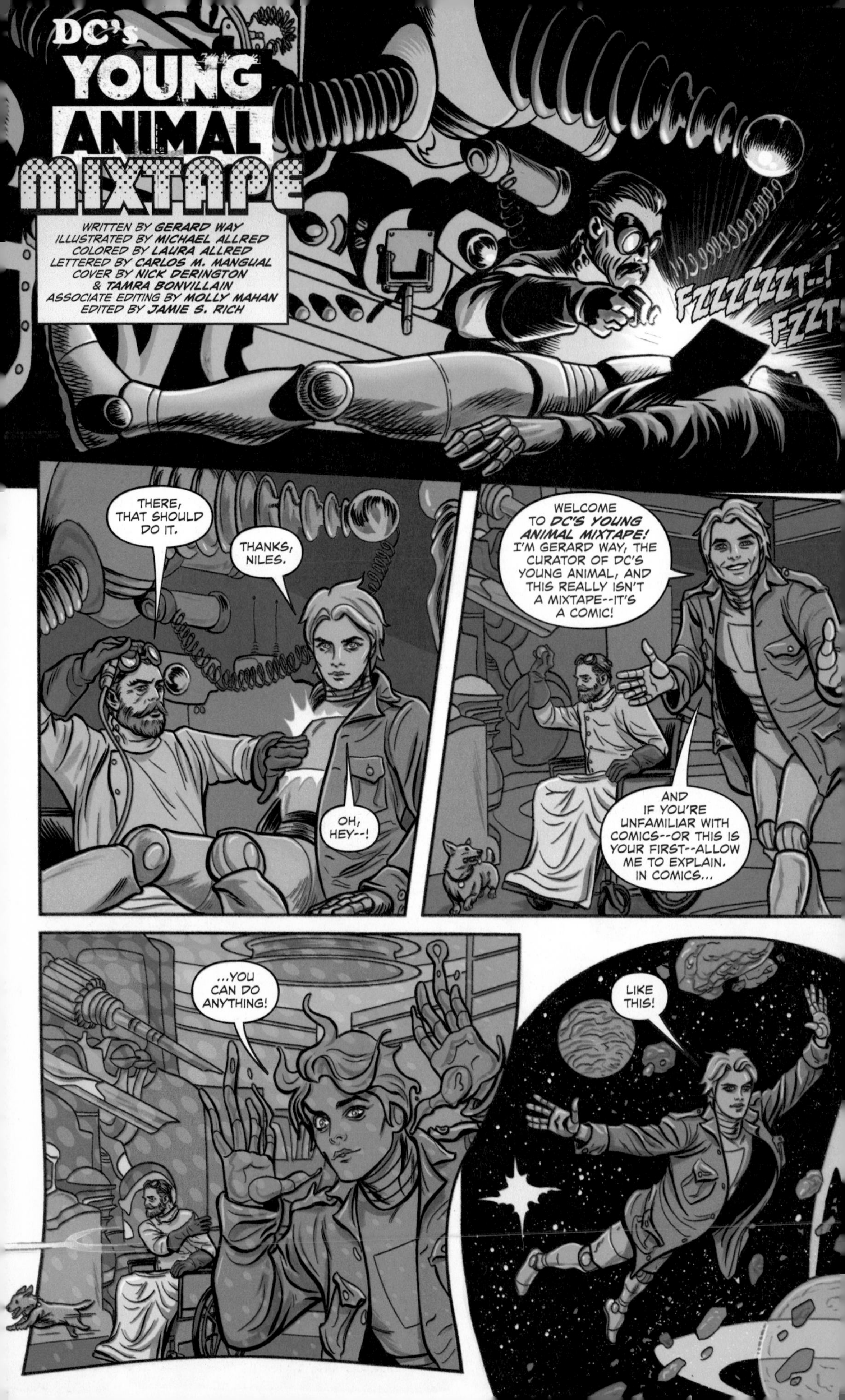
DC's
YOUNG
ANIMAL
MIXTAPE
WRITTEN BY GERARD WAY
ILLUSTRATED BY MICHAEL ALLRED
COLORED BY LAURA ALLRED
LETTERED BY CARLOS M. MANGUAL
COVER BY NICK DERINGTON
& TAMRA BONVILLAIN
ASSOCIATE EDITING BY MOLLY MAHAN
EDITED BY JAMIE S. RICH
FZZZZZZT..!
FZZT
THERE, THAT SHOULD DO IT.
THANKS, NILES.
OH, HEY--!
WELCOME TO DC'S YOUNG ANIMAL MIXTAPE! I'M GERARD WAY, THE CURATOR OF DC'S YOUNG ANIMAL, AND THIS REALLY ISN'T A MIXTAPE--IT'S A COMIC!
AND IF YOU'RE UNFAMILIAR WITH COMICS--OR THIS IS YOUR FIRST--ALLOW ME TO EXPLAIN. IN COMICS...
...YOU CAN DO ANYTHING!
LIKE THIS!

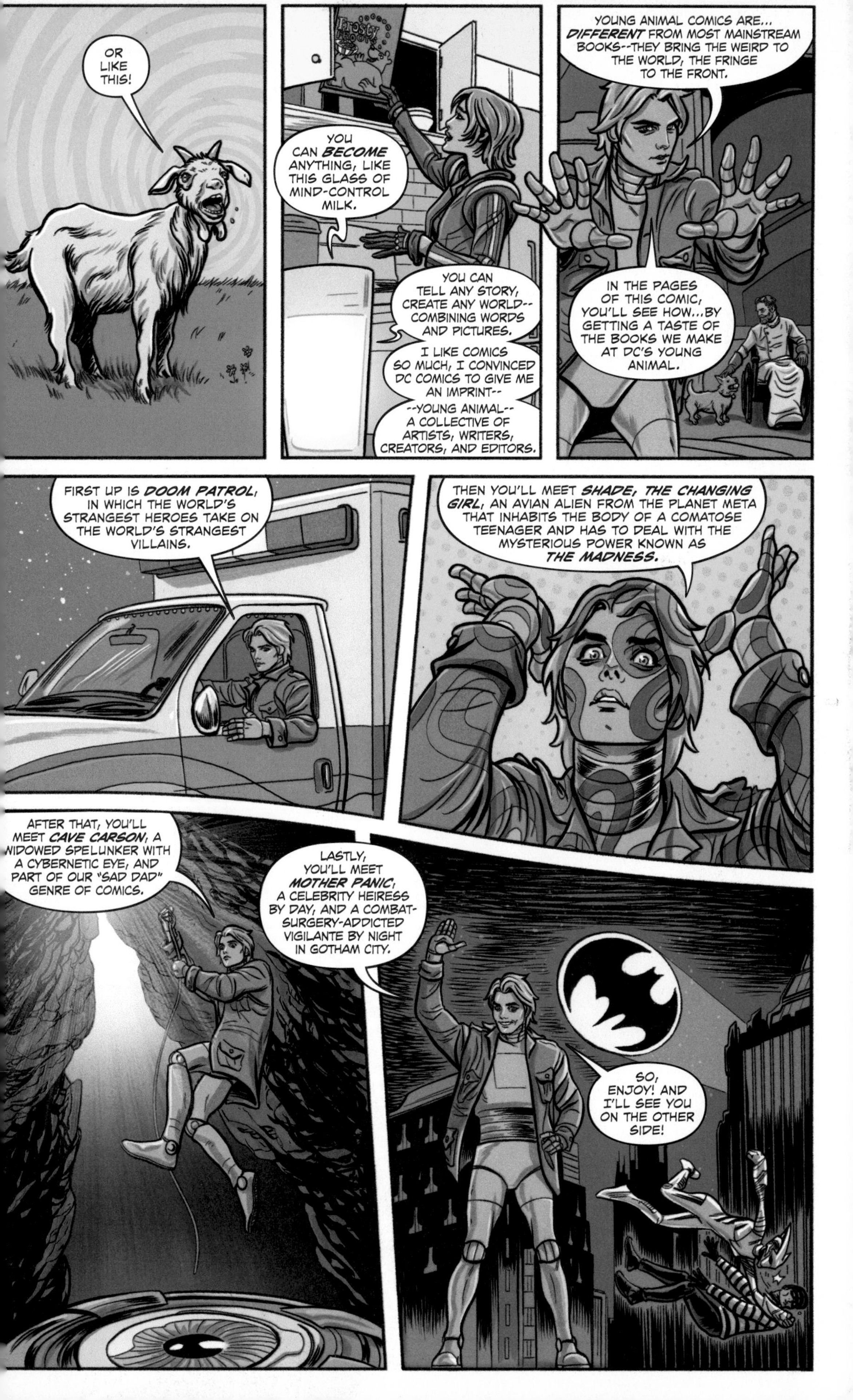
OR LIKE THIS!
YOU CAN BECOME ANYTHING, LIKE THIS GLASS OF MIND-CONTROL MILK.
YOU CAN TELL ANY STORY, CREATE ANY WORLD-- COMBINING WORDS AND PICTURES.
I LIKE COMICS SO MUCH, I CONVINCED DC COMICS TO GIVE ME AN IMPRINT--
--YOUNG ANIMAL-- A COLLECTIVE OF ARTISTS, WRITERS, CREATORS, AND EDITORS.
YOUNG ANIMAL COMICS ARE... DIFFERENT FROM MOST MAINSTREAM BOOKS--THEY BRING THE WEIRD TO THE WORLD, THE FRINGE TO THE FRONT.
IN THE PAGES OF THIS COMIC, YOU'LL SEE HOW...BY GETTING A TASTE OF THE BOOKS WE MAKE AT DC'S YOUNG ANIMAL.
FIRST UP IS DOOM PATROL, IN WHICH THE WORLD'S STRANGEST HEROES TAKE ON THE WORLD'S STRANGEST VILLAINS.
THEN YOU'LL MEET SHADE, THE CHANGING GIRL, AN AVIAN ALIEN FROM THE PLANET META THAT INHABITS THE BODY OF A COMATOSE TEENAGER AND HAS TO DEAL WITH THE MYSTERIOUS POWER KNOWN AS THE MADNESS.
AFTER THAT, YOU'LL MEET CAVE CARSON, A WIDOWED SPELUNKER WITH A CYBERNETIC EYE, AND PART OF OUR "SAD DAD" GENRE OF COMICS.
LASTLY, YOU'LL MEET MOTHER PANIC, A CELEBRITY HEIRESS BY DAY, AND A COMBAT-SURGERY-ADDICTED VIGILANTE BY NIGHT IN GOTHAM CITY.
SO, ENJOY! AND I'LL SEE YOU ON THE OTHER SIDE!

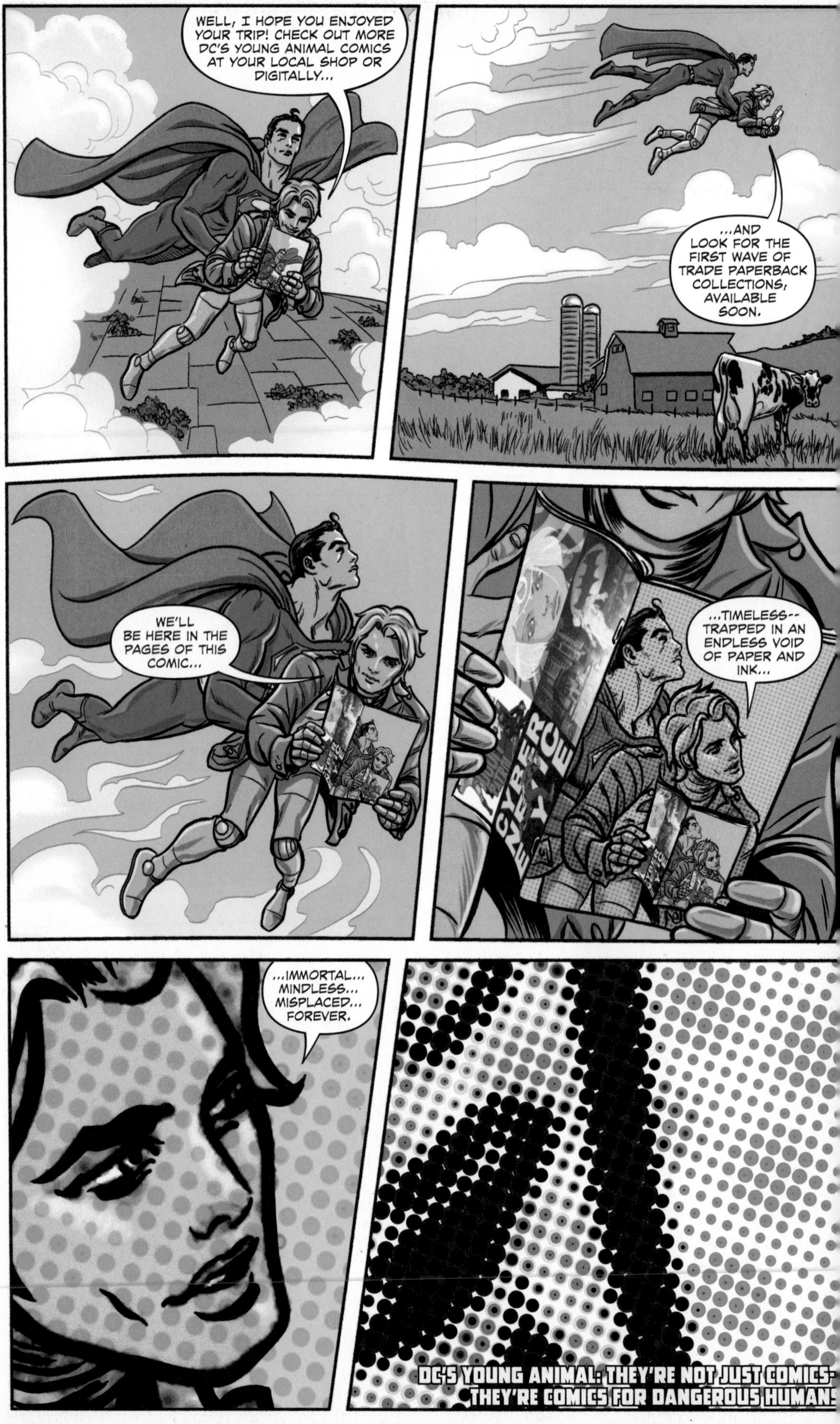
WELL, I HOPE YOU ENJOYED YOUR TRIP! CHECK OUT MORE DC'S YOUNG ANIMAL COMICS AT YOUR LOCAL SHOP OR DIGITALLY...
...AND LOOK FOR THE FIRST WAVE OF TRADE PAPERBACK COLLECTIONS, AVAILABLE SOON.
WE'LL BE HERE IN THE PAGES OF THIS COMIC...
...TIMELESS-- TRAPPED IN AN ENDLESS VOID OF PAPER AND INK...
CYBER
...IMMORTAL... MINDLESS... MISPLACED... FOREVER.
DC'S YOUNG ANIMAL: THEY'RE NOT JUST COMICS-
THEY'RE COMICS FOR DANGEROUS HUMANS

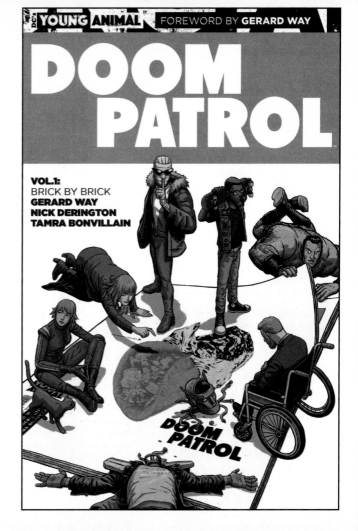

DC's YOUNG ANIMAL

MOTHER PANIC
VOL. 1: A WORK IN PROGRESS
JODY HOUSER with TOMMY LEE EDWARDS

CAVE CARSON HAS A CYBERNETIC EYE VOL. 1: GOING UNDERGROUND

SHADE, THE CHANGING GIRL VOL. 1: EARTH GIRL MADE EASY

DOOM PATROL VOL. 1: BRICK BY BRICK